THE DOCTRINE OF THE HERT

The Doctrine of the Hert is the fifteenth-century English translation of *De doctrina cordis*, a thirteenth-century Latin treatise addressed to members of the religious orders. A devotional bestseller, *De doctrina* circulated throughout Europe between the thirteenth and fifteenth centuries and was translated into six different languages. The text progressively pairs the seven gifts of the Holy Spirit with seven key actions of the heart, leading its audience toward contemplative union with God.

Exeter's full critical edition of the Middle English translation provides a much-needed resource for students and scholars working on *De doctrina cordis* and its vernacular versions. The book provides a full textual commentary along with a comprehensive list of the variants, a glossary and an index of scriptural quotations. The editors' authoritative introduction examines current thinking upon *De doctrina*'s authorship and envisaged primary audience. It also incorporates recent scholarly breakthroughs in the understanding of late medieval female spirituality.

Christiania Whitehead is Associate Professor in Medieval English Literature at the University of Warwick. Her fields of interest lie in medieval allegory and female spirituality.

Denis Renevey is Chair of Medieval English Literature and Language at the University of Lausanne, Switzerland. He has published widely in the field of vernacular theology and female religious writings.

Anne Mouron is a fellow of St Bede's Hall, an independent college in Oxford. She writes on late medieval devotional literature in English, French and Latin.

EXETER MEDIEVAL TEXTS AND STUDIES

Series Editors: Vincent Gillespie and Richard Dance

Founded by M. J. Swanton
and later co-edited by Marion Glasscoe

The Doctrine of the Hert

A Critical Edition
with Introduction and Commentary

edited by
Christiania Whitehead,
Denis Renevey
and
Anne Mouron

UNIVERSITY
of
EXETER
PRESS

Cover image: 'The Eucharistic Banquet'. Abtei St Walburg, Eichstaett, Germany. Reproduced by kind permission of the Lady Abbess and nuns of Abtei St Walburg.

First published in 2010 by
University of Exeter Press
Reed Hall, Streatham Drive
Exeter EX4 4QR
UK
www.exeterpress.co.uk

British Library Cataloguing in Publication Data
A catalogue record for this book is available from the British Library.

Paperback ISBN 978 0 85989 778 5
Hardback ISBN 978 0 85989 777 8

Typeset in Adobe Garamond 11/13
by Carnegie Book Production, Lancaster

Printed in Great Britain
by Short Run Press Ltd, Exeter

Mixed Sources
Product group from well-managed forests and other controlled sources
www.fsc.org Cert no. SA-COC-002112
© 1996 Forest Stewardship Council

FSC

Contents

Foreword

Despite the number of years we have spent reading, talking and writing about *The Doctrine of the Hert*, we always go back to this text with renewed interest and with a sense that much remains to be said about its different vernacular versions and contexts. We are delighted to be able to make the text available to a larger audience and it is to our colleagues that we owe our first debt of gratitude. In the course of our numerous presentations on the *Doctrine* at various international conferences and guest lectures our idea of publishing a modern critical edition of the text has been met with enthusiasm. Some colleagues kindly joined us to exchange ideas about the Latin *De doctrina cordis* and its vernacular versions at the Rhetoric of the Anchorhold conference which took place in July 2005 at Gregynog Hall, Newtown, Powys, where we were able to test our ideas in a strand of sessions specifically devoted to the *Doctrine*. Although the output of those sessions finds its most direct manifestation in Renevey and Whitehead (eds), *A Companion to The Doctrine of the Hert: The Middle English Translation and its Latin and European Contexts* (also published by University of Exeter Press, 2010) which accompanies this volume, it also has a bearing on this edition of the *Doctrine*. We also exchanged views on the *Doctrine* at the Leeds and Kalamazoo International Medieval congresses, the 2004 Paris and 2007 Lausanne Medieval Translator conferences, the Medieval Club of New York and at Keio University, Japan. On each of those occasions we benefited from the insightful comments of our colleagues.

We are most grateful to Anna Henderson, our commissioning editor at the University of Exeter Press, and to Vincent Gillespie and Richard Dance, the series editors. Their insightful, practical and scholarly comments have brought many new dimensions to the edition, while their tact and tolerance in the face of occasional setbacks and delays has been consistent and generous-spirited. We would like to extend special thanks to Penelope Cookson for her expert assistance with the translations from medieval Latin in this volume.

We would also like to thank the staff of the following libraries: the Bodleian Library, especially the staff in the Lower Reading Room, Upper Reading Room and Duke Humphrey; and the staff of the Fitzwilliam Museum and Trinity

College Library in Cambridge, and of the University Library in Durham, who readily made manuscripts of the text available to us during our visits.

The book was published with subsidies from the Faculty of Letters of the University of Lausanne and the University of Warwick. We are grateful to both institutions for their support.

Although we have only had recent personal contact with Sister Elisabeth Candon (formerly Sister Mary Patrick Candon), we nevertheless would like to acknowledge our debt to her own edition of the *Doctrine*, which was submitted as her doctoral dissertation to the University of Fordham in 1963. Her work has been on our desk at all times and has been a great source of inspiration to us.

Introduction

Human nature, the human heart, the spirit, the soul, the consciousness
itself – call it what you like – in the end, it's all we've got to work
with. It has to develop and expand, or the sum of our misery will
never diminish.[1]

Long before McEwan made one of his characters, June, speak about expansion
of consciousness, *The Doctrine of the Hert* invited its multiple readership to think
about and work on this subjective phenomenon. In fact, the *Doctrine* is one of
the many devotional texts from the medieval period to have been concerned
about this important psychological aspect. Although, as we shall see below,
the original Latin text of the *Doctrine, De doctrina cordis*, became a devotional
bestseller soon after its composition in the thirteenth century and was translated
into several vernacular languages, it has received insufficient attention in the
twentieth and twenty-first centuries, despite the pioneering work of several
scholars. Indeed, although medieval English devotional literature and its
cultural significance are currently at the forefront of medieval English studies,
with a number of scholarly articles and books devoted to anchoritic literature,
devotional texts written for and by women, Wycliffite biblical and theological
texts, and vernacular theologies more generally, the *Doctrine* has received only
passing attention as part of this comprehensive discussion. Yet *The Doctrine
of the Hert* matters as a significant contribution to this debate, and also yields
important information which assists in shaping a perspective for medieval
English devotional literature within the larger picture of continental trends.

We are pleased to put right those many years of neglect by producing
this edition of the Middle English version of the *Doctrine*, together with a
companion volume to accompany it.[2] This is the first printed edition of the
Middle English version of our text. We trust that the edition and its attendant
companion volume will be of use to several generations of scholars who we
hope will pick up some of the points raised in the various parts of this edition

---

[1]   Ian McEwan, *Black Dogs* (London, 1998), p. 172.
[2]   D. Renevey and C. Whitehead (eds), *A Companion to The Doctrine of the Hert: The
Middle English Translation and its Latin and European Contexts* (Exeter, 2010).

in order to make clearer sense of this fascinating text and its place within the larger corpus of devotional texts. Before addressing several textual issues, it is appropriate to mention here how we, as an editorial team, became immersed in the study of the Middle English *Doctrine*. Coincidentally, at various points of our doctoral and post-doctoral studies at Oxford, under the advice of our supervisor Vincent Gillespie, each of us tackled the version of the text found in Bodleian, MS Laud Misc. 330. In the case of Anne Mouron, the *Doctrine* became one of the first texts that she transcribed as part of a larger project on the transcription and edition of devotional texts. Christiania Whitehead wrote one of her first doctoral pieces on the *Doctrine*, included some of it in her doctoral thesis and used some of the textual evidence from it in her book, *Castles of the Mind: A Study of Medieval Architectural Allegory*. The *Doctrine* came to the attention of Denis Renevey as he was reading devotional texts in the search for material on the devotion to the Holy Name of Jesus. If, with the exception of one occurrence, the search for that material proved disappointing within the *Doctrine*, nonetheless the fascinating imagery found in the text left a lasting trace. Several talks and papers on the *Doctrine* have appeared between this first encounter, more than a decade ago, and the time of publication of this edition. Without the use of an unpublished thesis by Sister Mary Patrick Candon (now Sister Elizabeth Candon), keeping such regular company with this text would have been difficult, if not impossible.[3] We are immensely grateful to Sister Candon for the superb work she accomplished with her own edition of the *Doctrine*, which was submitted, according to the official academic language, 'in partial fulfilment of the requirements for the degree of doctor of philosophy in the department of English at Fordham University, New York, 1963'. Our debt to Sister Candon's work is immense and abundantly acknowledged in all parts of this edition.

The field of vernacular medieval religious writings as an object of academic investigation has undergone radical transformation in recent years, so much so that a presentation of *The Doctrine of the Hert* to a larger public in the form of an edition must take into account those changes and contextualize the text, as far as an edition allows, with reference to many newly conceived premises about the field. In addition, since Candon's dissertation, considerable work has been carried out by Guido Hendrix on the Latin *De doctrina cordis* and its manuscripts.[4] We are therefore in a more privileged position today to

---

[3]   Sister M.P. Candon, '*The Doctrine of the Hert*, Edited from the Manuscripts with Introduction and Notes' (unpublished doctoral dissertation, Fordham University, 1963). Hereafter cited as Candon, *Doctrine*.
[4]   For a comprehensive bibliography of Guido Hendrix's books and articles on *De doctrina*, see Renevey and Whitehead (eds), *Companion*, pp. 74–6.

engage in comparative work between the Latin source text and its Middle English adaptation. That privileged position has led us to argue that the Middle English *Doctrine* is an adaptation rather than a translation of the Latin text, and to shape a context for the treatise in relation to new, though controversial, evidence about its authorship. These scholarly developments, as well as the fact that we have opted for a different base manuscript from that used by Candon for her own edition, demonstrate the need for a new edition of the Middle English text. We have had to begin from scratch, albeit always of course working with Candon's dissertation on our desks.

Although this edition is the result of a team effort, it is nevertheless appropriate to explain how the work has been shared between the editors. Following our initial joint transcription of sample passages from the four Middle English manuscripts to establish a base manuscript, Christiania Whitehead was responsible for the transcription, formatting and modern punctuation of the McClean manuscript, together with the recording of the textual variants. The Middle English glossary, the index of Biblical quotations, the modern English translations of Latin and medieval French extracts in the textual commentary and the discussion of the changes in translation between Latin and Middle English texts in the introduction (Part 7) were the responsibility of Anne Mouron. The textual commentary, together with the manuscript descriptions in the introduction (Part 8), was the responsibility of Christiania Whitehead. The remaining parts of the introduction were written by Denis Renevey. At every stage we exchanged ideas, and we hope that, as a result, the edition is much more than the sum of its parts.

1. *De doctrina cordis*

The edition of the fifteenth-century Middle English *Doctrine* we present here is an adaptation of a mid-thirteenth-century text, *De doctrina cordis*, also known as *De praeparatione cordis*. This Latin text circulated widely during the late medieval period, as attested by 208 extant manuscripts found in European libraries, and 70 more no longer extant but for which we retain catalogue information.[5] Manuscripts are found in modern Belgium, the Netherlands, Germany, Switzerland, Austria, Great Britain, France, Italy and Spain.[6] They

---

5 For a list of the Latin medieval manuscripts, see G. Hendrix, *Hugo de Sancto Caro's traktaat De doctrina cordis. Handschriften, recepte, tekstgeschiedenis en authenticiteitskritik*, Documenta Libraria 16/1 (Louvain, 1995). Hereafter, Hendrix, *Hugo I*.
6 Hendrix, *Hugo I*, p. xxvii.

date from the thirteenth to the fifteenth centuries, with a greater number of manuscripts dating from the latter.[7] In view of the progressive loss of interest in *De doctrina* from the first decades of the sixteenth century onwards, it is likely that most of the manuscripts found in the several European libraries where they have been preserved up to this day, reached monastic or religious institutions near their current place of location before the end of the sixteenth century. The evidence for more than 270 medieval manuscript copies of *De doctrina* shows that it was a popular religious text, effectively a devotional bestseller; it also shows that, although not copied as often as such 'juggernaut' texts as James of Milan's *Stimulus amoris* (more than 500 manuscripts), it nonetheless satisfied the needs of a wide readership.[8] One of the reasons for its success may reside in the fact that its structure made it possible for the text to be used for a variety of different functions.

A study of the different textual manifestations of *De doctrina* that survive in Latin manuscripts offers useful information about those different functions. From an early date the text existed in different versions, and it is possible that the author of *De doctrina* devised those versions himself from the inception of the project. Indeed, Leiden, Bibliotheek der Rijksuniversiteit, MS BPL 2579, which is regarded by Hendrix as the apograph of the original version of the Latin text, possibly contains information which would also make it an autograph manuscript.[9] This manuscript contains notes such as 'vacat' which would make it possible for a copyist to compose a long or short version of *De doctrina* according to authorial intention. The long version of *De doctrina* is called the IP redaction because of the words 'ignaros predicatores' in its prologue, whereas the short version is called the HV redaction as a result of the substitution of the critical comment against preachers with the words 'in hoc verbo'.[10] Hendrix also identifies different versions of the text by reference

---

[7]   For a detailed description of each manuscript itemized by Hendrix, see Hendrix, *Hugo I*, pp. 13–105.

[8]   I am grateful to Allan Westphall, University of St Andrews, who provided us with this information in a private communication. For more information on the *Stimulus amoris*, see F. Eisermann, *Stimulus amoris: Inhalt, lateinische Überlieferung, deutsche Übersetzungen, Rezeption* (Tübingen, 2001).

[9]   Hendrix, *Hugo I*, p. xxix.

[10] Ibid., pp. xxviii–xxix. See also D. Renevey and C. Whitehead, 'Introduction', in Renevey and Whitehead (eds), *Companion*, p. 2; see also, in the same volume, M. Cré, 'A Middle Dutch Translation of *De doctrina cordis: De bouc van der leeringhe van der herten* in Vienna, Österreichischen Nationalbibliothek, MS 15231', pp. 210–11. Here are the whole IP- and HV-prologue sentences: 'Hoc dicitur contra ignaros predicatores qui, uim uerborum sacrorum ignorantes et per hoc eadem frangere et exponere

to certain lengthy passages that he calls 'macrovariants'. Even the short version of *De doctrina* is a sizeable text, enabling copists to abbreviate it or to select extracts from it depending on the use to which the copy was going to be confined. Without entering further into the details of the Latin manuscript tradition of *De doctrina*, the explanations above demonstrate its high degree of complexity.

A comprehensive history of the Latin manuscript tradition of *De doctrina cordis* is not currently within our reach. However, a brief consideration of its textual manifestation in Latin manuscripts offers evidence for its possible functions. In addition to the HV and IP redactions, the textual tradition of *De doctrina* shows that other, more radical, variants of the treatise, such as summaries, resumés, chapter excerpts and reordered renditions, fulfilled particular needs.[11] The I–voice of the Latin prologue positions itself as though impersonating the role of a preacher; one could therefore infer that the treatise that it introduces is made up of material for the use of preachers. As we will see in the following section, however, the structure of the HV and IP redactions of *De doctrina* is not 'preacher-friendly'; that is, it does not readily yield itself to use within a sermon. On the other hand, more radical versions of *De doctrina*, some of which are found in the manuscript company of preaching material, seem to have been assembled with this specific function in mind.[12]

2. The structure and content of *De doctrina cordis*

The Fourth Lateran Council of 1215 placed heavy emphasis on clerics' obligations to teach and preach. In addition, the advent of the mendicant friars and their academic involvement at the medieval universities caused them to engage with teaching and preaching, as well as theoretically debating the requirements for a good preacher and providing handbooks to support the *officium praedicatoris*. Although no claim can be made for *De doctrina* to have contributed to the kind of discussions found in, for example, such treatises as Henry of Ghent's

nescientes, ipsa uerba usque ad corda audientium non transmittunt'. And: 'In **hoc** verbo ammonetur predicator ut uerbum salutis diligenti et familiari expositione studeat eliquare ut sic ipsum uerbum facilius ad cor audientium transfundatur'. Hendrix, *Hugo I*, pp. 165–6.

11   For a more extensive discussion on this topic, of which this paragraph is a very brief summary, see C. Whitehead, '*De doctrina cordis*: Catechesis or Contemplation?', in Renevey and Whitehead (eds), *Companion*, pp. 57–72.

12   See, for instance, Basel, Öffentl. Bibliothek der Universität, MS B.x.4, of Dominican origin, in which selected chapters from *De doctrina* are found next to sermons. Whitehead, '*De doctrina*', p. 58.

Summa quaestionum ordinarium, written around 1275–76, the fact remains that *De doctrina* reflects those new interests in and preoccupations with the *officium praedicatoris*.[13]

However, *De doctrina cordis* is not an *ars praedicandi* nor a collection of *exempla*. As stated above, it circulated in several versions that may have been devised as such from the inception of the project. Although we will come back briefly to those different versions when discussing further the various uses to which *De doctrina* was put, it is appropriate at this point to offer information about *De doctrina* as found in the 1607 Naples edition, a reprint of an edition produced two years earlier in the same city. This edition, which remains extant only in Oxford, Bodleian Library, 8° L 12 Th. BS, provides the Latin text with which we compare the Middle English adaptation in a following section.[14]

De doctrina cordis is divided into seven books or treatises (both *liber* and *tractatus* are used in the table of contents of the Naples edition), with further subdivision into chapters. Book 1 is made up of thirty chapters and comprises more than half of *De doctrina*. The remaining books are less substantial, with six chapters for book 2, five for books 3 and 4, two for book 5, five for book 6, and two for book 7.[15] Each book deals with an aspect of the heart which is linked to one of the gifts of the Holy Spirit, so that the following pairs are created: 1) *praeparare – donum timoris* (to prepare the heart with the gift of fear); 2) *custodire – donum scientiae* (to guard with the gift of knowledge); 3) *aperire – donum pietatis* (to open with the gift of piety); 4) *stabilire – donum fortitudinis* (to stabilize with the gift of fortitude); 5) *dare – donum consilii* (to give with the gift of counsel); 6) *levare – donum intellectus* (to lift with the gift of understanding); 7) *scindere – donum sapientiae* (to cut with the gift of wisdom).[16] The organization of the treatise around the seven gifts of the Holy Spirit recalls preaching material similarly organized in this way. In addition,

---

[13]   For a recent illuminating discussion about the duty of the preacher, see A. Minnis, *Fallible Authors: Chaucer's Pardoner and Wife of Bath* (Philadelphia, 2008), pp. 36–97; see also S. Wenzel, *Latin Sermon Collections from Later Medieval England: Orthodox Preaching in the Age of Wyclif* (Cambridge, 2005), esp. pp. 288–96 on the friars.

[14]   Hendrix, *Hugo I*, pp. xxviii. The Naples 1607 edition is nearly identical to the first printed edition of 1506 (Paris), which differs only in the divisions and chapter headings from one of the earliest manuscripts of *De doctrina*: Oxford, Bodleian Library, MS Lat. th. f. 6, s. xiii (last third).

[15]   See the index in *Speculum concionatorum, ad illustrandum pectora auditorum, in septem libros distributum*, Auctore F. Gerardo Leodiensi, Ordinis Fr. Praedicatorum Lectore celleberrimo (Naples, 1607), Oxford, Bodleian Library, 8° L 12 Th. BS, pp. xiv–xv; henceforth cited as *De doctrina*.

[16]   See *De doctrina*, p. 5.

the division of the material into smaller thematic portions shows the influence of thirteenth-century academic practices in which the friars played a significant role. Indeed, it is possible that *De doctrina* may have come under the influence of the same Parisian masters and their disciples as the thirteenth-century vernacular *Ancrene Wisse* with regard to the division of the text into small parts, enabling a non-sequential reading of parts of the treatise.

Although the arrangement of the Latin text as found in the 1607 Naples edition does not yield itself to ready-made preaching use, the division described above would make the extraction of passages to be used for that purpose relatively easy. Hence it should come as no surprise to learn that some Latin sermons refer to *De doctrina* as a source of additional information in relation to their own content.[17] As well as contributing to sermons, the manuscript contexts of *De doctrina* also indicate that it may have functioned as a catechetical aid. Elsewhere, it seems to have functioned as a treatise of guidance, with the monastic novitiate as its probable target audience.[18] The variety of uses to which the Latin text was put, even without making reference to its vernacular transformations, makes it a perfect example of a text 'en mouvance'.[19]

3. Authorship

The application of 'mouvance' to *De doctrina*, a Latin text transmitted via the written medium, is at odds with the usual application of this term to vernacular anonymous texts whose means of transmission was oral. However, vernacularity apart, the process of transmission and adaptation of *De doctrina*, briefly sketched in the section above, bears interesting similarities to that of *Ancrene Wisse*, a treatise shaped anew by its anonymous author to fit the tastes of its changing readership. The author of the *Ancrene Wisse* participated in the process of disseminating his 'oeuvre', or work, into several equally valid texts. The same may be said of the author of *De doctrina*, who, according to Guido Hendrix, oversaw the production of the version of the text extant in Leiden,

---

[17] Whitehead, '*De doctrina*', p. 61.

[18] Ibid., pp. 61–3.

[19] See P. Zumthor, *Essai de poétique médiévale* (Paris, 1972); for the use of this term in the context of medieval English religious literature, see B. Millett, 'Mouvance and the Medieval Author: Re-editing *Ancrene Wisse*', in A.J. Minnis (ed.), *Late-Medieval Religious Texts and their Transmission* (Cambridge, 1994), pp. 9–20; see also her on-line article at http://www.soton.ac.uk/~wpwt/mouvance/mouvance.htm (last accessed 8.9.08).

Bibliotheek der Rijksuniversiteit, MS 2579, which offers suggestion for devising further different versions of the work.

But who was the author of *De doctrina cordis*? Is he, as in the case of *Ancrene Wisse*, growing more evasive as time goes by?[20] The list of possible authors, including Robert Grosseteste, Gerard the Carthusian, Hugh of St Cher, the Cistercian Gerard of Liège, Albert the Great, the Dominican Gerard of Liège, Alphonse of Spira and Albert of Brescia, has been cut down recently to two foregrounded names, those of Hugh of St Cher and the Cistercian Gerard of Liège.[21] As editors of the Middle English version of *De doctrina*, we leave it to experts of the Latin text to support one author against the other, and we provide here only a brief summary of the evidence that has been used in each case. Having reviewed early manuscript ascriptions of *De doctrina* to the Dominican friar Gerard of Liège, in 1931 André Wilmart suggested, on the basis of the literary content of *De doctrina*, that a Cistercian scholar with the same name – Gerard of Liège – would be a more plausible candidate for authorship. Although Guido Hendrix initially accepted this hypothesis, from the 1980s onwards his view changed to favour Hugh of St Cher (d. 1263), Dominican provincial, cardinal and papal legate.[22] The many reminiscences and imagistic and thematic associations to Hugh's *Postillae* were one of the main reasons that led Hendrix to propose Hugh of St Cher as the author of *De doctrina*.[23] After a careful reassessment of the evidence offered by Hendrix, Nigel Palmer offers arguments in favour, in his view, of Wilmart's original attribution of *De doctrina* to the Cistercian Gerard of Liège, who probably

---

[20] Since the suggestion made by E.J. Dobson in 1976 of Brian of Lingen, which has not been favourably received, no other suggestion has been made. The current evidence allows only a specification of the author's institutional affiliation with the Dominican order. For an account of the current state of research on this point, see *Ancrene Wisse: A Corrected Edition of the Text in Cambridge, Corpus Christi College, MS 402, with Variants from Other Manuscripts*, ed. by B. Millett with the assistance of R. Dance, EETS OS 326 (2006), pp. xvi–xix; see also E.J. Dobson, *The Origins of Ancrene Wisse* (Oxford, 1976), pp. 312–68.

[21] For such a list, see Candon, *Doctrine*, pp. xlii–l.

[22] This is only a brief summary of Palmer's own recapitulation of the authorship question; see N. Palmer, 'The Authorship of *De doctrina cordis*', in Renevey and Whitehead (eds), *Companion*, pp. 19–56.

[23] The full title of the work is *Postillae in universa Biblia juxta quadruplicem sensum, litteralem, allegoricum, moralem, anagogicum*. For an edition of the text, see Ugonis de S. Charo, S. Romanae Ecclesiae tit. S. Sabinae Cardinalis primi Ordinis Praedicatorum, *Opera omnia in universum Vetus & Novum Testamentum*, 8 parts in 5 vols (Cologne, 1621). Hereafter cited as Hugh, *Postillae*.

lived in a monastery in the southern Low Countries, from which Cistercian literary culture flourished. In addition to *De doctrina*, Gerard of Liège is strongly linked to the *Septem remedia contra amorem illicitum*, the *Quinque incitamenta ad Deum amandum ardenter*, and the *Tractatus super septem verba dicto a Domino Jesu Christo pendente in cruce*. Another work that can be associated with him is *De duodecim utilitatibus tribulationum*. Gerard of Liège worked with a mixed Cistercian audience in mind, and showed himself to be greatly influenced by Hugh of St Cher's works in particular and by the Parisian schools in general.

4. Vernacular versions

In addition to the number of extant Latin manuscripts, another measure of the wide transmission and circulation of *De doctrina* is the number of late medieval vernacular versions that circulated throughout Europe. There are four extant manuscripts of two Dutch versions, four of one Middle English version, four of three French versions, seven of several German versions, one of an Italian version and several late-fifteenth- and early-sixteenth-century early printed editions of a Spanish version.[24] *De doctrina* shows itself to have been part of a pan-European devotional phenomenon, satisfying broad devotional needs within the confines of the monastery, the convent, the beguinage and the lay world. Although each version bears the mark of the Latin original, its new garb also reflects a high degree of adaptability and attests to specific devotional and linguistic demands. One of the Dutch translations, for example, written in Western Flanders dialect, is the only vernacular version to make use of the IP redaction of the Latin text. It was aimed at the community of Augustinian canonesses of St Trudo, initially part of the congregation of St Victor, and affiliated in 1456 with the Windesheim Chapter, a grouping of priories inspired by the *devotio moderna* movement. As purity of heart was one of the main concerns of *devotio moderna*, and the flaming heart, St Augustine's symbol, was highly visible throughout St Trudo abbey, *De doctrina* proved an appropriate text to satisfy the devotional needs of the canonesses in the course of their conventual reform. Another copy of the text was made for the Carmelite convent of Sion in Bruges.

The French tradition, with four extant manuscripts, is another interesting

---

[24] For detailed discussions and bibliographical information about those vernacular versions (with the exception of the Italian version), see relevant chapters in Renevey and Whitehead (eds), *Companion*. The information on those versions is borrowed from our companion volume.

case in point. In the case of one manuscript, Troyes, Bibliothèque municipale, MS 1384, the manuscript provenance is indicated as Clairvaux and is dated from the fifteenth century. The very plausible argument put forward by Anne Mouron – that the vernacular text was produced for the use of lay brothers within the Cistercian monastery of Clairvaux[25] – throws light on the use made of vernacular texts in the fifteenth century. Although the laity became an avid audience for vernacular devotional texts at this period, nonetheless, one should not omit to survey the role played by monastic orders, not only in copying and circulating vernacular texts, but also in making use of them for their personal devotional consumption. On the other hand, Oxford, Bodleian Library, MS Holkham Misc. 42 inserts a passage into the section on the sacrament of the altar that makes reference to the hunting practices enjoyed in courtly circles. Even if it is not possible on the basis of this inserted passage to definitely assign a courtly audience to the text, it nevertheless assumes one familiar with such practices, possibly outside a monastic setting. The early date for MS Holkham Misc. 42, the thirteenth century, is exceptional amongst vernacular versions of *De doctrina*. Of the four French manuscripts, two of them (MSS Holkham and Douai) are copies of the same translation, while MS Troyes offers a different primary version of the Latin text. The fourth manuscript, Paris, Bibliothèque nationale, MS fr. 13272, offers an adaptation rather than a translation of a Latin version, and includes a series of changes that would appear to suggest a fifteenth-century secular readership.[26] This slightly more in-depth consideration of the French vernacular dissemination of *De doctrina* serves to show how much remains to be uncovered in order to fully understand the complex dissemination of the text throughout Europe.

The six extant German vernacular versions are dated after the Council of Constance (1414–18) and should be read in the context of the monastic reform programmes which issued from that council and also that of Basel (1431–49).[27] In that context, the discussions in *De doctrina* upon exemplary

---

[25] A.E. Mouron, 'The French Translations of *De doctrina cordis*', in Renevey and Whitehead (eds), *Companion*, pp. 199–206.

[26] For a detailed analysis of Bibliothèque nationale, MS fr. 13272, see A. Mouron, 'The *Livre de l'instruction du cuer de l'ame devote*: A Medieval French Translation of *De doctrina cordis*', in D. Renevey and C. Whitehead (eds), *The Medieval Translator/ Traduire au Moyen Age* 12 (Turnhout, 2010), pp. 237–50.

[27] For information on these councils, see the *Catholic Encyclopedia* online at: http://www.newadvent.org/cathen/04288a and htmhttp://www.newadvent.org/cathen/ 02334b.htm (last accessed 16.9.08).

religious life within a community would be useful both to novices and also to religious leaders in monastic, mendicant or canonical settings wanting to implement reform programmes within their own communities. Some of the German versions give particular emphasis to passages working to that effect: that is, providing practical information on how best to lead the religious life.[28] For example, the German version of *De doctrina* found in Munich, Bayerische Staatsbibliothek, Cgm 447, was used, along with other reform texts, to trigger a reform campaign at the Benedictine convent of St Walburg in Eichstaett. The manuscript is entirely made up of reform texts and specific extracts of *De doctrina*. Reform was enacted via texts with a didactic and practical agenda; nonetheless, these were not the only means used by the ecclesiastical authorities: in the case of the convent of St Walburg, the abbess, Elisabeth of Rechberg, was also dismissed, and the improvement of vernacular competence was helped by the support of the nearby convent of Rebdorf. It seems that although Augustinians, Benedictines, Dominicans and Franciscans used different means to achieve reform, nonetheless, the devotional texts used for that aim were often similar. Both full and truncated German versions of *De doctrina* served that purpose and need to be read with reference to this context, lest the significance of the truncated versions be downplayed.

Did the influence of *De doctrina cordis* remain limited geographically speaking to Northern Europe, with manuscripts of the Latin text and vernacular versions circulating mainly in the Low Countries, Germany, Austria, Switzerland, England and northern France? If the current location of medieval manuscripts is anything to go by, most of them are indeed found in libraries in these countries, with fewer manuscripts of the Latin version currently located in libraries of eastern countries, or in Italy and Spain. Only one extant manuscript contains an Italian version of *De doctrina*, and there is no extant manuscript of the Spanish version: the first available version in Spanish is found in an early printed book published in Salamanca in 1498. *Del enseñamiento del coraçon* went through several reprints: in Toledo in 1510, again in the same city in 1525, and in the southern city of Baeza in 1551. The evidence gathered so far points to a monastic or conventual readership for this Spanish version.[29]

---

[28] This is also the case for some Latin versions circulating in Germany; see K.-H. Steinmetz, 'De doctrina cordis and Fifteenth-Century Ecclesial Reform: Reflections on the Context of German Vernacular Versions', in Renevey and Whitehead (eds), *Companion*, pp. 223–37.

[29] See A.J. Lappin, 'The Spanish Translation: *Del enseñamiento del coraçon* (Salamanca, 1498)', in Renevey and Whitehead (eds), *Companion*, pp. 238–52.

On the basis of the evidence gathered so far for the continental vernacular versions, it would seem that most were initially aimed at an enclosed audience, whether monastic or conventual. This is rather surprising, considering the growing importance devout lay readers have been assumed to have had in the production of devotional texts in the fifteenth century. *De doctrina*, in its Latin and vernacular versions, offers sound, practical, and orthodox teaching, supported by creative analogies, that would have fulfilled the needs of monks, nuns and friars living in times of considerable religious turmoil. Although we must assume that the text reached a lay audience relatively speedily, the fact that it was first circulated within the walls of monastic and conventual houses makes it a slightly odd, reactionary text when compared to most other late-fourteenth- and fifteenth-century productions or translations.

5. *The Doctrine of the Hert* and fifteenth-century English religiosity

Was the English context for the Middle English text equally imbued with reformist intentions? *The Doctrine of the Hert* is only one of a vast corpus of texts translated from Latin in the late fourteenth and fifteenth centuries. In the mid 1990s, the well-known article by Nicholas Watson upon the impact of Arundel's Constitutions on the production of original vernacular texts, sketched a post-Arundelian scene marking the end of a golden age in the production of original vernacular theologies. The time for original vernacular productions was gone: with a few probable exceptions, the Constitutions made it impossible for succeeding generations of vernacular religious authors to emulate the likes of Rolle, Hilton or the author of *The Cloud of Unknowing*.[30] The religious writing activity that the Constitutions tolerated consisted in the translation and adaptation of canonical, reactionary texts which could easily inhabit an oppositional position to the heretical texts of the Lollards. Translations of texts attributed to Rolle, who died in 1349 and whose texts therefore did not fall under the ban of vernacular texts written during the time of Wyclif, circulated in the early fifteenth century, along with several

---

[30] N. Watson, 'Censorship and Cultural Change in Late-Medieval England: Vernacular Theology, the Oxford Translation Debate, and Arundel's Constitutions of 1409', *Speculum*, 70 (1995), 822–64. The composition of Julian of Norwich's *A Revelation of Love*, the long text which resulted from the series of visions she received at the age of thirty, may have taken place in part after 1409. For a recent edition of Julian's writings, see *The Writings of Julian of Norwich: A Vision Showed to a Devout Woman and A Revelation of Love*, ed. by N. Watson and J. Jenkins (University Park, Pennsylvania, 2006).

others all equipped with an impeccable orthodox pedigree.[31] Fifteenth-century English religiosity expressed in the vernacular bears the marks (or the scars) of the tension felt by the religious authorities as a consequence of Wycliffite and other heresies, the Constitutions being only the most evident visible deployment of that anxiety. Nonetheless, as Kerby-Fulton's book makes quite clear, the English scene, although in some respects idiosyncratic, remains intimately linked to pan-European religious phenomena.[32] In that respect, the reformist use to which vernacular versions of *De doctrina* were put on the continent may serve as a useful context from which to assess the English situation.

The Doctrine of the Hert is found in four fifteenth-century manuscripts: Cambridge, Fitzwilliam Museum, MS McClean 132 (hereafter M), Durham, University Library, MS Cosin V.III.24 (hereafter C), Oxford, Bodleian Library, MS Laud Misc. 330 (hereafter L), and Cambridge, Trinity College, MS B.14.15 (hereafter T).[33] In addition, we know of the existence of a fifth manuscript of the *Doctrine*, now lost, which was listed in the will of a Norwich gentry widow, Margaret Purdans.[34] The information gathered from all the extant manuscripts, together with the lost one, offers some understanding of the reading context in which the *Doctrine* circulated. In M and C, our text is found with two other texts written for the special attention of 'a religious woman'. These are *A letter of religious gouernance sent to a religious woman* and *A letter sent to a religious womman of þe twelue frutes of þe Holy Gost and first of þe frute of charite*.[35] M and C seem to have been compiled as books of devotion and guidance for the attention of enclosed women. The *Doctrine* was adapted to suit the needs of a non-*litteratus* audience, who would have missed the significance of the allusions to classical and patristic texts. L places the *Doctrine* in the company of a brief penitential lyric which appears at the end of the manuscript in a different hand. This lyric appears in a longer version in British Library, MSS Additional 37049

---

[31] For a survey of English religious vernacular translations, see V. Gillespie, 'Religious Writing', in R. Ellis (ed.), *The Oxford History of Literary Translation in English, Volume I: to 1550* (Oxford, 2008), pp. 234–83.

[32] See K. Kerby-Fulton, *Books under Suspicion: Censorship and Tolerance of Revelatory Writing in Late Medieval England* (Notre Dame, IN, 2006).

[33] Full manuscript descriptions and library catalogue details are provided in a following section of this Introduction.

[34] Margaret Purdans, St Giles', Norwich, Widow 1481 (Dioc. Reg. Caston 163), quoted in H. Harrod, 'Extracts from Early Wills in the Norwich Registries', *Norfolk and Norwich Archeological Society*, 4 (1855), 335–6.

[35] *A Deuout Treatyse Called the Tree and xii Frutes of the Holy Goost*, ed. by J.J. Vaissier (Groningen, 1960).

and 37605. The penitential, affective and performative character of the lyric is emphasized in Additional 37049 by its association with an image of Christ offering his wounded heart to a praying layman.[36] It is also interesting to note that the prayer that concludes the *Doctrine* in this manuscript is the same as that found in Middle English manuscripts of Marguerite Porete's *Mirouer des simples ames*, which are all of Carthusian origin. Considering the interest that Carthusian authors showed in converting communal devotional performances into mental visualizations for private, individual use, it is not at all unlikely that they might have showed an interest in copying a text like the *Doctrine* for the satisfaction of their own devotional needs or those of a female community under their spiritual care.[37] The clear address to a female readership in all the manuscripts of the *Doctrine* shows that the Middle English version had that particular audience in mind. Although some evidence, such as Margaret Purdans' will, points in the direction of a lay female audience, most of the manuscript evidence indicates a primary audience of nuns. On the last flyleaf of T, for instance, a note makes reference to 'dame Crystine seint nicolas', abbess of the convent of St Botoph without Algate in London, who bequeathed the *Doctrine* to the use of all future abbesses of that house. It is interesting to note that on two occasions T substitutes 'menoresse' for 'mynche' and 'sistir': T seems to have been copied for a specific audience of Franciscan nuns, with the Aldgate nuns as the obvious primary readership. Information about the now lost fifth manuscript of the *Doctrine* indicates Franciscan ownership as well. Margaret Purdans, whose family connections are detailed by Mary Erler, bequeathed her own copy of the *Doctrine* to the East Anglian Franciscan convent of Bruisyard.[38]

Unlike other continental vernacular versions, the Middle English *Doctrine* was specifically written for the attention of a female audience. As the section below, on the changes made in translation from Latin to English, shows clearly, the alterations brought to the text are made with that audience in mind, an audience that the translator considers in his own prologue, which he substitutes for the Latin one, to be 'unavisid' and 'unkunnyng' in devotional

---

[36] For an image of this folio, see J. Brantley, *Reading in the Wilderness: Private Devotion and Public Performance in Late Medieval England* (Chicago and London, 2007), plate 7.

[37] For an extensive discussion of the use made of communal and performative visual and textual material within the charterhouse, see Brantley's fine analysis of British Library, MS Additional 37049 in *Reading in the Wilderness*, pp. 167–209.

[38] See Mary Erler's chapter, 'A Norwich Widow and Her "Devout Society": Margaret Purdans', in M. Erler, *Women, Reading, and Piety in Late Medieval England* (Cambridge, 2002), pp. 68–84.

knowledge.[39] By pruning the Latin version of many scriptural, patristic and classical references the adaptor creates a piece in which the striking and extended images thronging the text appear to float free of their initial scriptural or literary base. This structural audacity apart, the *Doctrine* does not seem to have filled as daring a role as that found, for instance, in the German context. The careful abbreviation of the text by the adaptor for his audience shows him to have been aware of the need to spell out and simplify basic religious points. This is not to say that the text remaining in the Middle English version is spiritually unambitious, since the seventh book on ecstatic love, even if reduced in size, nevertheless offers sophisticated concepts for spiritual consumption and possible performance. It is therefore much more difficult to assert that the Middle English *Doctrine* was one of the tools used by religious reformers in their campaign against heretical views and lax discipline in nunneries, as may have been the case for the German versions. On the other hand, the care with which the translator/adaptor reworks his material for his female audience, with the effect of de-clericalizing the Latin text and turning it into a devotional tool, may reflect a certain anxiety as to the diminished level of post-Arundelian tolerance for over-ambitious and learned texts written in the vernacular.

6. Themes and images

As a devotional text, *The Doctrine of the Hert* offers captivating information about the way in which medieval religious and lay readers made use of textual images in shaping their devotional identities. The *Doctrine's* provision of images still fascinates modern readers as it shows an author/translator's bold and extravagant use of puzzling images to trigger devotional feeling. The exploration of the kitchen imagery, with its spiritual culinary recipes, is one case in point.[40] Deployed in the text without being strongly anchored in their

---

[39] See D. Renevey and C. Whitehead, "'Opyn þin hert as a boke": Translation Practice and Manuscript Circulation in *The Doctrine of the Hert*', in J. Jenkins and O. Bertrand (eds), *The Medieval Translator* 10 (Turnhout, 2007), pp. 125–48 (131–3, 137).

[40] For a discussion of kitchen imagery and the household, see D. Renevey, 'Household Chores in *The Doctrine of the Heart*: Affective Spirituality and Subjectivity', in C. Beattie, A. Maslakovic and S. Rees Jones (eds), *The Medieval Household in Christian Europe c.850–c.1550: Managing Power, Wealth, and the Body* (Turnhout, 2003), pp. 167–85; see also C. Batt, D. Renevey and C. Whitehead, 'Domesticity and Medieval Devotional Literature', *Leeds Studies in English, New Series*, 36 (2005), 195–250; and V. Gillespie, 'Meat, Metaphor and Mysticism: Cooking the Books in *The Doctrine of the Hert*', in Renevey and Whitehead (eds), *Companion*, pp. 131–58.

original biblical context, these images gain a new lease of life. The ambiguity created by this free-floating contextualization is not without danger: the spiritual culinary recipes proposed by the *Doctrine* play in a such a heightened manner with all the sensory faculties that those faculties are barely left behind when the reader tries to decode the spiritual message. Lettuce, lamb, chicken and roasts do not lose their culinary potential to touch man's appetites when applied to devotional values.[41]

Rather than discussing the most vivid themes and images in the *Doctrine*, this section attempts to understand the visual map designed by the author/ translator, which the audience is invited to internalize in order to facilitate the development of its devotional subjectivities. In addition to the organization of the text into seven books addressing various operations of the heart in relation to one of the gifts of the Holy Spirit, this map is a further important structural device. Here, in schematic form, is the visual map that is offered for the consumption of the readers (see diagram on p. xxv).

The images used to construct the spiritual itinerary that the nuns are invited to follow are deployed more pervasively in the first three books of the treatise. However, even within those books the aim is not to make use of an overly varied number of visual referents. Rather, core visual concepts, such as 'household preparations', the 'preparation of meat' or the 'besieged castle' are developed in considerable detail. The attention to detail helps the reader to easily internalize and memorize those concepts. For example, the second book makes very detailed use of the besieged castle as a visual concept.[42] Its employment leads to a detailed description of 'a castelle þat is set in a straunge lond, besegid with enemyes, stuffid with a kynges tresoure'.[43] However, the internalization of this visual concept also includes several other images associated with the context of the besieged castle, such as the castle porter who monitors those going in and out.[44] Even horses are a part of this landscape, and the fact that they may be bridled or unbridled introduces a discussion about discretion in speech. The ship, another possible element in medieval warfare, reinforces the same point.[45]

It is striking to note how the visual concepts which serve as structural foundations in the early books of the *Doctrine* recede in the final books to

---

[41] See *Doctrine of the Hert*, pp. 20, 24–7.
[42] For a study of besieged castles, see C. Whitehead, *Castles of the Mind: A Study of Medieval Architectural Allegory* (Cardiff, 2003), pp. 87–116.
[43] See *Doctrine of the Hert*, p. 47, lines 6–7.
[44] Ibid., p. 52, lines 220–6.
[45] Ibid., p. 53, line 248–p. 54, line 266.

Book 1	Book 2	Book 3	Book 4	Book 5	Book 6	Book 7
Preparing the heart with the gift of dread	Keeping the heart with the gift of pity	Opening the heart with the gift of knowledge	Keeping the heart stable with the gift of strength	Giving the heart with the gift of counsel	Lifting up the heart with gift of understanding	Cutting the heart with the gift of wisdom
House made ready to receive a worthy guest	The besieged castle	The open book		The merchant	The native country	The lover
Meat prepared to be consumed		The open door		The barber		
Spouse preparing herself to please her husband						

become briefer images simply strengthening one point or another. One even notices a possible apophatic tendency in book 7, with reference made to 'Seynt Denyse' on the topic of ecstatic love.[46] However, images are not completely absent from the last books of the *Doctrine*, and so one cannot make that claim too strongly. But it is interesting to see that the *Doctrine*, perhaps in a manner reminiscent of the more ambitious *Cloud of Unknowing* text, progressively reduces the initial structural role given to visual tools in the final stages of the spiritual programme that it proposes.

7. *The Doctrine of the Hert* as a translation

In the absence of a modern edition of *De doctrina cordis*, it is difficult to assess how widely the Latin text varied from manuscript to manuscript, but it seems certain that these differences were not restricted simply to the text's prologue.[47] In these circumstances, it is not possible to establish which surviving Latin manuscript (if any) the translator used, and therefore a detailed and lengthy analytical comparison of the Latin and the Middle English is not feasible. When one compares the Middle English text with the 1607 Latin edition, it is possible to state, however, that the Middle English *Doctrine* is an adaptation rather than a translation of the Latin treatise. Indeed, the massive reduction of the Latin text alone would be sufficient to justify treating the Middle English as an adaptation.[48] But there are other changes between the Latin and this vernacular version which need to be remarked upon.

The only proper addition featuring in the *Doctrine of the Hert* is its new prologue, which is not a translation of the Latin prologue but an altogether different introduction composed by the translator.[49] It very clearly indicates that this vernacular rendering has a non-*litteratus* audience of nuns in mind:

> I ... have compilid this tretice ... to the worship of God principally, and to edificacioun of symple soules.[50]

---

46   Ibid., p. 86, line 63.
47   Some of the Latin manuscripts, for example, have a fourth sign of virginity. See G. Hendrix, *Le manuscript Leyde Bibliothèque de l'Université, BPL 2579, témoin principal des phases de redaction du traité 'De doctrina cordis'* (Gent, 1980), introduction, p. vi. See also Hendrix, *Hugo I*, pp. 170–1.
48   For a more detailed assessment, see A. Mouron, '*The Doctrine of the Hert*: a Middle English Translation of *De doctrina cordis*', in Renevey and Whitehead (eds), *Companion*, pp. 83–108.
49   Additions of a few words long are not taken into account. For a comparative analysis of both the Latin and English prologues, see ibid., pp. 99–104.
50   *Doctrine of the Hert*, p. 3, lines 20–3.

The simple souls are later referred to as 'mynche[s]',[51] i.e. nuns. As a result of this new audience, the Middle English version is less intellectual and more didactic, less meditative and more devotional than the Latin version, and these changes can be noted in various ways.

The didactic stance of the Middle English version is perhaps first most obvious in the seven-book division, according to the seven gifts of the Holy Ghost, which is given more prominence in the vernacular version. Indeed, such a method of arranging material according to one of the lists of catechetical material is very much favoured by didactic manuals.[52] In its chapter 'Diuisio sequentis operis in septem Tractatus', the Latin text links each book to one of the seven gifts of the Holy Ghost:

> dicendum est, quod dono Timoris cor praeparatur, dono Scientiae custoditur, dono Pietatis aperitur, dono Fortitudinis stabilitur, dono Consilij datur, dono Intellectus leuatur, dono Sapientiae scinditur.[53]

The next and only reference to any of the seven gifts occurs at the beginning of book 7:

> 'Scindite corda vestra'. Scissionem quam facit contritio praetermittentes; ad tractandum de illa, quae pertinet *ad donum sapientiae* iuxta nostrum propositum, considerationis nostrae oculum conuertamus.[54]

Furthermore, in the Latin and in other of the vernacular versions, notably in medieval French,[55] the seven-book division is made much less visible by the

---

[51] See list of chapters in *Doctrine of the Hert*, p. 4, lines 41–54.

[52] For vernacular treatises, see, for example, *Dives and Pauper*, *Speculum vitae*, *Ancrene Wisse*, part IV, etc. This is also the case in Gower's *Confessio amantis* and Chaucer's *Parson's Tale*. For Latin texts, see M.W. Bloomfield et al., *Incipits of Latin Works on the Virtues and Vices, 1100–1500 AD* (Cambridge, MA, 1979), now supplemented by R. Newhauser and I. Bejczy, 'A Supplement to Morton W. Bloomfield et al. *'Incipits of Latin Works on the Virtues and Vices, 1100–1500 A.D.'*, Instrumenta Patristica et Mediaevalia 50 (Turnhout, 2008).

[53] *De doctrina*, p.5. (It is said that the heart is prepared by the gift of dread, it is kept by the gift of knowledge, it is opened by the gift of pity, it is made stable by the gift of strength, it is given by the gift of counsel, it is lifted up by the gift of understanding, and it is cut by the gift of wisdom.)

[54] *De doctrina*, p.276, our emphasis. ('Cut your hearts'. Passing over the cutting which contrition causes, let us turn the eye of our consideration to dealing with that cutting which belongs to the gift of wisdom, according to our plan.)

[55] See *De doctrina*. For manuscripts in medieval French, see Douai, Bibliothèque municipale, MS 514; Troyes, Bibliothèque municipale, MS 1384; Paris, Bibliothèque nationale, MS fr. 13272. These are henceforth referred to as MS Douai, MS Troyes and

subdivision of each book into chapters.[56] Book 1, for example, is divided into thirty-two chapters in the 1607 edition.[57] One would be forgiven, therefore, for forgetting that the seven gifts of the Holy Ghost have been mentioned at all.

The Middle English text, however, retains only the seven-book division. There are no subdivisions into smaller sections. This seven-book division is also given more prominence by the translator, who says in his prologue: 'I ... have compilid this tretice ... dividid *into seven chapitres*',[58] and who provides a list of contents at the end of the Prologue.[59] In this list the translator most clearly links each book to one of the seven gifts of the Holy Ghost. The first, for example, reads: '*Capitulum primum.* How and in what wise a mynche shuld make redy here hert to God be þe yifte of drede'.[60]

In addition to this, and with the exception of Book 1, the translator reiterates the role of each gift in the opening paragraphs of each book. For example, the third paragraph on the opening page of book 3 reads:

> Certeyn, sister, it is ful necessarie for to know þis, for many þer ben þat wenyn here boke of here conscience is opyn, and it is schitte. Why, trowist þou? Trewly, for: 'þei bysien hem moche for to know many outward þingis', as Seynt Bernard seith, 'and litel or nought here owne conscience.' Thenk, sister, þerfor, *be þe yifte of connyng*, þat þin hert or þi conscience is a boke wherin þou shuldist rede in þis lif.[61]

MS Paris respectively. MS Douai, being the closest to *De doctrina*, is usually preferred as the first witness. Note also that the Pseudo-Bernardine text, *Liber de modo bene vivendi ad sororem* (*PL* 184, cols 1199–306), which is divided into seventy-two chapters in Latin, keeps its chapter division in its fifteenth-century Middle English translation, *The Manere of Good Lyvyng* (ed. by A. Mouron (Turnhout, forthcoming)). Similarly, the Middle English translations of Aelred of Rievaulx's *De institutione inclusarum* are also divided up into relatively short chapters. One of the two translations even adds rubrics to each chapter in order to help the reader. See *Aelred of Rievaulx's De institutione inclusarum*, ed. by J. Ayto and A. Barratt, EETS 287 (1984), MS Bodley 423.

[56] Note, however, that it has not been possible to check every surviving manuscript of the text.

[57] For a list, see Appendix B, pp. 209–12.

[58] *Doctrine of the Hert*, p. 3, lines 20–4, our emphasis.

[59] The Latin 1607 edition also has a list of contents at the beginning, but the emphasis is on the list of chapters which divide each book. See *Index eorum, quae summatim infra continentur, De doctrina*, no pagination.

[60] *Doctrine of the Hert*, p. 4, lines 41–2.

[61] *Doctrine of the Hert*, p. 59, lines 9–14, our emphasis. Note that this paragraph is not in the Latin. See *De doctrina*, p. 191. It is neither in MS Douai, fol. 100r, nor in MS Troyes, fol. 92v.

At the beginning of book 2, which in the Middle English is linked to the gift of pity, and not as in the Latin to the gift of 'scientiae', the translator emphasizes pity with a pun on words. The second paragraph reads:

> ¶ Were it not gret *pite* þat such a castelle shuld be robbed and put into enemyes hondis? Yis, certeyn. ¶ We must be governyd *with þe spirit of pite* in doble wise, lest þis castelle be distroyid.[62]

If the seven gifts of the Holy Ghost are barely alluded to in the Latin, the vernacular reader, on the contrary, is certainly made aware of them.[63]

The emphasis on the seven-book division, and even more so the lack of subdivision into smaller sections, in the Middle English text are not simply cosmetic changes, but impact on the way the audience reads the text, or hears it read. The reader or listener is faced with much larger units, as confirmed by the manuscript layout: in all four surviving manuscripts of the Middle English text there are no breaks within the seven books, no larger capitals which mark the beginning of a new section and would provide the reader with a clear indication as to where he can pause.[64] By contrast, the 1607 Latin edition further facilitates the reader's task by adding notes in the margins.[65] This lack of obvious breaks in the Middle English version suggests a different pace of reading.[66]

---

[62] Ibid., p. 47, lines 7–10, our emphasis. The Latin text begins by comparing the heart to a vessel or dish. The comparison to a castle comes later. Note that at the end of book 4, the translator also refers to the relevant gift of the Holy Ghost: 'be þe spirit of gostly strengthe', Ibid., p. 76, line 313. The Latin does not do so. See *De doctrina*, p. 244.

[63] Note that the seven gifts of the Holy Ghost often feature in vernacular didactic manuals compiled after Lateran IV, among such other lists as the Ten Commandments, the Creed, the Seven Deadly Sins, and so on. See, for example, Oxford Bodleian Library, MS Bodley 938, fols 6v–7r; Oxford, Bodleian Library, MS Rawlinson C 209, fol. 11v; Oxford, Bodleian Library, MS Laud Misc. 524, fols 20r–v.

[64] Paragraph signs feature in McClean, Laud and Trinity manuscripts, but they frequently indicate very short units, often simply what has been punctuated as one sentence. MSS Laud and Trinity have fingers in the margin, but these emphasize specific points and not the beginning of new sections. MS McClean has none.

[65] This is most noticeable in book 1 which, in the Middle English as in the Latin, is about half of the entire treatise in length. In the much shorter Middle English version, as Candon has observed, the 'same unequal proportion between the first and the other chapters are kept; as in the Latin, the English first chapter is longer than the other six combined.' Candon, *Doctrine*, p. lx.

[66] See below, p. xxxvi.

One reason why the absence of smaller sections is possible in the Middle English is the much shorter length of the text. If the Middle English is slightly more than half the Latin treatise in length, by and large the reduction has not been achieved by the omission of specific sections of the text, but by a constant reduction throughout the volume as a whole, and this for various reasons.[67] The Middle English *Doctrine* was written for a female audience of nuns, but it is uncertain whether this was also the case for the original *De doctrina*.[68] Indeed, the vernacular version at times omits material which would be better suited for a male audience. For example, the figure of the barber, which is used in book 5 to discuss how to accept or give correction, is greatly reduced in the Middle English.[69] As Candon has noticed, moreover, references to 'profane authors' are regularly omitted by the translator.[70] In book 2, for example, when the Latin reads:

> Nam in correctione attendendus est status personarum, quae corripiuntur ... Vnde, cum sene, et veterano parcius agendum est, *vt dicit Seneca,* et Apostolus I. ad Timoth. 5. Seniorem ne increpaueris, sed obsecra vt patrem.[71]

the Middle English translates:

> The states of every persone shuld be considered: old folk shuld not be blamed as scharply as yong folk, for Seynt Poule seith: *Seniorem ne increpaueris sed obsecra vt patrem.* 'Blame not' he seith, 'sharply an old man, but pray him for to amende his defautes as þou woldist pray þi fadir'.[72]

---

[67] A few entire sections, though, have been omitted by the translator. See Mouron, 'The *Doctrine of the Hert*: a Middle English Translation', pp. 94–8.

[68] As Hendrix has noted, the Latin manuscripts come with two slightly different prologues. One of the two, the IP-prologue, is clearly addressed to 'ignar[is] predicator[ibus]'. See Hendrix, *Hugo I*, pp. 165–9.

[69] *De doctrina*, pp. 250–1; *Doctrine of the Hert*, p. 79, lines 67–83. It is noteworthy that the *Liber de modo bene vivendi*, which in all likelihood was written for a woman, does not experience this reduction of material when it is translated into Middle English, under the title *The Manere of Good Lyvyng*, for the Bridgettine sisters of Syon.

[70] See Candon, *Doctrine*, p. lxi.

[71] *De doctrina*, p. 187, our emphasis. (For in correcting other people, one must pay attention to the position of the person to be chastised ... Hence, with the aged and the old, it must be done more moderately, as Seneca and the Apostle (in the first epistle to Timothy 5:1) say 'do not rebuke an elder, but entreat him as you would your father'.)

[72] *Doctrine of the Hert*, p. 57, lines 397–401.

The reference to Seneca has disappeared from the English vernacular version.[73] It is important to recognize, however, that, as for material unsuitable for a female audience, such omissions are not the result of the change in language but in audience. MS Troyes, a French translation aimed at the monks of Clairvaux, translates the same passage thus:

> Car on doit regarder l'estat des personnes que on vuet reprenre … Dont si comme dit Seneques: on doit plus deporter les anciens et espargnier. Et saint Pol dit: *Seniorem ne increpaveris sed obsecra sicut patrem.* Tu ne dois pas reprenre ung ancient mais proier ausi comme pere.[74]

The reference to Seneca remains in the French vernacular text.

This difference of audience rather than of language in the retention or omission of profane authors is even more striking in MS Paris. Unlike the Middle English, this medieval French adaptation of *De doctrina* does not specify that it is aimed at a female audience, and probably was not.[75] It also begins with a new prologue, but one which initially quotes secular authors:

> Pour quoy dit *le poete Ovide* contre les foles amours: Obvie au commencement et resiste que pechiez ou faulte ne soit faicte. Car trop tard l'on donne medicine a maladie qui de long temps a priz racine. *Et Senecque dit en ses tragedies*: Celluy qui au commencement obvie a temptacion et virtueusement resistet seurement est victorieu.[76]

---

[73] Note that Seneca is quoted in the *Ancrene Wisse*: '*Seneca: Ad summam uolo uos esse rariloquas, tuncque paucilocas.* "Þet is þe ende of þe tale", seið Seneke þe wise; "Ich chulle þet ȝe speoken seldene, ant þenne lutel"'. *Ancrene Wisse: A Corrected Edition of the Text in Cambridge, Corpus Christi College, MS 402*, ed. by B. Millett, EETS 325 (2005), p. 30. Seneca is also quoted in the *Book for a Simple and Devout Woman*, which is a Middle English translation of Peraldus' *Summa de vitiis et virtutibus*: 'Forþi Senek wel seiþ þer he þus seiþ: *Si vis te diuitem facere non est pecunie adiciendum sed cupiditati detrahendum est.* – "If þu coueitest to be riche, ne gedere þu no godes togidere, bot wiþdraw þyn herte from ȝernynge of godes"'. See *Book for a Simple and Devout Woman*, ed. by F.N.M. Diekstra (Groningen, 1998), p. 169.

[74] MS Troyes, fol. 90v. (For one must pay attention to the status of the people one wishes to rebuke … Hence, as Seneca says, one must exempt and spare old people even more. And St Paul says: *Seniorem ne increpaveris sed obsecra sicut patrem.* 'You must not rebuke an old man, but entreat him as you would entreat your father'.)

[75] For an assessment of this interpolated medieval French version of the text, see Mouron, '*Livre de l'instruction du cuer de l'ame devote*', pp. 237–50.

[76] MS Paris, fol. 1r, our emphasis. (For this reason, the poet Ovid says against foolish loves: resist them in the beginning so that no sin or fault ensue. For medicine is administered too late to a disease which has taken root for a long time. And Seneca

If, as D.N. Bell has noted, 'from the early fourteenth century onwards, most nuns ... were unable to read and understand a non-liturgical text in Latin',[77] it is not surprising that references to 'profane authors' have disappeared from the Middle English text. However, in many instances, patristic references have also been left out by the translator. Consider the following passage:

> Propter hoc tale dicit Sapiens Ecclesiastae 7. Meliorem esse diem mortis, die natiuitatis. Vnde mors Sanctorum, Natale eorum in Martyrologijs appellatur; quia tunc quasi moriuntur ad mortem, et nascuntur ad vitam. Vere moriuntur ad mortem qui de vita praesenti exeunt. Nostrum vero viuere (*dicit Cassiodorus*) quotidie interire est. Vere etiam tunc nascitur ad vitam: quia (*sicut dicit Augustinus*) Mors, quam constabat esse vitae contrariam, facta est iustis instrumentum, per quod transitur ad vitam.[78]

and its Middle English version:

> Of þe wiche blissid deth spekith Salamon þus: *Meliorem esse diem mortis quam nativitatis.* That is: 'he commendith rather the day of oure holy dygheng þan þe day of oure wrecchid birth'. So þat the deth of holy creatures is clepid in holy chirch þe day of here birth, for þan they dyghen from deth and ben boryn to lif. Oure living in þis lif, *as doctouris seyn*, is noþing ellis but every day for to begyn to digh.[79]

Although the specific references have gone, the translator here acknowledges *auctoritates* in a general phrase 'as doctouris seyn'.[80] More often, however, there is

says in his tragedies: he who says no to temptation in the beginning and virtuously resists is surely victorious.)

[77]   D.N. Bell, *What Nuns Read: Books and Libraries in Medieval English Nunneries*, Cistercian Studies Series 158 (Kalamazoo, 1995) p. 66.

[78]   *De doctrina*, p. 81, our emphasis. (For this reason the wise man says in Ecclesiastes 7:2 that the day of one's death is better than the day of one's birth. Hence the death of the saints is called their birth day in the martyrologies; for then, as it were, they die to death and are born to life. Truly those who leave this present life die to death. Indeed our living (says Cassiodorus) is to die each day. Truly then they are also born to life, for (as St Augustine says) death, which was well known to be opposed to life, was made for the just person the means by which they cross over to life.)

[79]   *Doctrine of the Hert*, p. 27, lines 852–8, our emphasis.

[80]   Cassiodorus may be less commonly referred to in vernacular works, but he features at least once in the *Ancrene Wisse*. See *Ancrene Wisse*, ed. by Millett, p. 106. Note that, in MS Troyes, fol. 39r, both patristic quotations are retained, although translated into medieval French.

no such acknowledgement: the references are simply omitted.[81] In this respect it is interesting to note that if the Middle English usually first quotes biblical verses in Latin, which are then translated into Middle English, the case is different for patristic quotations, which are only quoted in Middle English:

> So seyth Seynt Bernard: 'His mete is my penaunce'.
> Seynt John Crisosteme seith: 'Yif thi penaunce like the, it liketh God'.
> For, as Seynt Austyn seyth: 'Penaunce restorith ayen al that was lost'.
> 'This vice' as Seint Gregor seith, 'is a perlious vice'.[82]

It is important to note, moreover, that the absence of patristic quotations in Latin is very much the translator's choice. MS Douai usually (although not always) quotes patristic authorities in Latin first:

> Dont y dist Cassiodorus: *Pax vera est habere concordiam cum moribus probis et litigare cum viciis.* C'est a dire Vraie paix est avoir concorde a bonnnes coust[umes] et tenchier aux visces.[83]

And so does the author of the *Ancrene Wisse*.[84] Other translators prefer to avoid Latin altogether for biblical as well as for patristic quotations.[85]

---

[81] For example: 'Noli ad nihilum te offerre, quae tanto pretio es a Christo comparata. Apende te ex pretio, dicit *Augustinus*', *De doctrina*, p. 52, our emphasis. (Do not bring yourself to nothing you who were bought by Christ for such a great price. Augustine says, evaluate yourself in accordance with this price.) 'Bringe not þi soule to nought þat so preciously is bought', *Doctrine of the Hert*, p. 19, lines 561–2.

[82] Respectively, ibid., p. 11, lines 260–1, p. 12, lines 269–70, p. 13, line 304, p. 15, lines 408–9, and so on. Note that there is one occasion when the same omission of the Latin occurs with scriptural verses in book 3. Indeed, all the quotations from Revelation are given only in Middle English. See ibid., p. 60, line 43–p. 64, line 198. Is the Latin omitted because the material quoted is part of the argument of the passage (i.e., the seven clasps of Revelation are equated to the seven impediments which prevent one from opening one's heart), or perhaps because Revelation is not as well known to a *non-litterata* audience as other books of the Bible?

[83] MS Douai, fol. 12v. (And Cassiodorus says this: *Pax vera habere concordiam cum moribus probis et litigare cum viciis.* That is to say, true peace is to have concord with good customs and to quarrel with vices.)

[84] For example: 'Of þis wit seið Seint Austin, *De oodoribus non stago nimis. Cum assunt, non respuo; cum absunt, non require.* "Of smealles", he seið, "ne fondi Ich nawt mucheles. ʒef ha beoð neh, of Godes half; ʒef feor, me ne recche"'. *Ancrene Wisse*, ed. by Millett, p. 41.

[85] This is the case for *The Manere of Good Lyvyng*. The same is also true for Nicholas Love's *The Mirror of the Blessed Life of Jesus Christ: A Reading Text*, ed. by M.G. Sargent (Exeter, 2004).

In addition to the omission of profane authors and patristic quotations, many biblical quotations are also left out from the Middle English translation. A brief look at both the Latin and the Middle English suggests not only that the vernacular version has reduced the overall number of quotations, but that it has also reduced the range of biblical books it quotes from, and this is especially noticeable with the Old Testament. If both versions have a majority of quotations from Isaiah, from the Psalms and from Solomon's books (i.e., Proverbs, the Song of Songs and Ecclesiasticus), the Latin also quotes from the smaller prophets (i.e., Micah, Hosea, Habakkuk, Daniel, Nahum, etc.) and has a greater number of quotations from other books of the Old Testament (i.e. Exodus, Kings, Jeremiah, Ezechiel, etc.). The emphasis on Wisdom literature and the New Testament in the Middle English implies a more devotional outlook.

It is important to realize, moreover, that often the omission of profane authors, as well as of patristic and biblical quotations, does not occur in isolation but together. In other words, it is the greater part of the text's exegesis which has been left out by the translator, as is the case, for example, in the following excerpt:

> Virgo est anima, quae a corruptione peccati est libera, quando integra est per incorruptionem, quando [vn]um diligit, [vn]um quaerit, [vn]um petit. Illud vnum, quod est necessarium, quod facit charitas, cuius officium est vnire. *Attende, quod virgo, quae oleum non habet in lampade excluditur in Euangelio a nuptijs caelestibus. Matthaei 25. Lampas sine oleo, virginitas sine charitate, Bernardus: Subtrahe oleum, lampas non lucet: sic subtrahe charitatem, et integritas, siue castitas non placet. Sed notandum, quod si quaerat signa integritatis sponsus, vel virginitatis in sponsa ipsa, ei tenebitur exhibere, sicut dicit Lex, Deuter. 22.* Notandae autem sunt de multis tres conditiones, quae virgini praecipue conueniunt, et virginitatem quodammodo attestantur, quae sunt, Verecundia in vultu, Paupertas in rebus, et Simplicitas in sermone.[86]

---

[86] *De doctrina*, pp. 93–4. (The soul is a virgin when it is free from the corruption of sin, when incorruptibility keeps it pure, when it loves only one, when it looks for one thing only, and when it asks for one thing only. That one thing which is necessary, is done by charity, whose function is to unite. Notice that in the Gospel according to Matthew 25, the virgin who has no oil in her lamp is excluded from the celestial marriage. The lamp without oil represents virginity without charity. St Bernard says: *Subtrahe oleum, lampas non lucet.* In the same way, take away charity and purity, and chastity does not please. But note that if the Bridegroom looks for signs of purity or of virginity in the bride herself, she is compelled to show them to him,

Here the Latin explores the relationship between virginity and charity with a quotation from the gospel, a reference to St Bernard and one to the Old Testament. All three have been omitted by the translator:

> Thi soule is a mayde and a virgine whan it is kept clene fro corruptible þoughtes, and lovyth but o þing, and axith but o þing, and seketh but o þyng, þe wiche is charite that knyttith and onyth a soule to God. But now, þre condiciouns þer ben þat acordith wel to a mayde. On is shamefastnes, another is poverte, and þe þrid is symplenes in wordis.[87]

In this instance the passage left out is relatively brief, but on other occasions the translator omits several pages from the Latin.[88] When one remembers that at least one of the two Latin prologues addresses itself to preachers, it is hardly surprising that exegesis should be an important part of the text. Neither is it surprising that the Middle English text, which is aimed at 'suche that ben unkunnyng in religioun',[89] and more specifically nuns, should omit it. Indeed, yet again, it is the audience rather than the language which explains these omissions. MS Troyes, which, as has been pointed out above, is a medieval French translation of *De doctrina* aimed at the monks of Clairvaux, translates the same passage thus:

> L'ame est vierge qui est franche de toute corrupcion qui est par amo[ur entiere][90] qui desire et aimme une chose et quiert une chose et tout ce fait charite. Pren ce garde que la vierge qui n'ot point d'oile en sa lampe fu forsclose des noces du ciel. La lampe sans oile est virginites sans charite. Donc dit saint Bernard: *Subtrahe oleum lampas non lucet. Subtrahe caritatem castitas non placet.* Oste l'oile de la lampe elle ne luira pas. Oste charite et ta chastete ne plaira pas. Mais ce fait bien a noter que se le espeus quiert en ses pense les ensaignes de verite que elle li est bien tenue a monstrer ensi le dit la loy. Trois choses especialment sont

as the law says in Deuteronomy 22. Now note that there are three conditions among many that are especially suitable for a virgin and which, in a measure, bear witness to virginity. These are modesty of expression, poverty in possessions, and simplicity in words.)

[87] *Doctrine of the Hert*, p. 30, lines 967–73.

[88] For examples of pages omitted by the translator, see Textual Commentary, *Capitulum primum*, notes 88, 103, 115, 148 etc.

[89] *Doctrine of the Hert*, p. 3, line 6.

[90] MS Douai, fol. 53r reads 'enterre par dilection'; MS Paris, fol. 57r: 'entiere par dilection'.

ensaignes et tesmongnage de virginite: vergoingne en la face, povretes en choses, simplestes en paroles.[91]

Not only has the quotation from St Bernard been retained (which perhaps is to be expected in a Cistercian copy of the text), but also the reference to the Law.

The omission of a considerable part of the exegesis also impacts on the way the Middle English text is read. The Latin text is not only read, but must also be contemplated, as Peter of Celle explains:

Lectio autem est pascua uberrima in qua animalia pusilla cum magnis assidue pascendo praeparant holocausta Domino medullata, cum intra se ruminantes dulcissimos divinae scripturae flores, nil aliud corde et ore continent.[92]

As the above passage from *De doctrina* shows, exegesis demands a slow and concentrated reading, as it examines a point from various angles, and thus induces reflection, since the reader is to build a whole picture from the various angles examined. In other words, whereas the Latin text is multi-layered, the Middle English one is often single-layered, and can thus be read (at a faster pace) rather than meditated upon. If reading the Latin text can also be seen as a repetitive process, the Middle English on the contrary often avoids repetition.

De quibus dicit Salomon Prouerb. 15. Non amat pestilens eum, qui se

---

[91] MS Troyes, fol. 45v. (The virgin soul is free from all corruption, and is pure through love. It desires and loves one thing only, and looks for one thing only, and all this is done by charity. Note that the virgin who had no oil in her lamp was excluded from the heavenly marriage. Hence St Bernard says: *Subtrahe oleum lampas non lucet. Subtrahe caritatem castitas non placet.* Take away the oil from the lamp, and it will not shine. Take away charity and your chastity will not please. But note this well that, if the bridegroom looks in his thought for signs of truth, the virgin is bound to show them, thus says the law. Three things especially are a sign and a proof of virginity: shame in the face, poverty in things and simplicity in words.) For the same passage in MS Douai see fols 53r–53v. MS Douai does not have the reference to the Law, but it is impossible to claim with any certainty that this omission is due to the translator. It could simply be the Latin manuscript he used.

[92] Peter of Celle, *L'École du cloître*, ed. and tr. by G. de Martel, SC 240 (Paris, 1977), p. 232. (Reading is a very rich pasturage, in which small and large animals prepare fat holocausts for the Lord by continual browsing, when they ruminate within themselves the sweetest flowers of divine scripture and have nothing else in their hearts or in their mouths. Peter of Celle, 'The School of the Cloister', in Peter of Celle, *Selected Works*, tr. by H. Feiss (Kalamazoo, 1987), pp. 63–130 (103).)

corripit. Imo ad modum equi scabiosi, qui cum tangitur super vulnus, fremit, et recalcitrat. *Tales assimilantur Diabolo, qui corrigi non potest. Vnde dicit idem Ecclesiastici 21. Qui odit correptionem, vestigium est peccatoris. Peccatorem vocat hic Diabolum per antonomasiam, cui multum assimilatur, qui correptionem odit, sicut vestigium valde simile est pedi, quasi dicat: Vestigium Diaboli habet in corde, qui correptionem, et reprehensionem odit.*[93]

In this excerpt, for example, the highlighted lines may be regarded as simply repeating the point made by Proverbs 15:12: that is, that a sinner does not like correction. The repetition disappears from the Middle English:

Of such spekith Salamon and seith: *Non amat pestilens eum qui se corripit.* That is: 'a contagious synner loveth not his reprover.' But such on farith as a scabbid hors, þat as sone as it is touchid upon the galle, it begynneth to wynce.[94]

Moreover, it is noteworthy that, unlike other devotional texts, the Middle English reader is not told to read and re-read the text.[95]

Reading the Middle English text, then, is not so much an intellectual exercise demanding reflection and meditation as a practical one. The different Middle English prologue sets this out quite clearly. The translator has this to say about how to read the treatise: 'thei mow, be the grace of almyghty God, come to sadnes of *good lyvyng*, yif þey wil do theyre bisynessis *for to rede and undirstonde* that they fynde write in this same tretice, not only with the lippis of the mouthe, but also and namly with the lippis of the soule'.[96] Reading goes

---

[93] *De doctrina*, p. 77, our emphasis. (About whom [i.e., hearts which react impatiently when reprimanded] Salomon says in Proverbs 15:12 'a noxious person does not love the one who chastises him.' Always, in the manner of a mangy horse whose wound is touched, he grumbles and kicks back. Such people are compared to the Devil who cannot be corrected. Hence Salomon again says in Ecclesiasticus 21:7: 'he who hates reproof walks in the footstep of a sinner.' Here, he compares by antonomasia the sinner who hates reproof to the Devil, as a footstep [*vestigium*] is greatly similar to the foot; as if he said, he who hates reproof and reprimand has the imprint [*vestigium*] of the Devil in his heart.)

[94] *Doctrine of the Hert*, p. 25, lines 794–7.

[95] *The Manere of Good Lyvyng*, for example, states in its prologue: 'reverent suster, rede overe this boke, and rede it thorogh agayn and agayn, and ye shall know in it, howe ye shall love God and your neyghbour …', Oxford, Bodleian Library, MS Laud Misc. 517, fols 1v–2r.

[96] *Doctrine of the Hert*, p. 3, lines 25–8, our emphasis.

hand in hand with understanding, not with 'rumination'. Indeed, whereas the Latin prologue begins: 'Praeparate corda vestra Domino: Verba sunt Samuelis, I. Reg. 7',[97] the very first words of the Middle English prologue, even if in Latin, are: '*Intelligite, insipientes in populo; et stulti, aliquando sapite*'.[98] And this understanding must result in good living. This is made clear again a few lines down: 'Wherfore I beseche almyghty God that al thoo, the whiche han this tretice in honde, mow so *rede and undirstonde* it, that it mow be to theim *encrese of vertue and of stable lyvyng*'.[99] The same emphasis also emerges through the rather didactic vocabulary used throughout the prologue and in the first two sentences of book i, words such as 'enforme', 'enformyng', 'edificacioun', 'informacioun', 'enformyd', 'informaciouns' and 'techith'.[100]

Emphasizing the reading and understanding of the text, rather than providing the reader with material for meditation, considerably alters the tone of the treatise. In this respect, it is essential to note that the translator's omissions are not restricted to substantial and lengthy passages in the Latin, with the implication that he otherwise translates the text accurately. For even when the translator broadly follows the Latin text, he usually rewrites the text rather than translating it, at times quite drastically, as in the following example. The text explains that there are 'þre condiciouns ... þat acordith wel to a mayde. On is shamefastnes, another is poverte, and þe þrid is symplenes in wordis':[101]

> He wille þat his spouse be ashamed to be seyn in st[r]etes and townes. Such shamefastnes bryngeth in holynesse of vertuos lyvyng, and þat is a gret grace, as Salomon seith: *Gracia super graciam mulier sancta et verecunda*. 'It is a grace passyng many oþer graces' he seith 'a womman to be bothe holy and shamefast'.[102]

This short paragraph is the translator's rendering of the first condition, 'shamefastnes'. A comparison with the Latin text demonstrates the extent of the translator's rewriting:

---

[97] *De doctrina*, p. 1.

[98] *Doctrine of the Hert*, p. 3, line 1, our emphasis. ('Understand, ye senseless among the people: and, you fools, be wise at last', Ps. 93:8, *Douai Bible*). The *Doctrine of the Hert* is not the only didactic manual in the vernacular to begin with a Latin quotation. See *Ancrene Wisse, Dives and Pauper*, the *Desert of Religion*, etc.

[99] Ibid., p. 4, lines 37–40.

[100] Ibid., pp. 3–5.

[101] Ibid., p. 30, lines 971–3.

[102] Ibid., p. 30, lines 974–9

Nam, si verecundiam commendans Apostolus I. ad Timoth. 2. iniungit maritatis, multo fortius virginem Christi verecundiae charactere vult signari; vt etiam videri in publico erubescat. Rebecca viso Isaac operuit vultum suum. Genes. 24. Esto ergo verecunda Christi virgo, Gallice, *ne blande abbandone.* Esto verecundia exemplo illius virginis, quae ab Angeli aduentu ad ipsam intrantis expauit, et turbata extitit in sermone, cogitans apud se qualis esset illa salutatio. Bernardus in Homelia super Missus est. Quod t[u]rbatur virgo, virginei est pudoris, quod tacuit apud se de modo salutationis insolito cogitans, prudentiae fuit. Ista duo, Verecundia, et Prudentia coniunguntur, quia vna sine altera non sufficit. Sunt enim aliqui ex verecundia indiscreti, vt audita, rarius distinguant, et ideo indiscrete respondent. Alij de Prudentia praesumentes, inuerecundi, et odiosi efficiuntur. Vtrumque beata Virgo obseruauit, quam verecundia turbatam, Gallice *Effroyee,* Prudentia cogitantem reddidit, et tacentem. Esto ergo virgo Christi prudens, et verecunda, vt gratiam super gratiam consequaris: iuxta verbum Ecclesiastici 36. dicentis: Gratia super gratiam mulier sancta, et pudorata. Sanctitas, quae idem sonat, quod munditia, refertur ad prudentiam, sicut effectus ad causam. Prudentia enim conseruatrix est munditiae.[103]

---

[103] *De doctrina*, pp. 94–5. (For, if the Apostle in 1 Timothy 2, recommending modesty, enjoins it to married women, all the more strongly does he want the virgin of Christ to be imprinted with the mark of modesty, so that indeed she would blush to be seen in public. In Genesis 24, when Rebecca had seen Issac, she covered her face. Therefore, be a modest virgin of Christ, in French, 'ne blande abbandone'. Be modesty itself, following the example of that famous Virgin who was much afraid, when the Angel came to her, and who was troubled by his words, as she wondered what that salutation could be. See what St Bernard says in his homily on *Missus est*. That the Virgin was troubled is a sign of virginal modesty; that she kept silence, wondering about the unusual manner of this salutation, was a sign of prudence. These two, modesty and prudence, are joined together because one is not sufficient without the other. For there are some people who are modest through a lack of discretion, so that they rarely discriminate what they hear, and, on that account, answer without discretion. Others, presuming they are being prudent, show a lack of modesty, and make themselves hateful. The Blessed Virgin observed both the one and the other, when modesty made her troubled, in French 'effroyee', and prudence made her think and be silent. Be therefore a modest and prudent virgin of Christ, so that you may attain grace upon grace, according to the words of Ecclesiasticus 26: *Gratia super gratiam mulier sancta, et pudorata.* Holiness, which has the same ring as moral purity, belongs to prudence, as the effect [does] to the cause. For prudence is the keeper of moral purity.)

Whereas the intellectual approach of the Latin could be considered formal and distant, the Middle English is more down-to-earth, almost conversational. Such rewriting of the text occurs throughout, and its cumulative effect completely transforms the original treatise.[104]

This more conversational tone can also sometimes be noticed in the way the translator presents his material. Whereas the Latin author reveals a rather scholastic frame of mind by some of the words he chooses, the Middle English avoids such terms. For instance, when the Latin reads:

> Attende autem, quod in tribus consistit praeparatio hospitij cordis tui. *Primo* vt mundetur, *secundo*, vt ornetur, *tertio*, vt portae eius custodiantur.[105]

the Middle English translates:

> Now <s>ister, yif thou wilt receyve worthily this blissed champioun, *first* thow must make clene thyn hous of thin hert, and þan þou must aray it, and *aftirward* kepe wele þe yates of þe same hous.[106]

The reduction of lists, which Candon was the first to remark upon,[107] could also be explained by this conversational tone.[108]

The latter also results in a more intimate approach. Although we know nothing about the identity of the translator, it is not impossible that he may have played some advisory role to the audience of nuns. He may even have been their confessor. It is striking that the number of addresses to the 'Sister' is greatly increased in the Middle English:

> *Nolite iudicare, et non iudicabimini.* 'Demeth not' he seith, 'and ye shul not be demed.' As thow he seyde thus: yif ye mow not eschew suspicious

---

[104] For reference specifically to the beginning and ending of each book, see below, pp. xliii–xlvi.

[105] *De doctrina*, p. 7, our emphasis. (But note that the inn of your heart must be prepared in three ways. First it must be cleansed, secondly it must be fitted out, thirdly its doors must be guarded.)

[106] *Doctrine of the Hert*, p. 7, lines 71–3, our emphasis. It is interesting to note that in medieval French, MS Troyes, a Clairvaux copy (i.e., for a monastic audience), translates 'primo', 'secundo', 'tertio' by 'premierement ... apres ... apres', fol. 2r, but MS Paris, which was probably designed for a secular but educated audience, possibly one of priests, has the more literal translation: 'premierement ... secondement ... tiercement', fol. 2r.

[107] Candon, *Doctrine*, pp. lx–lxi.

[108] It is noteworthy that the *Liber de modo bene vivendi*, which has a great number of 'Sister' addresses, does not have such lists, and that *Ancrene Wisse*, which only rarely addresses the sister, does.

demyngis because of freelte, fleeth than in any wise dome of ful diffinicioun, þat ye yive no ful sentence of þing that ye ben in doute of. Be war now, *sister*, þat þou deme not (and specialy noo good þingis) evyl, but doo as þe bee doth, þe wiche turnith bitter juse of floures into swetnes of hony. Yif þow here evyl, be ware þow yif no feith lightly þerto, but suppose the best. An envious soule cannot do so, but it farith as an ereyne. It tornith what that ever it soketh into venym; þat is, it tornith good into evyl. *Sister*, have thow þe hert of a bee, and turne þe werst into the best by trew compassioun of other defautes, considering sharply þin own defautes and merciably þe defautes of oþer. Lo, *sister*, þis is the stole of Cristis sete in þin hert, that is, for to deme þinself and be ware for to deme other.[109]

Indeed, this passage replaces in the Latin a 'lengthy section on the subject of right judgment with examples from which the translator has taken that of the bee and the spider'.[110] Although the Latin passage is much too long to be quoted here in its entirety, its beginning is amply sufficient, even in the absence of biblical and patristic quotations, to demonstrate how the Middle English creates a more intimate tone:

Nolite iudicare, et non iudicabimini. Vnde dicitur super Apostolum: Si suspiciones vitare non possumus, quia homines sumus; iudicia tamen, et diffinitiuas sententias continere debemus. Sed cum plures sint mali, quam boni, et frequentius fiant mala, quam bona, mouet quosdam cur non liceat dubia in peius interpretari, sicut in melius? Ad quos est reponsio: quod anima hominis est ad bonum cognoscendum. Vnde cum in illa sit ex parte operis discretio, et cognoscibilitas, quo animo fiat: debet anima secundum naturam suam magis existimare bonum, quam malum. Noli ergo, o anima te ipsam denaturare, mala de incertis, et dubijs existimando.[111]

---

[109] *Doctrine of the Hert*, p. 15, lines 382–97, our emphasis.

[110] Candon, *Doctrine*, p. 166.

[111] *De doctrina*, p. 29. ('Do not judge, and you will not be judged.' Hence it is said about the words of the Apostle: if, because we are men, we cannot avoid being suspicious, nevertheless we must refrain from judgments and definitive decisions. But since there are more bad than good people, and since bad actions occur more often than good ones, it makes some people question why doubtful things cannot be explained in a bad sense as well as in a good one? The answer to these people is that the soul of man exists in order to know good. Hence, since the soul can only partially understand an action and know the intention by which the action is performed, the soul, in accordance with its nature, must appraise the action to be good rather than evil. Do not, therefore, o soul, behave degenerately by judging uncertain and doubtful matters to be evil.)

The Latin philosophical and abstract discussion has gone from the Middle English, which chooses concrete examples instead, and addresses its message directly to the sister.

Addressing the sister at regular intervals not only makes for a more intimate tone; the translator also intervenes in order to guide his audience through her reading. For example, he regularly precedes his address to the sister by the interjection 'lo', in order to attract her attention to a specific point. This can be already seen in the above-quoted passage – 'Lo, sister, þis is the stole of Cristis sete in þin hert, that is, for to deme þinself and be ware for to deme other'[112] – but it also occurs on many other occasions:

> Loo, sister, seven þinges ben rehersid of þe hert: that is, to make it redy, to opyn it, to kepe it ...[113]

> Lo, sister, upon that stole of dome in þin conscience must oure lord sitte, and þerfor make the redy.[114]

> Lo, sister, þus have I declared how þou must make redy þin hert as an hous ... now, be the grace of God, I shal telle the how þou shalt make redy þin hert to God as meete þat must be etyn.[115]

> Lo, sister, þus have I declared þe how þou shalt make redy þin hert as mete ... Now shal I shew þe how þou shalt make it redy as a wyf maketh here redy ... for to plese here housbonde.[116]

> Lo, sister, bi þis mayst þou know þat þe wordis of oure lord sownyth swetly to devout repentaunt synneris.[117]

Another regular usage of the 'Sister' address is to make the reader aware of causes and consequences by adding the 'Sister' after 'therefore', as, for example, in the following excerpts:

> The bed of þis Helyse, Jhesu Crist, is pees and rest of conscience, as Davith seyth: *In pace factus est locus eius.* 'His place' he seyth, 'is made in pees'.

---

[112] *Doctrine of the Hert*, p. 15, lines 396–7, our emphasis.
[113] Ibid., p. 5, lines 25–6. Note that on several occasions (but not always), 'lo' translates the Latin 'ecce'. However, it is not followed in the Latin by an address to the sister.
[114] Ibid., p. 14, lines 357–8, our emphasis.
[115] Ibid., p. 19, lines 566–9, our emphasis.
[116] Ibid., p. 27, lines 868–71, our emphasis.
[117] Ibid., p. 46, lines 1588–9, our emphasis.

And perfor, sister, whan that evyr þou puttist þin hert in rest, thow puttist oure lord Jhesu Crist in his bed.[118]

A tornament is callid no bateyle but rather a prevyng of strength. Such tornementis usith the flessh and the soule ever stryvyng, and yit þe conscience may be in rest, for it is not overcome with no synne, þow þe flessh and the spirit provyd theire strengþe togedre. *Therfor sister,* be wel ware þat þou consent not to the wikkid styring of the flessh in the stry[v]ing to the souleward.[119]

Goo never withoute such a serjaunte of drede … And þan shal thi yates of thi five wittes be wel kept, for ther may never dedly synne entre wiþin the, but yif it come in by on of þi five yates. *Therfor, sister,* þe nedith also to have a porter for to kepe þi yates. Þis porter shal be discrecioun.[120]

Note that the translator is not unique in using these addresses. The *Liber de modo bene vivendi ad sororem* written for a nun follows the same usage.[121] This suggests once more that it is the audience rather than the language which determines these changes.

In each book of the text, moreover, there are two specific locations where the possible pastoral role of the translator comes to the fore. First he replaces the formal, if not rhetorical, introduction to each new book in the Latin text by a more conversational approach. The Latin text begins book 2 with these words:

Post tractatum de praeparatione Cordis secundum diuersas facies, sub multiplici diuisione diffusum: restat vt ad tractandum de Cordis custodia, cor, et stylum conuertamus.[122]

The Middle English reads instead:

Aftir this longe chapitre, þe wiche techith a mynche to make redy here hert, I purpose, be the grace of God, to declare how she shuld also kep here hert.[123]

---

[118] Ibid., p. 9, lines 157–60, our emphasis.

[119] Ibid., p. 9, line 183–p. 10, line 188, our emphasis.

[120] Ibid., p. 19, lines 530–5, our emphasis.

[121] For example: 'Ergo soror charissima', *PL* 184, col. 1201A; 'Igitur, soror dilecta', *PL* 184, col. 1201B; 'Igitur, honesta virgo', *PL* 184, col. 1204C, etc.

[122] *De doctrina*, p. 155. (After the treatise on the preparation of the heart of which we have considered different aspects and explored many divisions, we must turn our heart and stylus to the treatise on the keeping of the heart.) For book 3, see p. 191; book 4, p. 212; book 5, p. 244; book 6, p. 255; and book 7, p. 276.

[123] *Doctrine of the Hert*, p. 47, lines 1–3.

The translator highlights the didactic purpose of the chapter ('techith').[124] He replaces the formal first person plural ('conuertamus') by the more direct first person singular ('I purpose'). The rhetorical 'stylum'[125] has gone, and a reference to the 'grace of God' has been added.[126] Although this is not the case here, at the beginning of most of the other books he addresses his words to the reader by using second person singular pronouns.[127] On two occasions he goes further by appealing directly to the sister. Book 3, for example, begins:

> Sister, in to maner of wises I fynde þat þe hert must be opennyd. It shuld be openyd as a boke wherein thow shuldist rede ...[128]

This conversational tone is even more obvious at the beginning of book 7:

> Because *I have declarid þe* how þou shuldist lift up þin hert and whi, now *shal I* in þis last chapitre, ... *telle þe* how þou shalt cut þin hert.[129]

If the translator's pastoral role is made obvious at the beginning of each book in the Middle English version, it also holds true in the concluding lines of each book, when they are compared to the Latin. The Latin text ends book 3 with a quotation from Cicero and book 6 with one from St Augustine,[130] but with the exception of book 7, every other book in the Latin ends with an abrupt impersonal formula:

---

[124] This didactic purpose is also emphasized in later books. In book 4, the translator says: 'First þou shalt undirstonde', ibid., p. 68, line 3. There is nothing equivalent in the Latin. See *De doctrina*, p. 212. In book 5 'Attendentes cui cor dandum, quare, et quomodo dandum' (*De doctrina*, p. 244) becomes: 'Therfor, first *þou must know* to whom þou shuldist yive þin hert', *Doctrine of the Hert*, p. 77, line 6, our emphasis.

[125] 'Stilum prendere', for example, is a formula found in Cicero's writings.

[126] At the beginning of book 7, he says: 'be þe grace of God and þi devoute prayeris', *Doctrine of the Hert*, p. 85, lines 2–3.

[127] See books 4, 6, 7. Respectively, ibid., p. 68, line 3; p. 80, lines 1–3; p. 85, lines 1–3.

[128] Ibid., p. 59, lines 1–2, our emphasis. The Latin reads instead: 'Expedito tractatu de custodia cordis, et oris, ad tractandum de eiusdem Apertione, nostrae considerationis oculum conuertamus. Secundum autem duplicem faciem, de cordis apertione tractare intendimu. Est enim cor tanquam liber, qui aperiendus est ad legendum' (*De doctrina*, p. 191). See also book 5: 'Wete right wel, *sister*, þe nedith þe yifte of counseyle', *Doctrine of the Hert*, p. 77, lines 7–8, our emphasis.

[129] Ibid., p. 85, lines 1–3, our emphasis. The Latin reads: 'Dicto de cordis eleuatione, de eius scissione dicendum est, ad quod nos inuitat Dominus per Ioelem 2' (*De doctrina*, p. 276). The translator also says at the beginning of book 6: 'But how þou shalt lifte up þin hert to God and whi, *I shal telle þe*', *Doctrine of the Hert*, p. 80, lines 2–3, our emphasis.

[130] See *De doctrina*, respectively, pp. 212, 275.

Et haec dicta de ornamentis animae sufficiant.
Et haec dicta de custodia cordis, et linguae sufficiant.
Et haec dicta de cordis stabilitate sufficiant.
Et haec de cordis datione dicta sufficiant.[131]

In the Middle English, however, the translator usually repeats what he has been talking about and addresses the sister directly:

Thus, sister, þou must kepe þin hert, as Salomon seith: *Omni custodia serva cor tuum.*

Lo, sister, þus shalt þou opyn þin hert, bothe to God and to þin evencristen.[132]

The *ending* of several books further demonstrates the pastoral role of the translator, through his addition of sermon-like endings:

Thus have I declared þe þe þirtene ornamentes þat oure lord hath yif to the for to be arrayed with, yif þou wilt plese him as a gostly wif shuld plese here hosbonde, and so endith þe first chapitre of makyng redy of þin hert to God. *Cum Gloria in secula seculorum. Amen.*

Of þees þingis, sister be wel ware, for as it is rehersid in þe begynnyng of þis chapitre: *Optimum est gracia stabiliri cor.* 'The best þing for to stable þe hert in is grace', be þe spirit of gostly strengthe. *That grace God graunte us. Amen.*[133]

Although the translator has utterly altered the tone of the treatise with these changes at the beginning and end of each book of the text, it is interesting to

---

[131] *De doctrina*, book 1, p. 155; book 2, p. 190; book 4, p. 244; book 5, p. 255. Respectively, (And let these words about the soul's ornaments suffice: And let these words about the keeping of the heart and of the tongue suffice: And let these words about the establishing of the heart suffice: And let these words about the giving of the heart suffice.)

[132] Respectively, book 2, *Doctrine of the Hert*, p. 58, lines 441–2; book 3, ibid., p. 67, lines 336–7. See also books 4, 5 and 6, respectively ibid., p. 76, lines 311–14; p. 79, line 95; p. 84, lines 144–7.

[133] Respectively, book 1, ibid., p. 46, lines 1598–601; book 4, ibid., p. 76, lines 311–14, our emphasis. See also book 6 and book 7, respectively, ibid., p. 84, lines 144–7; p. 92, lines 257–9. Note that book 7 is the only one in the Latin text to end with such a formula: 'Illa autem, quae expectantibus se, praeparauit, sunt cognitio aperta summae veritatis, dilectio perfecta Diuinae bonitatis, securitas aeternae possessionis, quae in eo, et per eum habentur. Quo perducat nos Deus, qui est benedictus in saecula saeculorum. Amen' (*De doctrina*, p. 294).

note that this tone is not original to him, and nor is it confined specifically to vernacular works. It is, however, a style encountered in other texts aimed at a female audience. The *Liber de modo bene vivendi ad sororem*, for example, similarly addresses the sister and ends its chapter with sermon-like formulas. Its preface begins: 'Charissima mihi in Christo soror, diu est quod rogasti, ut verba sanctae admonitionis scriberem tibi', and ends: 'Omnipotens Deus custodiat, et ab omni malo te defendat, et cum omnibus tecum Deo pariter servientibus ad vitam perducat aeternam, venerabilis soror. Amen'.[134] Once more, the translator's method can be explained by an intention of adapting his text to a female audience.

Conclusion

Whereas the Latin text is an intellectual treatise aimed at educated readers (most probably preachers) accustomed to an exegetical style, the Middle English version, written for poorly educated nuns, has become a more practical, didactic and devotional text. It seems that the changes implemented by the translator are due to the difference in audience, rather than to the move from Latin to vernacular. In addition, and unlike other texts written or adapted for a female vernacular audience, the translator has not added material, such as glosses, in order to make the text more explicit.[135] Instead, he has chosen a much more drastic method: omitting a considerable amount of the original text and thus simplifying his text rather than providing it with explanations.

---

[134] *Liber de modo bene vivendi ad sororem*, PL 184, cols 1199A, 1199C–1200A. Respectively, (My dearest sister in Christ, you have asked me for a long time to write to you words of holy admonition: Let Almighty God keep and protect you from all evil, and let him bring you, and all those equally who serve God with you, to eternal life, venerable sister. Amen.)

[135] See, for example, *The Myroure of Our Ladye, Ancrene Wisse, The Manere of Good Lyvyng*, etc.

8. Middle English manuscript descriptions

Cambridge, Fitzwilliam Museum, MS McClean 132 (M)[136]

CONTENTS:
The Doctrine of the Hert, fols 1r–93v.
A letter of religious gouernaunce sent to a religious woman, fols 94r–117r.
A letter sent to a religious womman of þe twelue frutes of þe Holy Gost and first of þe frute of charite, fols 117v–198r.

A vellum manuscript measuring 222mm x 153mm. 199 fols. 25 lines per page, with ruled horizontal lines and vertical marginal lines. Fifteenth century. Collation: 1⁸–25⁸ (wants 8).

The entire manuscript is written in one excellent, clearly legible, fifteenth-century, bastard anglicana hand. It has subsequently been corrected throughout, either by the same or by another contemporary hand. Top line ascenders extend far into the top margin. Each book begins with an illuminated capital in gold, blue and pink, the capitals to the first book of the *Doctrine* on fol. 2v and to the opening of the two *Letters* being the most elaborate.

Rubrication is used to distinguish the following parts of the text: scriptural quotations in Latin and English, including those paraphased or in indirect speech; patristic quotations in English; the articles of the creed (fol. 71v forward); some proper names (e.g. fol. 46v: 'Cecile', 'Valerian'); some keywords within numbered lists (e.g. fol. 66v forward: the impediments to opening the book of the conscience); other keywords.

Signatures among the two *Letters*: 'John Savern', 'francis Rosse', 'francis Mallam'. On the last leaf, in a fifteenth-century hand: 'ihesu make me pore off hart and meke off spret'.

Modern binding by Zaehnsdorf.

M is listed as no. 83 in B. Quaritch's catalogue for December 1893 as follows: 'This is a very rare treatise or set of treatises, of ascetic character, written for the use of some house of Nuns'. The same words form part of a longer printed notice inserted within M:

> Doctrine of the Herte. MS on vellum. 193 leaves, 25 lines to page, with ornamental painted initials; bound in old russia and lettered "Ancient

---

[136] M.R. James, *A Descriptive Catalogue of the McClean Collection of Manuscripts in the Fitzwilliam Museum* (Cambridge, 1912), pp. 278–9. See also *Deuout Treatyse*, ed. by Vaissier, pp. x–xiv; Candon, *Doctrine*, pp. xiii–xiv.

Sermons MS". About 1460. This is a very rare treatise ... house of Nuns; perhaps, if we may judge from the southern and metropolitan character of the language, for the ladies of Sion.

Yif is the form for if, and elsewhere we find that yift=gift, yiuen=given, ayenst=against. That is, the old ȝ has been entirely replaced by y, and the þ is used side by side with the *th* throughout the book.

M then had a binding of c. 1780 with a double eagle on the back. It had earlier been no. 314 in an auction sale.

Since Quaritch's London bookshop was one of the most thriving centres of antiquarian exchange in the late nineteenth century, there are innumerable sources and disbanded libraries from which this manuscript could have been bought.[137] It is probably that Quaritch sold M to Frank McClean (1837–1904), who bequeathed it with the rest of his collection to the Fitzwilliam Museum, Cambridge.

The following notices are also found inserted into the front of M:

1. The Doctrine of the Herte. Small 4to.
   MS on vellum, beautifully written; old russia binding. About 1460.
   A set of interesting sermons by an eloquent preacher, addressed to women.

A handwritten notice from 1903 lists the quires of M, 8 folios in each:

2. 1–8
   9–16
   17–24
   25–32 etc.

3. An English Manuscript of the XIVth century, written in red and black gothic characters on 198ll. of vellum, with painted ornamental intials, russia. 4to.
   An interesting and important MS, illustrating the state of the language in the time of Wycliffe and Chaucer.

---

[137] S. de Ricci, *English Collectors of Books and Manuscripts (1530–1930) and their Marks of Ownership* (Cambridge, 1930), ch. 13: 'Bernard Quaritch and his Clients'.

Durham, University Library, MS Cosin V.III.24 (C)[138]

CONTENTS:
The Doctrine of the Hert, fols 1–69v.
Fols 70v–71v blank.
A lettre of relygyous gouernaunce sent to a relygyous woman, fols 72v–91v.
A lettre sent to a relygyous woman of þe twelue frutys of the hooly goost, fols 92v–150v.

Vellum and paper manuscript of mid-fifteenth century, probably written for an East Anglian nunnery. 558mm x 380mm. Collation for the *Doctrine*: 1–2[16], 3[16] wants 12–15 after fol. 43 replaced by 2 leaves, 4[14], 5[14] wants 10 after fol. 69 and 12–13 after fol. 70.

Written by four scribes as follows:

Scribe I: fols 1–43v line 5, except for passages by scribe II. 22–31 long lines per page. A mixed cursive hand. Some capitals simply elaborated with leaf work and human faces. Latin and English scriptural quotations are underlined. Spellings are East Anglian.[139]

Scribe II: fols. 17r–v, 32r–v, 30r lines 8–15, 39r lines 5-foot, 43v lines 6-foot (duplicating fol. 44r lines 1–23 by Scribe III), and fols 141r–v; also marginal corrections throughout. 22–4 long lines per page. A small anglicana hand.

Scribe III: fols 44–69v, 92–140v, 142–150v. Named on fol. 124v as William ('Wyth mercy and pyte / Prey for þe wryhtere of thys dyhte William'). 27–30 long lines per page. An anglicana formata hand. Spellings East Anglian, Bury St Edmunds.[140] Chapter headings and quotations underlined. Copying poor.

Scribe IV: fols 72–91v. Named on fol. 91v as Robert Baile ('Nunc finam fixi penitet me si male scripsi / Baile Robertus in celum sit benedictus. / Amen'). Pricking and ruling. 24–6 long lines per page. An anglicana formata hand. Spellings East Anglian, south of Bury St Edmund.[141]

---

[138] E.V. Stocks and A.I. Doyle, 'Draft Catalogue of Medieval Manuscripts in the University Library' (unpublished catalogue, Durham University). *Deuout Treatyse*, ed. by Vaissier, pp. xiv–xxiv. Candon, *Doctrine*, pp. ix–xi.

[139] A.I. Doyle notes similarities with the written style of John Shirley, a literary entrepreneur (d. 1456). Candon, *Doctrine*, p. ix.

[140] A. McIntosh, M.L. Samuels, M. Benskin, with the assistance of M. Laing and K. Williamson (eds), *A Linguistic Atlas of Late Medieval English*, 4 vols (Aberdeen, 1986), vol. 1, 87, 240, vol. 2, 490: CP 8480, Bury St Edmunds.

[141] Ibid., vol. 1, 87, 240, vol. 2, 482: LP 8310, south of Bury St Edmunds.

A London scrivener named Robert Baile is known 'after 1451'.[142] In addition, there are various mentions of a Carmelite prior named Robert Bale, from the priory of Burnham Norton in Norfolk, known for the writing and collecting of books.[143] Scribe III seems likely to have been a commercial copyist. Scribe II demonstrates the same hand as Cambridge University Library, MS Hh.i.11, fols 45–53v, a mid-fifteenth-century manuscript also made for a nunnery.[144]

There is evidence that the *Doctrine* was copied by Scribes I and III working simultaneously to some extent at least. There are also marginal + signs throughout the MS, indicating the necessity for correction. A black dot indicates that correction has been carried out. The amount and care of correction suggests that C was prepared as an exemplar for further and fairer copies. Unfilled spaces are left for initials throughout all three texts. A mid-nineteenth-century binding, with one clasp.

ANNOTATIONS:

Fol. ii top, 'amen quod Iohannes Waynfleett' in red. s. xv[2]. Probably the younger brother of William Waynflete, Bishop of Winchester, of the Patten family of Lincolnshire.[145] William's intimacy with Henry VI assisted his younger brother's multiple clerical appointments which included non-residentiary Canon of York, Canon of St Paul's, London, and Dean of Chichester.[146] Died 1479.

Fol. iir (added, s. xv/xvi) in red: 'O Jhesu ful of myght markyd in þi mageste / Save our kyng bothe day and nyght / In every place wher so he be. Quod Welles'. The same verse is repeated in black in the same hand, further down the page, with 'day' omitted, and unsigned, ending 'he be et cetera'. This page also shows medieval pen trials and scribbles.

Fol. iv: 'Geo. Davenport. 1664'. Fol. iiv: Davenport's list of contents and notes from Thomas James and Pits on the *Doctrine*. Davenport also foliated the *Doctrine* and the two *Letters* separately in pencil, and wrote 'Finis' in ink, and

---

[142] G.P. Warner and J.P. Gilson, *Catalogue of Old Royal and King's Collections of Western Manuscripts in the British Museum* (London, 1921), vol. 2, p. 236. Baile is also named as a warden of the Mistery of Scriveners in 1450. C. P. Christianson, *Directory of London Stationers and Book Artisans: 1300–1500* (New York, 1990), p. 108.

[143] *Victoria County History of Norfolk* (London, 1906), vol. 2, p. 426. *Dictionary of National Biography* (Oxford, 1921–22), vol. 2, pp. 962–63.

[144] Stocks and Doyle, 'Draft Catalogue'.

[145] R. Chandler, *The Life of William Wayneflete* (London, 1811), p. 4.

[146] John Le Neve, *Fasti Ecclesiae Anglicanae* (London, 1967), vol. 3, p. 22; vol. 4, p. 49; vol. 5, p. 28; vol. 6, pp. 74, 94; vol. 7, p. 5.

'G.D. 1664' in pencil on fols 69v, 91v and 150v. George Davenport, the chaplain to Bishop Cosin of Durham, collected many of the manuscripts that make up the Cosin contribution to Durham Cathedral library.

Oxford, Bodleian Library, MS Laud Misc. 330 (L)[147]

CONTENTS:
The Doctrine of the Hert, fols 1r–70v.[148]
Fols 71r–76r blank.
'O man unkynd', fol. 74v.

A vellum manuscript measuring 208mm x 140mm. 75 fols. 26–9 lines per page. Very faint framing lines. Fifteenth century. A folio has been lost at the beginning, so that most of the introduction is lacking; a second folio is lost between fols 6v and 7r. Collation 1⁶, 2–9⁸. Catchwords on all quires.
Written throughout in a single, clearly legible, bastard anglicana hand. A small number of corrections, both in the original hand in a darker ink, and in a second contemporary hand. Chapter capitals are elaborately decorated in blue and red, filling a three-line square. Some pointing fingers in margins.

Paraphs are in red. In addition, rubrication is used to emphasize precisely the same quotations and keywords as in MS McClean: scriptural quotations in Latin and English, including those paraphased or in indirect speech; patristic quotations in English; the articles of the creed (book 4); some proper names; some keywords within numbered lists (e.g. the impediments to opening the book of the conscience); other keywords. The seven impediments to opening the book of the conscience, and the twelve articles of the creed are numbered in the margin.

ANNOTATIONS:
Fol. 70v, in the same hand as the *Doctrine*:

> Syke and sorowe deeply,
> Wepe and morne sadly,
> Preye and þenk deuoutly,
> Love and long contynuely.

---

[147] H.O. Coxe, *Bodleian Library, Quarto Catalogues II. Laudian Manuscripts* (Oxford, 1973), pp. 253–54. S.J. Ogilvie-Thomson (ed.), *The Index of Middle English Prose, Handlist XVI: Manuscripts in the Laudian Collection, Bodleian Library, Oxford* (Cambridge, 2000), p. 41. Candon, *Doctrine*, pp. viii–ix.
[148] The treatise is defined in Coxe's catalogue as 'Regula monacharum'.

A.I. Doyle comments that these unusual lines are also found within Middle English manuscripts of Margarete Porete's *Mirouer des simples ames*, all of which are of Carthusian origin.[149]

Fol. 74v, in a different, fifteenth-century hand:

> O man unkynd
> Thow haue in mynd
> > My pennys smerte,
> Behold and see
> That is fore the
> > Percyd myne herte.
> And ȝyt I wold
> Or that I schuld
> > Thy sowll forsayk,
> On crosse wyth payne
> Scharpe deth agayne
> > Ffor thi luffe take.
> Ffore thys I aske
> None so taske
> > Botte luffe agayne,
> Me thane to luffe
> All thynge abuffe
> > Thow anyhe be fayne.[150]

A longer version of this lyric is also found in London, British Library, MS Addit. 37049 (where it is accompanied by an illustration of Christ offering man his wounded heart);[151] in BL, MS Addit. 37605, transcribing the inscription of the lyric on the walls of Almondbury Church, Yorkshire, dated 1522, and in New Haven, Beinecke Library 410 (roll).

Fol. 1r (bottom), 'Liber Guilielmi Laud Archiepi. Cantuar. et Cancellarii Vniuersitatis Oxon. 1633'. Archbishop Laud's famous book collection was largely acquired between 1633 and 1641, and was specifically designed for the use of the University of Oxford. MS Laud Misc. 330 formed part of his first donation.

---

[149] Candon, *Doctrine*, p. ix.
[150] J. Boffey and A.S.G. Edwards, *A New Index of Middle English Verse* (London, 2005), no. 2504, p. 164.
[151] D. Gray, *Themes and Images in the Medieval English Religious Lyric* (London, 1972), illustration 2, opp. p. 23; R. Woolf, *The English Religious Lyric in the Middle Ages* (Oxford, 1968), plate 1, opp. p. 186.

Cambridge, Trinity College Library, MS B.14.15 (T)[152]

CONTENTS:
The Doctrine of the Hert, fols 1r–75v.

A vellum manuscript measuring 216mm x 144mm. 79 fols. 30 lines per page. Ruled and framed. Early fifteenth century. Collation: 1–9⁸, 10⁶.

The manuscript is written by two scribes:
  Scribe I: fols 1–49r, in a neat, legible, bastard anglicana hand. Elongated ascenders into top margin. Decorated capitals at the beginning of each chapter, filling a three-line square.
  Scribe II: fols 49r–75v, in a legible cursive hand. Less ornate capitals, filling a two-line square. There are occasional corrections by a third scribal hand.

Occasional pointing fingers in margin. There are also a number of pen drawings in the margins: on fol. 13r, of a boar or pig playing bagpipes (beside a passage describing God's gift of 'oxen and schepe ... to cloþ mankynde ... and ... oþer unresonable bestis'); on fol. 27r, in the bottom margin, of an animal wearing a flowing coat with a fur collar; on fol. 32r, beside the passage describing the tenth arrayment of the soul, of a courtly lady with pointed headdress; on fol. 49r, beside the description of the Apocalyptic rider who holds scales, of a man in tunic and pointed shoes holding a pair of scales. At fol. 25r, a note in the margin reads: 'Of þe weddyng in profession'; at fol. 39r, Latin notes in the margin refer to the follies of spiritual battle, and the five follies are numbered in the margin.
  Rubrication is used throughout to distinguish Latin and English scriptural quotations, including those in indirect speech, patristic quotations in English, and other keywords. The Trinity MS contains a closing explicit and couplet on fol. 75v, not found in the other Middle English manuscripts: 'Here endith a tretice made to religious wommen which is clepid the doctrine of the hert'. 'Crist Jhesu his mede he hym rewarde / That this tretice bigan and the ende made'.

ANNOTATIONS:
The first fly-leaf is from a fifteenth-century account roll of deaneries and tithes:

---

[152] M.R. James, *The Western Manuscripts in the Library of Trinity College, Cambridge* (Cambridge, 1900), vol. 1, pp. 415–16. Candon, *Doctrine*, pp. xi–xiii.

f
Dec^a de Clyston
Dec. de Langacre et Lymby.
s
Distr. Dec. de Clyfton Vppelande.
Dec^a de Becre.
Dec^a de Craneford.
f
Dec^a Clysthydon.

On the last fly-leaf:

Hit ys to witt þ^t dame Cristyne seint nicolas of ye menoresse of london dowghtyr of nicolas Seint Nycolas squier 3eff þis boke aftyr hyr dysses to þe offyce of þ^e [erasure] and to þ^e offys of ye abbessry perpetually þe whyche passed to god out of þ^s worlde þe 3ere of owre lorde m.cccc.l.v þ^e ix day of marche of whoys soule god haue merci.

Additional information about Christine St Nicholas can be gathered from a 1446 entry in the Calendar of Close Rolls, where we learn that she was already the prioress of the minoresses of St Botolph without Aldgate, London, in 1446, and that her family owned land in the parish of St Nicholas at Wade, in the Isle of Thanet in Kent.[153] This, taken in conjunction with the fact that the Trinity MS twice substitutes the word 'menoresse' for the more general 'mynche' or 'sistir', suggests that the manuscript may have been prepared specifically for the Aldgate convent.[154] By the early fifteenth

---

[153] *Calendar of Close Rolls*, 25 Henry VI, 1446 (London, 1937), vol. 4, p. 441: '... and Thomas Seynnycolas esquire, both of the Isle of Thanet and all of Kent ... Quitclaim of the manor of Seyntnycolas co. Kent, and of all lands, rents, revisions and services in the parish of St. Nicholas atte Wade in the Isle of Thanet late of Christina Seynnycolas now prioress of the house of minoresses without Aldgate, London, and sometime of Nicholas Seynnycolas her father, with warrentry against John, prior of Christ Church Canterbury and his successors. Dated 21 November'.

[154] Other books owned by the Aldgate convent include London, British Library, MS Harley 2397, containing three texts by Hilton, which was given by Elizabeth Horwode, abbess of the London minoresses to the Aldgate convent for the use of her sisters, and Oxford, Bodleian Library, MS 585, a vernacular rule for enclosed minoresses (*A Fifteenth-Century Courtesy Book and two Fifteenth-Century Franciscan Rules*, ed. by R.W. Chambers, EETS OS 148 (1914, repr. 1963). For an informative account of the strong literary culture centred upon the Franciscan convent of St Botolph without Aldgate, see C.M. Meale and J. Boffey, 'Gentlewomen's Reading', in L. Hellinga

century there were four houses of minoresses in England, at London and at Waterbeach, Denny and Bruisyard in East Anglia. Interestingly, a second of these is cited in connection with a *fifth* manuscript of the *Doctrine*, now unfortunately lost. This fifth manuscript is listed in the 1481 will of Norwich gentry widow, Margaret Purdans, as follows:

> And to the Convent of Nuns at Brosyerd, after the decease of the Lady Margaret Yaxley, I give the book called *Le Doctrine of the Herte* ... Also, to the Nunnery of Thetford, an English book of *St Bridget* ... Also, to Alice Barley a book called *Hylton*.[155]

Recent research by Mary Erler has created a very detailed picture of Margaret Purdans, revealing an extraordinary array of connections to members of the Norwich governing classes, East Anglian hermits and anchoresses, fellows and masters of Cambridge colleges, eight East Anglian nunneries and the major London houses of Syon and Sheen. In addition, Erler identifies Lady Margaret Yaxley, a Franciscan nun at Bruisyard, as a member of Purdans's extended family: her son-in-law's sister, to be precise.[156]

On the front fly-leaf is stuck a drawing on paper, possibly a crest, of a black child, three-quarter length, with a fillet round its head, holding a plant with pink flowers. Below is written:

> S. Batman his Booke. Saxon ʒe
> 1455/ / Hor(?)e / 1575/

On fol. 1r, as a heading, Batman has written 'The doctrine of the harte'. On the last folio there is space for another attached drawing, now lost, and beneath:

> Nicephorus
> Aʒ the drau(?)er ʒerr(?)ed Who
> Hiet. S. B./5575/ mundi.

On the end fly-leaf, below the information on Christine St Nicholas, two additional paragraphs in a later hand may also be by Batman. They are as follows:

and J. B. Trapp (eds) *The Cambridge History of the Book in Britain, vol. III. 1400–1557* (Cambridge, 1999), pp. 526–40 (531–4).

[155] Margaret Purdans, St Giles', Norwich, Widow 1481 (Dioc. Reg. Caston 163), quoted in Harrod, 'Extracts from Early Wills', 335–6.

[156] Erler, *Women, Reading, and Piety*, pp. 68–84. For further information, contextualising this bequest and speculating on Margaret's reading of the *Doctrine*, see Reneavey and Whitehead, '"Opyn þin hert as a boke"', pp. 141–5.

The opinion of Sartaine Saxons is that whosoever wareth in his hat or cappe Pocokes fethers or bearith them in there handes: yf thei charnce to stumble they shall break som parte of there body as Arme, legg, Ribb or neack.

The note of A. Jwe which for the interest of a his money required a ^{li} of the mans fleshe to whom he lent the money, the bande forfait and yet the Jwe went wthoute his purpose / the parti notwithstandeng condemnid by lawe / the question whether he coulde cut the fleshe wthoute spilling of bloode/.

Stephen Batman (d. 1584) was a translator, author, and domestic chaplain to Archbishop Parker, for whom he collected a considerable library. His polemical Protestant writings indicate shared religious interests with Parker, a member of the Cambridge Reformers and one of the founders of Anglicanism.[157] Batman owned several other medieval manuscripts,[158] possibly a testament to an Elizabethan antiquarian interest.

9. Choice of base manuscript

C is a difficult manuscript, with a great number of deletions. It is written in several different hands and is not an easy manuscript to read. By contrast, the first impression given by T is of a neat and legible manuscript. However, it is full of mistakes which are due mainly to eye-skip and repeated words. L and M are both neatly written. They are perfectly legible and the script is precise. L, however, has two folios missing, which include the whole of the prologue. Notwithstanding this lack, which could easily be supplemented by M, both manuscripts stand as potentially valuable base manuscripts for any edition.

The extant manuscripts can be divided into two groups, LT and CM, with T following L until fol. 49r, after which it follows CM. CM is the

---

[157] S. Batman, *Christall Glass for Christian Reformation treating 7 deadly sins* (London, 1569); *Joyful News out of Helvetia from Theophr. Paracelsum, declaring ruinate fall of the papal dignitie* (London, 1575); *The golden booke of the leaden goddes, wherein is described the vayne imaginations of heathen pagans and counterfaict Christians* (London, 1577).

[158] M.B. Parkes, 'Paleographical Description and Commentary', in Geoffrey Chaucer, *Troilus and Criseyde. A Facsimile of Corpus Christi College, Cambridge MS 61*, intro. by M.B. Parkes and E. Salter (Cambridge, 1978), pp. 12–13; M.B. Parkes, 'Stephen Batman's Manuscripts', in M. Kanno et al. (eds), *Medieval Heritage: Essays in Honour of Tadahiro Ikegami* (Tokyo, 1997), pp. 125–56.

chronologially-later group in terms of spelling and grammar. Out of the two manuscripts, evidence points to M as preceding C, with the latter copying M or a descendant of M. So, for example, in M, fol. 32r (*Doctrine of the Hert*, p. 32, line 1045), the phrase 'long time in here youth' is retained in L and T, crossed out in M, and omitted in C, suggesting that C has responded to M's deletion. Similar instances can be found in M, fol. 90r (p. 89, lines 142–4), where L retains gender-specific pronouns, M deletes them and C omits them entirely, and in M, fol. 93r (p. 91, line 243), where L reads 'þer for', M reads 'þer for, and C responds to M again by giving only 'þer'.

One notices a similar relationship with LT. Because T omits many small words that are correctly present in L, it is clear that T has copied L or a descendant of L. For example, at fol. 19r (p. 20, line 598), M reads 'ayenst þe fire, is undirstonde þe blissed sacrament', L deletes 'is undirstond', and T reads 'aȝenst þe fire þe blessid sacrament'. Similarly, at fol. 33v (p. 34, line 1109), M reads 'melody and mirthe, but yit not so moche', L reads 'myrthe and melody, but ȝet not so myche', and T reads 'mythe and melody, ȝet not so myche'. And at fol. 60v (p. 58, lines 419–20), M reads 'Oute of þe rote of Jesse shuld þe yerde of correccioun come', L reads 'Oute of þe rote of Jesse schuld þe ȝard of correccion come', and T omits 'of correccion' entirely. There are several further examples.

However, as stated above, after fol. 49r T stops following L and starts following M or a descendant of M. This reliance upon M coincides with a change of scribal hand. From fol. 49r T follows M more faithfully than C: that is, there are far fewer variants to report between M and T than between M and C. Although this change of exemplar is pronounced and unambiguous, it does not mean that T's second hand does not go back to L for occasional checks. This may be the case, for instance, at fol. 85r (p. 82, line 102), where L reads 'desert', also given by T, whereas M reads 'maite', followed by C with 'myht'. Two other instances of the use of L by T's second hand occur on fol. 85v (p. 83, line 111: 'wyn'), and fol. 89v (p. 88, line 110: 'maner'). We are thus presented with the likelihood that M, L and T all co-existed together at some point in a scriptorium.

It is clear that all four manuscripts derive from a single lost archetype, alpha, containing the original Middle English translation of some version of the Latin text. The four manuscripts are far too close in their readings to derive from more than one independent translation. That said, the two manuscript groups do vary to some degree in their closeness to the Latin text. By and large, M and C are closer to the Latin original than L and T (first hand). Since we may presume the lost archetype, alpha, to represent the most faithful rendition of the Latin text, it would seem that manuscripts in the CM tradition have adhered more closely to this archetype, whereas manuscripts in the LT tradition have allowed small errors and omissions in transcription to creep in.

Some examples of comparative closeness to the Latin original are as follows. At p. 28, lines 888–9, the Latin reads 'Per sacerdotem, Christum intellige, qui animae virgini, lege matrimonij copulatur'.[159] M and C translate this correctly as 'Bi þis prest þou shalt undirstonde Jhesu Crist, þe wiche is coupled bi gostly matrymony to every clene soule', whereas L and T omit the sentence entirely. At p. 18, lines 509–10, the Latin reads 'Cum autem cibus visus non mutet corpus, nisi gustatus, vel comestus …'.[160] M and C translate this freely as 'For as longe as mete is uneetyn, so longe it is uncorporate', whereas L and T omit the sentence entirely. Again, on p. 83, lines 140–1, in the course of a list of the twelve fruits of the tree of life, M, C and T (second hand) correctly include the sixth fruit: 'undedlynes withoute passibilite', translating the Latin phrase: 'ibi immortalitas absque passibilitate',[161] whereas L, by this time working alone, erroneously omits the phrase. Again, on p. 7, line 27, p. 21, line 614 and p. 36, line 1204, M and C follow the Latin text in not naming 'þe prophete' responsible for various biblical quotations, while L and T provide names for the 'prophete' in question, occasionally erroneously.

Candon provides many further examples (generally of single words or short phrases) where M and C correspond more closely to the Latin text than L and T (first hand).[162] However, while in the great majority of instances M and C correspond more closely to the Latin, there are also a small number of instances where the opposite proves true, and where L, or L and T, offer a closer translation of the Latin text.[163] Candon argues convincingly that two of these instances may constitute a purposeful divergence on the part of M, C and T (second hand). At p. 73, line 186, M, C and T (second hand) read 'bi penaunce and oþer sacramentis, and also bi indulgences'. L omits 'and also bi indulgences', as does the Latin text.[164] In book 3, in a passage discussing the black sun and red moon predicted in the Apocalypse, L reads: 'By þe blak sonne þou schalt undirstond gret prelates of holy chirche as archebischoppis and bischoppis … By þe rede mone þou schalt undirstond lesse prelatis as abbotes, prioures, and prestes, and suche oþer mene gouernoures of holy chirche',[165] offering a fairly close translation of: 'Quid per Solem, nisi maiores praelati vt

---

[159] *De doctrina*, p. 85.
[160] Ibid., p. 48.
[161] Ibid., p. 275.
[162] Candon, *Doctrine*, pp. xxiv–xxvii.
[163] Ibid., pp. xxvii–xxx.
[164] *De doctrina*, p. 226.
[165] Fol. 48r, Candon, *Doctrine*, p. 107.

Episcopi, et Archiepiscopi designantur … Per lunam autem minores praelati, vt Abbates, Archidiaconi, Decani, Presbyteri, et huiusmodi …'.[166] M, C and T, on the other hand, offer a markedly vaguer translation of the Latin: 'Bi þe blak sonne þou shalt undirstonde gret prelatis and governouris of holy chirche … Bi þe red mone þou shalt undirstonde lesse prelates as curatis of chirches, sovereynes of religioun, and such oþer mene governoures of holy chirche' (p. 63, lines 176–80), where the precise ranks of clergy targeted for criticism within the ecclesiastical hierarchy are diplomatically left unspecified.

Despite noting the majority of instances in which M, C and T (second hand) offer a closer translation of the Latin *De doctrina*, Sister Candon finally opts for L as her base manuscript on the basis of the questionable supposition that scribes in the line of transmission from which M and C are descended *adjusted* the text so that it would more closely resemble the Latin of which it is a translation.[167] Since the evidence to support such adjustments is not at all clear, we have decided to regard closeness to the Latin original as our paramount consideration in selecting a manuscript, regardless of relative dates (as stated above, orthography and grammar suggest that M and C were copied somewhat later in the fifteenth century than L). M, C and T (second hand) are plainly closer to the Latin *De doctrina* than L and T (first hand) in a great majority of instances. Of the three, M is by far the superior manuscript in terms of legibility, clarity and precision. It is also, clearly, an *earlier* manuscript within its own textual tradition than either C or T (second hand). M thus became our unambiguous choice of base manuscript for this critical edition.

The stemma we propose is as follows:

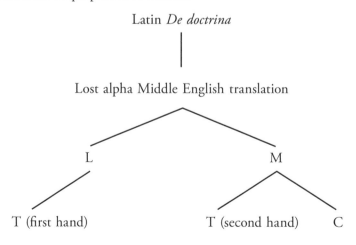

Latin *De doctrina*

Lost alpha Middle English translation

L M

T (first hand) T (second hand) C

---

[166] *De doctrina*, p. 201.
[167] Candon, *Doctrine*, pp. xxx–xxxi.

10. Language and dialect

Candon offers a substantial analysis of the language of *The Doctrine of the Hert* found in the four extant manuscripts.[168] In the first place she considers phonological characteristics (both vowels and consonants) and notices similar sound changes between all manuscripts. Most of the exceptions are nevertheless worthwhile detailing since many of them are found within our base manuscript, Cambridge, Fitzwilliam Museum, McClean 132 (M). The only difference with vowel spellings is found in M, for instance, with Old English 'á' + 'ȝ' written 'augh', while the other manuscripts write 'aw'. Consonental spellings are slightly less regular, with M again often proving the exception. While OE 'sc' is written 'sch' in all other manuscripts, M has 'sh' instead. OE final 'd' is almost consistently retained in all manuscripts except in M where it becomes 'th' (final 'th' appears only twice in T, once in C, and never in L). OE 'f' is written 'f' initially in all manuscripts. However, Candon makes reference to the fact that, in the word 'vouchsafe', which occurs six times in the text, while the OF 'v' becomes 'f' in L and C, it is retained in M and T. Old English palatal 'ȝ' is written 'ȝ' in all manuscripts with the exception of M, where it becomes 'y'.

In her discussion of accidence, Candon notes that plural endings in all manuscripts are '–es', '–is', '–ys' and '–s'. M and C include both 'eeryn' and 'eris' within the same sentence. The genitive plural of personal pronouns is usually 'her', 'here', 'þeire' and 'theire'; however, the latter two forms appear very infrequently except in M. The third-person personal pronoun as object is 'hem', with rare appearances of 'þeym(e)' and 'theim' in M only.

The forms of the third-person plural ending in all manuscripts are '–en' or '–yn', with a few cases where all manuscripts occasionally have '–eth' or '–ith'. The present participle of verbs in all manuscripts is '–ing' or '–yng'. The manuscripts share the same forms for the verb 'to be', with the single exception of 'hamme' found only once in M for the first-person singular, which is otherwise 'am'. For the verb 'to have', the plural form 'han' is found consistently in M, often in C, and rarely in T and L, where 'haue' is found instead. The forms of the verb 'schal' show some degree of variation between the four manuscripts in the initial consonantal group: while L and T consistently have 'sch', M has 'sh'; C has 'x' in fols 1–43 and 'sch' in fols 44–69, following a change in scribal hand.

Candon then offers a summary arguing for strong phonological and morphological resemblances between the four manuscripts, while acknowledging a few features which make C distinct. She makes use of the work of

---

[168] Candon, *Doctrine*, pp. lxxxa–lxxxt.

Moore, Meech and Whitehall in placing the language of the manuscripts in East Anglia and in locating the scribes of the Cosin manuscript within the Norfolk area.[169] According to Candon, all four manuscripts were written in the first part of the fifteenth century, as can be attested by the presence of medial 'd' rather than 'the' in words such as 'fadir' and 'modir': that particular sound change prevailed in the fifteenth century. One other feature in favour of the early fifteenth century is the consistent use of 'hem' instead of 'þeyme'. 'Þeyme', which is only attested (rarely) in M, came down from the north early in the century and soon began to establish itself as the accepted form.[170]

A check of M based on ten items used in the *Linguistic Atlas of Late Medieval English* shows the degree to which this manuscript reaches a degree of standardization specific to the fifteenth-century East Midland/London area.[171] THESE is spelt as 'thes' (on 14 occasions in M),[172] 'thees' (6), 'þes' (11) and 'þees' (32). The only occurrence for SHE is as 'she' (64). HER appears as 'hir' (1) and 'her' (7). There is only one spelling form used for IT, that is 'it' (368). Variants for THEY are all of the 'they' type: 'they' (18), 'þey' (44), 'þei' (116) and 'þeie' (21). THEM appears as 'hem' (133) most of the time, with the exceptions of three occurrences of the 'theim' type: 'theim' (1), 'þeyme' (1) and 'þeym' (1). THEIR appears most of the time as the 'her' type: 'her' (131), with only six occurrences of 'þeir' (6). SUCH appears as 'such' (178) and 'suche' (56). WHICH appears only with initial 'w–', with 'w(h)ich' (3) and 'whiche' (20). There are seven occurrences of the EACH variant, with 'eche' (7).

In fact, the language of M has many of the features of the Type 4 variety discussed by Samuels and summarized in Horobin.[173] Type 4, also called 'Chancery Standard', replaced Type 3 in the early fifteenth century in London. This language displays forms which are found in the central Midland dialects, with the supplementation of forms found only in the North Midlands. Of the forms 'theyre', 'thorough', 'such(e)', 'gaf' and 'not', which made their way south from the North Midlands, M includes the following occurrences: 'theyre'

[169] S. Moore, S.M. Meech and H. Whitehall, 'Middle English Dialect Characteristics and Dialect Boundaries', *University of Michigan Publications, Language and Literature* 13 (1935), 1–60.
[170] Candon, *Doctrine*, p. lxxxt.
[171] McIntosh, Samuels and Benskin (eds), *Linguistic Atlas*.
[172] This, and all following figures in brackets, refer to the number of occasions that the Middle English spelling in question appears in M.
[173] Horobin makes use of M.L. Samuels, 'Some Applications of Middle English Dialectology', *English Studies*, 44 (1963), 81–94, repr. in M. Laing (ed.), *Middle English Dialectology: Essays on Some Principles and Problems* (Aberdeen, 1989), pp. 64–80; see S. Horobin, *Chaucer's Language* (New York, 2007), pp. 34–40.

(1) and 'theire' (5), 'such(e)' (234) and 'not' (317). On the other hand, M has '3af' (2) rather than 'gaf', 'they' (18) and 'hir' (1), which are features of Type 3 language. The evidence points to M's language as occupying a transitional stage between Type 3 and Type 4.

Bibliography

This bibliography lists only manuscripts and early printed texts cited in this critical edition. For a comprehensive list of manuscripts and early printed texts of *De doctrina* and its vernacular versions, and for a comprehensive list of Guido Hendrix's publications on *De doctrina*, please see the bibliography at the end of D. Renevey and C. Whitehead (eds), *A Companion to the Doctrine of the Hert: The Middle English Translation and its Latin and European Contexts* (Exeter, 2010).

Manuscripts

De doctrina cordis:
Basel, Öffentl. Bibliothek der Universität, MS B.x.4
Leiden, Bibliotheek der Rijksuniversiteit, MS BPL 2579
Oxford, Bodleian Library, MS Lat. th. f. 6

The English translation: *The Doctrine of the Hert*:
Cambridge, Fitzwilliam Museum, MS McClean 132
Cambridge, Trinity College, MS B.14.15
Durham, University Library, MS Cosin V.III.24
Oxford, Bodleian Library, MS Laud Misc. 330

French translations: *Le traitiers de la doctrine du cuer*:
Douai, Bibliothèque municipale, MS 514
Paris, Bibliothèque nationale de France, MS fr. 13272
Oxford, Bodleian Library, MS Holkham Misc. 42
Troyes, Bibliothèque municipale, MS 1384

German translation:
Munich, Bayerische Staatsbibliothek, Cgm 447

Pseudo-Bernard, *The Manere of Good Lyvyng*:
Oxford, Bodleian Library, MS Laud Misc. 517

The Clensyng of Mannes Sowle:
Oxford, Bodleian Library, MS Bodley 923

'O man unkynd':
London, British Library, MS Additional 37049
London, British Library, MS Additional 37605
New Haven, Beinecke Library 410 (roll)

Lorens d'Orléans, *La Somme le Roi*:
London, British Library, MS Additional 28162

Early printed editions

De doctrina cordis:
De doctrina cordis 1st edition (Paris, 1506), Oxford, Bodleian Library, Vet.
E1.f.1.
*Speculum concionatorum, ad illustrandum pectora auditorum, in septem libros
distributum*, Auctore F. Gerardo Leodiensi, Ordinis Fr. Praedicatorum
Lectore celleberrimo, 2nd edition (Naples, 1607), Oxford, Bodleian
Library, 8° L 12 Th. BS.

Spanish translations of *De doctrina*:
Del enseñamiento del coraçon (Salamanca, 1498).
*Doctrina cordis de sant buena ventura en romance: nueuamente corregido y
enmendado* (Toledo, 1510).
*Doctrina cordis de sant buena ventura en romance: nueuamente corregido y
enmendado* (Toledo, 1525).
*Doctrina cordis del serafico dotor sant buena ventura en romance: muy util y
provechoso para todos los fieles christianos: nuevamente corregido y emendado*
(Baeza, 1551).

Alcok, John, *An exhortacyon made to Relygyous systers in the tyme of theyr
consecracyon by the Reuerende fader in god Johan Alcok bysshop of Ely*,
printed by Wynkyn de Worde (London, 1497).
Batman, Stephen, *Christall Glass for Christian Reformation treating 7 deadly
sins* (London, 1569).
—, *Joyful News out of Helvetia from Theophr. Paracelsum, declaring ruinate fall
of the papal dignitie* (London, 1575).
—, *The golden booke of the leaden goddes, wherein is described the vayne
imaginations of heathen pagans and counterfaict Christians* (London,
1577).

Hugh of St Cher, *Postillae*:
Ugonis de S. Charo, S. Romanae Ecclesiae tit. S. Sabinae Cardinalis primi
Ordinis Praedicatorum, *Opera omnia in universum Vetus & Novum
Testamentum*, 8 parts in 5 vols (Cologne, 1621).
Peraldus, Guillaume, *Summa de vitiis et virtutibus*:
Guilielmo Peraldo, *Summae Virtutum ac Vitiorum*, 2 vols (Antwerp, 1588),
Oxford, Bodleian Library, Douce P 806, 807.

Primary sources

Aelred of Rievaulx, *Opera ascetica, Liber de speculo caritatis, Epistola beati
Bernardi abbatis Clarevallis ad Ælredum abbatem 1–5*, ed. by A. Hoste and
C.H. Talbot, *CCCM* 1 (Turnhout, 1971).
—, *Aelred of Rievaulx's De institutione inclusarum*, ed. by J. Ayto and A. Barratt,
EETS 287 (1984).
Ambrose, St, *Hexaemeron*, *PL* 14, cols 123–275.
*Ancrene Wisse: A Corrected Edition of the Text in Cambridge, Corpus Christi
College, MS 402*, ed. by B. Millett with the assistance of R. Dance, EETS
OS 325, 326 (2005, 2006).
Anselm of Laon, *Enarrationes in Matthaeum*, *PL* 162, cols 1227–499.
Aquinas, Thomas, St, *Liber de Veritate Catholicae Fidei contra errores Infidelium:
Summa contra Gentiles*, ed. by D.P. Marc, C. Pera and D.P. Caramello,
3 vols (Rome, 1961–67).
Augustine, St, *Epistolae*, *PL* 33, cols 1–1093.
—, *Confessionum Libri XIII*, ed. by L. Verheijen, *CCSL* 27 (Turnhout, 1981).
—, *Confessions*, tr. by H. Chadwick (Oxford, 1991).
—, *De civitate Dei*, ed. by B. Dombart and A. Kalb, *CCSL* 48 (Turnhout,
1955).
—, *De Genesi ad litteram*, ed. by J. Zycha, *CSEL* 28.1 (Vindobonae, 1894).
—, *De nuptiis et concupiscentia*, *PL* 44, cols 415–75.
—, *Enarrationes in Psalmos*, *CCSL* 40 (Turnhout, 1956).
—, *Liber de bono conjugali*, *PL* 40, cols 373–95.
—, *Saint Augustine. Marriage and Virginity*, tr. by R. Kearney and ed. by
D.G. Hunter (New York, 1999).
—, *Tractatus in Johannis evangelium*, ed. by D.R. Willems, *CCSL* 36 (Turnhout,
1954).
Bede, Venerable, *In Lucae evangelium expositio*, ed. by D. Hurst, *CCSL* 120
(Turnhout, 1960).
Benedict, St, *The Rule of St Benedict*, tr. by J. McCann (London, 2nd edn
1976; repr. 1989).

Bernard of Clairvaux, St, *Sermones super Cantica canticorum*, in *Sancti Bernardi Opera*, ed. by J. Leclercq, C.H. Talbot and H.M. Rochais, 8 vols (Rome, 1957–77), vols 1–2.

—, *On the Song of Songs*, tr. by K. Walsh and I. Edmonds, 4 vols, Cistercian Fathers Series 4, 11, 31, 40 (Kalamazoo, 1971–80).

—, *Sermones*, in *Sancti Bernardi Opera*, ed. by Leclercq and Rochais (1966–70), vols 4–6.

—, *Epistolae*, in *Sancti Bernardi Opera*, ed. by Leclercq and Rochais (1974), vols 7–8.

—, *Sermones de diversis*, PL 183, cols 537–747.

Biblia sacra, ed. by A. Colunga and L. Turrado (Madrid, 8th edn 1985).

Biblia Latina cum Glossa Ordinaria, facs. repr. of editio princeps Adolph Rusch of Strassburg 1480/81, intro. by K. Froehlich and M.T. Gibson (Turnhout, 1992).

The Holy Bible, Douai Version Translated from the Latin Vulgate (Douay, A.D. 1609: Rheims, A.D. 1582) (London, 1956).

Revised English Bible with the Apocrypha, The (Oxford and Cambridge, 1989).

Boethius, *De consolatione philosophiae*, ed. by L. Bieler, *CCSL* 94 (Turnhout, 1984).

—, *The Consolation of Philosophy*, tr. by V.E. Watts (Harmondsworth, 1969).

Book for a Simple and Devout Woman, ed. by F.N.M. Diekstra (Groningen, 1998).

Book of Vices and Virtues, The, ed. by W. Nelson Francis, EETS OS 217 (repr. 1998).

Chaucer, Geoffrey, *The Riverside Chaucer*, ed. by L.D. Benson (Oxford, 3rd edn 1987).

Cicero, *Laelius de Amicitia Liber*, ed. by K. Simbeck (Lipsia, 1917).

Contemplations of the Dread and Love of God, ed. by M. Connolly, EETS 303 (1994).

Cassiodorus, *Expositio psalmorum*, ed. by M. Adriaen, *CCSL* 97 (Turnhout, 1958).

David of Augsburg, *Formula novitiorum*, ed. by P.P. Collegii S. Bonaventurae (Quaracchi, 1899).

Desert of Religion, The, A. McGovern-Mouron (ed.), 'An Edition of the *Desert of Religion* and its Theological Background', 2 vols (unpublished doctoral dissertation, University of Oxford, 1996).

Deuout Treatyse Called the Tree and xii Frutes of the Holy Goost, A, ed. by J.J. Vaissier (Groningen, 1960).

Doctrine of the Hert, The, Sister M.P. Candon (ed.), '*The Doctrine of the Hert*, Edited from the Manuscripts with Introduction and Notes' (unpublished doctoral dissertation, Fordham University, 1963).

'*Exhortacion*' *from Disce Mori, edited from Oxford, Jesus College, MS 39, The*, ed. by E.A. Jones, Middle English Texts 36 (Heidelberg, 2006).

Fifteenth-Century Courtesy Book and Two Fifteenth-Century Franciscan Rules, A, ed. by R.W. Chambers, EETS OS 148 (1914, repr. 1963).

Gregory the Great, St, *Homiliae in Evangelia*, ed. by R. Etaix, *CCSL* 141 (Turnhout, 1999).

—, *Forty Gospel Homilies*, tr. by D. Hurst, Cistercian Studies Series 123 (Kalamazoo, 1990).

—, *Moralia in Job*, ed. by M. Adriaen, *CCSL* 143A and B (Turnhout, 1979, 1985).

—, *Morals on the Book of Job*, English translation, Library of Fathers of the Holy Catholic Church 18, 21, 23, 31 (Oxford, 1844–50).

—, *Regulae pastoralis. Règle Pastorale*, ed. and tr. by B. Judic, C. Morel and F. Rommel, *SC* 381–2 (Paris, 1992).

—, *Pastoral Care*, tr. by H. Davis, Ancient Christian Writers 11 (Westminster, Md; London, 1950).

Grosseteste, Robert, *Le château d'amour de Robert Grosseteste*, ed. by J. Murray (Paris, 1918).

Guillaume de Deguileville, *The Pilgrimage of the Lyfe of the Manhode*, ed. by A. Henry, EETS 288 (1985).

Henry of Lancaster, *Le Livre de Seyntz Medicines: The Unpublished Devotional Treatise of Henry of Lancaster*, ed. by E. J. Arnould, Anglo-Norman Text Society 2 (1940).

Hilton, Walter, *The Scale of Perfection*, ed. by T.H. Bestul (Kalamazoo, 2000).

Hugh of St Victor, *Quaestiones et decisiones in Epistolas D. Pauli*, *PL* 175, cols 431–633.

Isidore, St, *Sententiae*, ed. by P. Cazier, *CCSL* 111 (Turnhout, 1998).

—, *Synonyma de lamentatione anime peccatricis*, *PL* 83, cols 825–67.

Jacob of Voragine, *Jacopo da Varazze: Legenda aurea*, ed. by G.P. Maggioni (Florence, 1998).

Jerome, St, *Epistolae*, *PL* 22, cols 235–1182; *PL* 30, cols 13–307.

Julian of Norwich, *The Writings of Julian of Norwich: A Vision Showed to a Devout Woman and A Revelation of Love*, ed. by N. Watson and J. Jenkins (University Park, Pennsylvania, 2006).

Langland, William, *The Vision of Piers Plowman*, ed. by A.V.C. Schmidt (London, 2nd edn 1995).

Lombard, Peter, *Commentaria in Psalmos*, *PL* 191, cols 61–1297.

Love, Nicholas, *The Mirror of the Blessed Life of Jesus Christ: A Reading Text*, ed. by M.G. Sargent (Exeter, 2004).

Manere of Good Lyvyng, The, ed. by A. Mouron (Turnhout, forthcoming).

Mechthild of Hackeborn, *Liber Specialis Gratiae*, ed. by H. Oudin (Paris, 1877).

Medieval English Prose for Women: Selections from the Katherine Group and Ancrene Wisse, ed. and tr. by B. Millett and J. Wogan-Browne (Oxford, 1990).

Peter Comestor, *Historia scholastica*, ed. by A. Sylwan, *CCCM* 191 (Turnhout, 2005).

Peter of Celle, *L'École du cloître*, ed. and tr. by G. de Martel, *SC* 240 (Paris, 1977).

—, *Selected Works*, tr. by H. Feiss (Kalamazoo, 1987).

Plato, *Phaedo*, in *Platonis Opera*, ed. by E.A. Duke et al. (Oxford, 1995), vol. 1.

Pseudo-Anselm, *De custodia interioris hominis*, in R.W. Southern and F.S. Schmitt (eds), *Memorials of St Anselm*, Auctores britannici medii aevi 1 (Oxford, 1969), pp. 354–60.

Pseudo-Bernard, *Liber de modo bene vivendi ad sororem*, *PL* 184, cols 1199–306.

—, *Meditationes piisimae de cognitiones humanae conditionis* (also known as *Tractatus de interiori homine*), *PL* 184, cols 485–507.

—, *Tractatus de interiori domo*, *PL* 184, cols 507–51.

Pseudo-Chrysostomus, *Opus imperfectum in Matthaeum*, *PG* 56.

Pseudo-Thomas, *De venerabili sacramento altaris*: St Thomas Aquinas, *De venerabili sacramento altaris* (Rome, 1931).

Regle des fins amans, Le, ed. by K. Christ, in B. Schädel and W. Mulertt (eds), *Philologische Studien: Karl Voretzsch Festschrift* (Halle, 1927), pp. 192–3.

Richard of St Victor, *De judiciaria potestate in finali et universali judicio*, *PL* 196, cols 1177–85.

Robert de Sorbon, *De consciencia et De tribus dietis*, ed. by F. Chambon (Paris, 1902).

Sedulius Scottus, *Collectaneum miscellaneum*, ed. by D. Simpson, *CCCM* 67 (Turnhout, 1988).

Seneca, *Naturalium quaestionum*, ed. by A. Gercke (Stuttgart, 1970).

Weye of Paradys, The. The Middle English 'Weye of Paradys' and the Middle French 'Voie de Paradis', ed. by F.N.M. Diekstra (Leiden, New York, Copenhagen, Cologne, 1991).

William of Nassington, *Speculum vitae: A Reading Edition*, ed. by R. Hanna, 2 vols, EETS OS 331, 332 (2008).

—, *Speculum vitae*, ed. by J.W. Smeltz, microfilm (Ann Arbor, MI, 1977).

William of St-Thierry, *Epistola ad fratres de Monte Dei. Lettre aux frères du Mont-Dieu*, ed. and tr. by J. Déchanet, *SC* 223 (Paris, 1975).

Secondary sources

Astell, A.W., *The Song of Songs in the Middle Ages* (Ithaca, NY and London, 1990).

Batt, C., D. Renevey and C. Whitehead, 'Domesticity and Medieval Devotional Literature', *Leeds Studies in English, New Series*, 36 (2005), 195–250.

Bell, D.N., *What Nuns Read: Books and Libraries in Medieval English Nunneries*, Cistercian Studies Series 158 (Kalamazoo, 1995).

Blommestijn, H., 'Self-Transcendence in Bernard of Clairvaux', in F. Imoda (ed.), *A Journey to Freedom* (Sterling, VA, 2000), pp. 230–65.

Bloomfield, M.W. et al., *Incipits of Latin Works on the Virtues and Vices, 1100–1500 AD* (Cambridge, MA, 1979).

Boffey, J. and A.S.G. Edwards, *A New Index of Middle English Verse* (London, 2005).

Boitani, P. and A. Torti (eds), *The Body and the Soul in Medieval Literature* (Cambridge, 1999).

Brantley, J., *Reading in the Wilderness: Private Devotion and Public Performance in Late Medieval England* (Chicago and London, 2007).

Chandler, R., *The Life of William Wayneflete* (London, 1811).

Christianson, C.P., *Directory of London Stationers and Book Artisans: 1300–1500* (New York, 1990).

Cohen, J.J., *Christ Killers: The Jews and the Passion from the Bible to the Big Screen* (Oxford, 2007).

Constable, G., *Three Studies in Medieval Religious and Social Thought* (Cambridge, 2nd edn 1998).

Cornelius, R.D., *The Figurative Castle: A Study of the Medieval Allegory of the Edifice* (Bryn Mawr, 1930).

Coxe, H.O., *Bodleian Library, Quarto Catalogues II. Laudian Manuscripts* (Oxford, 1973).

Cré, M., 'A Middle Dutch Translation of *De doctrina cordis: De bouc van der leeringhe van der herten* in Vienna, Österreichischen Nationalbibliothek, MS 15231', in Renevey and Whitehead (eds), *Companion*, pp. 208–22.

D'Avray, D.L., *Medieval Marriage Sermons: Mass Communication in a Culture without Print* (Oxford, 2001).

—, *Medieval Marriage: Symbolism and Society* (Oxford, 2005).

De Lubac, H., *Medieval Exegesis: the Four Senses of Scripture*, tr. by M. Sebanc (Grand Rapids, MI and Edinburgh, 1998).

De Ricci, S., *English Collectors of Books and Manuscripts (1530–1930) and their Marks of Ownership* (Cambridge, 1930).

Dobson, E.J., *The Origins of Ancrene Wisse* (Oxford, 1976).

Dolan, T.P., 'The Rhetoric of *Ancrene Wisse*', in *Langland, the Mystics and the Medieval English Religious Tradition*, ed. by H. Phillips (Cambridge, 1990), pp. 203–13.

Doyle, A.I. (ed.), '"Lectulus noster floridus": An Allegory of the Penitent Soul', in R.G. Newhauser and J. A. Alford (eds), *Literature and Religion in the Later Middle Ages: Philological Studies in Honor of Siegfried Wenzel*, Medieval and Renaissance Texts and Studies 118 (New York, 1995), pp. 179–90.

Eisermann, F. *Stimulus amoris: Inhalt, lateinische Überlieferung, deutsche Übersetzungen, Rezeption* (Tübingen, 2001).

Erler, M., *Women, Reading, and Piety in Late Medieval England* (Cambridge, 2002).

Gillespie, V., 'Mystic's Foot: Rolle and Affectivity', in M. Glasscoe (ed.), *The Medieval Mystical Tradition in England*, II (Exeter, 1982), pp. 199–230.

—, 'Religious Writing', in R. Ellis (ed.), *The Oxford History of Literary Translation in English, Volume 1: to 1550* (Oxford, 2008), pp. 234–83.

—, 'Meat, Metaphor and Mysticism: Cooking the Books in *The Doctrine of the Hert*', in Renevey and Whitehead (eds), *Companion*, pp. 131–58.

Gordon, J.D., 'The Articles of the Creed and the Apostles', *Speculum*, 40 (1965), 634–40.

Gray, D., *Themes and Images in the Medieval English Religious Lyric* (London, 1972).

—, (ed.), *A Selection of Religious Lyrics* (Oxford, 1975).

Harrod, H., 'Extracts from Early Wills in the Norwich Registries', *Norfolk and Norwich Archeological Society*, 4 (1855), 335–6.

Hebron, M., *The Medieval Siege: Theme and Image in Middle English Romance* (Oxford, 1997).

Hendrix, G., *Le manuscript Leyde Bibliothèque de l'Université, BPL 2579, témoin principal des phases de redaction du traité 'De doctrina cordis'* (Gent, 1980).

—, 'Le *De doctrina cordis*, source directe du *Chastel perilleux*', *RTAM*, 50 (1983), 252–66.

—, *Hugo de Sancto Caro's traktaat De doctrina cordis. Handschriften, recepte, tekstgeschiedenis en authenticiteitskritik*, Documenta Libraria 16/1 (Louvain, 1995).

Horobin, S., *Chaucer's Language* (New York, 2007).

Innes-Parker, C., 'The Lady and the King: *Ancrene Wisse*'s Parable of the Royal Wooing Re-Examined', *English Studies*, 75 (1994), 509–22.

—, '*Ancrene Wisse* and *Þe Wohunge of Ure Laurerd*: The Thirteenth-Century Female Reader and the Lover-Knight', in J. Taylor and L. Smith (eds), *Women, the Book and the Godly* (London, 1995), pp. 137–47.

Jager, E., *The Book of the Heart* (Chicago, 2000).

James, M.R., *The Western Manuscripts in the Library of Trinity College, Cambridge* (Cambridge, 1900).

—, *A Descriptive Catalogue of the McClean Collection of Manuscripts in the Fitzwilliam Museum* (Cambridge, 1912).

Kerby-Fulton, K., *Books under Suspicion: Censorship and Tolerance of Revelatory Writing in Late Medieval England* (Notre Dame, IN, 2006).

Langholm, O., *Economics in the Medieval Schools. Wealth, Exchange, Value, Money and Usury according to the Paris Theological Tradition, 1200–1250* (Leiden and New York, 1992).

Lappin, A.J., 'The Spanish Translation: *Del enseñamiento del coraçon* (Salamanca, 1498)', in Renevey and Whitehead (eds), *Companion*, pp. 238–64.

Leclercq, J., 'San Bernardo "cuciniere di Dio"', in *Bernardo Cistercense. Atti del XXVI Convegno storico internazionale Todi* (Spoleto, 1990).

Le Neve, J., *Fasti Ecclesiae Anglicanae* (London, 1967).

Lottin, O., *Psychologie et morale aux XIIe et XIIIe siècles* (Leuven-Glembloux, 1942–60).

McIntosh, A., M.L. Samuels, M. Benskin, with the assistance of M. Laing and K. Williamson (eds), *A Linguistic Atlas of Late Medieval English*, 4 vols (Aberdeen, 1986).

Meale, C.M. and J. Boffey, 'Gentlewomen's Reading', in L. Hellinga and J.B. Trapp (eds), *The Cambridge History of the Book in Britain, vol. III. 1400–1557* (Cambridge, 1999), pp. 526–40.

Millett, B., 'Mouvance and the Medieval Author: Re-editing *Ancrene Wisse*', in A.J. Minnis (ed.), *Late-Medieval Religious Texts and their Transmission* (Cambridge, 1994), pp. 9–20.

Mills, W.E. and R.A. Bullard, *Mercer Dictionary of the Bible* (Macon, GA, 1990).

Minnis, A., *Fallible Authors: Chaucer's Pardoner and Wife of Bath* (Philadelphia, 2008).

Minnis, A.J. and A.B. Scott, assist. D. Wallace, *Medieval Literary Theory and Criticism c.1100–c.1375* (Oxford, rev. edn 1991).

Moore, S., S.M. Meech and H. Whitehall, 'Middle English Dialect Characteristics and Dialect Boundaries', *University of Michigan Publications, Language and Literature*, 13 (1935), 1–60.

Mouron, A.E., 'The French Translations of *De doctrina cordis*', in Renevey and Whitehead (eds), *Companion*, pp. 185–207.

—, '*The Doctrine of the Hert*: a Middle English Translation of *De doctrina cordis*', in Renevey and Whitehead (eds), *Companion*, pp. 85–108.

—, 'The *Livre de l'instruction du cuer de l'ame devote*: A Medieval French Translation of *De doctrina cordis*', in D. Renevey and C. Whitehead (eds),

The Medieval Translator/Traduire au Moyen Age 12 (Turnhout, 2010), pp. 237–50.

Newhauser, R. and I. Bejczy, *A Supplement to Morton W. Bloomfield et al. 'Incipits of Latin Works on the Virtues and Vices, 1100–1500 A.D.'*, Instrumenta Patristica et Mediaevalia 50 (Turnhout, 2008).

Ogilvie-Thomson, S.J. (ed.), *The Index of Middle English Prose, Handlist XVI: Manuscripts in the Laudian Collection, Bodleian Library, Oxford* (Cambridge, 2000).

O'Sullivan, R.A., 'The School of Love: Marguerite Porete's *Mirror of Simple Souls*', *Journal of Medieval History*, 32.2 (2006), 143–62.

Palmer, N., 'The Authorship of *De doctrina cordis*', in Renevey and Whitehead (eds), *Companion*, pp. 19–56.

Parkes, M.B., 'Paleographical Description and Commentary', in Geoffrey Chaucer, *Troilus and Criseyde. A Facsimile of Corpus Christi College, Cambridge MS 61*, intro. by M.B. Parkes and E. Salter (Cambridge, 1978).

—, 'Stephen Batman's Manuscripts', in M. Kanno et al., (eds), *Medieval Heritage: Essays in Honour of Tadahiro Ikegami* (Tokyo, 1997), pp. 125–56.

Patterson, L.W., 'Ambiguity and Interpretation: A Fifteenth-Century Reading of *Troilus and Criseyde*', *Speculum*, 54.2 (1979), 297–330.

Pennington, M.B., *A School of Love: The Cistercian Way to Holiness* (Canterbury, 2000).

Pollard, W.F., 'Richard Rolle and the "Eye of the Heart"', in W.F. Pollard and R. Boenig (eds), *Mysticism and Spirituality in Medieval England* (Cambridge, 1997), pp. 85–106.

Renevey, D., *Language, Self and Love: Hermeneutics in the Writings of Richard Rolle and the Commentaries on the Song of Songs* (Cardiff, 2001).

—, 'Household Chores in *The Doctrine of the Hert*: Affective Spirituality and Subjectivity', in C. Beattie, A. Maslakovic and S. Rees Jones (eds), *The Medieval Household in Christian Europe c.850–c.1550: Managing Power, Wealth, and the Body* (Turnhout, 2003), pp. 167–85.

— and C. Whitehead, '"Opyn þin hert as a boke": Translation Practice and Manuscript Circulation in *The Doctrine of the Hert*', in J. Jenkins and O. Bertrand (eds), *The Medieval Translator* 10 (Turnhout, 2007), pp. 125–48.

— and C. Whitehead (eds), *A Companion to the Doctrine of the Hert: The Middle English Translation and its Latin and European Contexts* (Exeter, 2010).

Rouse, M.A. and R.H. Rouse, 'From Flax to Parchment: A Monastic Sermon from Twelfth-Century Durham', in R. Beadle and A.J. Piper (eds), *New*

Science out of Old Books: Studies in Manuscripts and Early Printed Books in Honour of A.I. Doyle (London, 1995), pp. 1–13.

Samuels, M.L., 'Some Applications of Middle English Dialectology', *English Studies*, 44 (1963), 81–94, repr. in M. Laing (ed.), *Middle English Dialectology: Essays on Some Principles and Problems* (Aberdeen, 1989), pp. 64–80.

Steinmetz, K.-H., '*De doctrina cordis* and Fifteenth-Century Ecclesial Reform: Reflections on the Context of German Vernacular Versions', in Renevey and Whitehead (eds), *Companion*, pp. 223–37.

Stocks, E.V. and A.I. Doyle, 'Draft Catalogue of Medieval Manuscripts in the University Library' (unpublished catalogue, Durham University).

Sutherland, A., '"Comfortable wordis" – the Role of the Bible in *The Doctrine of the Hert*', in Renevey and Whitehead (eds), *Companion*, pp. 109–30.

Swanson, R.N., *Religion and Devotion in Europe, c.1215–c.1515* (Cambridge, 1995).

Turner, D., *Eros and Allegory: Medieval Exegesis of the Song of Songs* (Kalamazoo, 1995).

Warner, G.P. and J.P. Gilson, *Catalogue of Old Royal and King's Collections of Western Manuscripts in the British Museum* (London, 1921).

Watson, N., 'Censorship and Cultural Change in Late-Medieval England: Vernacular Theology, the Oxford Translation Debate, and Arundel's Constitutions of 1409', *Speculum*, 70 (1995), 822–64.

Wenzel, S., *Latin Sermon Collections from Later Medieval England: Orthodox Preaching in the Age of Wyclif* (Cambridge, 2005).

Wheatley, A., *The Idea of the Castle in Medieval England* (York, 2004).

Whitehead, C., *Castles of the Mind: A Study of Medieval Architectural Allegory* (Cardiff, 2003).

—, '*De doctrina cordis*: Catechesis or Contemplation?', in Renevey and Whitehead (eds), *Companion*, pp. 57–82.

Wilkins, D., *Concilia Magnae Britanniae et Hiberniae* (London, 1737).

Woolf, R., 'The Theme of Christ the Lover-Knight in Medieval English Literature', *Review of English Studies*, 13 (1962), 1–16.

—, *The English Religious Lyric in the Middle Ages* (Oxford, 1968).

Zumthor, P., *Essai de poétique médiévale* (Paris, 1972).

Editorial Procedures

The following text of *The Doctrine of the Hert* is based upon Cambridge, Fitzwilliam Museum, MS McClean 132, fols 1r–93v. Occasional emended readings are taken from Oxford, Bodleian Library, MS Laud Misc. 330 and Cambridge, Trinity College Library, MS B.14.15, and are indicated with square brackets [...], and with footnotes. Moments where MS McClean becomes illegible through smudging or holes in the page are indicated with pointed brackets <...>.

Italics are used throughout the *Doctrine* text for material in Latin. Abbreviations in the manuscript, including the ampersand, are silently expanded in accordance with the way the word is usually spelled out in full. Manuscript spelling is followed, but *u/v* and *i/j* have been normalised in accordance with modern spelling conventions. Word division and capitalization are modern, as are sentence division and punctuation, although guided by manuscript practice. Paragraphing and sectional divisions are similarly editorial.

Rubrication is not indicated individually within the text, but the principles by which MS McClean is rubricated throughout are noted in full in the Manuscript Description.

The application of appropriate quotation marks is not always clear from the text. In general, quotation marks have been used for all Middle English translations of Latin scriptural quotes, even in instances where the translation deviates considerably from the Latin. They are also used for all Middle English patristic quotations, and for moments where the text intends to reproduce direct speech.

It should be noted that the scribe of MS McClean frequently fails to distinguish clearly between 'c' and 't', and between 'n' and 'u'. While other marks of abbreviations are applied consistently, there is also some ambiguity surrounding the use of a horizontal flourish through the ascender of final 'h'. In some instances, it would make orthographical sense to expand the flourish to 'he'; in many instances, it would not. In the face of this inconsistency, these flourishes have been ignored.

Within the Middle English text, the footnotes provide information about the physical condition of the McClean manuscript, including the presence of illuminated capitals, marginalia, deletions and holes in the manuscript. They also offer additional information on emended readings taken from the other manuscripts. The endnotes act as a textual commentary, detailing the substantial changes between the Latin *De doctrina cordis* and the Middle English text, identifying source material, citing analogous passages and explicating obscure references within the text.

The Textual Variants record all additions, omissions and subsitutions of words and phrases in MSS Laud, Trinity and Cosin, together with all changes in word order. All changes of number, tense and gender are also noted, together with deletions and additions in superscript or in the margin. Differences of spelling from one manuscript to another, and dialectal differences, are not noted.

Throughout the following edition, commentary and textual variants, Cambridge, Fitzwilliam Museum, MS McClean 132 is consistently abbreviated as M; Durham, University Library, MS Cosin V.III.24 as C; Cambridge, Trinity College Library, MS B.14.15 as T, and Oxford, Bodleian Library, MS Laud Misc. 330 as L.

The Doctrine of the Hert

Prologue

(fol. 1r)

Intelligite, insipientes in populo; et stulti, aliquando sapite.[1] As Seynt Austyn seyth, thes wordis ben undirstonde in this wise: 'ye that ben unkunnyng in the nombre of Goddis peuple inwardly undirstondith, and ye that ben unavisid, yif ye have grace of any gostly kunnyng,
5 sumtyme savorith sadly in hert.'[2] Myght not wel thees wordes be undirstonde of suche that ben unkunnyng in religioun, the whiche also nowadayes ben moche unstable in theire lyvyng, folowyng rather the ensample of seculer folk than the ensample of sad goostly religious folk? I trowe yis.
10 Suche symple soules[3] it is charite to enforme, namly seth oure lord yivyth us in charge, seiyng be the prophete Ysaye thus: *Loquimini ad cor Jerusalem.*[4] That is, 'spekith to the hert of Jerusalem.' This word, 'Jerusalem', is nothing ellis to mene in this place but symple chosyn soules, to the hertis of whom oure lord wold that we spake. O, ho durst
15 be recheles in enformyng of such symple soules, which oure lord bought with his precious blode and therto also hathe chosyn to his spouses, as ben thoo that dwellyn in religioun? Many, I wote wel, þer ben that speken to the body ouȝtward, but few to the hert inward of symple soules, and (fol. 1v) that is pite.
20 I, þerfore, oon of thoo whiche oure lord hath clepid to his servise in religioun,[5] alþogh I be no trew servaunt of his, have compilid this tretice that is clepid 'the doctrine of the herte', to the worship of God principally, and to edificacioun of symple soules,[6] wherein is comprehendid an informacioun of hertis dividid into seven chapitres,
25 in the whiche thei mow, be the grace of almyghty God, come to sadnes of good lyvyng, yif þey wil do theyre bisynessis for to rede and undirstonde that they fynde write in this same tretice, not only with the lippis of the mouthe, but also and namly with the lippis of the soule. Clene and chast soules ever desiryn so for to rede that thei myght feele
30 it savourly withinforth. Hertly redyng is a gracious meene to goostly felyng.[7] In this wise, þerfor, shuld this tretice be rad or herd, and than wil oure lord worche be his grace, namly, þer the hertis be clene that redith it or herith it.

Seynt Gregor seith in an omelie upon this text of Seynt John: *Unccio eius docet nos de omnibus.*[8] 'The soule' he seith, 'is ful febly enformyd   35 be þe voyce withoughtforth, but yif it be anoynted be þe (fol. 2r) grace of þe holy gost withinforth.'[9] Wherfore I beseche almyghty God that al thoo, the whiche han this tretice in honde, mow so rede and undirstonde it, that it mow be to theim encrese of vertue and of stable lyvyng. Amen.   40

Capitulum primum. How and in what wise a mynche shuld make redy here hert to God be þe yifte of drede.[10]

Capitulum secundum. How and in what wise a mynche shuld kepe here hert to God be the yifte of pite.

Capitulum tercium. How and what wise a mynche shuld opyn here hert   45 to God be þe yifte of kunnynge.[11]

Capitulum quartum. How and in what wise a mynche shuld stable here hert to God be þe yifte of strengthe.

Capitulum quintum. How and in what wise a mynche shuld ȝyve here hert to God bi þe yifte of counseile.   50

Capitulum sextum. How and in what wise a mynche[12] shuld lefte up here hert to God be þe yifte of undirstondyng.

Capitulum septimum. How and in what wise a mynche (fol. 2v) shulde cutte here herte be the yifte of wisdom.

Capitulum primum.[a] **How and in what wise a mynche shulde make redy here herte to God be the yifte of drede.**[1]

Religious[b] sister, seven informaciouns I rede in holy writ to teche a symple soule for to dispose here hert to grace.

¶ The first is that Samuel the prophete techith us to make redy oure hertis, whan he seith thus: *Preparate corda vestra Domino.*[2] 'Make redy' he seith, 'youre hertis to God.'

¶ The secunde is that Salomon techeth us to kepe oure hertis to God, whan he seith: *Omni custodia serva cor tuum.*[3] 'With al maner of bisines kepe thin herte' he seith, 'to God.'

¶ The thrid is that the boke of Machabeorum techith us to opyn oure hertis to God, where it is write þus: *Adaperiat Dominus cor vestrum.*[4] 'Oure lord' he seith, 'opyn youre hertis to hym.'

¶ The fourth is that Seynt Poule techith us to stable oure hertis to God, whan he seith thus: *Optimum est gracia stabiliri cor.*[5] 'The best þing that is to stabil the hert with is grace.'

¶ The fifte is that Salomon techith us to yive oure hertis, whan he seyth thus: *Justus cor suum tradet ad vigilandum diluculo ad Dominum, qui fecit illum.*[6] 'The rightwisman' he seith, 'shal yive his herte for to wake to oure lord in þe erly mor- (fol. 3r) nyng.'

¶ The sixte is that Jeremy þe prophete techith us to lifte up oure hertis to God, where he seith thus: *Levemus corda nostra cum manibus ad Deum.*[7] 'Lifte we up' he seith, 'oure hertis with oure werkis to God.'

¶ The seventhe is that Johel the prophete techith us to cutte oure hertis, where he seith thus: *Scindite corda vestra.*[8] 'Cuttith' he seith, 'youre hertis.'

¶ Loo, sister, seven þinges ben rehersid of the hert: that is, to make it redy, to opyn it, to kepe it,[9] to stable it, to yive it, to lifte it up, and to cutte it. ¶ Thes seven, withoughten þe seven yiftes of the holy goost, mow not perfightly be performyd, the which ben thees, for to begynne

---

[a] A blackened area in M makes these two words illegible.
[b] Illuminated capital 'R' covering two lines. In C, a two-line square space is left for an illuminated letter at this point. In T, an illuminated 'R' takes up a three-line square.

at the laste to the first: þe yifte of the drede of God, the yifte of
kunnyng, the yifte of pite, the yifte of strength, the yifte of counseyle,   30
the yifte of undirstondynge, and þe yifte of wisdom.[10] ¶ Bi the yifte of
the drede of God the hert is made redy, bi the yifte of kunnyng it is
kept, be þe yifte of pyte it is openyd, be the yifte of strength it is stabled,
be the yifte of counseyle it is yivyn, be the yifte of undirstondyng it is
lifte up, and be þe yifte of wisdom it is cutte.   35

¶ And how thow shalt make þin hert redy I shal telle the. The hert
muste be made redy in (fol. 3v) thre maner of wises: that is, as an hous
is made redy to receyve a worthi gest, as mete to be made redy for to
be etyn, and as a spouse maketh here redy to plese here housbonde.[11]

¶ As for the first. This worthi gest, whom an hert made redy shuld   40
receyve, is oure lord Jhesu Crist, that sekith amonges his childryn a
restyng place, the whiche to here helth hath tendirly yivyn his herte
blode, and þerfor he, beyng wery and woundid, axith of hem a restyng
place in þeire hertis. ¶ That he was wery for laboure in his passioun
the prophete Ysaie berith witnes, where oure lord be the same prophete   45
saith thus to clene hertis: *Hec requies mea. Reficite lassum.*[12] 'This is my
restyng place' he seith, 'refresshith me þat am wery.' Sister, receyve this
blissid lord, this gracious lord, and þis worthi gest, into þin hert þat is
his restyng place after his laboure.
     ¶ We ben cause of his grete laboure and werinesse, þat was woundid   50
to the dethe for oure wikkidnesse. ¶ What unkynde wrecchis be we
that wil not gladly receyve suche a champion into oure hous of oure
hertis, the whiche for oure love wagyd batayle with oure enemy and
had the victorie and the maystry, comyng fro the batayle al for- (fol. 4r)
sprenclid with blood, blew, wery, and woundid.[13] And what is he that   55
wil not meete with such a glorious champioun comyng home to his
hous, seth it so is that angelis of heven, whos kynde he toke not upon
hym but only the kynde of man, mette with hym styhing to heven on
Assencioun Day, joying and mekly merveyling of the body of mankynde,
the whiche he brought with him, seying thees wordes: *Quis est iste, qui*   60
venit de Edom, tinctis vestibus de Bosra? Iste formosus in stola sua.[14] 'What
is he, this' thei seide, 'that comyth ought of the world woundid, whos
clothis ben sprenclid with blood of tribulacioun? Certeyn, his clothing
becomyth hym right wel for he is ful semly þeryn.' O, yif angelis shewid
suche reverence to him in his Assencioun, whom he bought not with   65
his blood as he dede mankynde, whi shuld not we than mete him in
þe way and receyve hym with reverence, comyng to oure hertis axing

rest aftir his werynesse?[15] I drede but yif we receyve hym he wil another
tyme shame us and seye: *Hospes fui, et non collegistis me.*[16] 'I come to
70   yow as a gest' he wil sey, 'and ye wold not receyve me.'

¶ Now <s>ister, yif thou wilt receyve worthily this blissed (fol. 4v)
champioun, first thow must make clene thyn hous of thin hert, and þan
þou must aray it, and aftirward kepe wel þe yates of þe same hous.[17]
    ¶ The brome wherewith the hous of þin hert shuld be made clene is
75   drede of God, for as Salomon seith: *Timor Domini expellit peccatum.*[18]
'Drede of God puttith away synne', and þat is be confessioun. Seynt
Austyn seith: 'A soule þat knowith here synnes and of that knowleche
becometh dredful is anone enduced to be shryvyn.'[19] Cnowleche of the
synnes be þe mouthe in confessioun is noþing ellis but puttyng ought
80   filthes of the hous of oure herte be the dore of the mowth with þe brome
of the tunge.[20] But first, or thow go to confessioun, thow must serche
thi conscience bi bisy examynacioun and aftirward swepe it bi diew
confessioun. Thus dede Davith, the prophete, whan he seide: *Excercitabar
et scopebam spiritum meum.*[21] 'I' he seyde, 'with bisy inquisicioun serchid
85   my conciens and afterward swepte it be confessioun.'
    ¶ But summe þer ben that in confessioun tellyn bi pride and elacioun
here good dedes and hyden here evyl dedes. ¶ I may likne al tho to such
þat delyvere þeym of þeire good blood and kepe here bad blood within.
(fol. 5r) ¶ Sister, thow shalt not do so, but lete ought thi corrupt blode
90   of synne be the vayne of þi mowthe and kepe in þi good blood.[22] Telle
it not presumptuously but mekely be way of counseyl.[23]
    ¶ Merveyle not thow I calle þe mowthe a veyne, and synne corrupt
blood, for so I fynde write in the proverbes of Salomon: *Vena vite os
iusti.*[24] 'The mowth of a rightwisman is a vayne of lif.' Whan is thi
95   mowth, sister, a vayne of lif? Trewly, whan þou puttist ought fro þin hert
þe corrupt blood of synne be the lawncete of sorow and contricioun. Of
þis corrupt blood desired þe prophete[25] to be delyvered, whan he seyde
thus: *Libera me de sanguinibus, Deus, Deus salutis mee.*[26] That is: 'lord
God, my lord Jhesu, þou that lovest þe helþe of my soule, delyvere me
100   I beseche þe, from the corrupt blood of synne.' ¶ By this, thow mayst
considere that þe soule is as moche greved and more for to be delayed
fro confessioun whan it hathe nede, as þe body to be delayed fro blood
leete or mynucioun whan it is replete with corrupcioun.
    Of o þing be war: thow mayst never yif trew rekenyng in confessioun
105   but yif thow remember the longe afore, as a lordis catour, the whiche
shal yive a rekenyng to his lorde, (fol. 5v) first he rekenyth by himself.
Right so shuldest thou do, erþan thou come to confessioun, rekene

thin defautes bi thiself: how thou hast despendid thi lordis good the
whiche he hathe lente to the, that is, the yiftes of nature, the yiftes of
fortune, and þe yiftes of grace.[27] Thou wost wel also, yif a catour shuld   110
yive trew rekenyng, he writeth bothe the dayes and the causes in his
boke, how that he hathe dispendid his lordis good. So must thow do.
Rekene wel the circumstaunces of thin synnes: where and how and by
what causes thow hast synned, and þan go to confessioun and yif thi
rekenyng to thi lordis auditoure, that is, to þi confessoure, sittyng ther   115
in thi lordis name.[28]

¶ Many þer ben the whiche don as slow servauntes don, that whan
they shuld swepe here hous and putte ought the filth, they caste grene
risshes above and hide the filth. So don ypocrites; whan thei shuld
schew the unclennes of here synnes, thei hide it and telle þe fayrenesse,   120
and so cast aboven the filth the bewte of good werkis. Do not thou so
but first make al clene the flore of thi conscience fro al maner of filthes,
not only fro dedly synnes, but also fro venial (fol. 6r) synnes.[29] And
than axe counseyle of thi confessoure how vertuously thou mayst lyve
afterward, and þan throw grene risshes upon the clene flore.[30]   125

¶ And leve it wel, water of contricioun is a necessarie þing to clensyng
of the flore of þe conscience, for right as dust may not clerly be swept
ought of an hous withought water, so may not filthes of synne withoute
contricioun.[31] ¶ Thus þan bi verri contricioun and trew confessioun as
it is declared, the hous of thin hert must be clensid and made clene,   130
that oure lord mow devoughtly be receyved.

¶ Thus moche as for the makyng redy of the hert that is caused be
drede, as Salomon seith: *Qui timent Deum preparabunt corda sua.*[32] 'Tho
that dredyn God' he seiþe, 'shulle make redy theire hertis.'[33]

¶ It is not inow that þin hert be only swept and made clene for to   135
resceyve thi lord Jhesu, but also that it be arayed.[34] ¶ What profite is
it to a gest for to be resceyved into an hous that is clene swept, but yif
it be arayed? How and in what wise thin hous of thin hert shuld be
arayed, I shal shewe the bi ensample as I fynde write.

¶ Helyse, the prophete,[35] had in costome for to go ofte bi a devoute   140
wommanys hous, the whiche had an housbonde (fol. 6v) acordyng in
good lyvyng to here devoute purpose, as the Boke of Kynges tellith.[36] ¶
This devout womman perceyvid wel and set good eygh þat þe prophete
comme ofte bi here hous. She seyde to here housbonde thus: 'I perceyve
wel that this man, þe whiche ofte tymes gooth by oure hous, is a blissed   145
man, therfor I pray yow make we to him a litel hous, and set therin
a litel bedde, and a mete-table and a stole, and also a candilstik with

light that, whan that evyr he comyth bi us efte sones, he mow rest and
dwelle therin.'

150   In the same wise yif thou wilt receyve oure verry prophete Helyse,[a]
Jhesu Crist, into þe litel hous of thin hert, thow must ordeyne for hym
gostly thees foure thinges: a bed, a met-table, a stole, and a candilstik
with light. ¶ By this bed thow shalt undirstonde pees and rest of
conscience; be this met-table, penaunce; be this stole, the dome of þin
155   own conscience, and bi this candilstik with light, the knowleche of thi
conscience.[37]

¶ The bed of þis Helyse, Jhesu Crist, is pees and rest of conscience, as
Davith seyth: *In pace factus est locus eius.*[38] 'His place' he seyth, 'is made
in pees.' And þerfor, sister, whan that evyr þou puttist þin hert in rest,
160   thow puttist oure lord Jhesu Crist in his bed.[39]

¶ But (fol. 7r) now thou woldist wite what pees a soule shuld have
to be able for to resceyve oure lord? I shal tel the. A soule is in pees
for to resceyve oure lord whan it is not in wil to synne no more as it
hath don, no desireth no þingis ayen that is forsake,[40] no is brokyn
165   with adversite, ne reysid up with prosperite. ¶ Nevertheles, al tymes of
pees excludith not labouris and tornamentis, but rather, in pees tyme
betwene kyngdome and kyngdome, yonge pepil and bacheleris shewyn
theire strength be torneementis.[41] ¶ Also, pees tyme betwene kyngdome
and kyngdome excludith not þeves, but rather þan theves ben most
170   plente and usyn theire þefte.

¶ As for the first: that tyme of pees betwene reawme and reawme
excludith not laboures, right so it farith in a pessable conscience, and
that I may wel prove be Seynt Poule. ¶ Ho wold sey that he was not
in trew pees of conscience? Yit he seith himself in his epistolis that he
175   was in moche laboure and ofte tymes in prison, schorgid and betyn
ought of mesure, ofte tymes in poynte of dethe, in gret hungir, in gret
thrust, in moche fastyng, and suffryng gret cold.[42] ¶ Yif thou suffre
suche þingis paciently, sey not that thow hast lost pees, for in tyme of
pees thow must suffre suche (fol. 7v) thinges.

180   ¶ Also tyme of pees betwene reawme and reawme excludith not
tornamentis, but rather þan yonge bacheleris wil use þeire strength in
tornamentis, thow it be unlefful.[43] So it farith in pessable consciences.
¶ A tornament is callid no bateyle but rather a prevyng of strength.
Such tornementis usith the flessh and the soule ever stryvyng, and yit
185   þe conscience may be in rest, for it is not overcome with no synne,

---

[a] Two words have been erased beneath 'prophete Helyse'.

þow þe flessh and the spirit provyd theire strengþe togedre.⁴⁴ Therfor
sister, be wel ware þat þou consent not to the wikkid styring of the
flessh in the stry[v]ingᵃ to the souleward, for thow she steryth þe soule,
sey not thow hast lost pees, for in tyme of pees thow must suffre suche
stryvyngis.⁴⁵   190

❡ I seyde also that pees betwene reawme and reawme excludith
not þefte, but rather þan, þefte is most usid. ❡ Be þees þeves thow
shalt undirstonde smale negligences, omyssions, ydille daliaunces, and
seculer apportes, the whiche ben cause of mysspendinge of tyme.

❡ Thes smale þeves bringen in gretter þeves. So I rede in the Boke   195
of Kynges that the smale þeves of Sirie lad oute the doughter of Israel
and toke her as a prisoner.⁴⁶ Therfore be right wel ware of such smale
trespaces, lest thei bringe (fol. 8r)ᵇ with hem gretter and lede oute the
soule prisoner into the fendis dawnger, and yif thei come, þei wil bothe
dispoyle and robbe. Whi? Trewly, for þe smale þeves that were within   200
afore openyd þe yatis of thin hert and lete hem in.⁴⁷

Of suche þat so openyth the hert be consentyng to synne, pleynyth
Job, seiyng thus: *Venerunt latrones et fecerunt viam per medium.*⁴⁸ That
is, 'thevis come and made hem a way in the myddis.' Thevis makyn a
way in the myddes of thin hert, sister, whan þin hert (þe whiche shuld   205
be as a close gardyn to oure lord,⁴⁹ brynging forthe floures of meknes,
paciens, and of al vertu) is made a commune gardyn to thin enemy,
bringing forth ydel daliaunce, wikkid þoughtes, negligences, and oþer
þornis and breris of vicious living. And the cause is that þin gardyn is
not y-heggid wit siker keping as a close gardyn shuld be.⁵⁰   210

Salomon seith: *Ubi non est sepes, diripietur possessio.*⁵¹ 'Leve it wel, ther
that is noon hegge of sikir wardyng þer shal thin enemy entre and robbe
þe.' Therfor kepe wel þin gardyn of thin hert and be not moche aferd
of suche þeves, althow thei come and profre hem for to entre.

And sey not þat thow hast lost pees, thow þou suffre suche tribula-   215
ciouns and temptaciouns, for oonly pees of hert þat alle (fol. 8v)
commun vertuos lyveris han may not put away suche trobles, but only
softnes of hert. For it is more to be esy and softe in hert þan for to be
pessable in hert,⁵² for in a pessable hert oure lord hathe a place, but in
an esy softe hert he hath a dwelling habitacioun, as the prophete Davith   220
seith: *In pace factus est locus eius.* 'His place' he saith, 'is made in pees.'
*Et habitacio eius in Syon.*⁵³ 'And his dwellyng place is in Syon.'

ᵃ Probably a scribal mistake, since the text continues with two references to
'stryvyngis'. Emended reading from L.
ᵇ There are no paraph signs on fols 8r and 8v.

Be this word, 'Syon', thow shalt undirstonde contemplacioun, the whiche may not be had withoute a softe spirit and an esy. But yit pees
225 most make way afore, for he that is pessable may sone come to the grace of contemplacioun and ellis not, for right as þou mayst not se thi face in a trobled water, right so þou mayst not se God with a trobled hert.[54]

Yif thow wilt þerfore ordeyne to oure lorde in thin hert a place of rest and also a dwellyng place of esines, be pessable and esy in spirit,
230 for he wil not rest in the but yif thou desire to rest in hym, as the prophete seith: *Super quem requiesset spiritus meus nisi super humilem et quietum.*[55] 'Upon whom' he seyth, 'shal my spirit of contemplacioun rest but on him that is mekly pessable and quiete in spirit? Trewly, upon noon ellis.'[56]

235 ¶ But þis rest and (fol. 9r) quietenesse must be kept in thin hert and lokkid up with a kay; thow maist not be liberal for to speke. ¶ The trew keper of pees is þe kaye of taciturnite, for it is a commune seiyng: he that is stille in al thing, in al thing he fynte rest.

¶ Thenk that he, the whiche dwellith in thin hert, wil be þin avoket
240 in al maner of causes, for to answere for the as he dede for Mary Mawdeleyne. Yif thow wilt be stille, he axith no noþer reward of the for his salarie but stilnesse. Knowist thou not wel how he answerid for Marie Mawdeleyne to the pharise, Symon, the wiche grutchid at the mete and seyde thus: 'Yif he this were a verry prophete he myght sone
245 wite what this womman is, for she is a synner.'[57] To this she answerid noþing, but she wept, and oure lord answerid for here.

¶ Also, to here sister Martha þat playnid upon here to hym, she answerid noo word but oure lord answerid for here.[58] ¶ Also, another tyme ayenst Judas, that tretoure, the wiche grucchid whan she anoynted
250 oure lordis feete and seyde: 'Why is þis precious oynement so lost? It myght had be sold and yiven to powre men',[59] she answerid not, but oure lord answerid for here. (fol. 9v)

Lo sister, how oure lord answerith for hem þat suffren and be stille and softe in spirit. ¶ Suche softnes and stilnes is keper of verry pees,
255 Jhesu Crist.[60]

¶ The secunde þing that must be ordeynid in the litel hous of thin hert for þis Helyse, Jhesu Crist, is a mete-table, be the wiche is undirstonde verry penaunce.[61]

¶ They settyn a mete-table afore oure lord that ordeyneth hem for to
260 do penaunce for here synnes. So seyth Seynt Bernard: 'His mete is my penaunce.'[62] He that mekly doth penaunce and hath gladnes and delite theryn, he biddith oure lorde to þe fest. The condicioun of al tho that

biddyn þeire frendis to the fest; whan thei ben set and servid, because
thei wold chere þeire frendes, first they begynne and tast of the same
mete and than rehete þeire frendes. Right so, thi gladnes and meknes   265
of thi penaunce, þe wiche is the duresse of religioun that þou suffrest
for Godis sake, is cause that he wille sitte with the and ete with the.
This etyng of oure lord is the gladnes of the in thi penaunce. Oure
lord is fed with thi meknes and gladnes, for Seynt John Crisosteme
seith: 'Yif thi penaunce like the, it liketh God, and yif it mislike the,   270
(fol. 10r) it[a] may not plese God.'[63] Woldist thow þat it shuld plese God
that mysliketh the? Nay, it may not be.

   ¶ But now, yif thow wilt wel plese this gest, Jhesu Crist, the wiche
thou hast bede to mete, þou must first honestly aray thi mete-table, as
Salomon seith: *Transi et orna mensam tuam.*[64] 'Go' he seith, 'and aray   275
thi mete-table.' Be þis word 'goyng', thou shalt undirstonde bisines
and quyknes, that thou be not dul ne slow ne unlusty in doyng of
thi penaunce. ¶ And also, ther I say 'aray thi mete-table', undirstonde
gladnes in doyng of thi penaunce, as Salomon seith in anoþer place thus:
In omni dato hillarem fac vultum tuum.[65] 'In every yifte that thou yivyst   280
to oure lord in the[b] fest of penaunce, schew glad chere.' ¶ Thus chere
thi gest, Jhesu Crist, that voucheth saf to sit with the at the fest of thi
penaunce, and serve hym not with many disches, for he is homly ynow.
He holdith him wel apayed to eete with the of the same plater of gladnes
that thou shewist to him. Yif thou yive him gladnes of thi penaunce, he   285
wil yive þe mercy and gostly gladnes of everlastyng blisse.

   ¶ Of this mercy I fynde a figure in holy writ that Kyng Davith
seyde to the sone of (fol. 10v) Saul (the wiche was callid[66] Misybosecch)
whan he seyde þus: *Misybosecch, faciam in te misericordiam et restituam
tibi omnes agros patris tui, et tu comedes panem in mensa mea semper.*[67]   290
'Misibosecch' he seide, 'I shal shew the mercy and restore the to thi
fadres londes, and thou shalt eete with me brede evyr at myn owne
table.' ¶ Þis word, 'Misibosecch', is no more to undirstonde but a
shamefast mowth, and it betokeneth a repentaunt synner that with
shame sheweth his synnes.[68]   295

   ¶ Than the wordis of Davith to the sone of Saule, Misibosecch, ben
the wordis of oure lord to every repentaunt synner. As thow he seide to
every repentaunt synner thus: I shal shewe the mercy because thou hast

---

[a] M reads 'it it' (fols 9v–10r). The initial 'it' has been lightly erased in black (the
quotation is in red letter).
[b] There is a small space between these two words, and between the paraph and
'Thus' on the following line, as a result of a flaw in the vellum.

doo rightwisnes of thiself in accusyng of thi synnes bi confessioun and
300 punshing gladly thi synnes in doyng of penaunce. And also I shal restore
the ayen to thi fadres londes. ¶ Be thes londes þou shalt undirstonde the
heritage of heven that was in maner lost fro the by thi synne, þe wich
oure lord yeldeth ayen with al the goodes þerof to a repentaunt synner.
For, as Seynt Austyn seyth: 'Penaunce restorith ayen al that was lost.'[69]
305 Also, he seith: 'Thow shalt eete with me brede evere (fol. 11r) at myn
own table.'[70] He eetith brede ever at oure lordis table that ever deliteth
and list for to do penaunce. For brede in holy writ ofte tymes is callid
penaunce, tribulaciouns and persecuciouns, be þe wiche þou shuldist be
fulfillid and wex fat gostly be the meke suffraunce of hem.[71] ¶ Of such
310 bred oure lord was fulfillid himself, þat is, with reproves and shames.
As ofte, þerfore, as any shames and reproves in religioun ben put to
þe, þonke oure lord þat hath yive the of the same brede that he eete
hymself. ¶ This is a cloystreris bred; ete it gladly, sister. It is hard with
such that etith þis brede grucchingly.[72]
315 ¶ Ther ben also summe þat puttyn away from hem þe penaunce of
the duresse of religioun. What don thei, trowist thou? Trewly, in as
moche as in hem is, thei put Crist away from hem, þe wiche stondith
afore hem and ministreth to hem the plater of penaunce, and seith
þus: *Filia tinge buccellam in aceto.*[73] 'Dowter, wete thi mossel in myn
320 ayselle.' By this mossel is undirstonde tribulaciouns and temptaciouns
that a clene soule suffreth, wiche ben but litel in maner of a mossel in
comparison of Cristis passioun, the wiche is undirstonde be the ayselle.
In that medicinable (fol. 11v) sause, wete thi litel mossel of tribulacioun
and temptacioun. ¶ Put it not away fro the, but tempere thi sorowis
325 with his sorowis, and þou shalt fynde it þan a savery mete.
¶ There is also anoþer maner of sauce, the wich stont upon oure
lordis owen table. ¶ That sauce, yif it be usid, maketh al maner mete
of penaunce swete. What is that sause, trowist þou? Trewly, mynde of
endeles reward. ¶ Of that sause spekith Seint Austyn and seith that:
330 'þenkyng of endeles mede lessith the strengthe of penaunce.'[74] This is
callid sause of aromatik, for what that ever is ete therwith is made swete.
¶ Of the wiche sause oure lordis spouse seith in the Boke of Love thus:
Messui mirram meam cum aromatibus meis.[75] 'I have repe my myrre' she
seith, 'with myn aromatik.' ¶ Be this myrre thow shalt[76] undirstonde
335 temptacioun and tribulaciouns in religioun, and bi this aromatik thou
shalt undirstond mynde of endeles reward. ¶ Than thou repist wel þi
myrre with thin aromatik, whan þou temperist al maner sorowis that
þou suffrest with hoope of endeles reward.[77]

¶ The thrid þing that must be ordeyned in the litel hous of þin
(fol. 12r) hert for this Elise, Jhesu Crist, is a stole to sitte upon. Of this   340
stole spekith the prophete Davith þus: *Justicia et iudicium preparacio*
sedis tue.[78] 'The ordenaunce' he seith, 'of thi sete, Jhesu, is dome and
rightwisnesse.'

¶ Yif a gret lord shuld come to thin hous, woldist thou not make
redy for hym a sittyng place? Good sister, þan[a] make redy a sittyng   345
place to almyghty God, the wich comyth to þin hert, that is, examyne
þin conscience and deme thiself gilty, and so punshe and chastise
thiself by rightwisnes, that þou mow receyve that blessyng that the
prophete spekith of and seith: *Beati qui custodiunt iudicium, et faciunt*
iusticiam in omni tempore.[79] 'Blessid ben al tho that kepyn trew dome   350
of examinacioun of hemself, and done therto diew satisfaccioun of
rightwisnes in al tyme.'[80] ¶ Sister, kepe such trewe dome and diew
satisfaccioun, and punshe þiself in the chapitre of thin hert every day,
that þi soule mow be made hole fro the woundis of synne, for as Job
seith: *Qui non amat iudicium sanari non poterit.*[81] 'He that loveth not   355
for to deme himself gilti, he may not be hoole fro synne.'[82]

¶ Lo, sister, upon that stole of dome in þin conscience must oure lord
sitte, and þerfor make (fol. 12v) the redy, for thow must stonde afore him
as afore thin visitoure to be punshid for thi defautes. Resceyve therfor
lowly of hym blames and reprovis for þin defautes, for he it is, as holy   360
writ seith, that blameth and chastiseth every child that he resceyveth.[83]

¶ But first, er þis blessid visitour come, make redy his sittyng place,
that is, deme thiself and noon oþer. ¶ Usurpe not upon þe þe jurisd-
iccioun of anoþer for to deme oþer, for þat longith not to þe. And
specialy bewar of mysdemyng of oþer mennys consciences suspeciously   365
and folily, þe wiche consciences ben unknowe to þe.[84] Al maner
folious domes of other, Seint Poule inhibiteth and seith: *Nolite ante*
tempus iudicare, quoadusque veniat Dominus: qui illuminabit abscondita
tenebrarum, et manifestabit consilia cordium.[85] 'Deme not' he seith, 'afore
the tyme of the general dome, that is, unto the tyme þat oure lord shal   370
come and make cler þe privee þingis of derknes, and make opyn the
counseiles of hertis.'

¶ There ben thre maner of domes.[86] Oon is dome of suspicioun, that
is, whan we han suspicioun of anoþer be þing seyn in him or herd of
him. This is, as summe doctouris seyde, litel synne or noone, so it go   375
no ferther (fol. 13r) than himself. ¶ Another is dome of light credence:
whan we in dowty þingis, sopose evyl of annoþer, not affermyng it

---

[a]   This word is added as superscript with ^.

for soth, but lightly yivyng feith and credence þat it shuld be so. This,
summe doctoures holdyn but venial synne,[a] in as moche as it is not
380 affermyd for soth. ¶ The thrid is dome of ful diffinycioun and sentence
in evyl. This maner of demyng is dedly synne, þe wiche is forbede be
oure lord, where he seith thus: *Nolite iudicare, et non iudicabimini.*[87]
'Demeth not' he seith, 'and ye shul not be demed.' As thow he seyde
thus: yif ye mow not eschew suspicious demyngis because of freelte,
385 fleeth than in any wise dome of ful diffinicioun, þat ye yive no ful
sentence of þing that ye ben in doute of.
¶ Be war now, sister, þat þou deme not (and specialy noo good
þingis) evyl, but doo as þe bee doth, þe wiche turnith bitter juse of
floures into swetnes of hony. Yif þow here evyl, be ware þow yif no
390 feith lightly þerto, but suppose the best. An envious soule cannot do
so, but it farith as an ereyne. It tornith what that ever it soketh into
venym; þat is, it tornith (fol. 13v) good into evyl. ¶ Sister, have thow þe
hert of a bee, and turne þe werst into the best by trew compassioun of
other defautes, considering sharply þin own defautes and merciably þe
395 defautes of oþer.[88]
¶ Lo, sister, þis is the stole of Cristis sete in þin hert, that is, for to
deme þinself and be ware for to deme other.[89]

¶ The fourth þing þat must be ordeyned in the litel place of thin hert
for þis Helyse, Jhesu Crist, is a candilstik with light. Be þis candilstik
400 with light undirstonde knowleche of thiself.[90] ¶ Mannys hert is as a
derk hous but yif it have light of his own knowlech. It hath as moch
light as it hath knowlech.
¶ Sory mow they ben that so precious a candille of here own
knowlech spenden rather abowten oþer outward þinges þan aboute
405 here own gostly profight. 'Wheþer thei ben not suche' as Seynt Bernard
seith, 'that bisyin here wittes to know many outeward þinges and ben
ferre fro the knowlech of hemself.' I trow yis.[91] What is it ellis but the
synne of curiosite? ¶ 'This vice' as Seint Gregor seith, 'is a perlious
vice, for the more bisi a man is to serche þe lif of anoþer (fol. 14r), the
410 lesse he knowith himself.'[92] ¶ Amonges suche curiouse hertes oure lord
Jhesu wil not be herbourid. He farith not as a nyght crowe that hatith
light, but he wil þat þi light be set an hygh, that he may se the and so
entre into þin hert.[93]
¶ Set up thi light upon a candilstik, that thow may see þiself and
415 examine thiself, and þan will þe fende, þe wiche sekith for to slepe in

---

[a] An 's' has been erased on the end of 'synne'.

derkenesse, fle fro the. ⁊ Wel ben thei at ese that mow sey, as Abya
seyde to Jeroboam, stonding on high upon an hille: 'With us is a
candilstik of gold and light þerin.'⁹⁴ This man, Abya, that stod upon
the hille, betokeneth every rightwisman that abideth perseverauntly in
the heith of vertuos lyvyng. Such on stondith alway ayenst Jeroboam,   420
þat is, the fende, and seyth, in puttyng away of hym and resceyvyng
of Crist, that he hathe light of knowlech set in a goldyn candilstik
of his hert.

⁊ Therfore it was þat oure lord seyde to his spouse thus: *Revertere ut
intueamur te.*⁹⁵ 'Come ayen' he seith, 'dere spouse, that we mow beholde   425
thee.' As thow he seyde thus: 'Bow thi knowleche upon thiself, that so
longe hathe be extendid aboute outward þinges, than (fol. 14v) shal I
merciable see thee.' For oure lord wil not be harbourid in a place ther
the herbergoure is oute. ⁊ Thus also, to turne ayen to þe hert, oure lord
biddith every synful soule bi the prophete Ysaye, seiyng thus: *Redite,*   430
*prevaricatores ad cor.*⁹⁶ 'Turne ayen' he seith, 'þe trespasoures to youre
hertes.'⁹⁷

⁊ Yif thou þus, sister, have light in the, than wil the prophete Helise,
that is oure lord Jhesu, make his dwellyng place in the.⁹⁸

⁊ Thogh þin hous, sister, be þus clensid and arayed, yit yif oure lord   435
shuld dwelle þerin, þe yates þerof must wel be kept. ⁊ The yates þat
shuld be kept ben thi fyve wittis, that is, tastyng, touching, seyng,
heryng, and smellyng.ᵃ Bi þes five yates þe soule goth oute to outeward
þingis, and outeward þingis comyth into the soule.⁹⁹

⁊ The keping of thees yates is noþing ellis but puttyng away of   440
delectaciouns of þe five wittes. The soule gooth oute be þe yates whan
she puttith here to outeward bisynes þat longeþe to actyf lif, the whiche
shuld be usid with gret sadnes and gret drede. For right as lordis, whan
thei gon fer from home, þei hane afore hem serjauntes with maces in
her hondis, for to avoyde the peple that thei shuld not oppresse here   445
lord, (fol. 15r) so a clene soule shuld do whan she goth oute to speke,
to heere, to see, or for to do any actyf honest mynistracioun, shuld
ever have afore here drede, as a serjaunte with a mace in his honde, of
remembraunce of the paynes the wiche ben in helle, to put away the
company of wikkid þoughtes þat wold oppresse a clene soule.   450

⁊ Such a serjaunt wantid Dyna, the doughter of Jacob, whan she went
oute for to behold wymmen of a straunge regioun, for the wiche goyng
oute she was ravisched and oppressid of Sichem, the sone of Emor.¹⁰⁰

ᵃ   These five sense nouns are all capitalized in M.

Curiosite in seyng of vanites and heryng of tithingis was cause of this,
455 the wiche is a way of corrupcioun.[101]

¶ Such a serjaunte wantid Esau, whan he went oute on huntyng and
lost þe blessing of his fadre, but Jacob had it, for he be lefte at home.[102]
By this Esau ben undirstonde þoo, the wiche ben unrestful at home
in here own conscience and sekeris of outeward comfortis, to whom
460 þe eyre of the cloystor is unholsome, and þer is noþing so hevissom to
hem as is rest. Al such ben hunteris of flesshly lust, þe wich lesyn þe
blessing of here fadre, almyghty God.

¶ By Jacob þat be left at home, ben undirstonde restful and
pessable cloystreris, the whiche han al here joy in rest of cle- (fol. 15v)
465 ne consciences.[103] ¶ So shuld þi joy be, sister, ever inward in a clene
conscience. ¶ In that hous shuld be thi restyng place, and þer shuldist
þou praye, þer shuldist þou use þi meditacioun and also contemplacioun,
and close fast the yates of þi five wittes, and þan devoutly behold þi
fader, þi spouse, þi love, and þi lord, in þe privitees of þin hert.

470 ¶ Overmore, whan that ever þou be put to outeward bisynes, go never
withoute a serjaunte of drede afore the with a mace in his honde, ouþer
of remembraunce of deth, or of purgatorie, or of þe dredful dome, or
ellis of helle. And þan, I fere not but þat þou shalt escape synne in thi
bisynes.

475 ¶ But þer ben to maner of dredes: drede of God, þat is love drede,
and drede of peynes, þe wiche is clepid servile drede. Whan þat ever
þou goist oute with drede for peynes, þou hast afore the a serjaunte
paynted upon a cloþe with a mace in his honde, semyng as thow he
wold smyte, þe wiche is noo quyk serjaunte. ¶ Neverþeles, to somme
480 suche maner of drede doth good, for it makith hem aferd for to synne
for drede of payne. But þer doth noone so moche good as doth the
quyk serjaunte that is love drede, with a (fol. 16r) mace in his honde
of þretenyng, but yif þou leve to synne only for love.[104] For so seith
Salomon: *In timore Domini declinat omnis a malo.*[105] 'In the drede of
485 God' he seith, 'a clene soule bowith away fro synne.' ¶ And yif thou
only for drede of peyne levest for to synne, thou woldist synne yif thou
wistist not for to be punschid.

¶ The fende aspieth ful sclily[a] to what synne þou art most disposid,
and þat synne he profreþ most, wenyng that þou hungrist lustes, and
490 þerof he profreth the such mete as he hath for to sclake þin hunger.
¶ Do thou þan as a daungerous delicat womman, resceyve noon of

---

[a] M is unclear. This word could begin 'sc' or 'st'. The latter would be a
mistake.

his meete, but þrow it ayen in his face! What is desire of the flesh but
hunger of lustes? What is desire of the eyghen but hunger of richesse?
What is pride of this present lif but hunger of worshippes?[106]

So þan, generaly, I may say þat every synner persheth in hunger,   495
and that was wel provyd bi the sone þe wiche wastyd his fadres good
in another lond, lyvyng lecherously, whan he seyde thus: *Quanti
mercennarii in domo patris mei abundant panibus, ego autem hic fame
pereo!*[107] 'How many hired men ben at home in my fadres hous' he
seyde, 'and have abun- (fol. 16v) daunce of liflode, and I sterve here   500
for hunger!' ¶ By þees hired men thou shalt undirstonde rightwis[a]
soules of þe blisse of heven, the wiche have wel servid oure lord in this
lif for hevenly mede, þat now in blisse ben fed and fulfilled with lif
everlastyng. And the synful soule, the wiche in this lif hath lyvyd in
lustes, in endeles payne shal sterve in hunger.   505

¶ But now, sister, of o þing take hede. Whan that ever the fende
profreth to the meetes of foule temptaciouns, þe wich ben to þin hert
abominable, it is not in þi power for to withstonde such profres, but
it is in thi power for to receyve hem or not for to receyve hem. ¶ For
as longe as mete is uneetyn, so longe it is uncorporate. ¶ Be wel war,   510
therfor, þat nouþer thou tast ne eete of his metis. It is a gret differens
of tastyng of mete and of etyng of mete. Yif þou tast mete, þou asayst
it undir thi tonge withoute swolwyng, but yif thow eete it, þou drawist
it into thi body.[108] Right so, þer ben summe that in no wise wold synne
dedly by consentyng in synne, but yit ofte tymes þey taste of synnes by   515
delectaciouns, whan þei (fol. 17r) suffre here hertes to tary therin.[109]

¶ Lo, sister, how foule it is for to taste of the fendes meetes, and yit it is
moche fowlere for to ete of hem. ¶ Neverþeles, ofte tastyng is equypollent
to a draught, as it is wel proved by hem that ofte tastyn wyne. Right
so, ofte to have delectacioun in synnes bringeth in conscente. ¶ Yif   520
thou drede deth of soule that cometh be consentyng of synne, be aferd
to delite in þoughtes of synne, for þough such lusty þoughtes in synne
propirly sle not þe soule, yit they disposyn a soule to deth.

¶ Good sister, be wel war of such wrecchid metes. Nouþer tast
of hem, no eete of hem, and þan be[b] not aferd þow he profre to þe   525
þoughtes of blasfemy, or ayenst þi beleve, or of oþer maner of abomina-
ciouns of synne, for he may never do the dissese with hem, yif þou kepe
þe fro receyvyng of hem ouþer be tastyng or be eetyng.

¶ Thus, sistir, whan that ever þou art put oute to honest actif

---

[a]   M reads 'rightwisnesse'.
[b]   M reads 'be ne not'.

530 occupacioun be obedience, goo never withoute such a serjaunte of drede, and namly of love drede, as it is rehersid. And þan shal thi yates of thi five wittes (fol. 17v) be wel kept, for ther may never dedly synne entre wiþin the, but yif it come in by on of þi five yates.

¶ Therfor, sister, þe nedith also to have a porter for to kepe þi yates.
535 Þis porter shal be discrecioun.[110] Þis porter may be no sleper, for yif discrecioun slepe, what merveyle is it þough þeves entre in bi þi yates? Thus I rede in holy writ þat Ysboseth was killed in his bed, in as moche as þe womman that wynwed whete, þe wiche shuld had kept þe yate, was aslepe.[111] Seynt Gregor expounyth þis in þis wise: 'A womman
540 wynneweth whete whan discrecioun departith vices fro vertues, and whan þat þis womman, discrecioun, slepith, þan entren in enemyes for to sle here lord, Ysboseth, þe soule.'[112] Suffre not, sister, þerfore, þe porter of þi yate, discrecioun, slepe, lest enemyes entre and sle þi soule. Yif þei entre, leve it wel, þei wil make of þi conscience a commune
545 market place, the wiche shal be þan a place of crye and noyse and not a place of restful silence, a place of propre goodes and not a place of commune goodes, and a place of byhyng and sellyng and where shal noþing be unsold.[113]

¶ Now wel may such a synful (fol. 18r) soule be callid a place of crie
550 and noyse, where þe þondring of oure lord be þretenyng may not be herd, and where also ben noyseful þoughtes and unpessable, every of hem stryving wiþ other. A synful soule may also be wel callid a place of propre goodes and not of commune goodes, where charite wantith, þe wiche preferrith evermore commune goodes afore propre goodes. ¶
555 A synful soule is also a place of bihing and selling where is put to sale þe best juelle, þe wiche is þe soule, as Salomon seith: *Animam suam venalem facit.*[114] 'Such a synner' he seith, 'puttiþ his soule for to be sold to þe fende for a lewyd foule mony of delectacioun.'

¶ Be þerfor wel war, sister, þat þou wilfully make not of thi fadres
560 hous of heven, the wiche is þi conscience, a commune market place to þe fende, and bringe not þi soule to nought þat so preciously is bought. ¶ He þat bought it lefte no bloode in þe purse of his skyn for rawnsummyng of þi soule. Þerfor, it is right nedful for to kepe wel þi yates, þat þou mow be jocunde and mery with Crist alone in þi restful
565 conscience.[115]

¶ Lo, sister, þus have I declared how þou (fol. 18v) must make redy þin hert as an hous, þe wiche is made redy for to receyve a worthi gest. And þerfor now, be the grace of God, I shal telle the how þou shalt make redy þin hert to God as meete þat must be etyn.

¶ Oure lord Jhesu, that so tendirly and so merciably hath made   570
himself redy to þe for to be etyn in the blessid sacrament of the aughter,
axith the same of the that thou make þin hert redy for to be etyn of him.
¶ Thus techith Salomon þe prophete, seiyng þus: *Cum sederis ad mensam
principis, diligenter attende que sunt posita ante faciem tuam. Et scito quia
talia te oportet preparare.*[116] 'Whan þou art set' he seith, 'at þe kynges   575
table, take hede what is set afore the.' ¶ Thou art set at þe kynges table,
whan þou knelist at Godis borde for to be fed with þe blissed body of
þat kynge in þe sacrament of þe aughter. ¶ Therfor, take hede what is
y-set afore þe for to be receyved into þi soule, for it is hevenly liflode,
þe wiche come down from heven.[117] ¶ It is also an undefoulid lamb þat   580
must be etyn and receyvid with soure letuse of contricioun.[118] ¶ It is also
hevenly manna, þe wich hath þe tast of al maner of swetnes.[119]

¶ Take (fol. 19r) now right good hede, and I shal telle the what þis
manna menyth. ¶ We rede in holy writ þat oure lord reynid down
from heven manna to þe children of Israel for to be fed with in desert,   585
in figure of þe blissed sacrament of þe aughter. The wiche manna in
kynde was such þat it meltid ayens þe sonne as snow, and it wax hard
ayenst þe fyre.[120]

¶ It obeid to melt ayenst þe sonne, because it was an hevenly þing as
þe sonne was, but to þe fire, þe wiche was an erthly þing, it wold not   590
obeie, but withstode it and wax hard þerayenst. ¶ By þis, þou mayst
undirstonde a grete difference betwene þe heete of þe sonne and þe
heete of þe fyre. ¶ The heete of þe sonne makith herbis to grow, be the
wiche is undirstonde charite, þat makeþ vertuos to encresse in þe soule.
But þe heete of þe fire distroyeth herbes, be þe wiche is undirstonde þe   595
heete of fleschly lust, þat distroith al vertuos.

¶ Thus þan, bi þis manna, as I seyde, þe wiche meltith ayenst þe
sonne and hardeneth ayenst þe fire, is undirstonde þe blissed sacrament
of þe aughter, Cristes flessh and his blood. ¶ Whan þat ever þis blissed
sacrament is receyvid of a soule þat hath þe heete of þe sonne, þe   600
(fol. 19v) wiche is charite, it meltith al in teris, ouþer in outeward teris
or inward or ellis bothe, and in love and devocioun. ¶ But whan it is
receyvid of a soule þat is encombrid with þe heete of fleshhly lust, such
a soule wexith obstinate, as ben al such þat receyvyn Cristes flessh and
his blood in dedly synne.   605

¶ Preve þerof þiself, sister, that receyvist that blissed sacrament:
wheþer þou have the heete of þe sonne that is charite, or þe heete of
þe fire þat is flesshly lust. For ouþer thou must nedis melte in teris bi
swetnesse of love, yif thow receyvist it in charite, or ellis þou must wex
hard in ostinacie, yif þow receyvist it in dedly synne.[121]   610

¶ Thou must also considere in þis blissed sacrament the gret largenes of divine love þe wiche is shewid to mankynde, and that is in many wyses.[122] On is that he yivith frely to mankynde al creatures beneth man to þe use of man, as the prophete seith: *Omnia subiecisti sub*
615 *pedibus eius.*[123] 'Al thing' he seith, 'oure lord hath made subjecte to the use of mankynde', bothe oxyn and schepe ben dispoylid for to clothe man, and oxyn ben flayne for to covere mennys feete, and so of oþer unresonable bestis.

¶ The secunde largnes (fol. 20r) of divine love is that he hath graunted
620 to man the princes and dukes of his houssold, þat is, al angelis, to the servise of man. 'For al the angelis that ben in heven' as Seint Poule seiþ, 'ben made servisable to hem that shuld take þe heritage of helth.'[124] ¶ Thes princes wardyn us and defendyn us from the violence of al oure gostly enemyes whiles we lyvyn in þis lif.

625 ¶ The þrid largenes of divyne loue is þat he hath yive to mankynde himself, and þat is in many maner of wises. Þat is, as a broþer and as a felaw, whan he comme down and toke flessh and blood of oure lady Seint Marie, and so was made man. Than was Crist made oure brother and oure felaw, ye and oure servaunt, in þat he was bete and suffred
630 passioun for us. ¶ Also, he hath yivin himself to us as a mayster, in as moche as he hath taught us, for he seith hymself: *Vos vocatis me Magister et Domine, bene dicitis: sum etenim.*[125] 'Ye clepe me mayster and lord' he seith, 'ye say wel I am so.' ¶ Also, he hath yivin himself to us in ensample be his meke conversacioun of living, as he seith himself:
635 *Exemplum dedi vobis, ut quemadmodum ego feci, ita et vos faciatis.*[126] 'I have yi- (fol. 20v) ven yow ensample that right as I have don, do ye.'

¶ Also, he hath yiven himself to the passioun for us, into a grete[a] price for oure rawnsom. Thus seith Seint Poule: *Empti enim estis precio magno.*[127] 'Ye ben bought' he seith, 'with a gret price.' ¶ Also, he hath
640 yiven his blissid body in the sacrament of þe aughter for oure meete,[128] as for þe most worthiest yifte þat ever he yaf to mankynde, as he seith himself: *Caro mea vere est cibus: et sanguis meus, vere est potus.*[129] 'My flessh' he seith, 'is very gostly mete, and my blode is very gostly drynke.' This is an excellent shewyng of love to mankynde: it passith
645 al his oþer yiftes. ¶ Thus shalt þou considere þe excellent benefices[b] of the sacrament of the aughter.

---

[a] The 'r' is added as superscript with ^.
[b] The McClean scribe frequently replaces 't' with 'c'. The word here and in subsequent usages translates as 'benefits'.

¶ But now þe nedeth for to ordeyne for his mete (þat hath ordeyned his blissed body for thi mete) as it is rehersid afore in þe auctorite of Salomon: *Scito quia talia te oportet preparare.*[130] That is: 'beholde and take hede what is set afore the whan þou sittest at Godis borde', for so　650 þou must ordeyn for him. He hath yiven himself for þi mete; yive þou now þiself for his mete.[131]

How and in what wise thow shalt make þiself redy to his mete, it is write in (fol. 21r) holy writ bi ensample of Jacob and Ysaac. 'Sone' seide Rebecca to Jacob, 'I herd thi fadre speke to thi brother, þat he　655 shuld bringe him home summe mete bi his huntyng, that he myght have his blissyng er than he dyede. Þerfor, sone, listen to my counseyle and go to the flok, and bringe home fro þennys too þe best kydes þat ben amonges hem, þat I mow þerof make summe soupyng for thi fadre, wherof y wote wel he wil gladly eete.'[132] By this Jacob, þou shalt　660 undirstonde every repentant synner. Bi Rebecca, þe modir of þis child, Jacob, thou shalt undirstonde grace, þe wiche is þe modir of every repentaunt synner, and[a] techith how thei shuld make here repentaunt lif mete, able to be ete and receyvid of here hevenly fadre, Jhesu Crist.[133] ¶ By thes too kydes, þou shalt undirstonde þe body and the soule of　665 every repentaunt synner.

¶ Take þou þerfor, sister, þees too kedes, þi body and thi soule, and make þerof mete, able to be etyn and receyvid of hym, þin hevenly fadre, Jhesu Crist. First, þe nedith for to flee þes too kydes, for þi fadre wil not ete hem with þe skynnes. ¶ Thi bodi is wel flayn whan it is　670 dispoylid and made nakid from al maner temporale goodes. (fol. 21v) ¶ Thi soule is wel flayn whan it is dispoylid and made nakid from here own willes. ¶ Thes ben þe principles of þi gostly ordenaunces: first that þou forsake temporale goodes, and þan þin own willes.

¶ Isaac, þin hevenly fader, is no best. He wil not ete þe with þi　675 skynne, þat is, he wil not receyve suche cloystreris þat ben bothe wilful and propretaries, but he wil gladly receyve al symple cloystreris þat wantyn such skynnes. ¶ Thou must nedis flee þin hert fro þe olde skynne of his own wille, and also þi body fro þe skynne of temporal goodes, þat þou mow to þi lord be made able for to be receyvid.　680

¶ But now take hede þat a skynne, þe more sotil it is and þynne, þe worse it is, and þe harder for to be flayn fro þe body.[134] Right so, because þat þe propre willes of a soule is more sotil, in as moche as it is withinforth, þan temporal goodes, þe wiche ben oughtward, therfore it

---

[a] 'and techith' are run together. A diagonal dash has been added in between, probably by the original hand.

685　is moche more harder a cloystrer to spoyle himself from his own willes
þan from temporal possessiouns.

 ¶ Also, þe skynne þat is upon þe hede of a best is more harder to
be flayn þan any oþer party of the body. Whi, trowst þou? Trewly,
for in the hede ben al þe five sensable wittes, and every sensible witte
690　(fol. 22r) tyghth sumwhat. ¶ By þis hede, þou shalt undirstonde such
cloystreris þe wiche þenkyn þat thei ben more discrete, more witty, and
more kunnyng þan oþer, and þerfor al such naturel witty cloystreris ben
[more]ᵃ lothe to be spoylid and be made nakid from here own willes
þan oþer symple cloystreris. ¶ For þer such high wit is, þer is moche
695　indignacioun and ofte tymes conflicte, multipliyng of many wordis,
and pride of kunnyng.¹³⁵ Thei han gretᵇ indignacioun whan þei ben in
any wise withstonde from here own willes. Þei wene þat þei han gret
wrong yif oþer ben clepid to counseyle and not þey. ¶ Such oure lord
þreteneth bi þe prophete, and seith: *Ve qui sapientes estis in oculis vestris,*
700　*et coram vobismetipsis prudentes.*¹³⁶ 'Woo' he saith, 'be to yow þat ben
witty in youre own sight and afore youreself prudent.'

 ¶ Also, take hede þat right as an eele is a slyper fissh for to be flayn,
right so summe cloystreris ben so slyper in new fyndyng wittes and
resones for to excuse hem, þat unnethe þei mow be flayn from here own
705　willes. ¶ Thes ben þe skynnes of þe londe (fol. 22v) of Madian, of whom
the prophete spekith and seith: *Turbabuntur pelles terre Madian.*¹³⁷ 'The
skynnes' he seith, 'of þe lond of Madian shul be trobled.' Madian is
no more to sey but contradiccioun. ¶ What ben þees s[k]ynnesᶜ of þe
londe of Madian, but such þat defendyn and mayntene here own willes
710　and ever redy for to shew forth wordis of contradiccioun, þe wiche I
drede shul be trobled at þe last day of jugement with an horrible drede
of dampnacioun, and such namly þat now weryn an abite of religioun
and han þerunder a seculer soule?¹³⁸ ¶ Do away, sister, yif þou wilt not
so be trobled, þe s[k]ynne of þin own wille, and þan make redy þin
715　hert for to be receyvid of oure lord.

 ¶ And whan þou art so flayn, þou must rost þin hert at þe fire of
tribulacioun.¹³⁹

 ¶ Sister, whan þou entrest first þe cloyster of þi religioun þou
puttist þin hert into Godis kychyn, þer for to be rostid in þe fire of
720　tribulacioun.¹⁴⁰ For right as a lordis kychyn shuld not be withoute fire,
right so shuld not a cloyster be withoute tribulacioun,¹⁴¹ but þe fire of

---

ᵃ　Emended reading from L and T. M reads 'right lothe'.
ᵇ　'r' added as superscript with ^.
ᶜ　M erroneously reads 'sclynnes' at this point.

tribulacioun must be norshid, as Salomon seyth: (fol. 23r) *Custodiens fornacem in operibus ardoris*.[142] 'The oven' he seith, 'of þe cloyster must be kept in þe workis of heete.' ¶ The werkis of heete, he seith, be noþing ellis but instituciouns and statutes of the ordir þat norshyn þe fire of   725
hardnes in religioun, the wiche a rawgh hert þat was never provyed, is rostid and made redy for to be receyvid of Cristes mouth, yif it have lardir of charite, ellis it farith in the rostyng as a lene hen: it wil raþer bren þan rost.[143]

¶ But because þat lene hennes shuld not brenne in þe rostyng for   730
defaught of lardir, þei shuld be lardid with þe lardir of oþer. Right so, al such in religioun þat wantyn þe fatnesse of devocioun and charite, þe wiche is þe fatnesse of þe hert, shuld be lardid be þe charitable ensample of other, and so to be made myghty in pacience for to suffre duresse of religioun, lest þat by unpaciens and defaught   735
of charite rather þey bren, never able to be receyvid of God, þan rost kyndly. ¶ The[r]for, sister, suffre þe fatnes, the wiche is charite of thi sistren, to drepe intoo þin hert,[144] considering the gret devocioun, þe meknes, þe pacience, and the obedience of hem: how mekly and how (fol. 23v) gladly þey obeye.   740

¶ Of such take ensample, and not of hem þat with angwisse bere the crosse of obedience with Symon,[145] þat of everything the wiche is put to þeyme of here sovereynes wil dispute and make questiouns.[146] ¶ A lene hen is not wont to be rosted with another lene hen, but with a fatte hen. Right so do thou in thi rostyng: take noon ensample of hem   745
þat lakken devocioun, meknes, and paciens, but of hem þat ben replete with devocioun and charite.

¶ Lo, sister, þre þinges I have rehersed to the, how thow shalt make þiself redy for to be receyvid of God. On is how thow must be flayn. Anoþer is how þou must be rostid. And þe þrid is how þou must be   750
lardid and anoynted. Be fleyng away of þi skynne is undirstonde poverte in forsakyng superfluyte of temporal goodes and of thin own propre wille. Bi rostyng þou shalt undirstonde suffraunce of tribulacioun and adversite in religioun. And by þe lardyng þou shalt undirstonde þe anoyntyng of charite.   755

¶ The first and þe secunde avaylyn right nought withoute the þrid. What (fol. 24r) profite is it for to be made poure of temporal goodes and of þin own wille, and also for to be rostyd in the fire of tribulacioun, yif þou wante fatnes of charite? Trewly, noon. Witnes of Seint Poule, seiyng thus: *Si distribuero omnes facultates meas in cybos pauperum, et tradidero*   760
corpus meum ita ut ardeam, caritatem autem non habuero, nichil michi

prodest.[147] 'Yif I yive al my temporal goodes' he seith, 'to poure folk, as
for þe first, and þerto put my body to þe fire þat it brenne, as for þe
secunde, and have þerto no charite, as for þe þrid, it avayleth not.' For
765 noiþer forsakyng of temporal goodes and oure willes, noiþer proving
of tribulacioun in religioun, profiten right nought withoute fatnes of
charite.[148]

¶ Thes þre were wel founde in oure lord whan he suffred his passioun.
He was flayn whan his cloþis were take from hym and was put naked
770 upon þe crosse. He was rostid upon þe spite of þe crosse be þe Jues, þe
wiche were his kokis, in gret tribulacioun.[149] But he was not brennyd
because þe þrid wantid not, þe wiche was þe fatnes of charite that flowid
oute be þe fyve gret holis of his body.[150]

¶ What was ellis þe blood flowyng oute of his woundis, but þe holy
775 (fol. 24v) anoynement of charite? ¶ Good sister, put undir þe panne of
thin hert and gadre inow of þis precious oynment, and þan schalt þou
lakke no lardir in tyme of tribulacioun.[151]

¶ But now for to know whan þin hert is rostid inow in tribulacioun, I
shal telle þe by ensample þat kokes usyn. ¶ Thre toknes þer ben þat a
780 koke knowith whan flessh is rostid inow. ¶ On is þat yif þe flessh be so
tendre þat, be tastyng of þe kokes fynger, it folowith þe nayle. Another
is yif þe blood be ful dried up. And þe þrid is yif þe flessh lightly losith
fro þe bone. ¶ Good sister, undirstonde weel þees thre þinges and kepe
hem wel in þin hert. ¶ By the first tastyng of the fynger, undirstonde
785 suffraunce of reprovis; by þe secunde, ful forsaking of carnel affeccioun;
and bi þe þrid, undirstonde an holy desire for to be departid oute of þis
world and to be with Crist.

¶ As for the first, þou art asayed with the fynger of thi sovereyne
for to wite wheþer þou be wel rostid in tribulacioun or not, whan she
790 reprovyth þe sharply. And þan, yif þin hert folow mekly and obediently
þus withoute grotchyng þi reprover, it is a token þat þin hert is wel
rostid in tribulacioun. Be noon (fol. 25r) of þo that faryn as towgh
flessh, þe wiche wil never be tendre, as al such þat ben ever unpacient
whan þei ben reprovid. Of such spekith Salomon and seith: *Non amat*
795 *pestilens eum qui se corripit.*[152] That is: 'a contagious synner loveth not
his reprover.' But such on farith as a scabbid hors, þat as sone as it is
touchid upon þe galle, it begynneth to wynce. A good cloystrer farith
not so but lovyth him that reprovith here, as Salomon seith: *Argue*
sapientem, et diliget te.[153] 'Reprove a savery religious soule' he seith, 'and
800 she shal love þe.' Such a sad religious soule wil not grutche þough she
be reprovid.

⁋ What is þe cause, trowist þou, þat summe grucchyn in religioun
whan þei be repr[o]vidᵃ for here defautes? Trewly, for here soules ben
voyde and empty fro grace and gostly wisdom as a voyde tonne is. ⁋
Smyte a voyde and an empty tonne with an hamer, and it yivith a grete   805
sown. Right so don al such þat ben empti fro grace and gostly wisdom:
whan þey ben reprovid þei grutch and groyne with a loude voyce.

⁋ The secunde token for to know whan flessh is [rostid]ᵇ inow, is
whan þe blod is dried up in þe rostyng.¹⁵⁴ ⁋ In þe same wise, whan
al þi carnel affeccioun is withdrawe fro þin hert, it is a token (fol. 25v)   810
that þin hert is wel rostyd in tribulacioun. Is it not a merveylos þing þat
þine hert, þe wiche hath be so longe in Godis kechyn, is not yit dried
up from al maner affeccioun of carnel frendes, seth it so is þat Seynt
Ambrose seith: 'Continuel laboure tornith affeccioun'?¹⁵⁵ Yis, in soth,
for al the joye of a gostly cloystrer shuld not be outward but inward in   815
a clene conscience. What avayleþ it for to set þin hert to moche upon
þin kynrede or an þi carnel frendes? Better it were þat þei shuld have
joye of þe, þan þou of hem.¹⁵⁶

⁋ Than shuldist þou not bisy the to sore abought þi carnel frendes, yif
þou be onys trewly tornid in religioun, lest þei let þi gostly bataile; but   820
aftir þe ensample of oure lord, commytte al þi carnel frendes to John,
as he dede his own modir, diyng upon the crosse. Be John þou shalt
undirstonde grace. Committe þerfor al þi carnel frendes to grace and
praye for hem. So, sister, shalt þou do. Sette never þin hert to moche
upon þi carnel frendes.¹⁵⁷   825

⁋ The þrid tokene for to know whan flessh is [rostid]ᶜ inow is yif flessh
wil lightly be departyd fro þe bone. ⁋ Thou departist wel þe flessh fro
þe bone, whan þou desirest perfightly to be losid oute of þe flessh and
(fol. 26r) oute of þis present world, as Seint Poule dede.

⁋ Seth it so is, sister, þat þou shalt dye within a litel while, þou   830
wotist never how sone be verry nede, for þou mayst not alway lyve in
þis world, whi wilt þou not desire in hert holily for to be delyvered out
of such a peyneful prison? Desire it not for hevynesse of hert for þat
is synne, but desire it for holynesse of hert.¹⁵⁸ And þan þou desirest as
Seint Poule dede, whan he seide: *Cupio dissolvi, et esse cum Christo.*¹⁵⁹ 'I   835
desire' he seith, 'to be departid out of þis wrecchid world and be with
Crist with joye of conscience.' And so, þou mayst turne þi nedful deth
unto an holy deth bi a blissed desire of hert.

ᵃ   The 'o' is omitted in M in what seems to be a scribal mistake.
ᵇ   Reading supplied from L and T.
ᶜ   Reading supplied from L and T.

¶ Desire of deth, þat þou mow be with Crist in blisse endelesly, is
840   a token þat þou art wel rostid in þe fire of tribulacioun, for þe flessh
of þin hert is departith fro þe bon of þis present lif. This world may
wel be likned to a bon, for it is bareyn from alle vertu as a bon is fro
flessh.[160]

¶ Such a desire shuld al perfight soules han þat hopyn to fynde þe
845   tresoure of heven in here dygheng, þe wiche tresoure þei han sought
al here lif-tyme, and þerfor it is þat Salomon seith: *Justus sperat in*
(fol. 26v) *morte sua.*[161] 'A rightwisse soule' he seith, 'hathe al his hope
in his deth.' What merveyle is þat? Trewly, right none. For than al
his gostly enemyes shuld never more pursue ayenst him, and also he
850   is þan delyvered oute of prison, and also þan he is come to þe haven
of helth.

¶ Of þe wiche blissid deth spekith Salomon þus: *Meliorem esse diem*
mortis quam nativitatis.[162] That is: 'he commendith rather the day of
oure holy dygheng þan þe day of oure wrecchid birth.' So þat the
855   deth of holy creatures is clepid in holy chirch þe day of here birth, for
þan they dyghen from deth and ben boryn to lif.[163] ¶ Oure living in
þis lif, as doctouris seyn, is noþing ellis but every day for to begyn to
digh.[164]

¶ Thenk, sister, þat thou art but a presoner. The condicioun of a
860   presoner whan he knoweth wel þat he shal be delyverid, is þis: every
day and every houre he wayteth at þe dore whan his jayler wil come
and delivere him. Suche a desire and hope of delyveraunce, every day
and every houre must þou have, for so I rede had Seint Poule, whan he
seyde: *Quis me liberabit de corpore mortis huius?*[165] 'Ho shal delyvere me'
865   he seyde, 'fro þe body of þis wrecchid deth?' ¶ Such a desire also had
(fol. 27r) the prophete, whan he seyde: *Educ de custodia animam meam.*[166]
'Lord' he seyde, 'delyvere my soule oute of þis bodily preson.'[167]

¶ Lo, sister, þus have I declared þe how þou shalt make redy þin hert
as mete that shuld be etyn. Now shal I shew þe how þou shalt make
870   it redy as a wyf maketh here redy and arayth here for to plese here
housbonde.[168]

¶ Of þis maner redynes or arayment of Cristes spouse spekith Seint
John in þe Apocalips, and seith: *Venerunt nupcie Agni, et uxor eius*
preparavit se.[169] 'The gostly weddyng day of the lombe, Jhesu Crist' he
875   seith, 'is comen, and þe wif of þe same lambe hath made here redy
and arayed here.' ¶ Of þre þinges þou must take hede, þe wiche ben
rehersid in this clause of Seint John. On is what shuld be þe spouse
or þe wif of þis lamb, Jhesu Crist? Anoþer, what þis gostly weddyng

may be? And þe þrid, with what maner of arayment Cristis spouse
shuld be arayed?   880

⁊ As for þe first, what she shuld be, þat to þis lambe, Jhesu Crist, shuld
be coupled in gostly matrimonye, holy writ techith wher I fynde write
þus: *Sacerdos virginem ducet uxorem: et viduam et repudi[a]tam,*ᵃ *et
sordidam et meretricem non accipiet.*¹⁷⁰ That is: 'The prest shal have to
his (fol. 27v) wif a mayde or a virgine, and he shal in no wise take a   885
wedewe, ne a departid womman, ne a defoulid womman, ne a commune
womman.'¹⁷¹ ⁊ Good sister, undirstonde þis gostly and not flesshly.¹⁷²

⁊ Bi þis prest þou shalt undirstonde Jhesu Crist, þe wiche is coupled
bi gostly matrymony to every clene soule. ⁊ For every clene soule, han
þey synned never so wikkidly afore, yif þei ben ones trewly tornid to   890
God, þei ben callid maydenes or virgines, as Seint Jerome seith: ⁊ 'Ther
is a gret differen[c]eᵇ betwene gostly matrymony and bodily matrymony:
in bodili matrimony a virgine is corrupte, and in gostly matrymony a
soule þat is corrupt is made be grace a clene virgine ayen.'¹⁷³

⁊ Now þan, þou shalt undirstonde be þees foure kyndes of wymmen,   895
þat is: wedewis, departid wymmen, defoulid wymmen, and commune
wymmen, þe wiche shuld be putte away fro þe gostly matrimony of
Crist, the high sovereyn prest, foure maner kyndes of synners.¹⁷⁴

⁊ Bi the wedew, þou shalt undirstonde al such to whom þe use of
flesshly lust is cesid but not þe desire therof. Synne is withdraw in such   900
only for nede and not (fol. 28r) for charite.¹⁷⁵ ⁊ Wel may such on be
callid a wedew, for here husbonde, flesshly lust, is biried in here hert.¹⁷⁶
⁊ Of such a wedew spekiþ Seint Poule and seyth: *Vidua in deliciis vivens
mortua est.*¹⁷⁷ 'A wedew, þe wiche is undirstonde here a lecherous hert
lyvyng in delices, is dede fro vertu as long as she lyvyth so lustly.'¹⁷⁸ ⁊   905
I may wele liknee suche soules to a figure that I fynde in holy writ of
the childrin of Israel, the wiche lothed þe swete manna in desert and
desired flessh, the wiche thei forsoke in the lond of Egipt.¹⁷⁹ Good sister,
be wel ware. Desire never ayen þat þou hast onys forsake in the world,
and lothe never the swete manna of desert, þat is holy redyng, devout   910
prayer, and blissed meditacioun of þe cloyster.¹⁸⁰

⁊ Bi þe departid womman þou shalt undirstonde al such that þe

---

ᵃ M reads 'repudidatam' erroneously. The correct word, 'repudiatam' is added in
the margin. In addition, a second hand has marked the first 'a' of the word, in
the text, in black, and put a black mark beneath the erroneous 'd'.
ᵇ M reads 'differente' here. The scribe seems not always to differentiate between
'c' and 't'.

world hateth and forsaketh, and wil not of here servise. And neverþeles
suche on wil smatere with wordly bisines, albeit that þe world hath
915   despised here. ¶ Wel may such on be callid a wrecch of al wrecchis. ¶
Many ther ben of þis condicioun, for þough þey ben put out of wordly
mennys houssold (fol. 28v) by lothnes of here persones, yit þei desire
and make menys to entre in ayen, for to be fed with delicat mossellis,
and to lyve lustly in ryot and wordly pompe and pride. And þough
920   such suffrid desesis and tribulaciouns of the world, yit þei wil in no
wise forsake þe werld.[181]

¶ Bi the defoulid womman, þou shalt undirstond al such þat ben
defoulid with unclene affeciouns and desires in hert. ¶ There ben many
such þat defoulyn here hertis with unclene desires.[182] ¶ Good sister,
925   be none of þo, yif þou desirest to be coupled to oure lord in gostly
matrimonye. A spot of synne is more abomynable in þe and in such as
þou art, in þe sight of God, þan of any oþer. For right as in a white
clothe a spot of filthe aperith sonner þan in anoþer colourid cloth, right
so in a chast mayde a spot of synne semeth more fouler þan in anoþer
930   commune synner. Therfor seith Seint Jerome þus: 'The vertu of clennes
and virginite is a worthi vertu, yif it be kept clene fro spottis of filth',[183]
and þerfor, it is right nedful þat a mayde wassh ofte þe face of here
conscience bi trew confessioun.[184]

¶ Bi þe commune womman, þou shalt undirstond al such þat yiven
935   stede to every (fol. 29r) temptacioun and restyn þerupon. ¶ Such a soule
may wel be likned to a commune womman. For right as a commune
womman that haþ be long a foole in synne, after þat she is onys
encombrid with on of here flesshly loveris, she can never afterward
denygh his folyos wille, for she is so overcome bi him; right so, after
940   tyme þat she is onys oppressid and encombrid bi consentyng in synne
to here wrecchid lover þe fende, she hath never bolnesse afterward, but
yif þe gretter grace make it for to withstond hym and denygh him his
unlefful axyng. And so is such a soule brought into mochel mischef,
and þat is no merveile, for as Seynt Gregor seith: 'Every synne is so
945   ponderous of himself þat it drawith evyr dounward to other synnes.'[185]
Good sister, be þou wel ware of þis fals wrecchid lover þe fende, and
here not his voyce of synne whan he speketh to þe bi temptacioun.[186]
Have never delite in temptacioun, for she may never be clepid a chast
womman afore God, that gladly herith unclene wordis and dishonest
950   of flesshly loveris, alþough she never consente to here unclene willes.
Right so, a soule may in no wise be rekenyd in þe sight of God chast
and clene, þat gladly receyvith þe fen- (fol. 29v) dis tempaciouns and
deliteth þerin, wenyng þat she shuld never consente to him.

⁋ But sister, þe condicioun of a chast womman is þis: whan þat ever
an unclene lover spekith to here dishonest wordis of unclennes, with   955
a chast indignacioun of spirit and contricioun of hert she goth away
from him and so withstondith him. Do þou so. Withstonde al þe fendis
temptacioun, and he wil fle fro the, as Seint Jame seith: *Resistite diabolo,
et fugiet a vobis.*[187] 'Withstonde þe fende' he seith, 'and þan wil he flee
fro the.'[188]   960

⁋ Loo sister, thus have I declared to the what betokneth þees foure
kyndes of wymmen þat ben excludid fro þe gostly matrymony of the
high prest, almyghty Jhesu, the wiche wil only have coupled to him in
gostly matrymony a mayde and a virgine.

⁋ Therfor, yif þou wilt couple þi soule to oure lord bi gostly   965
matrymonye, þou must apere afore oure lord a chast mayde and a clene
virgine.[189] ⁋ Thi soule is a mayde and a virgine whan it is kept clene
fro corruptible þoughtes, and lovyth but o þing, and axith but o þing,
and seketh but o þing, þe wiche is charite that knyttith and onyth a
soule (fol. 30r) to God.[190]   970

⁋ But now, þre condiciouns þer ben þat acordith wel to a mayde.
On is shamefastnes, another is poverte, and þe þrid is symplenes in
wordis.[191] ⁋ Thes þre condiciouns oure lord axith of every mayde
and virgine þat he chesith to his spouse. ⁋ He wille þat his spouse
be ashamed to be seyn in st[r]etes[a] and townes. Such shamefastnes   975
bryngeth in holynesse of vertuos lyvyng, and þat is a gret grace, as
Salomon seith: *Gracia super graciam mulier sancta et verecunda.*[192] 'It is
a grace passyng many oþer graces' he seith, 'a womman to be bothe
holy and shamefast.'[193]

⁋ The secunde condicioun of a clene mayde shuld be poverte of   980
temporal goodes, for it is a commune seiyng:[194] yif a mayde have a
peny, it shal be seyde þat she hath receyvid it of sum corrupt lover.
⁋ Good sister, gadre no wardly good, for þin hosbonde, Jhesu Crist,
is rich inow. For a more worthi richesse mayst þou not bringe to thi
spouse, Jhesu Crist, þan for to be pore and despise richesse.[195] ⁋ Now   985
is þis gretly ayenst such sovereynes þat raþer lokethe after þe temporal
goodes of a womman þat cometh to religioun for to be a mynche, þan
(fol. 30v) after gostly goodes. That is right a grete synne for it smellith
symonye.[196]

⁋ The þrid condicioun of a clene mayde shuld be symplenes in   990
wordis. ⁋ It besemeth wel maydenes to be symple and softe in wordis.

---

[a]   Reading supplied from L. M reads 'stoetes' mistakenly.

¶ Thou art symple and softe in spekyng whan þou shewist þi synnes in confessioun purely and playnly, withoute any doblenes or peyntyng, right as they were don. This is to Godward.[197] ¶ Also, þou hast softnes
995 and symplenes in spekyng whan þou spekist charitablely and esyly, and withoute boystousnes to al creatures, for Salomon seyth: *Verbum dulce multiplicat amicos et mitigat inimicos*.[198] 'A swete word' he seith, 'a soft word and an esy, multiplieþ frendes and lessith or swagith the malice of enemyes.' ¶ Thus sister, shuldist þou have symplenes in confessioun,
1000 and softnes in wordis to edificacioun of al Cristen peple.[199]

¶ In this wise mayst þou know what Cristes spouse shuld be. Therfor, now shal I telle þe what is gostly matrymony, be the wich a mynche is coupled and knette to oure lord.

¶ There ben þre maner of gostly matrymonyes, like as þer is þre bodili
1005 matrymonyes. On is matrymony þat is bigonne. Anoþer is matrimony þat is (fol. 31r) confermid. And the þrid is matrimony that is perfight.[200] ¶ Gostly matrimony is bigunne betwene Jhesu Crist and þi soule, whan þou art come to religioun for to be provid as a novice. ¶ Gostly matrimony is confermyd, whan þou art professid and hast receyvid þe
1010 ryng.[201] ¶ Gostly matrimony is also made perfight, whan thi soule is knet and coupled unseparatly to þi spouse, Jhesu, bi perseveraunce, abidyng in the observaunce of the cloyster in maner tastyng of swetnes of joye.[202]

¶ Therfor, sister, yif þou be a novice, þenk þat þi weddyng is begunne
1015 betwene þe[a] and þi love, Jhesu. Yif þou be professid, þenke þat it is confermyd. And whan þou hast tastid þes swetnes of oure lord, þenke that thi weddyng in perseveraunce of þe cloyster in maner is made perfight. ¶ Of þees þre gostly weddyngis spekith oure lord be Jeromy, þe prophete, to every clene soule þe wiche is entred into religion, thus:
1020 *Recordatus sum tui, miserans adolescenciam tuam, et caritatem disponsa-cionis tue, quia secuta es me in deserto*.[203] 'I have mynde' he seith, 'of the, and merciably I þenke upon þi tendre age and upon thi charitable weddyng, because þou hast folowed me (fol. 31v) perseverauntly in desert.'

1025 ¶ Good sister, take hertly heede to þees comfortable wordis. For þer þat oure lord seith þat he þenketh merciably upon thi tendre age, undirstond that he menyth al þe while þou art a novice, for so longe þou art but tendre of age in religioun. ¶ And where he seith that he thenkiþ

---

[a] A mistake seems to have been erased between 'þe' and 'and'. ~~~ has been used to fill the space.

merciably upon thi charitable weddyng, undirstond þat he menyth of
thi professioun. ¶ And where he seith, because þou hast folowid hym   1030
in desert, undirstond þat he menyth of thi perfight weddyng, þat shal
be in heven withouten ende.

¶ As touching þe first, þou shalt wel knowe þat oure lord þenkiþ
merciably of thi tendre age in novishode, because þou hast commyttid
þiself for his love to þe duresse of religioun as a novyse. ¶ Of such tendre   1035
soules speketh Salomon in the Boke of Love, seying þus: *Adolescentule
dilexerunt te nimis.*[204] 'Yonge tendre novices' he seith, 'lovith the, Jhesu,
right moche.'

¶ Why seith he 'right moche'? Trewly, for the hert of a yonge creature
þat is trewly turnid to vertu lovith oure lorde more tendirly and more   1040
swetly þan many oþer þat ben provid of lenger tyme, be- (fol. 32r) cause
of the novelte of love. ¶ And þerfor, in that age specialy, shuld every
novice be wel ware þat she suffre not unclene þoughtes to rest in here
hert, þe whiche excludith oure lord from his dwellyng place. ¶ For yif
suche þoughtes rest in here hert longe tyme,[a] it is a gret grace yif þey   1045
mow be put away in age.

¶ Therfor every novice shuld þenk þat she is put to þe scole of love
whan she is put to religioun.[205] And yif she kunne not lerne þan for to
love him to whom she purposith to be weddid aftirward, she may not
wel know þe crafte of love whan she is weddid. ¶ It is but a light lesson   1050
þat she lernyth, but it must ofte be recordid. ¶ What is þat lessoun?
Trewly, love. ¶ Now is þis a short lesson and a frughtful. ¶ This is þe
lesson that oure lord techith to al his disciples, restyng his blissid body
upon þe chayer of the crosse. ¶ There he holdith scole for to teche
novices love, for he died þerupon, sister, for love of the. Suffre þerfor,   1055
sister, for his love, tribulacioun in religioun.

¶ But first, yif a novice wil for his love suffre tribulacioun and desese
mekly in religioun, she must repente here with (fol. 32v) sorow of hert
of al wordly loves that she lernid in the world. And so shal she be able
for to receyve the love of God, as Salomon seith: *Qui minoratur actu*   1060
percipiet illam.[206] 'He that wiþdrawith and maketh lesse in him al
outward wordly dedis shal perfightly, as it may be had in þis lif, receyve
such love.' ¶ Loo, sister, þus alle novices shuld offre hemself fully and
hooly to oure lord, departid fro al wordly bisynes.

¶ Al such hool departyng fro þe world stondith in to þinges. On is   1065

---

[a]   M reads 'time ~~in here youthe~~'. The phrase is omitted in C, but retained in L
and T.

that a novice take noþing with here into religioun of that the wiche is the worldis. Anoþer, that she leve noþing of heris in the world.

¶ As for þe first, I seyde that a novice shuld bringe noþing of þe world with here into religioun, lest the werld fynde ayenst here a chalaunge. ¶

1070 A novice bringeth with here into religioun þingis of þe world, whan she bringeth with here wordly worshipis, reportis and maneris of þe world, and also seculer daliaunce and disportis. Be wel ware, sister, þat þou have brought noþing with þe of the worldis, lest þe world fynde more with þe of his good þan of Godis good. 207

1075 ¶ Also, a novice shuld so fully be departid fro þe (fol. 33r) world that she leve noþing of heris in the world, as summe don that gon to religioun with here body and leve here hertis in þe world. I may likne suche to a flying hauke with his jessis, þat at þe last he is tayde with his jessis to a tre, and so is take. ¶ Therfore, sister, yif þou be trewly fled

1080 oute of þe world, cut awey fro þin hert þe jessis of wordly affeccioun, þe wich lettith þe flyte of contemplacioun to Godward. Thus clerly shuld a novice come to religioun.

¶ I sayde also, in the same auctorite of Jeromie, þat: 'oure lord merciably þenketh upon thi charitable wedding to him bi professioun.'208 ¶ In

1085 professioun þou art weddid to God, in as moche as þou hast made to him a bihest of obedience, of stabilnes in thi religioun, and also of trewe tornyng of thi maneris,209 so þat bi such promisse þou art bounde to þi spouse, Jhesu Crist, for ever, after the circumstaunces of þe same promisse.

1090 ¶ Playne not þerfor, good sister, and sey þou art streyghtly bounde, for the more streyghtly þou art bounde in religioun, þe more myghtly bi love wil Jhesu be bounde to the. ¶ But take hede what he seith: 'he þenkith upon þi charitable weddyng', for charite, þe (fol. 33v) wiche is the bonde of perfeccioun, as Seint Poule seith, maketh a soule perfightly

1095 for to consente to oure lord.210

¶ And þerfor, thi weddyng is confermed whan þou art professid. Albeit, sister, þat thou be þus coupled an knet to thi love, Jhesu, bi gostly weddyng confermyd in thi professioun, yit is he not so homly with the as thou woldist have him, for oþerwhile þou suffrest tempta-

1100 ciouns, oþerwhiles oþer maner of desesis bodili and gostly, þe wiche þou must nedes suffre as longe as þou art in þis world. And alþough oure lord, þi gostly spouse, be within þe sufferaunce of suche temptaciouns, yit he is not with þe as þou woldist have hym, for thou woldist have him to the, peraventure, al in swetnes and devocioun and in pure devoute

1105 love, as an hosbond shuld love his wif.

¶ Sister, I may likne the and al such professid mynches to a wif
þat is weddid to a lord in a fer contrey oute of his owne contrey.²¹¹ ¶
Thou wost wel, yif a lord wedde a wif fer oute of his owne cite and
lordship, he makith melody and mirthe, but yit not so moche as he
wold yif he were in his owne (fol. 34r) cite and lordship, but al þe joy,   1110
mirthe, and melody shal be whan she is brought home to his own cite.
Right so, sister, þe gret lord, þe kyng of heven, hathe weddid the in
this vale of teris, in þis wrecchid londe, þe wiche, þough al þe world
be his, yit propirly the blisse of heven is his owne cite and lordship,
and þin heritage. And þerfor, loke after no gret melody in þis world of   1115
þi weddyng, albeit þat oþerwhiles he shew the glad chere bi swetnesse
of devocioun, but not alway, for oþerwhiles þou suffrest temptacioun,
and þan I fere not, yif þou suffre mekely such temptacioun, he wil at
þe last bringe the home to his owne cite, where al gladnes withoute
sorow shal be shewid to the.   1120

¶ And þerfor it is that I seyde in the same auctorite of Jeromy þat: 'þou
hast folowid oure lord in desert.'²¹² ¶ By this word 'desert', þou shalt
undirstond þe blisse of heven where þi weddyng shal be made perfight.
That 'desert' is callid heven, it semyth wel be the wordis of oure lord in
the gospel, where he seith thus, in a parabole to the puplicanes and to   1125
the phariseis: *Quis ex vobis homo, qui habet centum oves: et si perdiderit
unam ex illis, nonne dimittit nonaginta* (fol. 34v) *novem in deserto, et vadit
ad illam que perierat?*²¹³ 'Whiche of yow' he seith, 'þat hath an hundrid
shep, yif he lost on of hem, wheþer he wold not leve abidyng in desert
nynty and nyne and go for to seke [þat]ᵃ shep þat he had lost?' Loo,   1130
sister, yif I expoune not al þis sentence for it nedith not, yit þou maist
know þat he beleft in heven, þat is, in desert, as Seynt Gregor seith,
þe high quere of angelis, and come for to seke mankynde. 'Whi' seith
Seynt Gregor, 'is heven callid desert? Trewly, for desert is no more for
to sey but "forsake".'²¹⁴   1135
¶ Man forsoke heven whan he synned. So þan þou mayst wel know
þat whan I say, þou hast folowid þi spouse in desert, þou shalt dwelle
with him in the blisse of heven wher þi weddyng shal be made perfight.
Thou folowist wel oure lord in desert whan þou art perseveraunte in
the observaunce of þe cloyster, þat in maner is callid a desert,²¹⁵ the   1140
wiche shal bringe þe to þe blisse of heven, for in such perseveraunce,
wedding is in somme wise coupled.²¹⁶ Thou wost wel, yif a kyng wedde
a lady in a straunge londe, she is not so mery as yif she were in here

---

ᵃ This reading is taken from L and T. M and C incoherently read 'þe to' here.

lordis kyngdom. So, thow þou be weddid to oure lord in þe cloyster,
1145   (fol. 35r) the wiche is the porche of heven, þou art not so glad in soule
as þou woldist be yif þou were with him in his kyngdom of þe blisse
of heven. And þerfor, sister, thow þou fynde no such comfort as þou
woldist have at þi weddyng in this straunge contrey, þat is to sey, in
þis lif, but tribulaciouns and desese, yit take it in maner for a fest, and
1150   whan þou comist to his owne contrey and kyngdom, þan wil he make
the there a gretter fest with myrthe and melody inow.

¶ Than wil thi spouse, Jhesu, wipe away al the teeris fro þin
eyghen þat þou hast wept for his love,[217] þe wiche hath be so long
fro þe, be endlesse swetnes. Than shal al the stretys of hevenly
1155   Jerusalem be arayed, and þan also shal þer be sunge of aungelis right
melodously, alleluya, at thi comyng home. ¶ Than shal be complete
þi perfight matrymony þat I spake of, yif þou folow oure lord wel
in þe cloyster.[218]

¶ Aftir this declaracioun of gostly weddyng, sister, I shal also declare
1160   þe the þre goodes of gostly matrimoni. For as ther ben þre goodes of
bodily weddyng, as doctouris seyn, þe wich ben fayth, childrin, and
sacramente, right so ther ben þre goodes of gostly weddyng: fayth,
(fol. 35v) childrin, and sacrament.[219]

¶ In bodily wedding, faith is undirstond trewth betwene a man and
1165   his wif, þat eche of hem shul be trewe to other. In þe same wise, in gostly
weddyng betwene oure lord and þe, þou must kepe trewth and fayth
in oned of spirit, in withdrawyng of þin hert from al maner of wordly
noyse and unquietnesse of it. And so, yif him, withoute any faynyng
purpose, trewly and faythfully, þin hert, þat þou mow sey, as Salomon
1170   seith in the Boke of Love thus: *Dilectus meus michi, et ego illi.*[220] That is:
'my wel belovyd Jhesu is attendaunt to me and I to him.'

¶ Also, þou shuldist love him aboven al creatures. Also, þou shuldist
plese him bi þi chast lyvyng. A mayde shuld ever þenk how she shuld
plese God. ¶ Be þe bonde of þis fayth and trewth, þou mayst so be oned
1175   to him, þat he wil fully be knyt to the. ¶ And in token þerof, þou hast
receyvid a ring of feyth and trewth in thi professioun.[221]

¶ The[a] secunde goode of bodily matrimony, as doctouris seyn, is
bringen forth of childrin. Right so, þou in thi gostly weddyng must
bringe forth gostly childrin, þe wiche ben good werkis.[222] ¶ As many
1180   good werkis as þou doyst, so (fol. 36r) many gostly childrin þou bringest
forth to God, þi spouse. Be war now þat þou bringe forth none evyl

---

[a]   'h' is added as superscript with ^.

childrin, þat is evyl workis, but whan þou hast any such, put hem away
fro þe bi trew confessioun.²²³

¶ The þrid good of bodili matrimony is þe sacrament of wedlok
laughfully done. For yif þis sacrament be laughfully done betwene   1185
to²²⁴ persones, þey mow never be departid unto þe deth of here bodies.
Right so, in thi gostly weddyng þou haste bounde þe be þi professioun
never to be departid from þi love, Jhesu, but perseverauntly for to serve
him in clennesse of religious lyvyng, like as he wil never be departid
fro the.²²⁵ ¶ Such perseveraunce shal receyve a crowne, as holy writ   1190
sayth: *Qui perseveraverit usque in finem, hic salvus erit.*²²⁶ That is: 'he
þat lastingly abideth in the servise of oure lord bi clennesse of religious
lyvyng, shal be saf and have a crowne in blisse withoute ende.' ¶ Many
þer ben þe wiche ben fervent in the begynnyng of here conversioun,
and in here ende negligent and slak.²²⁷   1195

¶ Loo, sister,ª þees þre goodes of gostly weddyng þou must kepe:
fayth and trewth of hert, bringing forth children of good werkis, and
thi sacrament of thi professioun (fol. 36v) perseverauntly, withoute
departyng.²²⁸

¶ Aftir this tretice of gostly matrimoni with þe gostly goodes þat   1200
longith þerto, I shall telle þe and declare the what ben þe ornamentis
of þi soule, Cristis spouse, with the wiche þou shuldist be arayed yif
þou wolt plese þi love, Jhesu. What þees ornamentis ben, he rehersith be
the prophete and seyde: *Lavi te aqua, et emundavi sanguinem tuum a te,
unxi te oleo. Vestivi te discoloribus, calciavi te jacincto; cinxi te bisso, indui*   1205
te subtilibus. Ornam te ornamento, dedi armillas in manibus tuis, torquem
circa collum tuum. Dedi inaurem in auribus tuis, et coronam decoris in
*capite tuo. Et ornata es auro et argento.*²²⁹ 'I have wassh the' he seith,
'with watir and clensid þi blod fro þe. I have anoyntid þe with oyle,
and arayed the with cloþis of dyverse colouris. I have shoed þi feet with   1210
shoes of jacincte, and girded þe with a girdille of bisse. I have cloþed
the with sotiltees, and made the faire with an ornament. I have yeve
þe broches for þin armes, and a bygh aboute thi nekke. I have yeve þe
ringis in þin eeris, and set a fayre crowne upon þin heede, and þou art
arayed with gold and (fol. 37r) silver.' ¶ Loo, sister, thirtene araymentes   1215
of þi soule ben rehersid in þees wordis of oure lord.

¶ First, he seith þat he hath wassh the with water, þat is with water
of bapteme, þe wiche come out of his side in his passioun, be þe

---

ª The 'r' is superscript.

wiche water he hath clensid þi blode, þat is þi synnes, fro the. ❡ What
1220 merveyle is it þough such water clense synnes? Trewly, none, for it
coome oute so boylingly fro þe hert of oure lord, made hoote be þe fire
of love aboundyng in his brist, þat it both clensith þe hert fro synnes,
and also scaldith þe fende.[230]

❡ Bi þis blissed water we ben wassh in oure bapteme, and not only
1225 with water, but also with blod, for of hem bothe oure lord hathe made
a lygh to clense synnes away fro oure hertes clerly, as Seint John seith:
Lavit nos a peccatis nostris in sanguine suo.[231] 'He hathe wassh us fro oure
synnes with his blode'; þer come no blode oute withoute water. ❡ With
such blissed lygh, sister, þou must clerly wassh þin hert, for þou hast
1230 defoulid it, peraventure, seth it wasse first wassh with bapteme.

❡ Thou wilt se abought þat þi vessellis and napry be clene, and þin
hert þou wilt suffre to be unclene. ❡ Hast þou more charge of thi
(fol. 37v) vessellis than of thin hert, the wiche is more precious þan
eny vesselle? Here now what oure lord seith: *Lava a malicia cor tuum.*
1235 *Usquequo morabuntur in te cogitaciones noxie?*[232] 'Wassh þin hert' he
seith, 'fro malice.' Thou woldist now wyte, peraventure, what þis
malice shuld be. It sewith in þe same auctorite, whan he seiþ: *Usquequo
morabuntur in te cogitaciones noxie?* That is: 'how longe shul noyghes
þoughtes dwelle in the?' As þou he seyde þus: þe tarying of unclene
1240 þoughtes maketh þe vessel of þin hert unclene.

For to wassh away such malice of hert fro the, oure lord Jhesu, þi
lavendir, hath not only ordeyned for þe a clensyng ligh of water and
blode in thi bapteme, but also an helyng bath of swet and teris,[233] þat
þou shuldist bothe be wasshe þeryn and be hole. ❡ Into þis bath þou
1245 must ofte entre, for it is medicinable.[234] ❡ For to entre into this bath is
noþing ellis but for to drenche þin affeccioun and þi þoughtes in Cristes
passioun, considering bothe þe shedyng of his blode and water, and also
þe swetyng and þe wepyng of his body. Þat wold God þou woldist dygh
only þi feet in his blode, as Davith (fol. 38r) seith: *Intinguatur pes tuus*
1250 *in sanguine.*[235] 'Wold God' he seith, 'þat þe feete of þin affeccioun were
made rede in þe liquore of his precious bloode.'[236]

❡ But now þou shalt undirstonde þat þer is sum maner of cloth þe
wich is dyed whiles it is wolle and summe whiles it is þrede. The cloth
þat is dyghed whiles it is wolle shal never leese his coloure but yif it be
1255 right foule fare with. But clothe, þe wiche is dighed whiles it is þred, it
wil ofte tymes chaunge colour. Right so, þou art dyghed whiles þou art
wolle yif þou lerne for to do weel whiles þou art yonge. ❡ Al such for
þe more party kepyn here coloure of vertu. ❡ And alþough such leven
not for to synne only yit for love, þey leve for drede or ellis for shame,

þe wiche I hope shal bringe in love and[a] drede. ¶ Thou art also dyghed   1260
whan þou art þred yif þou lerne to do welle in þin old age. Suche ofte
tymes wexyn right slow and dulle of vertu.

¶ The secunde arayment þat oure lord hath yive þe, is þat he hathe
anoynted the with oyle. Be þis oyle þou shalt undirstonde gostly
gladnesse, with the wiche þou shuldist anoynte (fol. 38v) thi soule whan   1265
thou art sory for synnes,[237] and whan þou fastist, wakist, and wepyst
for compassioun of the synnes of oþer, þat it mow be verified of the, as
Davith seyde: *Unxit te Deus tuus oleo leticie.*[238] 'Thi lord God' he seith,
'hath anoynted þe with his oyle of gladnes.' Therfor, sister, yif þou
wilt þat þi religious penaunce be acceptable to God, shew glad chere   1270
as Salomon seyth: *In omni dato hillarem fac vultum tuum.*[239] 'In every
yifte of gostly excercise þat þou yivist to God, be it in fasting, weping,
or of praying, shew glad chere.'[240]

¶ The þrid arayment þat oure lord hathe yif to þe, is that he hath arayid
þe with clothis of diverse colouris. Bi þees cloþes of diverse colouris,   1275
þou shalt undirstonde diversite of vertues þat arayeth þe soule mervey-
lously.[241] ¶ Summe trew soule is specially arayed with rightwisnes,
summe with mercy, summe with pacience, summe with meknes,
summe with devocioun, and summe with clennes and chastite.[242]

¶ Use wel, sister, þees vertues cloþes, and namly on holy festyval   1280
dayes, as in þe feste of Cristes nativite.[243] Aray þe principaly þat day and
al þe fest suwyng with clothes of meknes, þenkyng þat he appe- (fol. 39r)
rid to us as a child of mekenes. ¶ Thou werist wel þis cloth of mekenes
whan þou takist ensample to be meke be the mekenes of Crist. ¶ Also,
in his passioun tyme þou shalt be arayed with clothes of penaunce, þat   1285
is wepyng and wayling and dissiplines, for þan oure lord, Jhesu Crist,
in the chapitre of þe crosse, was sore i-dissiplined for us.[244]

¶ In the fest of his resurrexioun þou shalt be arayed with cloþes of
gladnes and joy, for þan [were][b] his disciplis joyful and glad for his
blissid resurrexioun. ¶ In þe fest of his assencioun þou shalt be arayed   1290
with cloþis of hope and love, for þan by love þou shuldist hope to come
þer he is. ¶ In festis of martires þou shalt be arayed with clothes of
pacience; in festis of confessoures, with cloþis of sad lyvyng;[245] and in
festis of virgines, with cloþis of charite and chastite. And so, aftir the
festes ben, þou shalt be arayed with clothes of diverse vertues.[246]   1295

---

a   'and' added in superscript with ^.
b   Reading supplied from L. M erroneously reads 'where'.

¶ Every sovereyn in religioun þat can conforme here to synneris only for to wynne hem to grace, is wel arayed with þis clothe of diverse colouris. ¶ A sovereyne shuld sey and be as Seynt Poule seith: *Omnia omnibus factus sum.*[247] 'I hamme made al þing' he seith, 'to al folk.'[248]

¶ Now, (fol. 39v) peraventure, þou woldist wite how a sovereyne shuld conforme here to synners and kepe here in vertuous lyvyng. I shal telle the. ¶ Thou wost wel þat a fowler þe wiche goth a-fowlyng, first he taketh with him a paynted brid, þat oþer wilde briddis shuld be þe more homly and familiar to come to þe nette of þe fowler. The cause why þat wilde briddes ben not aferd is in as moche as þey fle to such on that is like to hem. Right so shuld a sovereyne do in religioun.[249] First, she shuld conforme hereself, in al þingis þat no synne is in, to synners: as in lowly communicacioun, in meknes and homlynes of wordis, in yeldyng hereself a synner, and such oþer, so for to wynne oþer synners to grace. ¶ Whan a sovereyne is such on, þan is she wel arayed with þis cloth of diverse colouris.

¶ She shuld also, to al synners, hide here streyghtnes of lyving, þat is of abstinence, of wakyng, of weryng, of wepyng, and of lyghing.[250] In token hereof, I fynde in holy writ a figure þat Moyses hid his face whan he spake to þe puple.[251] So shuld every sovereyne do. ¶ A sovereyne hideþ wel here face to þe commune puple whan she (fol. 40r) hideth þe streyghtnes of here livyng for þe tyme þat she speketh to synners to draw hem to grace.

¶ Thus dede Seynt John þe Baptist. He hidde his face whan he prechid to þe puple, þat is, he hidde and kept pryve his streyghtnes of lyving to himself, and taught þe puple how þey shuld flee synne. ¶ Albeit þat he wold drink no wyne, yit he bad never þe puple for to do so. ¶ And alþou he werid sharp cloþis next his body, yit he bad never þe puple to were þe heyre. ¶ But o þing he bad hem do, þe wiche is a commune þing to al synners, only for to do penaunce.[252] ¶ Yif a sovereyn behave here thus to al synners for to wynne hem to grace, þan she is arayed wel with þis clothe of diverse colouris.

¶ The fourth arayment þat oure lord hath yive þe, is þis: he haþe yive þe to þi feet shoes of jacincte. Bi þis jacincte, þe wich is like to a clere colourid firmament, þou shalt undirstonde hevenly desire, whereafter thi foote, the wiche is þi gostly affeccioun, shuld be arayed.[253] Therfor, sister, make to thi foote of thi gostly affeccioun a shoo of al heven, as þou I myght seygh þus to þe: aray al þine affeccioun with hevenly desires, þat holy chirche (fol. 40v) may seye of þe, as Salomon seyth of þe kynges doughter of heven: *Quam pulcri sunt pedes tui in calciamentis, filia principis!*[254] That is, 'A! How faire, kynges doughter, ben þi feet of gostly affeccioun in schoes of hevenly desires.'

¶ Trewly, sister, it is right unsemly þat þou shuldist go barfoote fro such schoes, because þou art a kynges doughter. ¶ In tokene hereof, al   1340
bisshopes, whan þey sey here messis solemply, weryn sandalyes in here feet.[255]

¶ The fifthe arayment þat oure lord hathe yive þe, is þis: he hath girte the with a girdil of bisse or of fustian. Bi þis fustian, þe wiche is whittest, softest, and clennest of al clothes, þou shalt undirstonde þe   1345
whitnes and clennesse of chastite.[256] ¶ For right as such white fustian cometh to his whitnes by moche betyng afore, right so, with moche laboure and disciplines, a mynche may come to moche pure clennesse of chast lyvyng. ¶ This is þat girdille þat oure lord bad his disciples to were, whan he seyde þus: *S[i]nt lumbi vestri precincti.*[257] 'Gyrde   1350
up[a] youre lyndes' he seyde, 'with þe girdel of chastite be continente lyvyng.'[258]

¶ This girdelle shuld not only gyrde þi lyndes but also (fol. 41r) þi briste, in keping of clene þoughtes in þin herte, for yif þin hert be clene, þi body may be kept clene. ¶ With þis girdel, sister, þou moste   1355
girde the streyte, for al slak girderis mow make no bosome. ¶ What þat ever þei put in here bosome, yif þei ben slak girte, it fallith oute. Right so, yif þou be slak girte with þis girdel of chastite and suffrest þi þoughtes of þin hert fle oute and in as þei wille, and also þou fleest none occasioun of synne but trustist so moche to þiself – what þat ever   1360
þou seyst or herist, þou wenyst þat þou shalt not falle – þan what maner of good vertu þou puttist into þin hert, it must nedes falle away, for þou hast no bosome. ¶ Therfor sister, girde þe streyght þat þou kepe wel þi streightest poyntes of religioun, and so shalt þou flee unclennes of synne and occasioun þerof.   1365

¶ Tho maner of puple in þe world ben streight and fast girte: on is fightyng folk, and anoþer is servauntes. Right so, sister, we þat dwellyn in religioun dwelle in þe felde of batayle ever to fight with oure gostly enemyes.[259] It is nedful, þerfor, þat we be streight girte with þe girdel of chastite.   1370

¶ We ben also ordeynned servauntes for to serve a worthi kyng, (fol. 41v) Jhesu Crist, and þerfor, we must also be streight girte wiþ þe girdille of chastite, and not only fro þe dede of unclennesse, but also

---

[a] M reads 'up~~on~~'. The deletion is coherent.

fro unclene delectacions. Good sister, kepe wel þis girdel of chastite þat
1375   oure lord, þi spouse, haþe yive to the.[260]

¶ The sixte arayment þat oure lord hathe yive to þe, is that he hath
arayed þe with sotiltees. Bi þis sotelle cloth þou shalt undirstonde feyth
with al þe articles þerof, wiche articles ben þees: the incarncacioun of
Crist, his nativite, his passioun, his resurrexioun, his assencioun.[261] Of
1380   þes sotelle þredes, sister, þou must weve þe a stamyne of trew feith and
suffre it never come fro þi bak. For like as þe stamyne is þe first cloth
þat þou dost on, right so, faythe must be þe first vertu þat þou nedist
to be arayed with.[262] Al þes articles, sister, be þe grace of þe holy gost,
shul be declared to þe more opynly in þe fourthe chapitre suwyng,
1385   wiche techith for to stabil the herte.[263]

¶ The seventh arayment þat oure lord hathe yive þe is þat he hathe
arayed þe with an ornament. ¶ Be this ornament, wiche is not specified
in name of (fol. 42r) ful knowyng as oþer ornamentes ben afore, þou
shalt undirstonde þe excellent cloth of charite. ¶ This charite is a special
1390   cloþ of gostly weddyng, withouten wiche cloth þou art not able to entre
into þe weddyng fest, þat is, into holy chirche. ¶ And þerfor it was þat
oure lord, in maner merveylyng, þat we shuld þe sunner merveyle and
be astoned, seyde þus: *Amice, quomodo huc intrasti non habens vestem
nupcialem?*[264] 'Frend' he seyde, 'how entrest þou, þat hast not an þi
1395   weddyng cloth?'

¶ Is it not a merveylous þing, wenyst þou, þat a creature may dwelle
amongis godis puple in holy chirche and in þe cloyster withoute charite?
Yis, trewly.

¶ Fyve causes þer ben why þat oure lord merveylid of suche. On is
1400   for it cost him right moche to make the clothe of charite for to yive it
to his chosyn soules, and now he fyndeth hem naked fro þe same clothe
of charite. What cost was it þat he dede þerto, and whereof made he it?
Trewly, nouþer of wolle ne of silke. Wherof þan? Certayn, of his owne
bowelis and of is[265] herte blode. ¶ A more preci- (fol. 42v) ous cote and
1405   derrer bought myght no creature yif þe, þan is þe cote of charite, þe
wiche oure lord hath yiven to us. And yit we wil not were it, but in al
wisis go naked therfro.

¶ The secunde cause of his merveyle is þis: it is a cloth þat most
plesith him, and þerfor, he merveyleth þat we kept it not. That it is
1410   a cloth þat most plesid him, it was wel y-sene in his passioun, for he
suffred raþer his blissid body to be persid and torryn, þan his cote to be
devyded.[266] Be þat, it semyd þat he lovyd more his kote þan his body.

¶ Why shuld we be so bolde þan to departe and dyvyde þe kote of charite be scisme and discorde and strif in religioun?²⁶⁷ ¶ We departe not only þat kote fro us, but also þe lord þat owith þe kote, for where 1415 þat þe kote of charite is, þere wille oure lord be.

¶ The þrid cause of his merveile is: whi we ben not redily purveyed of þis kote of charite, sith it so is þat we must nedis shewe it, we not what oure, in the courte of heven, where shul be present holy apostelis, martires, confessoures, and virgines.²⁶⁸ And yif we ben not redily 1420 purveyed þerof, we shulle not dwelle in þat company. (fol. 43r) In comendacioun of trewe spouses in holy chirche, I rede thus: *Quesivit lanam et linum, et operata est consilio manuum suarum.*²⁶⁹ 'Cristes spouse is besy in sekyng every day and every tyme bothe wolle and flexe, for to worche þerof be here hondes of good werkis a clothe of charite.' 1425

¶ Bi þis wolle, sister, þou shalt undirstonde þe benefices wiche we receyve of þe manhode of Crist. ¶ And be þe flexe, þou shalt undirstonde þe benefices wiche we receyve of þe godhede of Crist. ¶ Of þes to benefices of his manhode and of his godhede, we shuld worche a kote of charite, ever revolvyng in oure mynde þe goodnes þat 1430 he hathe shewid to us in oure makyng, in oure rawnsumyng, and in oure preservyng. ¶ Suche ofte reme[m]braunceᵃ of þe benefices of God enflawmyth þe herte to love and charite.

¶ The fourthe cause of his merveyle is þis: þat we wil not hide oure owne schame, for charite is a kote þe which coveryth oure synnes and 1435 hydeth hem fro dampnacioun, as Salomon seith: *Universa delicta operit caritas.*²⁷⁰ 'Charite' he seith, 'coveryth and hydeth oure synnes, as þough þei hadde never be don.' ¶ O, how gret shame wer it, on of (fol. 43v) us for to go nakid afore a multitude of pupille? Trewly, right so, it shal be a gretter schame and schensship withouten ende, for to be founde 1440 nakid at þe day of dome, afore so grete a multitude, withoute þe kote of charite.

¶ The fifte cause of his merveyle is þis: þat in as moche as every soule knowith wel it may not be savyd withoute þis cloth of charite, he wondrith þat she makeþ none ordenaunce þerfor, þat is, for to seke 1445 love, pees, and be in charite with alle creatures.²⁷¹

¶ The eyte arayment þat oure lord hathe yif þe, is þat he haþeᵇ yif þe broches for þine armes.²⁷² Bi þis broches þat ben ornamentes for þin armes, þou shalt undirstonde bisynes of good werkis.²⁷³ Suche broches

---

ᵃ   M erroneously reads 'remenbraunce' at this point.
ᵇ   'e' added as superscript.

1450 of bisines shuldist þou offre to oure lord, as Salomon seith: *Datum brachiorum, et sacrificium sanctificacionis offeres Domino.*[274] 'Thou shalt offre' he seith, 'to God þe yifte of þin armes and þe sacrefice of þin holynes.'

¶ Thou shalt undirstonde [be the] yiftes of þin armes,[a][275] labouris
1455 werkis of þine hondes, as þe rewle of þi religioun techith þe, but be þe sacrifice of þin holynes, þou shalt undirstonde gostly (fol. 44r) excersise in redyng, praying, and contemplacioun.[276] To þis also þou art bounde be þe doctrine of þi religioun. And þerfor, offre devoutly þees to to God, for þees too, oure lord biddith þe to do, whan he seith þus:
1460 *Pone me ut signaculum super cor tuum, et pone me ut signaculum super brachium tuum dexterum.*[277] 'Put me' he seith, 'as a mark upon þin hert, and put me as a mark upon þi right arme.'

¶ Thou puttist wel oure lord as a mark upon þin hert, whan þou servist him with devocioun in redyng, praying, and contemplacioun.
1465 Thou puttist him also upon þi right arme as a tokne or a mark, whan þou usist necessarie actyf laboure and bisines only for a right entent, þat is, for þe blisse of heven in mynistracioun of þin sistres.[278]

¶ The nynthe arayment þat oure lord hathe yif þe, is þat he hath yive þe a bigh aboute thi nekke. Bi þis bigh, þe wich is an ornament for
1470 þe nekke dependaunt to the briste, þou shalt undirstonde discrecioun and temperaunce in spekyng, þe wiche longith moche to cloystreris to whom is grauntid a resonable tyme in places of silence for to take avisement and lerne discrecioun in speking.[279] (fol. 44v)

¶ Neverþeles, þer ben summe ydel religious folk þat gadir togedre in
1475 places of silence, wordis of superfluite and so, occupi here þoughtes in lernyng and answering of wordis raþer than in swetnes of devocioun.
¶ Alle suche I may likne to þe water of a mylle, þe wiche gadreth at þe clouse dore, abidyng þe dore tille it be openyd, and whan þe dore is openyd, it rennyth þorogh with an hasty cours.[280] Wheþer summe
1480 ydel cloystreris faryn not þus? Yis, I wene. ¶ As sone as þei come out of places of silens, anone þey breke oute with wordis of superfluite, þe wiche wordis ben cause ofte tymes of stryving and debate, as Salomon seith: *Qui dimittit aquam caput est iurgiorum.*[281] 'He þat leteth oute his water is heede and begynner of strif.'
1485 ¶ He leteth oute his water, þat cannot refreyne himself fro superfluite of unprofitable wordis, and suche on is þe begynner of discorde and

---

[a] Emended reading from C. M reads, somewhat confusingly, 'undirstond yiftes of þin armes ...'. See commentary for additional explanation.

strif in religioun, wherof also comyth breking of hertis. ¶ For right as
a verre or a glasse, whan it is ful of hoote scaldyng water, al to brestith
for violence of þe heete, right so þe hert of suche a religious persone,
yif it be ful of scaldyng water of wraþe, it brekith oute with stryvyng   1490
wordis and wor- (fol. 45r) dis of debate. ¶ Therfor, sister, be war þat þou
be not to liberalle in spekyng aftir þi longe silence, lest þou breke oute
in wordis of striving. ¶ But as ofte as wordis of reprovis or wrongis ben
put to þe, answere not þerto but do as an innocente child doth, þat of
whom þat evyr he be betyn, he rennyth to his modir. So do þou, what   1495
wronges þat ever þou suffre or reprovis, renne to þe passioun of Crist
wiche shuld be þi modir, and þou shalt fynde grete comfort.²⁸²

¶ It is better þat þou be overcome of oþer þan þou overcome oþer,
for as Seint John Crisostme seith: 'The best maner of victorie is to be
overcome in many þingis', ²⁸³ for bi silence we overcome þe unpaciens   1500
of oure hertes.

¶ Good sister, bi þees wordis lerne to tempere þi speche in bering
aboute þin nekke, gostly, þe ornament of þe bygh þat oure lord hath
yif to þe.²⁸⁴

¶ The tenth arayment þat oure lord hath yif to þe, is þat he hathe arayid   1505
þin erys with rynges. ¶ Bi þees rynges, þe wiche ben ornamentes of þe
eerys, þou shalt undirstonde obedience, as Salomon seith: *Inauris aurea
margaritis fulgens qui arguit aurem obedientem.*²⁸⁵ 'As a geldyn ryng' he
(fol. 45v) seith, 'schynyng with margery perlis arayth honestly þe eere,
right so, þe trew hert of a wise reprover arayeth religiously þe heris   1510
of him þat is verry obedient.' ¶ Therfor, sister, as ofte as þi sovereyne
biddith þe do any þing, or reprovith þe, or enformith þe, so ofte þin
eeryn ben arayed with rynges of gold. ¶ Thenk not þat whan þou art
reprovid or blamyd, þat þou art þe more abjecte and lower in the sight
of oþer, but þou art þe more richely arayed. ¶ Therfor, good sister, here   1515
lowly obedience of þi sovereyne, be it in biddyng or reprovyng.

¶ Thou shalt undirstonde þat oure lord hathe yif þe to eeris in
token þat þou shuldist obeye in to þingis,²⁸⁶ as holy writ seith: *Obedite
prepositis vestris et subiacete eis.*²⁸⁷ 'Obeith to youre sovereynes and lowly
be subiecte to hem.' In þat þat I sey þou shuldist obeie to hem, þou shalt   1520
undirstonde meke obediens, and þer I say þou shalt lowly be subiecte
to hem, þou shalt undirstonde low subieccioun in disciplines taking,
and reprovyng of religioun.

¶ Ther ben (fol. 46r) summe þe wiche ben lowli inow to do as þei
ben bodyn, but þei grutch and ben unpacient whan þei ben reprovid,   1525
whan þey ben disciplined, and whan þei ben put at penaunce for here

defautes. Al such han but on obedient eere. ⁊ And þer ben summe also,
þat nouþer wil do ne suffre gladly in religioun. ⁊ Al suche lakkyn both
eeris of obedience.[288]

1530   ⁊ The ellevenþ arayment þat oure lord hath yif þe, is þat he hath sette a
fayre crowne upon þine heede. Bi þis faire crowne þou shalt undirstonde
virginite, for to virgines oure lord yiveth himself specialy as a fayre
crowne in þe blisse of heven, þe wiche crowne is noþing ellis but an
excellent dignite þat specialy shal be yivyn to virgines.[289] ⁊ This crowne
1535   is clepid in Latyn *auriola*, þe wiche I may likne to a crown of gold with
a chapelet aboven, arayed with diverse swete flowres. ⁊ Oure lord is þis
crowne: he is a crowne of mede to al þat shal be saved, but yit he is a
more excellent crown to virgines, as I have rehersid.

    ⁊ Of þis excellente crowne, (fol. 46v) I fynde a figure in holy writ,
1540   where oure lord bad Moyses make a table in þe tabernacle, and in the
tabil a crowne, and upon þat crowne a litelle crowne, be þe wiche is
undirstonde *auriola*, wiche virgines shul receyve, sette above þe comune
crowne of glorified soules.[290] ⁊ In liknes of þat crowne, þe angele aperid
to Seint Cecile, the virgine, and to Valeriane, here hosbonde, bothe
1545   lyvyng togedre in virginite, bringyng to crownes in his honde.[291]

    ⁊ Yif crownys shuld be yiven to hem þat han overcome myghtly here
enemyes, why shuld not than virgines have crownys, þat overcomen here
flessh and lyvyn in flessh withoute flessh?[292] ⁊ Yif crownes ben yivin
to kynges and quenys, why shuld not virgines have crownes, þat ben
1550   spouses to þe kynge of heven?[293]

    ⁊ The twelthe arayment þat oure lord hath yive þe, is þat he hath
arayed the with gold.[a] Bi þis arayment of gold þou shalt undirstonde
þe trewe obediens þat a soule shuld have to þe preceptis of oure lord.
⁊ The preceptis of oure lord is likned to preciosite of gold, with þe
1555   wiche a trew cloystrer is (fol. 47r) wel arayed, whan here desire is set
fully for to fulfille hem, as Salomon biddith: *Pone cor tuum in mandatis
Altissimi et proderit tibi magis quam aurum.*[294] 'Put þin hert' he seith, 'to
þe biddyngis of almyghty God, for to fulfille hem, and it shal profite
þe more þan gold.'

1560   ⁊ On is for to put þe preceptis of God in þin hert, and anoþer is for
to put þin hert in his preceptis. Þou puttist þe preceptis of God in þin
herte whan þou hast mynde upon hem. Þis is good, but yit it is more
bettir whan þou puttist þin hert in his preceptis, for þan, þou fulfillist

---

[a]   M has double red diagonal dashes here.

hem more specialy þan for to only þenke upon hem.²⁹⁵ For in þat he
seith, þou shuldist put þin hert in his preceptis, he wil þat þou desire   1565
hertly for to fulfille hem, and for to governe þi lif after hem.²⁹⁶

¶ The þirteneth arayment, and þe last þat oure lord hath yif þe, is þat he
hathe arayed þe with silver. Bi þis silver, þou shalt undirstonde swetnes
of þe wordis of oure lord, for like as silver yiveth a swete sowne among
al oþer maner of metallis, right so, þe wordis of oure lord sownyth more   1570
swetly in þe eere of a (fol. 47v) clene soule þat is devoutly disposid for
to undirstond hem, þan þe wordis of any oþer creatures.

¶ Where ben swetter wordis to a clene disposid soule þan þe wordis
wiche was sayde to þe womman þat had synned in avoutri, as þe gospel
tellith: *Nec ego te condempnabo: vade, in pace et amplius noli peccare.*²⁹⁷   1575
'Womman' he seyde, 'I shal not condempne þe, go and be in rest and
pees, and be in wil never more for to synne.' ¶ Is not þis a swete word to
a repentaunt soule? Yis, certeyn, for þat is seyd to on, is seyde to alle.²⁹⁸

¶ Also, what is a more swetter word for repentaunt synners þan þat,
þe wiche was seyde to Mary Mawdeleyne: *Fides tua te salvam fecit: vade*   1580
*in pace.*²⁹⁹ 'Thi feith' he seith, 'and þi trew beleve þat þou hast in me
hath savyd þe, go now and be in rest and pees.'

¶ O wher, also, was a swetter word þan þat, þe wiche was seyde to
þe trew þef, hongyng on þe right side of þe crosse: *Hodie mecum eris*
*in paradiso.*³⁰⁰ 'Today' he seyde, 'þou shalt be with me in paradise.' ¶   1585
Were not þis, trowist þou, a comfortable word (fol. 48r) to a repentaunt
synner, whan he shal passe out of þis world? I trow yis.³⁰¹

¶ Lo, sister, bi þis mayst þou know þat þe wordis of oure lord
sownyth swetly to devout repentaunt synneris.

¶ With þis silver, sister, þou art wel arayed, whan þou occupiest þe   1590
in heryng of þe blissid wordis of oure lord, wheþer it be in redyng or
heryng of devout tretises, or ellis in heryng of devout sermonys, or swete
communicacioun sewyng to vertu. But she þat knowith holy lyves and
holy tretices, and herith devoute sermonys, and wil not lyve þerafter,
she hath silver, but she is not arayid with it.³⁰² ¶ Therfor sister, do þou   1595
as Seint Jerome techeth: 'Love to here or to rede or to commune devout
vertuos þinges, and it wil kepe þe fro vices.'³⁰³

Thus have I declared þe þe þirtene ornamentes þat oure lord hath yif to
the for to be arayed with, yif þou wilt plese him as a gostly wif shuld
plese here hosbonde, and so endith þe first chapitre of makyng redy of   1600
þin hert to God. *Cum gloria in secula seculorum. Amen.*³⁰⁴

Capitulum secundum. How and in what wise a mynche shuld kepe here hert to God be þe yifte of pite.[1]

Aftir[a] this longe chapitre, þe wiche techith a mynche to make redy here hert,[2] I purpose, be the grace of God, to declare how she shuld also kep here hert, aftir þe biddyng of Salomon where he seith þus: *Omni custodia serva cor tuum.*[3] 'Kepe wel þin hert' he seith, 'with al maner
5   of bisynesse.'

¶ I may likne an hert to a castelle þat is set in a straunge lond, besegid with enemyes, stuffid with a kynges tresoure.[4] ¶ Were it not gret pite þat such a castelle shuld be robbed and put into enemyes hondis? Yis, certeyn. ¶ We must be governyd with þe spirit of pite in doble wise,
10   lest þis castelle be distroyid. On is þat we presume not to moche of the strengthe of oure castelle, þat is of oure hertis. Anoþer is þat we hope mekly in þat lord þat oweth þe castelle of oure hertis, þat he wil socoure us whan we axe help devoutly of him.[5]

¶ How þis castelle is besegid in a straunge londe with enemyes, I shal
15   telle þe. ¶ Thou wost wel, as longe as we lyve in þis lif, we (fol. 49r) lyve in a presone and in a straunge londe fer fro oure owne contrey, þe blisse of heven, where þe castelle of oure hertes is bisiged be þe fend and his wikkid host, þe wiche: 'goth aboute roryng as a lyon sekyng whom he may devoure.'[6]

20   He sekith where he may fynde any entre into þis castelle.[7] Be þe yate of þe eyghe he shewith unclene formes and schappes of unclene and curious sightes, wherby he myght þe sunner distroye þe chastite of þe hert. ¶ He exciteth also us bi heryng of oure eeris, into lusty and lecherous songes, and þe tonge to reprove other, and þe hondes for to
25   smyte in yre. ¶ Also he promyttith wordly worshipis yif we wold leve gostly bisynes. ¶ And yif he may not thus privily begile us, he temptith us with opyn dedis so for to disceyve us yif he myght, ayenst whom we shuld be as redy for to withstonde as he is redy for to assayle.

---

[a]   M gives a two-line-square illuminated capital 'A'. In C, a two-line-square space is prepared for an illuminated capital (not finally added). T gives a three-line-square illuminated capital.

¶ Lo, sister, se and behold what adversarie þou hast. Kepe þerfor þe
castelle of þin herte fro suche an enemy þat so hathe besegid þe.   30

¶ Considere also and behold how sobirly al þo þe wiche ben besegid
in a castel lyvyn,[8] how litelle þey slepe, how silde, and with what drede
and how moche sleythe, þey (fol. 49v) gon oute of þe castelle whan þei
han nede, and how sone þei come ayen, how ofte and how bisily þei
serche þe wardis of þe castelle, with what noyse and with what bisynes   35
eche of hem exciten oþer to batayle, and yit, albeit þat þey ben þus
sorowfulle and dredfulle, þei synge oþerwhiles on hygh upon þe castel
wallis because here enemyes shuld be aferde.

¶ Thus shuldist þou do, sister, yif þou wilt wel kepe þe castel of þin
hert. Be sobre of þi lyvyng in etyng and drynkyng, for it besemyth right   40
nought him þat is besegid in a castel for to lyve in lustes. ¶ Also þe
nedith for to wake holily for thyn enemy slepith not. Put away al maner
of hevinesses of slewth and kepe þe within the castelle. Go not oute of
þi monasterie but it be right selde, and þat it be with sleith, and at þe
biddyng of þi sovereyne. ¶ Serche also bisily þe wardis of þin hert:[9] how   45
þin undirstondyng and þin affeccioun ben rewlid, and excite and stire
þiself and oþer þat ben with þe, to laboure and to synge devoutly in
the quere with gostly gladnes, þat bi such devout syngyng in þi castelle,
þe hoste of þe fendes, the wiche besegyn trew hertis, mow be aferd and
(fol. 50r) sey, as I fynde write thus: *Ve nobis: quia non fuit tanta exultacio*   50
ab heri et nudius tercius.[10] 'Alas, what may þis be? Þer was not so moche
joye yisterday and þre dayes agon as it is now.'

¶ Anoþer þing also, sister, þou must lerne of hem þat ben besegid in
castellis. ¶ Thou wost wel þat al þo þe wiche ben long tyme besegid in
a castelle and almost enfamynid, þey sende home to here kynge and   55
þe lordis of þe reawme for reskwyng[a] and socoure, þat þei vouchesaf to
come and breke þe sege or lesse þe nombre of þe host.[11] So must þou
do. Yif þe castel of þin hert be so sore besegid þat þe semyth þou art
almost yold to þe hondis of þin enemyes, þan privily sende home þe
messanger of prayer to þe lege lord of þi castel, Jhesu Crist, and to þe   60
lordis þat ben with him, þe wiche ben seyntes of heven, praiyng hem of
socoure and of helpe, þat þe host of fendes, þe wiche han besegid þin
hert, mow ouþer be lessynnyd or disperblid. And I drede not, sister, yif
þou do þus, þou shalt sone fynde comfort.

¶ A comfortable figure I fynde hereof in holy writ, where I rede þus: 65
Naas besegid a cite wiche was callid Jabes in so moche þat bi (fol. 50v)

---

[a] The 'k' in 'reskwyng' is partially smudged, following a small hole in the MS
at this point.

longe contynuaunce of þat besegyng, the puple þat were in þe cite were
almost enfamyned and so in poynt for to be yolde. At þe last, þei were
in so grete myschif þat þei sent to Naas for to be yold to hym and take
70 pees with him. He sent hem word ayen and seyde he wold take pees
with hem upon þis condicioun, þat þey shuld suffre hym to put oute
alle here right eyghen. And upon þis, he yaf hem respite into þe tyme
thei had sent home to here kynge,¹² and so to yif him an answere.

⁋ Word was sent home to þe kynge and to þe lordis and oþer puple
75 of þe reawme. Than þe pupil had grete compassioun þat such a cite
shuld be distroyed, be þe wiche þe kynge was þe sunner stired for to
reskewe þat cite and socoure þe pupil þerin. And so he dede. He brak
þe sege and killid a grete nombre of þat wikkid hoste, so þat þer were
not lefte alive twayn togedres, but ouþer þei were put at flyght or ellis
80 were killid.¹³ In þis figure, sister, þou mayst lerne gret comfort in þi
gostly batayle.

⁋ Bi þis Naas, þe wiche is no more to mene but a serpente, þou shalt
undirstonde þe fende, þat every day with his wikkid hoste besegith
Jabes, wiche is þe cite of mannys soule, (fol. 51r) impugnyng it with
85 gret diverse temptaciouns. So þat for such grevous temptaciouns,
many þer ben þat ben aboute for to yilde up þe cite of here soules
into here enemyes hondes, desiryng pees with þe serpent, Naas, þat is,
consentyng to synne wiche he stirith hem to, raþer þan for to live in
such grevous temptaciouns.

90 ⁋ O, sister, now is þis a wikkid pees, for to be in pees with oure
adversarie, þe wiche wil put oute oure right eygh. Þat is, he wil
benymme from us oure love þat we han to God, or oure gostly
knowleche, for ellis he wot wel þat he may not longe rejoyse us yif we
kepe with us oure right eygh.

95 ⁋ Shuld not þis be to us a grete feere for to lese oure right eygh? Yis.
Therfor, sister, take never pees with þis enemy, Naas, for certeyn, yif
þou do, he wil make þe blinde on þe right syde, and þat were pite now
for to lese al þe love and gostly knowleche of God and gostly þing for
a litel fals pees. But raþer, sende home be devoute prayer to þi lige lord,
100 Jhesu Crist, þe owner of þi cite, and to þe lordis and þe puple þat ben
þer with him, for socoure and help.

⁋ O, what pite and compassioun þe lordis and þe puple of heven
han (fol. 51v) of mennys soules here in erth þat ben so beseged. Þei
prayin þe kynge of heven ofte tymes for hem, þat he wold vouchesaf
105 to socoure hem and help hem, for as Seint Bernard seith: 'þogh seyntes
ben unpassible, þey ben not uncompassible.'¹⁴ And be here compassible
prayer oure lord þe sunner socourith hem and helpith hem. Now, sister,

behold and see how oure lord comyth with his hevenly host for to
socoure þi soule, þe wiche is besegid with þat serpent, Naas. The first
þing þat he dothe: he disperblith him and his host, and puttith hem to   110
flight, and yit not alle, for as it is rehersid in þis figure: 'summe he put
to flight, and summe were left stille.'

⁋ What menyth þis, trowist þou ? Treuly, noþing ellis but þogh oure
lord delyver þe fro gret temptacioun be compassioun of seyntes þat
prayed for þe, yit somme smale temptaciouns he suffreth to abyde ᵃ in   115
tokne þat þou be not to bold and to siker of þiself, for as Seynt Austyn
seith: 'The most temptacioun þat is, is not for to be temptid.'¹⁵

Good sister, gadre þe frute of þis figure þat I have rehersid and,
þogh þin hert be besegid with gret and dispitous temptaciouns, yilde
not up þe (fol. 52r) castelle ne take no pees with þin enemye, lest he   120
put oute þi right eygh of love and gostly knowleche, but raþer sende
messangeris of devout prayeris to oure lord, þe kynge of hevene, and to
his cosainys, seyntes of hevene, for socoure and help, þat so be praier
and compassioun of seyntes þou mayst þe sunner be holp. And yit,
þow he leve with þe summe maner of smale temptaciouns, grucch not,   125
for it is don to kepe þe in mekenes and drede, þat þou be not to siker
of þinself.

⁋ But o þing þou shalt wel knowe: a castelle may not longe be
kept yif it fayle men for to defende it and kepe it; right so þou mayst
not longe kepe þin hert in trew rest fro the fende, but yif þi þoutes   130
ben myghty and strong for to withstonde hym. ⁋ Thou wost wel, yif
wymmen or childrin be in a castelle þat is besegid, þei ben sone sent
oute for they mow lightly discomfort hem þat ben within, and also,
for cowardise and faynte hert, bringe in with summe sotilte, privily,
here enemyes. ⁋ Thus must þou do: put oute al childly þoughtes   135
and lusty affecciouns, and kepe within myghty þoughtes and affecci-
(fol. 52v) ouns.

⁋ Thi þoughtes ben wymmen and no men whan þei ben ocupied
aboute lustes and flesshly desires.¹⁶ Such þoughtes defendyn not thin
hert fro þe fende, but raþer bringen in þe fende. ⁋ Thi þoughtes also   140
ben childrin and no men whan þei desire to moche wordly þingis raþer
þan hevenly þingis, for al wordly þinges in comparisoun of hevenly
þinges ben but litel, and maken hem litel of price in þe sight of God
þat þenken moche upon hem.¹⁷

⁋ Sende oute, þerfor, fro þe castel of þin hert, bothe wymmen and   145
childrin, yif þou wilt kepe þin herte, as Salomon seyth be þe auctorite

---

ᵃ M reads 'abyde ~~in þe~~'.

þat is rehersid afore: *Omni custodia serva cor tuum*.[18] That is: 'with al maner of bisynes kepe perfightly þin hert.'[19]

⸏ Ther ben many gret folyes wher þorogh soules ben overcome in here
150 gostly batayle, of þe wiche, be the grace of God and þi devoute prayeris, summe I shal reherse to make þe þe more war.[20]
⸏ On is of such þat wil not do on here armoure unto þe tyme þei ben hurt and woundid. So don many in religioun, whan þei ben hurt and woundid, þan (fol. 53r) þey don on her armour of pacience and
155 here scheld of meknes; þan þei schet fast þe stabil dore whan þe hors ys stole. ⸏ Sister, in al wise be wel war of þis foly, go alway armyd with þe armour of paciens and þe scheld of meknes þat, whan þi gostly batayle begynneþ, þou mow withstonde þin enemy, þe fende, and alle his lymes. ⸏ Be stille and softe in spirit, and love wel þe vertu of taciturnite,
160 and þan shalt þou lightly overcome þin enemyes, for alle þe champions of oure lord suffren moche and speke litelle.[21]
⸏ The secunde foly is of hem þat don on such armoure þe wiche is to hevy for hem, and so ben overthrow in here owne harneyce and encombred, as don many new fervent soules þat, in þe begynnyng
165 of here conversioun, þei take so moche upon hem undiscretly of over moche fastyng and wakyng, þat þei lese here gostly myghtes for to pray devoutly. ⸏ Suche armour, to a soule þat is in batayle, is to chargous. Therfor sister, lete discrecioun, þe chyveteyn of þi gostly batayle, teche þe to be armyd, and not undescrecioun.[22]
170 ⸏ The þrid foly is of such, whan þey shuld goo to batayle and fight, þan þei caste (fol. 53v) away here armour, as al such þat casten and put away fro hem meknes whan elacioun and pride ariseth in here hertis. And whan þei ben tormentid with adversite of outewarde puple, þan þei cast away þe armoure of pacience. And whan þei ben sterid with
175 flesshly temptaciouns, þei put away here gostly strength in prayer and discrete fastyng and wakyng.[23]
⸏ Also, þey put away from hem gostly armour whan þei take none hede of holy ensamples of seyntes, for as Salomon seith: *Ibi mille clipei pendent et ex illa omnis armatura forcium*.[24] 'An infinite nombre of scheldes' he
180 seyth, 'may be founde in here lyvyng in withstondyng of synne, for of hem al trew soules taken here gostly armoure.' ⸏ And, þerfor, it is þat, in þe begynnyng of youre chapitres, ther is redde a lessoun of þe marteloge,[25] þat is of seyntes lyvis, wherein þou mayst here how summe were scorgid, and summe brennyd, and summe tormentid with diverse
185 tormentis, and paciently þei suffrid it for þe love of God, in tokne þat þou shuldist mekely and paciently suffre al reproves and blames of hem

þat ben þi presedentis in chapitre, and also þat þou shuldist so arme þe
in þe begynnyng of (fol. 54r) the day with such vertues of paciens and
meknes be þe ensamples of such holy seyntes, þat þou be not overthrow
be þin enemy.²⁶ ¶ Good sister, here devoutly such holy lessonys every   190
day afore chapitre, wherebi þou may wynne such gracious armoure.²⁷

¶ The fourth foly is of hem þat wil not distroye here enemyes al þe
while þei be litelle, but suffre hem to grow and wex myghti in age, and
þan it is hard to overcome hem. Right so, al þo þat suffre here first
steryng of synne²⁸ to grow into gret delectaciouns and aftirward into   195
consentyng of wrecchidnes, it is ful hard for to distroye hem. Þerfor,
sister, withstonde þe begynnyng of wikkid þoughtes, and þan shal þin
enemy never do þe harme.²⁹

¶ The fifthe foly is of hem þat wil not withstonde here enemyes at
þe narew yates of þe cite where þei myght sone overcome hem, as at þe   200
castel yates or at þe yates of þe cite, for few within þe castel or þe cite
mow overcome many withoute.³⁰ ¶ Be wel ware, sister, of þis gret foly.
And whan þin enemyes begynne to make asaught at þe yates of þin
hert, þat is at þe yates of þi five wittes, as whan he begynneth to make
þe here amysse, (fol. 54v) or to have delectacioun in syght, in spekyng,   205
in touching, and in smellyng, anone withstonde him and suffre hym
in no wise entre, as I have rehersid afore in þe firste chapitre, where I
spake of kepyng of þi five wittes.³¹ And bewar also of ydilnes, for þat
is on of þe feldes wherein þe fende wil fight with Godis champions.³²
Þerfor, good sister, be occupied ouþer in redyng or in praying or in holy   210
meditaciouns or ellis in summe honest actif bisines,³³ þat in no wise þe
fende fynde þe ydelle.³⁴

¶ Lo, sister, such folies, and many mo, þou must eschew, yif þou wilt
perfightly kepe þe castelle of þin hert after þe auctorite of Salomon,
where he seyth: *Omni custodia serva cor tuum*.³⁵ But because þe tonge   215
is most nessessarie of al þe wittes for to be wardid, yif þe castel of þe
hert shuld wel be kept, as Salomon seith: *Qui custodit os suum custodit
animam suam*,³⁶ 'he þat kepith wel his tonge kepith wel his soule'; þerfor,
sumwhat shal I sey, be þe grace of God, of þe kepyng of þi tonge.³⁷

¶ Thou wost wel, a lord þat hath a castel to kepe, he wil make noo   220
foole keper of þe yate, but he maketh a wise, sad man portour of þe
yate for to wite ho goth oute and ho comyth yn. So must þou (fol. 55r)
do. Make discrecioun keper and portoure of þi mowth, þe wiche is þe
grete yate and þe most perlious yate for to be kepte of þe castel of þin
hert, and lete discrecioun sitte alway at þat yate specialy, þat none come   225
in withoute his leve and his dome.³⁸

¶ For leve it wel, sister, yif discrecioun be not portoure of þi mouthe, I may likne þin herte to a cite withoute wallis, and to a vessel withoute coveryng, and to an hors withoute bridelle, and to a schip withoute
230 styrne. As to þe ferst, Salomon seyth þus: *Sicut urbs patens absque murorum ambitu, ita homo qui non potest in loquendo cohibere spiritum suum.*[39] 'Like as a cite' he seith, 'þat is not wallid abought, so is he þat cannot kepe and constreyne his spirit in spekyng.' Thyn hert, sister, lakkith wallis whan þi mowth is to liberalle in spekyng withoute þe
235 vertu of taciturnyte. It is no maystry þogh such a cite be sone i-wonne of enemyes.

¶ Also I seyde, yif þou lakke þe portour of discrecioun, þin hert is likned to a vessel withoute coveryng. Such a vessel ofte tymes is unclene, as oure lord seythe: *Vas, quod non habet operculum immundum erit.*[40] 'A
240 vessel þat is withoute coveryng' he seith, 'shal be unclene.' ¶ Al such ben vessellis with- (fol. 55v) oute coveryng that conne[a] kepe no counseyle, for what þat ever þey se or here, þei must nedis spek it forth. Ther is no portour of discrecioun, for a tyme of discrecioun shuld be kept in spekyng, and so to know wheþer it myght profight or disprofight wiche shuld be
245 spokyn. ¶ Where[b] is goode charitable discrecioun, whan o sister tellith of anoþer withoute charite, þat shuld not be tolde in such a wise? Suche an hert must nedis be unclene as long as it usith such condiciouns.[41]

¶ I seyde also þat, yif þou lakke þe portour of discrecioun, þin hert is likned to an hors withoute bridelle, and to a schippe withoute stirne, as
250 Seynt Jame seith: *Si enim equis frena in ora mittimus ad consensiendum nobis, et omne corpus eorum circumferimus. Et naves, cum sint magne, a ventis validis minantur, circumferuntur autem a modico gubernaculo. Ita et lingua modicum membrum est, et magna exaltat.*[42] 'Seth it so is' he seith, 'þat bridelis ben put in hors mowþes for to make hem consente to
255 us, be þe wiche bridelis we mow torne here bodies abought as we wil have hem, and also as schippis, be þei never so grete, albeit þat þei ben oþer- (fol. 56r) while dryven with boystous wyndes, yit þei mow be tornyd ayene with a litel styrne, right so it farith be þe tonge. But it be governyd, it ariseth right high and bringeth þe castel of þe hert into gret perile.'
260 ¶ Lo, sister, in what myschef þou art put yif þou cannot governe discretly þi tonge, for as an hors bridilles rennyth where he list, and a schippe styrneles stond in gret perile, so doth a cloystrer the wiche

---

[a] A hole in the parchment follows 'conne'. No words are lost.
[b] In M, 'where' is followed by an 'it' in the inner margin, which detracts from the coherence of the sentence. This 'it' is found in M and C, but omitted from L and T.

cannot governe his tonge. ¶ An hors þat shuld be wel rayned, it must
have a schort bridelle. So must þou do yif þou wilt speke withoute
defaute or stomblyng: put in þi mowth a bridel of sad spekyng, ellis,   265
but þou can þus governe þe, þou art a feble religious womman.[43]

¶ Thou mayst wynne gret frute, sister, in keping of þi tonge, as Salomon
seith: *De fructu oris sui unusquisque replebitur.*[44] 'Every man' he seith,
'shal be fulfillid of þe frute of his mowth.' ¶ O, what ben þees frutes?
Certeyn, þe frutis of the mowthe ben þees: prayer, þonkyng to God,[45]   270
confessioun of synnes, charitable correccioun of oure bretheryn and
sistren, and enformyng or teching of hem þat ben unkunnyng.[46] ¶ Lo,
(fol. 56v) sister, here ben fyve frutis, the wiche mow wel be clepid þe five
wordis þat Seynt Poule spekith of, where he seyth þus: *Malo quinque
verba loqui sensu meo quam decem milia linguis.*[47] 'I had lever' he seide,   275
'speke five wordis with felyng of my soule þan ten þousand wordis
spekyng only in my tonge.'

     ¶ The first of þes five wordis fonde wel þe trew þef þat henge on þe
right syde of Crist, þe wiche seyde to his felaw þat hynge on þe toþer
side þus: *Neque tu times Deum, qui in eadem damnacione es. Nos quidem*   280
digna factis recepimus: hic autem nichil mali fecit. Memento mei, Domine,
dum veneris in regnum tuum.[48] 'Nowþer þou dredist God' he seide, 'þat
art in þe same payne. Thou and I' he seyde, 'han receyved as we han
trespace. This lord dede never evyl. Have mynde on me, good lord,
whan þou comyst to þi kyngdome.'   285

     ¶ As for þe first, þer he seyde 'nowther þou dredist God', in þat he
correctid and blamyd charitably his felaw, as for þe [ferst]ᵃ fruȝt of
the tonge. And þer he seide to him that he was in þe same payine, he
charitably enformyd him, as for þe secunde fruȝt. And whan (fol. 57r)
he seide 'we han receyvid as we han trespaced', þer he accusid himself   290
þat þe tother shulde sunner know himself gylti, as for þe þrid frute. ¶
And þer he seyde 'this dede never evyl', þan he commendid oure lord
of gret goodnes, as for the fourth frute. But in þat that he, at þe last,
seyde 'lord, have mynde upon me whan þou comyst to þi kyngdom',
he prayed, as for þe fifth frute of þe tonge.[49]   295

     ¶ Thes ben five profitable wordis. ¶ In suche wordis, sister, shuld þi
tong be occupied.

¶ Neverþeles, five þinges þer ben þat must be considerid in spekyng yif
þou wilt speke wel. On is what þou spekist. Anoþer is whan þou spekist.

ᵃ   Emended reading from L and T.

300   The þrid is where þou spekist. The fourth is to whom þou spekist. And
       þe fifth is how þou spekist.[50]
          ¶ As for þe first, be wel ware what þou spekist, þat þi wordis be
       no wordis of noyous, ne dishonest wordis, ne unprofitable wordis.
       Al þo ben noyous wordis, þe wiche enducyn þe herer to erroure or
305   to schrewdnes. Inhonest wordis ben al þo þat sownnyn to unclennes
       or to ribawdry. Unprofitable wordis ben al þo þat nouþer profiteth
       þe herrer ne þe speker. ¶ I forbede not wordis of recreacioun, þogh I
       forbede noyous wordis, (fol. 57v) dishonest, and unprofitable wordis, for
       wordis of recreacioun, yif þei ben spokyn in tyme and for to put away
310   slewth and hevynesse of þe world, þei ben comfortable, profitable, and
       meritorie.[51]
          ¶ Þe secunde is: þou must be ware whan þou spekist.[52] As touching
       þis, þou shalt undirstonde þat 'þer is tyme of silence and tyme of
       spekyng', as Salomon seyth: *Tempus taciendi, et tempus loquendi*.[53] Tyme
315   of silence is whan þou art amonge þin elderis or þi sovereynes. Also,
       tyme of silence is whan þou art amonges suche þat raþer wil cacch þe in
       þi wordis þan be edified bi þi wordis. ¶ And tyme of spekyng is whan
       þi wordis ben take profitably.
          ¶ The þrid is: þou must be ware where þou spekist. As for þis, þou
320   wost wel þer ben certeyn places of spekyng and certeyn tymes of
       spekyng as þi religioun techith þe; governe þe þerafter.[54]
          ¶ The fourthe is: þou must be ware to whom þou shalt speke. In
       þis þou shalt considere þe persone, what he or sche is, to whom þou
       spekist. 'Yif it be a naturele fole, þou shuldist not speke moche with
325   suche on',[55] as Salomon seith, but commune and speke with such þat
       ben sad and wise, or such þat wold (fol. 58r) be reformyd to grace.[56]
       And as towching the communycacioun of sad folk, þou must considere
       first wheþer þou shalt speke to hem þing þat longith to hem, or þing
       þat longith to the.
330   ¶ Yif it be for þing þat longith to þe, se wheþer he be such on þat
       þou may be profited by or not, for þer ben many good sad folk wich
       have no discrecioun of counseyle. It is a yifte of þe holy gost for to
       have þe spirit of counseyle. Al sad folk hane not þat yifte. Þe holy
       gost yivith it where he wille.[57] ¶ Ferþermore, yif þou speke of þing þat
335   longith to him þe wiche þou spekist to, considere to þingis. On is: yif
       he þat þou spekist to hath no nede of þin exortacioun for, peraventure,
       he is warnyd of oþer whos wordis he settith more to hert þan þine. ¶
       Anoþer is: wheþer he be obstinat and wil receyve correccioun or not.
       Yif he be obstinat, it is no wit for to speke moche to him but raþer to
340   praye for him. ¶ Neverþeles, yif þou be a sovereyne and have charge of

a subjecte þat is obstinate, þou art bounde for to speke to such on, o tyme or oþer, for ensample of oþer.⁵⁸

❡ The fifte is: þou must be ware how þou spekist and in what maner of wise. ❡ Thi maner of spekyng (fol. 58v) shal stonde in þre þingis: in sownyng of þi wordis, in þin aport, and in significacioun of þi wordis.   345
❡ The sownyng of þi wordis shal be myld and esy withoute noyse of crying. ❡ Thin aport shal be sadly and manerly withoute castyng of þin armes or poyntyng of þin fyngres. ❡ The signifiyng ᵃ of þi wordis shal be trew withoute doble menyng or sophymes.⁵⁹

❡ Lo, sister, now þow knowist what þou shalt speke, whan, where,   350
to whom, and in what wise, and how. Yif þou kepe þis doctrine, þou shalt fynde þerin grete rest of soule.⁶⁰

❡ Yit o þing now þat fallith to my mynde be þe grace of God, I schal declare to þe more opynly, þe wich is touchid afore in on of þe five frutes of þe tonge, and it is þis: charitable correccioun or blamyng of   355
þe defautes of oure brethren and sistren.⁶¹ ❡ Of þis be wel ware þat þi blamyng b[e] ᵇ not to boustous ne to esy.

❡ Neverþeles, to þingis⁶² þou most undirstonde and know er þan þou begynne to blame, on is what þei ben, þe wiche ben bounden for to blame oþer for here defautes, and in what case þei shuld be blamed.   360
❡ As for þe first, þou shalt wele know þat we ben al bounden for to blame oþer for here de- (fol. 59r) fautes charitably, but yit summe ben more bounden þerto þan summe. And also in anoþer wise, as prelatis and soveraynes ben oþer wise bounden for to blame þan subjettis. ❡ Neverþeles, how subjettis ben bounden for to blame, I shal telle þe.   365

❡ A subjecte is bounden for to blame oþer þat trespacen for here defautes, except certeyn casis.⁶³ On is whan þer is none hope of amendement, as of obstinate folk and fooles. For such þou shuldist raþer praye þan speke, al þe while þou art a subjette and no sovereyne. Salomon seith: *Noli arguere derisorem, ne forte oderit te.*⁶⁴ 'Blame not a   370
scorner' he seith, 'lest he cast an hate to þe.' Such ben raþer werse after here blames þan better. Also in casis crymynalis, yif þou be a subjette and no sovereyne, speke not but raþer praye, namly wher no prof may be founde. Also, yif þe defautes of oþer be know to here sovereynes þe wiche shal be here juges, þan þe nedith not for to speke but raþer for   375
to praye. Also, þe nediþ not for to speke yif þou be occupied aboute a better þing or as good, þat is in prayer or meditacioun or ellis in somme

---

ᵃ   M reads 'singnifiyng' erroneously.
ᵇ   Amended to 'be'. M reads 'bo' erroneously.

oþer gostly excersise, for such blissid bisinessis amendith rather (fol. 59v) synneris þan þi speche, as long as þou art a subjette and no sovereyne.

380 ꝑ Yit þer is anoþer case þat þin blamyng may not avayle as long as þou art a subjette: þat yif a multitude or a gret potestate hathe trespaced. For such, prayer raþer avayleth of subjettis þan speche, but yif þere be any hope of amendement.

ꝑ Thus for to blame trespasoures, prelates or sovereynes ben not 385 bounden as subjettis ben. For a prelate or a sovereyne is bounde to blame as wel þe corrigible as þe uncorrigible, wheþer such on be þe better or þe worse, for ensample of oþer. ꝑ A sovereyne shuld never blame his subjette privyli for open defautes, albeit he know wel þat such on is uncorrigible, as I seyde afore, for ensample of oþer. ꝑ Of 390 such correccioun of opyn defautes spekith Isidere þus, and seith: 'Opyn synnes shuld not be purged be privi purgacioun but opynly blamyd.'[65]

Foure þingis þer ben þat every sovereyne shuld considere in blamyng of defautes of oþer.[66] On is discrecioun, anoþer is softnes or tranquillite, 395 þe þrid is charite, and þe fourth is profite.

ꝑ A sovereyne blamyth undiscretly þat to al indifferently shewith like (fol. 60r) penaunce in blamyng. ꝑ The states of every persone shuld be considered: old folk shuld not be blamed as scharply as yong folk, for Seynt Poule seith: *Seniorem ne increpaveris, set obsecra ut patrem.*[67] 400 'Blame not' he seith, 'sharply an old man, but pray him for to amende his defautes as þou woldist pray þi fadir.'

ꝑ Also, a sovereyne shuld blame softly and esily with tranquillite, as Seynt Poule seyth: *Servum Dei non oportet litigare: set mansuetum esse ad omnes cum modestia corripientem.*[68] 'Godis servaunt' he seith, 'shuld 405 not stryve in his blamyngis, but be myld and esy to alle folk, blamyng with tranquillite.' Neverþeles, as Seynt Austyn seith, it is not ayenst þis auctorite of Seint Poule þogh[a] al such be blamyd with rigerouste þat wil not be blamyd and correctid with esynes,[69] so þat þe entent of a sovereyne be set for to amende þe defautes of subjettis withoute cruelte. 410 Therfor, sister, yif þou be a sovereyne, put awey al maner of trobel in þi blames, and blame after þe ensample of oure lord, with al maner of esynes.[70]

A sovereyne also shuld correcte and blame with charite, not to hate hem þat ben blamyd but (fol. 60v) for to love hem, as Seynt John 415 seith: *Ego quos amo, arguo, et castigo.*[71] 'Hem þat I love, I blame and reprove.' ꝑ Neverþeles, þer ben summe þat wille not blame hem whom

---

[a] There is a manuscript hole in M after 'þogh'.

þei love not. Al such be no trew sovereynes, for þei shuld love al and
here blames shuld come oute of þe rote of charite, as þe prophete
seith: *Egredietur virga de radice Jesse.*[72] 'Oute of þe rote of Jesse shuld
þe yerde of correccioun come.' ¶ Bi þis yerde þou shalt undirstonde   420
correccioun of blame, and bi Jesse þou shalt undirstonde brennyng of
love and charite. ¶ Than þe yerde of correccioun comyth oute wel of
þe rote of Jesse whan a sovereyne correctith with þe yerde of charite. ¶
For what þat ever he be, sovereyne or subjette, þat blameth or accuseth
annoþer[73] only for to blame him maliciously and not for to correcte   425
him charitably, he synneþ þerin dedly, albeit þogh it be trew þat he
seith.

¶ Also, a sovereyne shuld blame profittably. A sovereyne blamyth
unprofittably whan wityngly she blameth anoþer þat is not here
subjette, knowynge wel þat sche is uncorrigible, where no profite is,   430
nouþer (fol. 61r) of here that is blamyd ne of oþer for to take ensample
bi. ¶ A sovereyne also blamyth unprofittably whan sche blamyth here
sovereynes wiche ben above here, knowyng wel þat þei ben untrettable.
For Seynt Austyn seith: 'Al such shuld be suffred for a while, and
correccioun shuld be seced for commune pees of holy chirche, and   435
pray for hem.'[74] Good sister, take hede þerfore, yif þou shuldist blame,
þat þi blamyng be discrete, esy, charitable, and profitable, and þan þi
blamyng shal be meritorie.

¶ How also correccioun shuld be receyvid, it is rehersid afore in þe
first chapitre.[75]   440

¶ Thus, sister, þou must kepe þin hert, as Salomon seith: *Omni custodia
serva cor tuum.*[a76]

---

[a]   A long decorated horizontal flourish, filling the remainder of the line, marks
the end of second book.

Capitulum tercium. How and in what wise a mynche shuld opyn here hert to God be þe yifte of kunnyng.[a1]

Sister,[b] in to maner of wises I fynde þat þe hert must be opennyd. ¶ It shuld be openyd as a boke wherein thow shuldist rede, and as a dore wiche shuld be openyd for to receyve him þat knokkith þereat.[2]

¶ As for þe first, þat it shuld be openyd as (fol. 61v) a boke wherein þou shuldist rede, þou must considere to þingis.[3] On is what ben þe lessonis þe wiche shuld be rad in þe boke of þin hert. Anoþer is what ben þe lettyngis þat letteth þe boke of þe hert or of þe conscience for to be openyd.

¶ Certeyn, sister, it is ful necessarie for to know þis, for many þer ben þat wenyn here boke of here conscience is opyn, and it is schitte. Why, trowist þou? Trewly, for: 'þei bysien hem moche for to know many outward þingis', as Seynt Bernard seith, 'and litel or nought here owne conscience.'[4] Thenk, sister, þerfor, be þe yifte of connyng, þat þin hert or þi conscience is a boke wherin þou shuldist rede in þis lif, for it is þi boke whereby þou shalt be demyd.[5] ¶ That boke shal be openyd at þe day of dome, and as oure lord fyndeth þan writen in þat boke, so wil he deme þe, ouþer to endeles peyne or to endeles joye.[c]

¶ Yif þou wilt wite þanne what lessonys þou shuldist rede in that boke, I schal telle þe. ¶ Thou shalt rede þerin lamentaciouns of sorow and penaunce caused be consideracioun of þin owne synnes, of periles, and of wretchidnesse of (fol. 62r) this world. ¶ Thou shalt also rede therin songes of joy and gladnes be consideracioun of everlastyng blisse. ¶ And þou shalt also rede þerin woo of everlastyng damnacioun of such þat shuld be damnyd.

¶ Thes ben þe þre lessouns þat Ezechiel fonde write in his boke:

---

[a] A second horizontal flourish fills the remainder of the line.
[b] An illuminated capital 'S' covers a two-line square. In C, a two-line-square space for a capital is left. In T, an illuminated capital 'S' covers a three-line square.
[c] The manuscript page of M is stained or slightly damaged here, but the words are still clearly visible.

lamentaciouns, songis, and woo.[6] Rede þerfor, sorowfully, þi defautes
and oþeris also, þat oure lord þe sunner wold vouchesaf for to foryif þe
þi synnes. And also rede þerin þe wrecchidnesse of þis world, þat þou
myght the sunner despise it.[7] ¶ Rede þerin songes of everlastyng blisse,
so to lerne for to desire it.[8] ¶ And rede also þerin woo of damnacioun,   30
þat þou myght þe better fle it.

¶ Lo, sister, upon þees þre short lessouns þou shuldist studie bisily.
Thees lessouns must ofte be radde, for þogh þou have no moo bokes,
it wil serve the al þi lyve.[9] ¶ Do not as oþer don þat redyn rather oþer
bokes þan here own, as al such þat negligently leven here owne hertes   35
unserchid and spyen after þe defautes of oþer. ¶ Such folk blameth
Ysidere and sayth: 'Defoule not þi mowth with (fol. 62v) the curiouse
serching of oþer folkis synnes; serche first þin owne. And of þat þat
longeth not to þe, axe no questiouns. What þat folke speken togedres,
desire not for to wite.'[10] Good sister, recorde wel þis þre lessouns þat   40
I have rehersid afore. Lete not þi boke al day be schet; opynne it ofte,
and se what is writen þerin.[11]

¶ Now shal I telle þe what ben þe lettyngis þat lettith the boke of þe
hert or of þe conscience for to be opynned.

¶ Seven lettyngis I fynde þat lettith þe boke of þe conscience for to   45
be opynned,[12] the wiche lettyngis ben callid seven claspis, of the wiche
Seynt John spekith in þe Apocalips, seying thus: *Dignus est Agnus qui
occisus est aperire librum et solvere septem signacula eius.*[13] 'The lambe'
he seith, 'the wiche was killid, is most worthi for to opyn þe boke of
oure hertis, and for to undo þe seven claspis of it.' ¶ This lambe is   50
Crist Jhesu, the wiche dyede upon the crosse for us. This lambe it is
þat only may opyn oure boke of oure hert of conscience. Therfor it was
þat Machabee, þat worthi duke, prayed for us to þe blissid lambe, þat
oure boke myght be opynned bi him, whan he seyde: *Adaperiat* (fol. 63r)
Dominus cor vestrum.[14] 'Oure lord' he seyde, 'þat blissid lambe, opyn   55
youre hertis and undo þe seven claspis of youre conscience.'[15]

¶ He undoth the seven claspis of oure conscience whan he puttith
away þe seven impedimentis þe wiche lettith us to opyn oure boke
for to rede þerin. ¶ Tho seven impedimentis ben þees: defens of oure
synnes, excusacioun of hem, considering raþer to þe defautes of oþer   60
þan oure owne, hiding of oure trespacis, quenching of oure good
purpose, communicacioun with synneris for þe more mayntenaunce of
oure owne synnes, and to moche occupacioun in wordly þingis.

¶ Loo, sister, þes ben þe seven impedimentis þe wiche mow wel be
callid þe seven claspis þat closid þe boke of oure consciences. ¶ Yif þe   65

boke of þe conscience shuld be openyd, þees impedimentis must nedis be avoydid.

¶ I may likne þees seven impedimentis to þe seven claspis þe wiche were schewid to Seynt John in the Apocalips, where I rede þus:[a][16] 'Whan þe angel had openyd þe first claspe, Seynt John herd a voyce as a gret þundir, and þan he sygh a whyght hors and a man sittyng above beryng in his honde a boghe.'[17] In þis revelacioun, sister, þou mayst (fol. 63v) know what þe first impediment betokeneth, þe wiche is clepyd defendyng of synne. Ther ben somme in religioun þat whan þei ben reprovid for here defautes, þei put oute here voyce as a gret þundir bi grucching and criyng, gretly tempestid in here hertis, and so defend here defautes.

¶ What doth such on more, trowest þou? Trewly, she berith in here hond a bogh and castith oute arowis. Be þis bogh þou shalt undirstonde a cursid tonge þat schetith oute arowys of scharp reprovys or cursyngis, and of wordis of despite. ¶ But be the whight hors, þat al such syttyn upon, þou shalt undirstonde a chast body, for þe more party al such þat presumen of here chast lyvyng ben more violente in spekyng, more scharp in rebewkyng, whan þei ben blamed for here defautes, þan oþer. Why is þat? Trewly, for þei hane moche vayn glorie of here chast lyvyng, wenyng þat it is inow for to be chast in body withoute mekenes.[18]

¶ The secunde impediment of þe openyng of þe conscience, þe wiche is clepid excusacioun of synne, is betokened be þe openyng of the secunde claspe, where I rede þus: 'Whan þe (fol. 64r) angel had openyd the secunde claspe, Seynt John sygh a rede hors and[b] a man sittyng above, þe wiche had power for to take away þe pees in erthe, and þat eche man shuld sle oþer.'[19] Bi þis rede hors þou shalt undirstonde a myschevous synner.

¶ Whan synneris eche of hem excuseth oþer, and wil hide eche oþer defautes, and put his defautes upon oþer and not upon himself, eche of hem sleth oþer and puttith away þe trew pees of hert þat shuld be in trew blamyng of defautes. ¶ Thus dede Adam in paradise, he put his defaute upon Eve, and Eve put hir defaute upon þe serpente. Thus eche of hem sleyn oþer, wenyng þerby for to be excusid. ¶ Therfor it was þat Davyth prayde to oure lord thus, and seyde: *Non declines cor meum in verba malicie, ad excusandas excusaciones in peccatis.*[20] 'Lord'

---

[a] 'apoc vi' is added in the margin of M in the scribal hand.
[b] 'and' added here in black as superscript, with ^. The rest of the quotation is given in red.

he seide, 'bow not down myn hert in wordis of malice for to excuse me
be excusacioun in synne.'

¶ The þrid impedyment is in considering raþer þe defautes of oþer þan   105
of hemself, þe wiche is betokened be þe openyng of þe þrid claspe in þe
Apocalips, where I rede þus: 'Whan þe angel had openyd þe þrid claspe,
(fol. 64v) Seynt John sygh a blak hors and on syttyng above, havyng in
his honde a balaunce.'²¹ Bi this blak hors þou shalt undirstonde also
a synner.²² And bi þe balaunce þou shalt undirstonde þe weyghyng of   110
oure goode dedys and oure badde. ¶ Al þo, þerfor, þat weyghyn more
hevyer oþer mennys defautes þan here owen, þei han a balaunce of gyle;
such weyghyn hevyer here owne good dedis and lightly oþer. 'Þis is
abominable balaunce in þe sight of God', as Salomon seyth.²³

Many sovereynes faryn þus, they loke ful narow to here subjettis   115
defautes and live hemself ful wantounely. ¶ Therfor, as collectoures
don of taxis in a cite, þey taxe pore puple and go hemself quyte, for
pore folk pay for hem. ¶ Right so don somme sovereynes in religioun:²⁴
þei make hard constituciouns and statutes of þe ordre, and put grete
charges upon þe nekkes of here subjettis, and þei hemself wil not kepe   120
þe lest poynte. ¶ I may also likne such to jaylouris þat han prisoneris to
kepe: þey hemself live largely and delicatly of þe prisoneris goodes, and
to þe prisoneris þei yiven right a streyte liflode. Also, þei come never
amonges here prisoneris (fol. 65r) but for to se wheþer they ben fast
tayde or none. ¶ In þe same wise done summe sovereynes of religioun: 125
þey lyven delicatly of þe goodes þe wiche ben yiven to þe cloystreris in
here owne chamber, and þei kepe streitely þe cloystreris with a scarse
liflode, and þough þei sey we ben al sistren and bretherin, yit here
disches ben not like.²⁵ ¶ Suche sovereynes comen never to þe cloyster
or sild, but yif it be certeyn dayes whan þei wil come to chapitre for to 130
tygh hem shorter and for to yive streyter preceptis.²⁶

¶ This is a fals balaunce. Good sister, do not þou þus yif þou be a
sovereyne, or whan þat ever þou be a sovereyne. ¶ God forbed it þat
alle were suche.²⁷

¶ The fourth impediment þat shettith þe boke of þe conscience is   135
hidyng of oure synnes, þe wiche is þe condicioun of ypocrites þat hiden
here synnes in confessioun, lest here name be lesse set by. Þis betokenyth
þe openyng of þe fourth claspe in the Apocalips, where I rede thus:
'Whan þe angel had openyd the fourth claspe, Seynt John sygh a pale
hors, and one sittyng above whos name was deth, and helle folowid   140
hym.'²⁸ Bi þis pale hors þou shalt undirstonde ypocrites that þorogh
doblenes of here hertes þei make here (fol. 65v) face rewly for to be hold
holy. The name of him þat sitte above þis pale hors is deth. What is þis to

mene? Trewly, noþing ellis but þe fende, þat brought deth into þis world,
sitteþ above suche ypocrites hertis, and þe more þei schew outeward
payntid holynes, the sikirer sitte he upon here hertis.[29] ¶ But yit, it is
a dredful word wich folowith, þat helle sewith him. Suche on, I drede,
helle folowith, for to receyve him but yif he or she amende.

¶ The fifte impediment is quenching of a good purpose conceyvid in
þe hert. Ther ben many þat han a purpose for to do wel, but þei ben
so withdraw with custome of synne þat þei strangle here good purpose
and bringen it to none effecte, and þat betokenyth wel be þe opynnyng
of þe fifte claspe in þe Apocalips, where I rede þus: 'Whan þe angel
had openyd þe fifte claspe, Seynt John sygh undir an awgter þe soules
of dede bodyes þat werin killid, and þe soules cryed with a gret voyce
and saide: "Lord God, venge oure blode."'[30] Bi þis awgter whereon
is offred sacrifice, þou shalt undirstonde the hert wherein is offred al
sacrifice of good (fol. 66r) lyvyng to God.[31] And be þo soules of dede
bodies þe wich cried venjaunce, þou shalt undirstonde goode devoute
purposes strangled in þe hert þat come never to effecte, þe wiche crien
venjaunce of God ayenst hem þat promitten and make a vow to lyve
religiously, and kepe it not. ¶ Therfor, sister, kepe þi first devout purpose
of religious lyvyng and quenche it not, as Seynt Poule seith: *Spiritum
nolite extinguere*.[32] 'Quenche not' he seith, 'þi religious purpose.'

¶ The sixte impediment is communicacoun with synners in
mayntenyng of oure owne synnes. This impediment lettyn many
on þat þei mow not opyn here boke of here conscience for to rede
þerin, folowyng on every side wordly synneris bi whos ensample and
communicacioun þei ben draw bakward. And þis is betokenyd in þe
openyng of þe sixte claspe in þe Apocalips, where I rede þus: 'Whan þe
angel had openyd þe sixte claspe, Seynt John sygh a gret ertheqwave,
and þe sonne was blak as an hery sak, and þe mone was rede as blode,
and sterrys fylle oute of hevyn.'[33]

Bi þis gret erthequave þou shalt undirstonde þe multitude of synneris,
for þe (fol. 66v) nombre of synneris is gretter þan þe nombre of devout
lyveris.[34] ¶ Bi þe blak sonne þou shalt undirstonde gret prelatis and
governouris of holy chirche fro whom þe light of kunnyng and þe hete
of charite is passid.[35] ¶ Bi þe red mone þou shalt undirstonde lesse
prelates as curatis of chirches, sovereynes of religioun, and such oþer
mene governoures of holy chirche, þe wiche ben tornid al to blode, þat
is, al to synful lyvyng.[36] ¶ Bi þe sterris þou shalt undirstonde subjettis
þat ben fal down to þe erth of wordly covetise. ¶ The ensample of such,
sister, lettith ofte tymes þat þe boke of oure hertis or consciences may
not be openyd.

¶ Þe seventhe impediment of þe conscience is to moche occupacioun   185
with wordly þingis. Suche mow not be occupied aboute here conscience
whom þe love of the world hath so tayde. Wordly occupaciouns makyn
so gret a noyse in þe hert, þat þe soule may not here what is red in þe
conscience, þogh it were openyd. And þis is betokened in openyng of
þis seventhe claspe in þe Apocalips, where I rede þus: 'Whan þe angel   190
had openyd þe seventhe claspe, þere was silence in heven, (fol. 67r) as it
had be half an houre.'37 Bi þis heven þou shalt undirstonde conscience.
And bi silens þou shalt undirstonde pees and rest of conscience, þe
wiche pees and rest is but schort amonges hem þat ben occupied to
moche aboute wordly bisynes. And þat may be undirstonde be þe half   195
houre þat I speke of, whan I seyde, unnethe half an houre in heven
is silens, þat is, in þe conscience of hem þat ben gretly bisied aboute
wordly þinges is litel rest.

¶ Lo, sister, þo seven impedimentis þat withdrawyn þe knowleche of
þe conscience, after þe moral undirstonding of þe seven revelaciouns in   200
þe Apocalips, I have declarid to þe schortly.38 Þerfor, I pray þe, whan
þou redist or herist þe blames of sovereynes, þe wiche ben in maner
schortly touched with fere and drede in þe þrid impediment, and in
þe sixte, þer þat I speke of prelatis and sovereynes of religioun, have
compassioun and pite upon hem, and þenke with compassioun þat þi   205
synne and myn is cause of here mysliving and of myn, as Job seith:
*Propter peccata populi regnare facit ypocritas.*39 'For þe synnes of þe puple'
he seith, 'Oure lord suffreth ypocrites for to regne in mysselevyng.'40

¶ Now (fol. 67v) þan, sister, yif þou wilt rede wel in the boke of þi
conscience, put away þees seven claspis, þat is, defende not þi synnes,   210
excuse þe not þerof, considere not oþer mennys defautes more þan þine
owne, hide not þi synnes bi ypocrisie, quenche not þi good purpose þat
is conceyvid in þin hert, folow not þe evil ensample of þe multitude
of synneris, and be not to moche occupied aboute wordly þingis.41 ¶
Pray, þerfor, to þe lambe, Jhesu Crist, wich dighed upon þe crosse, þat   215
he wolde vowchesaf, be his grace, opyn þi boke and undo þe sevenþe
claspes þerof, so þat þou mow rede withoute any impediment clerly
þerin; that, at þe day of jugement, whan alle bokis shulle be openyd,
þou myght in þe same boke offre to oure lord þe cause of þi savacioun,
and so to receyve of hym a sentence diffynytif,42 ever to be in blisse   220
withouten ende. Amen.43

¶ Sethe I have thus tolde þe how þou shuldist opyn þin hert as a boke,
I shal now teche þe how þou shalt open it as a dore for to receyve a
worthi gest.

225 ¶ This maner of openyng of þe hert is love, and þis gest þat knokkith
at þe dore is Crist Jhesu.⁴⁴ ¶ Thou openyst (fol. 68r) wel þe dore of þin
hert to hym, whan þou receyvist him bi love. ¶ So desired þe blissed
duke Machabee, as I rede in holy writ, þat þe hertis of hem to whom
he wrot to shuld be openyd be love, whan he prayed þus: *Adaperiat*
230 *Dominus cor vestrum in lege sua.*⁴⁵ 'Oure lord' he seyth, 'opyn [y]oureᵃ
hertis in his lagh.' What is þis lagh but love? ¶ Thou openyst wel þin
hert in his lagh, whan þou suffrest God and alle resonable creatures to
entre into þin hert be love and charite.

¶ First, how þou shalt opyn þin herte for to receyve God, I shal telle
235 þe, and after þat, how þou shalt opyn þin hert to al resonable creatures.
¶ Thou openyst þin hert to God whan þou clensist þi conscience by
confessioun and repente þe for þi myslyvyng. Thou openyst also þin
herte to God whan þou dost good dedis. ¶ He þat wold come in, sister,
stondith at þi dore and knokkith, and seith thus: *Ego sto ad ostium, et*
240 *pulso: si quis mihi apperuerit, intrabo ad illum.*⁴⁶ 'I stonde at þe dore'
seyth oure lord, 'and knokke. Hosoever wil opyn þe dore to me, I shal
entre into him.'

¶ In to maner of wises oure lord knokkiþ at þe dore of oure hertis
for to be lete in: oþer- (fol. 68v) while he knokkith with his hond, and
245 oþerwhile, with a rodde. ¶ He knokkith with his honde, whan he
maketh þe to have mynde of his gracious benefices and yiftes.⁴⁷ First,
how he made þe of nought, and how he rawsommyd þe whan þou
were in þe devylis daunger, with his precious blode; and how he hathe
graciously preservyd þe fro diverse periles, bothe bodily and gostly;
250 and how, yif þou contynue in vertu, he wil rewarde þe in þe blisse of
heven. ¶ Also, he knokkith at þe dore of þin hert with a rodde, whan
he chastiseth þe with diverse siknes and oþer maner of bodily disesis for
þe offenses þat þou hast don ayenst him. ¶ He wil not have þe damnyd,
but he wil have þe purgyd in þis lif.⁴⁸

255 ¶ Therfor, gode sister, for þe love of Jhesu, lete in Jhesu, and suffre
not Jhesu stond withoute. Opyn þin herte to him be prayer, and þi
mowthe be confessioun, thi spirit be love, and þin armes þat he myght
clippe þe.⁴⁹ Thou must undo to him whan he cometh al þi dores; lete
no dore be schet ayenst him, he is þi good frende. He lefte no dore
260 unopenyd to þe.

¶ Was not his side openyd for þe upon þe crosse? Þat he suffred for
to be don because he wolde þou had- (fol. 69r) dist fre entre to his hert,
in þe wiche wounde þou mayst be hid from al þi gostly enemyes. ¶

ᵃ M reads 'þoure' erroneously.

Openyd he not also alle his oþer yates of his woundes? The lest of hem
alle is moche inow for to receyve alle þe synneris in þe world to mercy.   265
Be not streyt þan in openyng of þi smale yates to him þat so grete yates
hath openyd for þe.[50]

¶ I seyde also, þou must opyn þe dore of þin hert to alle resonable
creatures, þat is, to al mankynde. ¶ Al þo þat schettyn þe dore of here
hert, wiche schewyn rather cruelte þan mercy to her evencristen, Seynt   270
Jhon reprovith and seith þus: *Qui viderit fratrem suum necessitatem
habere, et clauserit viscera sua ab eo: quomodo caritas Dei manet in illo?*[51]
'He þat sieth his broþer' he seith, 'at nede, and schetteth his dores of
mercy ayenst him, how may þe charite of God dwelle in such on?'
Sith it so is þan þat defaute of charite closith þe dore of pite to oure   275
evencristen, þan þe gracious havyng of charite is cause þat oure hertis
ben openyd merciably to oure evencristen. ¶ Lete in þerfor, bi pite, into
þin hert as þe prophete seith, al maner of puple: *Egenos vagosque induc in
domum tuam.*[52] 'Bringe in' he seith, 'into þe hous of þin hert al maner of
nedy puple and wayfaring puple by pite (fol. 69v) and compassioun.'   280
¶ Now, peraventure, þou wilt axe me a questioun and sey wheþer alle
maner of puple shuld be receyvid into oure hert or not, seþe it so is þat
Salomon seith: *Non omnem hominem inducas in domum tuam.*[53] 'Lede
not into þin hous of þin hert alle maner of puple.' How may þis be,
þou wondrist and merveylist, þat Ysaye biddith indifferently al maner   285
of puple to be lad in, and Salomon forbedith it? What menyth þis? I
shal telle þe. ¶ Thou shalt receyve into þin hert al maner of puple be
pite and charite, and few be pryvy communicacioun and familiarite.[54]
¶ Here hertis ben to commune þat receyvyn indifferently al maner of
puple to prive familiarite.   290

¶ Five þingis þer ben þat þe nedith for to know yif þou wilt chese þe a
familier frende. ¶ On is þat he be discrete, anoþer is þat he be good of
lyvyng, þe þrid is þat he be not wratheful, þe fourth is þat he be not
prowde, and þe fifthe is þat he be trew.

As for þe first, chese such on þat is discrete and be ware of þe frenchip   295
of folis. Þe frenchip of a foole durith but a litel while. Why? Trewly, for
it lakkith þe vertu of discrecioun, a litel þing may greve hym. Chese no
suche frendes but such þat for vertu lovyn þe and in (fol. 70r) vertu wil
norschyn þe, and never fayle of þis love fro þe, nouþer in prosperite ne
in adversite, as longe as þou lovyst God. Suche a discrete frende chese   300
unto þe.[55]

¶ The secunde þing þat shuld cause þe to chese a frende shulde be
goodnesse. Evyl folk con no frendes be. ¶ There may no trew frenschip

be but only amonges good folk.[56] How may he be a trew frend þat
305 lovyth no good lyvyng in effecte? For, as Seynt Austyn seith: 'He may
not trewly love a creature þat lovyth not him þat made creatures.'[57]
Therfor, amonges good folk þe bonde of love is most myghtiest.

¶ The þrid þing þat shuld cause þe to chese a frende is þat such on
be not wrathfulle, þe wiche shuld be chose. For Salomon seith: *Noli*
310 *esse amicus homini iracundo.*[58] 'Be not familier' he seith, 'to a man þat
is wrathfulle.' ¶ A wrathful man is like to a tre ful of þornys þe wiche
prikkith hem þat touchith it, and þerfor, þogh such shuld be lovyd
in affeccioun of charite, yit shuld þei not be receyvid into familiarite,
lest þei make þe such as þei be, for wrath is a contagious evylle. ¶ The
315 frenschip and love of mylde folk shuld be desired and chosyn, for it is
pesa- (fol. 70v) ble and it durith al tyme.

¶ The fourthe þing þat shuld cause þe to chese a frende is þat suche
on be not prowde. ¶ A prowde body can be no felaw for he wold evyr
be a lord, and such on can no frende be. ¶ In frenschip only evenhede
320 is considered: þat þe more be felaw with þe lesse; to þis love a prowde
body is not able, but raþer to strif and debate, as Salomon seith: *Ubi*
fuerit superbia, ibi et contumelia.[59] 'Ther þat pride is' he seith, 'þere is
strif and debate.'

¶ The fifte þing þat shuld cause þe for to chese a frende is þat such
325 on be trew and faythfulle. The trewth ligth in continuaunce of love in
al tyme, as wel in prosperite as in adversite, as holy writ seyth: *Omni*
tempore diligit qui semel amicus est.[60] 'He lovyth ever' he seyth, 'þat
is ones trewly made a frende.' ¶ To suche a frende may be mad no
comparisoun. ¶ The worthynes of gold and silver may in no wise be
330 likned to þe feith of such a frende.[61] Whi, trowist þou? Trewly, for such
a frende helpith more, boþe be lif and be dethe, þan doth any gold or
silver. A trew frende kepith, be his prayer and gostly bisynes, þe lif of
anoþer þat he (fol. 71r) lovith better þan doth gold or silver;[62] for so
seith Salomon: *Amicus fidelis medicamentum vite.*[63] 'A trew frende' he
335 seith, 'is a medicyne to good lyvyng bi his prayeris.'[64]

¶ Lo, sister, þus shalt þou opyn þin hert, bothe to God and to þin
evencristen.[a][65]

---

[a] Double horizontal flourishes indicate the book end.

Capitulum quartum. How and in what wise a^a mynche shuld
stabil here herte to God be þe yifte of strengthe.^{b1}

Off^c stabilnes of hert, Seynt Poule seithe in þis wise: *Optimum est
gracia stabiliri cor.*² 'The best þing þat is' he seithe, 'for to stabil þe hert
is grace.' First þou shalt undirstonde þat stabilnes is noþing ellis but a
stabil and a perseveraunte purpose of goodnes in þe soule. ¶ But because
the undirstonding of þe soule is ofte tymes blynded, þerfor I shal   5
declare to þe certeyn articles of þe feyth for to stabil þin undirstonding,
þat it be not variaunt ne be lad with every wynde of newe doctrines.
For alle suche þat ben so variaunt, Salomon reprovith whan he seith
þus: *Qui cito credit levis est corde.*³ 'It comyth' he seith, 'of þe vice of
lightnes, for (fol. 71v) to yive fayth sodeynly withoute avisement to every   10
ne<w>e^d doctrine.'⁴
   ¶ This is ayenst hem þat passyn away fro þe trew undirstonding
of doctouris and yif fayth to sone⁵ to þe spirit of errour and so, in
as moche as in hem is, þei defoule here trew feyth. ¶ And þerfor,
yif oure undirstondyng shuld be wel stabilid, it must nedes have þe   15
yifte of gostly [strength],^e for þat is necessarie to þe stabilyng of oure
undirstondyng^f in oure feyth.

¶ Because feith is nedful to þe stabelyng of oure undirstonding, þerfor,
be þe grace of God, sumwhat I shal sey of þe twelve articles of þe
feyth,⁶ after þe nombre of þe twelve apostelis þat made þe twelve   20
articles, þe wiche ben þe twelve fundamentis of þe high cite þat is very
Jerusalem.⁷ ¶ The first article of þe feith longith to God þe fadir, and
þe sexe wich folowyn to God þe sone. The first of þo sexe longith to

---

^a There is a small manuscript hole between 'a' and 'mynche', and between 'be'
and 'þe' in the following line.
^b Triple horizontal flourishes fill the remainder of the line.
^c M has an illuminated capital 'O' covering a two-line square. C leaves a two-
line-square space for such a capital.
^d A black smudge over the word makes the 'w' illegible.
^e M reads 'treuthe' here erroneously. Emended reading supplied from L and T.
^f There is a small manuscript hole between 'un-' and '-dirstondyng'.

his godhed, and five þat sewith, to his manhode; and þe five last, to
25 þe holy gost.

¶ The first article is: *Credo in Deum, patrem omnipotentem, creatorem*
celi et terre. 'I beleve in God fader, (fol. 72r) almyghty maker of heven
and of erthe.' Þou belevyst in God whan þou puttist al þi feithe in God
and lovyst him enterly in beleve.[8] There ben many þat beleve God, þe
30 wiche belevyn not in God. They beleve God þat belevyn þo þinges
trew þe wiche ben seyde of God, and they belevyn in God þat perfytly
loven him with hert and desire. Many han þe first beleve but few han
þe last beleve. It is more for to beleve in God þan for to beleve God.
Þou must also beleve him, with love, fadir almyghty.

35 ¶ The knyttyng of þes to[9] wordes is a swete conjunccioun of þe
fayth, for to þe fadir of mercy lakkith never goode wille, namly to his
childrin, and like as to þe fader of mercy fayleth never good wille, right
so to þe same fadir þat is almyghty, fayleth no powere for to fulfille
þat god wille. ¶ Ther ben many þat supposyn þei shul defayle or dygh
40 for hunger yif þei servyd God in poverte. Al such belevyn not fully in
almyghty God þe fader.

¶ Thou must also beleve þat almyghti God, þe fader in trinite, is
maker of heven and of erthe, þat is of visible þingis and of unvisible
þinges, for al visibles and unvisibles wiche ben (fol. 72v) conteyned in
45 heven and in erthe, almyghty God in trinite made of nought.[10]

¶ The secunde article whereon þe undirstonding of oure soules shuld
be stabled is þis: þat we shul beleve in Jhesu Crist his sone, only oure
lord. In Latine we sey þus: *Et in Jhesum Cristum, filium eius unicum,*
Dominum nostrum. [Þou][a] shalt undirstond þis article þus, and sey: 'I
50 beleve with love in Jhesu Crist, þat he is verry Jhesus oure savyoure,[11]
and þat he is Crist anoynted by benignite and myldenes. And also þou
shalt beleve þat Jhesu Crist is þe sone of God þe fadir, and God and
man himself. ¶ And also þou shalt beleve þat he is only oure lord.'
¶ Crist is only oure lord be creacioun and redempcioun. Ther is no
55 creature þat hathe lordschip of any oþer in þees to þinges, but only
oure lord Jhesu Crist, and þerfor he may wel be clepid and be belevyd
oure synguler lord, for þer is none suche but he.

¶ The þrid article, þe wiche is þe first þat longeth to þe manhode of
Crist, is: *Qui conceptus est de Spiritu Sancto, natus ex Maria Virgine.* That

---

[a] M reads 'Than' erroneously here. Emended reading from L and T.

is: 'I beleve with love in oure lord Crist Jhesu, þat he was conceyvyd of   60
þe holy gost and borne of oure lady (fol. 73r) Seynt Mary, sche beyng
modir and mayde.'[12]

¶ We must beleve þat þe holy gost toke of oure lady, þat blissid moder
and mayde, þe most pure þing þat was in here, and made þerof þe
blissid body of Crist. And he enspired þerin a soule, so þat anone he was   65
verry God and man, and perfite in grace, kunnyng, and blissidhode, in
þe same tyme þat he was conceyvid.[13] ¶ In his conceyvyng he wantyd
synne, and in his birthe he hurte not the pure virginite of his modir,
ne was to here cause of sorow in his birthe.

¶ The fourthe article is þis: *Passus sub Poncio Pilato, crucifixus, mortuus*   70
et sepultus. That is: 'I beleve with love in oure lord Jhesu Crist, þat he
suffred hard passioun undir þe juge þat was callid Pilate of Pownce,
crucified, ded, and beried.'

¶ Take hede wel to þis article: he suffred hard passioun under þe
juge Pilate, þat untrew creature, and was nayled to þe crosse and so   75
continuede in þat torment unto þe tyme he dide;[14] þat nowþer for þe
criyng of þe Juis ne of þe knyttes – wiche scornyd him and seyde: 'Yif
þou be kynge of Israel come downe of þe crosse'[15] – yit wold he not, in
tokene þat þou shalt not leve þe crosse of penaunce in religioun[16] for
no criyng, ne lettyng of þe fende, (fol. 73v) ne of oþer carnel frendes,   80
unto þe tyme þou dygh and departe oute of þis world.[17]

¶ Also in reprovyng of harde hertis, as Seynt Jerome seith: 'Al þe
elementes had compassioun of here makere. Þe sunne lost his light for
he myght not suffre to se þe deth of Crist, þe erthe quaked for sorow,
stones al to claterid, and þe veyle of þe temple dividid asondre and   85
gravys openyd, but we wrecchid lyveris hane no compassioun of him
for whom alone he dighed.'[18]

¶ He was also biried. ¶ O good sister, to him þat was biried for þe,
make a grave in þi soule for him by mekenes and poverte, and so hide
him within þe, þan wille he sey þat he hathe a gracious sepulcre.[19]   90
Dispise richesse, and þou shalt be riche; dispise wordly joy, and þou shalt
be glorious.[20] ¶ Loke þou birie him not nakid but wynde him in clene
sendelle. Þou wyndist him in clene sendel yif þou receyve him in a clene
pure soule.[21] ¶ Al bodies comunly ben beried for here corrupcioun. Leve
it wel, him nedith not for to be beried so, for he was uncorruptible, save   95
for þe: to teche þe for to bery þat incorruptible body in þi pure soule.

¶ The fifte article is þis: *Descendit ad inferna.* Thou must beleve þat
oure lord Crist Jhesu (fol. 74r) descendit into helle only in his soule,

for to delyvere oute of prison alle his derlinges þat were in lymbo.[22] ⸿
100 Lymbus is noþing ellis but þe porche of helle, were chosyn soules abode
þe visitacioun of oure lord for to be delyvered. ⸿ A, sister, now be we
unkynde, þat wil not folow oure lord be good lyvyng into heven, whom
oure lord sought and folowid into helle.

⸿ Þe sexte article is þis: *Tercia die resurrexit a mortuis.* 'The þrid day he
105 rose fro deth to lyve.' A, sister, [yif þou wilt axe me][a] wheþer he, þat
so arose be his owne strength so myghtly, may not now areyse bodyes
and soules fro deth to lyve graciously? Yis, trewly.

⸿ In tokene þat he was trewly risen, in flesch and blod glorified,
he aperid to his disciplis, visible and palpable openly. ⸿ This holy
110 resurrexcioun shuld be cause of þi gostly resurrexcioun: þat þi soule
shuld aryse fro deth of synne to gostly lyvyng. For as Crist rose
trewly, holy, and everlastyngly, in his body, so shuldist þou, be his
grace, arise in þi soule trewly, holy, and everlastingly. ⸿ He arose
trewly in flesch and blode, palpable and not fantastikly, as we rede
115 thus: *Surrexit Dominus vere.*[23] 'Oure lord arose trewly', and aperid to
Petre. ⸿ A (fol. 74v) fantastik and no trew resurreccioun schewyn al
ypocrites þat hane toknes of gostly lyvyng in word, in abite, and in
here aport outeward, and withinforth han quenchid þe lif of grace be
here corrup and malicious entente. ⸿ Þey han a name þat þey lyve, and
120 ben dede.[24]

⸿ Crist also arose holy in his body be integrite, in token þat þou
shuldist aryse holy bi grace in soule.[25] Many þer ben þat arisen fro
synne but not holy, for þei kepe privy synnes within hem. What profyte
is it to arise fro þe synne of lechery, and ligh stille in þe synne of pride
125 or of covetyse? ⸿ Also, I seyde þat Crist arose everlastyngly for, whan
he arose fro deth to lif, he myght never afterward dygh.[26] Right so
shuldist þou do, whan þou art onys arise fro deth of synne, digh no
more þerin.

⸿ Lo, sister, þis[b] trew, hole, and everlasting arising of þi soule
130 answerith to þe trew, hole, and everlastyng resurreccioun of Crist.

⸿ The seventhe article is þis: *Ascendit in celum, sedet ad dexteram Dei,*
patris omnipotentis, inde venturus est iudicare vivos et mortuos. Thou must

---

[a] Editorial addition. The sentence does not make sense as it stands in M and
other Middle English MSS.
[b] An emended reading from L and T. M reads 'þis is trew', which is less
coherent.

beleve bi love in oure lord Jhesu Crist: 'þat he ascendid into heven and
sitte even with þe fadir almyghty (fol. 75r) on his right side, and fro
þennes he shal come for to deme bothe þe quyke and þe dede.' ¶ Ther   135
þat oure lord Crist Jhesu is assendid it is ful nedful þat we ascende, for
þer þe hede is, þe body must folow.

¶ The syttyng on his faderis right side is noþing ellis but þat he is
evyn with his fadir in godhede. ¶ But now, peraventure, þou woldist
wite why it is seyde raþer þat he sitteþ þan he stondith on his faderis   140
right side. I shal telle þe. While he was here in erthe, al his lif was but
laboure of stondyng because he suffrid passioun, but now he restith in
godhede and manhode togedre aftir his laboure. ¶ Right so, yif þou
suffre here for Crist, þou shalt rest þere with Crist on his right side
with savyd soules.   145

¶ Therfor, sister, eschew not þe laboures of þin ordre be þe wiche þou
shalt have suche an holy sessioun þere. ¶ Be þis, þou mayst undirstonde
þat Crist Jhesu, þi spouse, hathe chose a sessioun þer for[a] him and for
þe. For him, in þat he is lik to þe fadir in godhede; for þe, in þat þou
laborist lowly in þe observaunces of religioun.[27]   150

He shal also come fro þennys to deme þe quyke and þe dede; þat is,
bothe good and evyl, or ellis suche þat in his comyng to þe dome ben
in body (fol. 75v) founde alive, þe wiche shule digh in a moment and
aftirward arise, and also, oþer þat weryn dede afore.

¶ O, how dredful he shal apere to hem þat shul be damned, whos   155
voyce shal seme to suche a þoundir clap, and how mekely he shal apere
to hem þat shul be savyde.[28] ¶ Upon þis, þou mayst axe me a questioun
and sey wheþer þe chere of Crist in his dome shal be chaungeiable or
none, þat is, wheþer it shal apere outeward to damnyd soules on, and
to savyd soules anoþer? ¶ To þis, I may answere thus. ¶ The dredful   160
chere or þe gladsume chere of Crist in his dome shal apere inwardly in
the consciencis of hem þat shal be demyd, and not outward, for every
man as he fyndith himself gylty in conscience or ungilti, so shal him
seme þat þe chere of Crist shal apere to him. ¶ Outewardly, þe chere
of Crist is unchaungeable, for with esynes he shal deme every man to   165
payne or to joy.

The first article þat longith to þe holy gost, and þe eyghteth in nombre,
is þis: *Credo in Spiritum Sanctum, sanctam ecclesiam catholicam.* 'I beleve
in þe holy gost and in holy chirche.' We must with love beleve in þe

---

[a] 'þer for' is written erroneously as one word. A dividing line between the two
parts of the word has been added to indicate the mistake.

170 holy gost, (fol. 76r) that he hathe ordeyned sacramentes in holy chirche for to foryif synnes.[29]

¶ Five articles longeth to þe holy gost. ¶ Thre longen to þe tyme of þis present lif, and twayn to þe tyme þat is to come.

¶ The first is: *Sanctam ecclesiam catholicam.* For to beleve in 'holy 175 chirche', þou shalt beleve þat þe holy gost is almyghty God and bi him holy chirche is halowyd. Þis is þe first article þat longeth to þe holy gost.

¶ The secunde article and þe nynthe in nombre, is: *Sanctorum communionem.* That is, for to beleve 'communyng of seyntes.' ¶ To þe holy gost also longith communyng of seyntes, þat is, onhed of membris 180 in þe body of holy chirche, for he o[n]eth[a] and knettith trew soules togedres as membris to þe body, in love and charite.[30]

¶ The þrid article and þe tenthe in nombre, is: *Remissionem peccatorum.* For to beleve 'foryifnes of synnes.' ¶ To þe holy gost longeth foryifnes of synnes.

185 ¶ Thou must beleve þat synnes ben foryive in holy chirche bi bapteme, bi penaunce and oþer sacramentis, and also bi indulgences.[31] ¶ Therfor, sister, it is a gret token þat þou hast þe holy gost, þe wiche foryiveth synnes, yif þou foryive þe trespaces of oþer þat is don to þe. ¶ Seth þe (fol. 76v) holy gost haþe yive þe mercy, denyghe no mercy to oþer.

190 ¶ The fourthe article and þe elevenyth in nombre, is: *Carnis resurreccionem.* That is, for to beleve 'þe risyng of oure bodies at þe day of dome.' ¶ Be not to tendir þerfor upon þi body, þat for a litel disposicioun to siknes þou leve not þe observaunces of þi religioun undone. Þenke yif þou continue mekly al tymes in þi religious laboure, þi body 195 shal be glorified, be it now never so weyke.[32]

¶ The fifte article and þe twelþe in nombre, is þis: *Vitam eternam.* That is, we must beleve 'everlasting lif.' ¶ Thou must beleve þat lif everlastyng is mede and reward to hem þat hane servyd oure lord Jhesu mekly and lowly.

200 ¶ Lo, sister, þes ben þe twelve articles upon þe wiche þe undirstonding of þi soule shuld be stabilid.[33]

¶ Now, seth I have told þe how þin undirstonding may be made stable, I shal now telle þe what þingis þo ben þat maketh oure beleve stedfast.

---

[a] M reads 'oueth' erroneously. Emended reading supplied from L, C and T.

¶ The first þing þat stabilith oure beleve ben m<era>cles.ᵃ The
meracles of oure beleve began upon Abel and his yiftes þat he offred to   205
God. ¶ Holy writ seyth: 'Oure Lord beheld Abel and his yiftes.'³⁴ What
þis behelding was I shal telle þe. ¶ Abel bele- (fol. 77r) ved myghtily in
oure lord, þat he wold accept his yiftes þe wiche he offred to him. And
in tokene þat he acceptid hem, he sent from heven a fyre and consumyd
his oblacioun. ¶ The feyth of Abel was cause of þis. ¶ So may I sey   210
of Noe and of Abraham, þe wiche were faithful and rightwis in here
lyvyng.³⁵ And at þe last he made his apostelis schew meracles bi feyth,
not only be here live, but also after here dethe, in confirmacioun of
oure feith.³⁶

¶ The secunde þing þat confermyth oure feith is þe witnes of holy   215
seyntes, as Seynt John þe Baptiste, þat come for to bere witnes of
oure feith. For we rede of him þus: *Venit ut testimonium perhiberet
de lumine.*³⁷ 'He come for to bere witnes of þe light of oure feith.' ¶
What witnes, trowist þou, bare martires of oure feith, whan we rede of
hem þus: *Testimonio fidei probati sunt?*³⁸ 'In witnes of þe feith þei were   220
founde wel provid.'³⁹

¶ The þrid þing þat confermyth oure feith ben revelaciouns of
prophetes of Ysay and Jeremy, and such oþer, þe wiche wrote oure beleve
as touching þe godhede and þe incarnacioun of Crist. And þei hemself
leved be þe same fayth þat we han now.   225

¶ The fourth þing þat confermyth oure feyth is þe gret comfort þat
Cristen (fol. 77v) men hane in here hertes of here beleve. The wiche
beleve, þer þat it is kept and hold devoutly, it purgeth hertis fro synne,
as Seynt Petir seith in his epistelis: *Fide mundans corda eorum.*⁴⁰ Þat is:
'oure lord clensith þe hertis of loveris bi trew bileve.' Ther is no secte   230
undir sonne þat han so gret comfort of here feyth as Cristen men han of
here feith. Therfor, al þo þat wil not bough to þe Cristen feith þe sunner
for such strong prevys, þey shul not be excusable afore God at þe day
of dome.⁴¹

¶ Thus moche of þe strengthe of Cristen feith I have declarid to þe   235
for to make þi soule stable.⁴²

¶ Neverþeles, foure þingis þer ben þat letteth þe stable undirstondinge
of þe soule. On is foly. Þou shalt never fynde stabilnes in a fole for every
fole is unstable, as Salomon seith: *Stultus ut luna mutatur.*⁴³ 'A fole' he
seith, 'is chaungeable as þe mone', fro þought to þought, fro o desire   240
to anoþer, fro o synne to anoþer synne.

ᵃ A black smudge renders part of word illegible.

¶ The secunde þing þat lettith oure stabilnes of soule is synne. The
hert of every grevous synner is as a balle. For right as a balle in commune
play is tossid fro on to anoþer, so þe hert of a grevous synner is tossid
245   fro o synne to anoþer in þe hondes of oure gostly enemyes. Of (fol. 78r)
such unstabilnes causid be synne spekith Jeremy, þe prophete, and seyth
þus: *Peccatum peccavit Jerusalem, ideo instabilis facta est.*[44] 'Jerusalem' he
seith, 'mannys soule,[45] hath synned and þerfor it is unstable.'

¶ The þrid þing þat lettith oure stabilnes of soule is unpacience. ¶
250   Every unpacient soule is unstable.[46] ¶ I may likne a pacient soule to a
schip þat is governyd by a sterne, as Salomon seith: *Qui paciens est multa
gubernatur sapiencia.*[47] 'He þat is pacient is governyd' he seith, 'with
moche wisdome.' For right as a schip for defaute of governaunce of a
styrne, is wynde dryve hider and þedir, and at þe last is hurte at summe
255   rokke; right so, an unpacient hert, in þe see of tribulaciouns for defaute
of paciens, is hurt and al forbrokyn be wrathe and indignacioun.

¶ The fourth þing þat lettith þe stabilnes of þe soule is lakkyng of
drede. Drede maketh a soule stable. ¶ I may likne drede to an ankir
for, whan schipmen han lost here ankir, þei make moche sorow.[48] ¶ So
260   shuld we be sory whan we han lost drede, for a schip withoute ankir
is an hert withoute drede.

¶ Ther ben to maner of dredes: a good drede and an evyl drede. The
good drede (fol. 78v) makith þe soule stabil, and þe evyl drede makith
it unstable. This evyl drede may be callid wordly drede and mannys
265   drede. ¶ He hathe drede of þe world þat raþer chesith for to synne þan
for to lese his possessioun of wordly good. ¶ Also he hathe drede of
man þat raþer chesith for to synne þan for to be[a] hurte bodily or lese
his bodily lyf.

¶ Al riche covetouse folk han wordly drede, þe wiche dredyn almost
270   al þing þat þei see. Yif þei se pore folk, þei wene þei ben þevis; yif þei
se riche folk þei wene þei ben ravenoures.[49] Such on is never siker ne
restful. Also wordly drede han al suche þa[t][b] ben to sore aferd for to
be seke in body, and þerfor, þei ben þe more tendre to hemself, and
norsche to moche þe flessh. They wene þat travayle, disciplines, and
275   duresse of religioun, shuld sle hem.[50] Yif þou wilt, þerfor, make þi soule
stable, avoyde suche fals dredis, and drede God only and þi sovereynes
for God. For Seynt Jerome seyth: 'The grettest sikirnes for to make þe
soule stable is only drede of God.'[51]

Yif þer come a þought to þe and sey þou shalt be dede, be not aferd

---

[a]   'be' is added as superscript with ^.
[b]   M mistakenly reads 'þan' here. Emended reading supplied from L, C and T.

but answere þerto and sey: 'Therfore I come into þis world for to go   280
hennys ayen.' It is but a foly for to drede to moche þat þou mayst not
eschew. (fol. 79r) Þer may none eschape it; þou art not the first, ne
peraventure, þou shalt not be þe last. ¶ Ferþermore, þi þought may
sey to þe þat þou shalt dygh whiles þou art yonge. Answere ayen þus,
and sey: 'It is best for to dygh whan me liketh best for to lyve, lest my   285
lyvyng displese God yif I lyve lenger.'[52] ¶ Thus avoyde þi þoughtes þat
wolde bringe þe to unstablenes.

¶ Overmore, þou shalt undirstond þat stabilnes of bodily abidyng in o
place causith gret stabilnes in soule, so þat þou may live plesauntly to
God in þe same place.[53] For as Seynt Bernard seyth: 'It is unpossible   290
a man or a womman to stable trewly here soule in o þing, þat cannot
first stable his body in o place perseverauntly.'[54]
   ¶ They ben gretly distempered in soule þat seketh rest in diverse
places. I may likne hem to such þat flen here owne schadew: ever þei
fyndeth hem like and oþerwhile wors because of here removyng, for,   295
whan þei come þer, þey wene for to fynde stabilnes, and þan þey ben
more distempered in soule þan þei were bifore. As a sike man þat hath
an axesse, þe wiche for distemperaunces of gret heetes, may not ligh
stil in his bedde: now he lyth on þe to side, now on þe tother, now he
þrowith (fol. 79v) oute his feet, now his armes. ¶ Thus don ofte tymes   300
such removeris and renneris aboute,[55] þat mow not longe rest in þe
silence of þe cloyster and in commune prayers of þe quere, but þey
stirt about from on office to anoþer, and whan þe belle ringith to þe
houres,[56] þan þey begynne first to occupie hem in here offices.
   ¶ Such mow also be likned to briddes in a cage, þat ever skippin   305
aboute fro perche to perche and kunne have no rest, and oþerwhile
þey han here billes at þe wyndow of here cage. ¶ Such þer ben, I trow,
þat stirten aboute fro dore to dore, fro grate to grate, and fro whele to
whele, for to here tithingis and for to be hold in ydelle daliaunce. Al
þo ben ful sike, I dar wel say.[57]   310

¶ Of þees þingis, sister, be wel ware, for as it is rehersid in þe begynnyng
of þis chapitre: *Optimum est gracia stabiliri cor.*[58] 'The best þing[a] for to
stable þe hert in is grace', be þe spirit of gostly strengthe. That grace
God graunte us. Amen.[59]

---

[a]   M reads 'þing is'.

Capitulum quintum. How and in what wise a mynche shuld
yif here hert to God be þe yifte of counseyle.

The[a] fifthe chapitre techeth for to yive oure hertis like as (fol. 80r)
Salomon seith in commendacioun of rightwis soules, þus: *Justus cor
suum tradet ad vigilandum diliculo ad Dominum, qui fecit illum.*[1] 'The
rightwisman' he seith, 'shal yive his hert for to wake to oure lord in þe
5   erly mornyng.'[2]

    ¶ Therfor, first þou must know to whom þou shuldist yive þin hert. ¶
And how it should be yif. ¶ Wete right wel, sister, þe nedith þe yifte of
counseyle for to know how it shuld be yive. ¶ Pray, þerfor, first to oure
lord, þe holy gost, þat he wold vouchesaf to graunte þe his gracious yifte
10 of counseyle, and þan þou shalt not erre in þi yiving.[3]
    ¶ To oure lord God it must be yiven: þi maker, þi reformer, and þi
lover; to him allone þat may fulfille þin hert, it shuld be yiven. For he
it is þat axith it as for his special porcioun, seying þus: *Prebe michi cor
tuum.*[4] 'Dowter' he seith, 'yive me þin herte.'[5] Sister, yif þin hert be
15 for to selle, þou haste founde a blissid marchaunt, þe wiche bought it
ful dere with moche price of his blode. ¶ And love was þe cause whi
þat he wolde schede so moche blode: only for to bygh þin hert. Yif þou
haddist a clothe þat were dere bought,[6] woldist þou not kepe it wel
more better þan anoþer cloth, because it cost þe moche? Moche more
20 þan, me þinkith, þou (fol. 80v) shuldist kepe wel þin hert, þe wiche was
bought right dere.
    ¶ Also, yif þin hert be for to be put away, þou shalt fynde þis blissid
marchaunt, Jhesu Crist, a violent revour. For þogh þou wilt lese his
good, leve it wel he wil not lese it for he bought it right preciously. ¶
25 Now, þou woldist wite how oure lord revyth from us oure herte. I shal
telle þe. ¶ He punchith us with diverse siknes and oþer tribulaciouns,
as a lord þat setteþ his dettoure in prisoun til he have his good ayen,
and so with schorging and þretnyng he maketh us glad for to yive him

---

his good ayen, þat we ben aboute for to benyme him, þe wich is oure
hert.[7]   30
Yif þin hert also be for to be yiven, to a better myght it never be
yiven þan to Crist Jhesu, þi love. Þou shalt not lese þeron, y warne þe
wel, yif þou yeve it to him, for he wil yive to þe his hert þerfore, for o
good turne axith anoþer. A! Now is þis a blissid chaunge.

 ¶ Neverþeles, he suffreth þe to kepe bothe þin hert and his, for in   35
þin brest he hath made his tresoure hucche. ¶ Therfor, yive to him
trewly þin hert be feith and meditacioun, and he wil yive þe þe kay of
his hert, for to come in whan þou wilt, þat is perfyt love. With þe key
of love þou mayst opyn his side (fol. 81r) and þere for to hide þe ayenst
þe pursuet of al þi gostly enemyes.[8] The nedeth not to be aferd of no   40
gostly enemy yif þou be in so siker ward.[9]

 ¶ Now, how þou shalt yive þin hert, I shal telle [þe].[a] ¶ Thou must yive
it to him bi perfite obedience.[10]
 ¶ As sone as þou art bounde to religioun, þer comyth on to þe in
Godis name, and axith of þe lownes of obediens unto þi deth.[11] ¶ Sche,   45
þis þat axith of þe obedience, is þi sovereyne. ¶ For, like as Crist Jhesu,
dyghing on þe crosse, offred to his fadir of heven his spirit, whan he
seyde: 'Into þine hondes, fadir, I yeld my spirit';[12] so shuldist þou do,
beyng dede to þe world in þe crosse of religioun, yeld þi wyl bi trewþe
into þe hondes of þi sovereyne in Godis name.   50
 ¶ Be wel ware, þerfor, yif þou have onys þus yoldyn þi wil into
þin sovereynes hondes, presume never to take it ayen, for þan þou
dost gret þefte and robbery. ¶ As ofte as þou strivist and wil not do
þe wil of þi sovereyne but raþer þin owne presumpt[u]es[b] wil, so ofte
þou arte noted for a cruel þef in þe sight of God. ¶ And þat may wel   55
be undirstonde be þe wordis of Ysay, þe prophete, were he saith in
persone of such presumptuose cloystreris þus: *Quare ieiunavimus, et non
aspexisti; humiliavimus animas nostras, et nescisti?*[13] (fol. 81v) As þogh
such wilful cloystreris myght sey to oure lord þus: ¶ 'Why hane we
fastid and þou wilt not considere it, and why hane we lowyd oure soules   60
and þou wilt not know it? Is not oure fastyng plesaunt and likyng to
þe, and oure lownesse in religioun also?' To þis oure lord answerith and
seith: 'No', and I shal telle þe why. *Quia in die ieiunii vestri invenitur
voluntas vestra.*[14] 'For in þe day of þi fastyng and þi lownesse þou hast

---

[a] Emended reading from L and T.
[b] M reads 'presumptnes' erroneously.

65 had þi presumptuose wille.' As þogh he seyde þus: þi fastyng and þi
lownes liketh me not because þou kepist þi propir wille.

  ⁋ It shuld fare be a cloystrer þat is undir obedience as it doth with
a man þat is schave under a barbouris ᵃ rasoure. ⁋ Thou wost wel: he
þat sit under a rasoure he suffreth þe barbour to turne his hede, now
70 on þe to side, now on þe toþer syde, now he suffreth him to opyn his
mowth, and now for to lefte up his chyn, and al þis he suffreth lest he
be hurte of þe rasoure yif he stroglid.

  ⁋ Right so shuld a cloystrer do. As longe as þou art under þe
governaunce of þi sovereyn in religioun, so longe þou art under þe
75 hondes of a barboure for to schave away þi synnes. Be not rebel ne
stryve not under þe rasour of cor- (fol. 82r) reccioun, but suffre it
lowly be it never so scharp, lest þou be hurt grevously in soule be þin
unobedience.

  ⁋ And right as a man sit most stille under þe hondes of a rewde
80 barbour, so must þou do under þe governaunce of a boystous sovereyne,
for holy writ seith: *Non tantum bonis et modestis, set et[iam]* ᵇ *discolis.*¹⁵
'Not only to esy sovereynes a mynche shuld obeye, but also to rewde
and boustous sovereynes.' ¹⁶

  ⁋ Therfor, sister, kepe wel þis vertu of obediens, and yive þin hert trewly
85 to God, and never chalange ayen þat þou hast onys yiven to here, for þe
lesse þou have of þine owne spirit, þe more þou hast of Godis spirit.

  But now, peraventure, þou woldist wete what þis gray mornyng
shuld be þat I spake of in þe begynnyng of þis chapitre, wher I seyde
a rightwis man shuld yive his hert for to wake to oure lord in þe erly
90 mornyng. I shal tel þe. Þou wakist wel in yiving of þin hert to oure lord
in þe erly mornyng, whan þou wakist aboute þi soule in getyng and
wynnyng of new vertues be þe erly mornyng of þe entre of religioun.
It is to þe a new day, entre of religioun, for al þis is new to þe whan
þou comyst to religioun.¹⁷
95 ⁋ Thus have I declared to þe how þou shalt yive þin hert to God.ᶜ
(fol. 82v)

ᵃ Emended from 'barboure is' to clarify genitive usage.
ᵇ Emended in accordance with the Middle English translation and the readings
of L, C and Vulgate. L reads '*set eciam*'. C and Vulgate read '*sed etiam*'. T reads
'*sed et*'.
ᶜ Double decorated horizontal line indicating the book end.

Capitulum sextum. How and in what wise a mynche shuld lifte up here hert to God be þe yifte of undirstonding.

The[a] yifte of undirstonding is nedful to þe for to lyfte up þin hert to God.[1] ¶ But how þou shalt lifte up þin hert to God and whi, I shal telle þe.[2]

First þyn hert must be lifte up be holy meditaciouns. ¶ In commendacioun of such þat han here hert lift up to God bi holy meditaciouns, Salomon seith þus: *Cogitacio eorum apud Altissimum.*[3] 'The þoughtes of devought folk ben in almyghty God' he seith.

¶ Thus, sister, set þi þought and meditacioun in almyghti God and in his preceptis, as Salomon seith in anoþer place: *Habe cogitatum tuum in preceptis Altissimi, et in mandatis eius assiduus esto.*[4] 'Have þi þought in þe biddingis of God', and because it is not inow only for to þenke on his biddingis but yif workyng sewe, þerfor it folowith: *In mandatis eius assiduus esto.* 'Be also besy in his preceptis.' Thou þenkest wel and art besy in þe preceptis of God, whan þou art not avoyded from hem by none encumberaunce of dedly synne. This is þat I sayde afore in þe first prologe: *Levemus corda nostra cum manibus ad Deum.*[5] 'Lifte we up oure hertis with oure workis to God.'

Now, peraventure, þou axist me and seyst: (fol. 83r) 'What and I þenk on my synnes, is my þought not lift up to God?' I shal telle þe: þer is to maner of þenkyng of synnes. On is with repentaunce for to sorow hem, anoþer is with lustes for to delite in hem.[6] Whan þou þenkist on þi synnes with repentaunces, þin hert is lift up wel inow, but whan þou þenkist on þi synnes with delectacioun, þin hert is depressid down. ¶ Deleccioun in suche wise is synne, and synne holdith þe lower place of þe soule, and þin hert þan is þere þat synne is. But whan þou þenkist upon synne repentauntly, þan is þin hert above synne.

¶ Thus þan, devout meditacioun, be it in God or in repentaunce of synne, is on of þo þat liftith up þe hert to God and is preysing to him,

---

[a] An illuminated capital 'T' covering a two-line square. The same is found in T. C leaves a two-line-square space for the same.

30   as Davith seith: *Cogitacio hominis confitebitur tibi, et reliquie cogitacionis diem festum agent tibi.*[7] 'The þought of a resonable man' he seith, 'in his synnes, is preising to oure lord, and þe remenaunt or þe relef of þo þoughtes shul make an holy fest to God.' ¶ Thou shalt undirstonde a man in þis place, a resonable creature and not unresonable. The þought

35   of a resonable creature on his synnes shal be praysing to God, for it is discrete and honeste.[8]

    ¶ Ne- (fol. 83v) verþeles, þe þought of a lusty synner on his synnes is not so, but it is occupied abought þe filth of flesshly lustis. ¶ Such þenken not as men but as hogges, and þerfor þeyre þoughtes ben no

40   preysyng to God, but raþer blasfemy.[9] The holy gost withdrawith him fro such þoughtes; yif he shuld be had ayen, al such lusti þoughtes must be put away.

    ¶ Therfor, sister, put away such lusty þoughtes and lifte up þin hert in holy þoughtes, þat it falle not fro þe hert to þe flessh, but þat it abyde

45   in þe hert with þe herte, þat þou mow sey as Davyth seyth: *Meditatus sum cum corde meo.*[10] 'I have beþought me with myn hert.'

    ¶ Many þer ben þat þenken in here hert, but few with here hert. He þenkith in his hert þat þenkith vanite.[11] ¶ Also, he þat þenkith and considerith not what he þenkith, he þenkith not with his hert, for his

50   hert rennyth where it wille. Þer is noþing so flittyng as is þe hert.[12]

    ¶ Sister, þenke þou, þerfor, with þin hert, wisly and discretly, þat it flit not aboute. Than may I sey of þe þat þi þought on God, or ellis on þi synnes repentauntly, is prai- (fol. 84r) syng to God. And þe remenaunt or þe relef of þo þoughtes makyn a gret fest to God in thy soule. What

55   ben þo releves þe wiche ben left? Trewly, pees and joy of hert. Thes ben þe releves of þat blissid table þat Davith spak of, [whan][a] he seyde: *Fuerunt michi lacrime mee panes die ac nocte.*[13] 'My teeres' he seith, 'han be to me loves[14] both day and nyght.'

    ¶ Whan þou repentist þe in þi þought of þi synnes þou spredist þe

60   table of penaunce,[15] and al þat leveþ of þat fest ben joy and pees of hert. ¶ This is a blissid table and þees ben blissid releves, and i-blissid ben al þo þat etyn of þe bred of suche teris. ¶ Lifte up, sister, þin hert, and cast up al þin þought in God, and he wil norssche þe with þees loves of teeris, þat þi soule may be fed with hem.[16]

65   ¶ The secunde þing þat lifteþ up þe hert is hope, as Salomon seith: *Qui sperat in Domino sublevabitur.*[17] 'He þat hopith in God' he seith, 'shal be lifte up.' Wel may hope be callid a lifter up of þe hert, for as

---

[a]   M reads 'whom' here. Emended reading from L and T.

þe prophete seith: *Qui ambulat in tenebris, et non est lumen ei, speret in nomine Domini, et in[n]itatur*^a *super Dominum suum.*[18] 'He þat goth in derkenes and hath no light, he shuld hope in þe name of Jhesu and   70
(fol. 84v) festyne him upon þe mercy of God, and þan he shal be lift up.'
Thou gost in derkenes whan þou lyvist in tribulacioun and adversites of þis world, but hope bringeth in light of comfort, yif þou hope in þe name of Jhesu and knytest þe to his mercy.[19] Therfor, yif þou wilt have light in derknes, hope in oure lord and so, be mene of þat hope, cleve   75
fast to his mercy, and he wil yif þe mercy.[20]

¶ The þrid þing þat liftith up þe hert is desire, for a clene desire is hungir of þe hert; desire maketh þe hert hungry for to have oure lord.
Oure lord is þe mete of a clene hert, but þis mete is aboven us. Þeþer þan, must we lifte up oure hert, þer þat oure mete is.   80

¶ Such an hungry hert in desire oure lord likneth to an egle, as he seith to Job: *Nunquid ad preceptum tuum elevabitur aquila, et in arduis ponet nidum suum? In petris manet, in preruptis silicibus, inde contemplatur escam suam.*[21] 'Wheþer an egle' he seith to Job, 'shal be lifte up at þi biddyng, and make his nest in high places? In stonys   85
he restith and in brokyn flyntes, fro þennys he lokith aftir his mete.'
¶ Bi þis egle, þe wiche is a solitarie brid and fleeth high and seeth sotelly, þou shalt undirstonde a solitarie contem- (fol. 85r) platif soule þat is departid fro þe love of wordly conversacioun,[22] in whos flight is undirstond contemplacioun, and in whos sight is undirstonde sotil   90
undirstonding.[23]

¶ Oure lord axid of Job þus, weþer such a contemplatif soule shal be lift up at his biddyng, as þough he seyde: Nay Job, not at þi biddyng but at my biddyng, for þe grace of contemplacioun comyth fro me. And whan it is so lift up bi contemplacioun at my biddyng,   95
þan shal she make here nest be desire in hygh hevenly þingis, and rest in stones, þat is, in þe ensample of holy seyntes, þe wich ben sad in lyvyng as stones.[24] And also she shal dwelle in brokyn flyntes, þat is, in contemplacioun of holy angelis, þe wiche ben callid brokyn flyntes, for o party of angelis in heven fille down and were brokyn,   100
wich was lucifer with his company, and o party abode stille.[25] ¶ They ben hoole be qualite of here maite,[26] and þei ben brokyn be quantite of here nombre.[27]

¶ And fro þennis, such contemplatif soules lokyn after here mete,

---

^a M reads 'inuitatur'. Emended in the light of the other ME manuscripts, Vulgate, and Latin *De doctrina*.

105   Crist Jhesu, þe wiche is mete of angelis and of clene soulis. This mete
       þou shuldist desire and hungir, sister.[28]

       ¶ The fourth þing þat liftith up þe hert is a right entente. ¶ Suche a right
       entente had Seynt Poule whan he seyde: *Nostra conversacio* (fol. 85v) *in
       celis est.*[29] 'The entente' he seith, 'of oure conversacioun is in heven', for
110   he enformed al his entencioun for to wyn heven blisse. Þus shuldist þou
       do, sister: lete þe entent of þi lyvyng be for to wyn blisse.[30]
       ¶ Thes ben þe foure lifteris up of þi soule: on is meditacioun; anoþer
       is hope; þe þrid, desire, and þe fourth, a blissid entente.[31]

       ¶ Now shal I telle þe why þou shalt lift up þin hert.
115   ¶ Foure causes þer ben why þou shalt lift up þin hert.[32] ¶ The first
       is for þin owne contrey is in heven above, and kendly every resonable
       creature hath a special love to his owne contrey. ¶ This world, þou mayst
       wel wite, is not þe contrey of þin hert, for þerin þou mayst fynde no
       rest but rather troble. In hevenly þingis, I hope þou fyndest grete rest.
120   Be þat þou mayst wel know þat heven is a contrey and þin heritage,
       kynges douter, and a place of gostly rest.[33] ¶ To þat contrey shuldist
       þou ofte lifte up þin hert.
       ¶ The secunde cause whi þou shuldist lifte up þin hert is because þi
       tresoure is þer and þi tresorer. Every good dede þat þou doyst, yif þou
125   do it for Godis love, þou puttist it in Cristes hucch and þou makist
       oure lord þi tresorer. Than be reson, 'þer þi tresor is, þer shuld þin
       (fol. 86r) hert be': *Ubi est thesaurus tuus, ibi et cor tuum erit.*[34] Make
       non þi tresorer but God, for he wil at þe last yilde manyfold double
       for a litelle.[35]
130   ¶ The þrid cause whi þin hert shuld be lift up is because þou hast an
       hevenly fadir, kynges douter. Hevenly children acorden wel to hane an
       hevenly fadir, and þerfor þou seyst whan þou prayist: *Pater noster, qui
       es in celis.*[36] In heven he is þat þo praiist to. ¶ Therfor, sister, to such an
       hevenly fadir be an hevenly douter,[37] sekyng, saveryng, spekyng, and
135   desiring hevenly þingis.
       ¶ The fourthe cause whi þou shuldist lift up þin hert is because al
       perfeccioun and fulnes of al good is above us in heven, where þou shalt
       fynde al þe good þat þou desirist. ¶ There þou shalt fynde helþe withoute
       siknes, yowthe withoute eldnes, fulfilling withoute lothnes, fredom
140   withoute servile subjeccioun, fayrenes withoute deformite, undedlynes
       withoute passibilite, abundaunce withoute necessite, pees withoute
       trobel, sikirnes withoute drede, knowleche withoute ignoraunce, glorie
       withoute confusioun, and joy withoute sorow.[38]

¶ Lo, sister, to þis place, þer al þees joyes ben in, þou shuldist lifte
up þin hert, and sey as Seint Austyn (fol. 86v) seith þus: 'O hevenly   145
Jerusalem, hous of ful gret clernes, he receyve me into þe, þat made
bothe þe and me.'[39] Amen.[a]

---

[a]   Double horizontal flourishes take up the remainder of line.

Capitulum septimum. **How and in what wise a mynche shuld cutte here hert be þe yifte of wisdom.**

Because[a] I have declarid þe how þou shuldist lift up þin hert and whi, now shal I in þis last chapitre, be þe grace of God and þi devoute prayeris, telle þe how þou shalt cut þin hert, as þe prophete seith: *Sindite corda vestra.*[1] 'Cuttith youre hertis' he seith. ¶ The cuttyng of þe hert þat verry contricioun causith I shal not declare in þis place, for þat cuttyng is know wel inow of every clene hert. ¶ Only of þe cuttyng þat longith to þe yifte of wisdom, after my first purpose, I shal declare unto þe be þe help of God.

¶ Thin hert is cut wel be þe yifte of wisdom whan it is discevered from al maner of carnalite, and whan it is so purgid from al maner unlefful affecciouns and made pure. Þan it saverith Crist Jhesu, and al þing þat is not Crist Jhesu, or not for Crist Jhesu, is unsavery to such an hert.[2] In fugure hereof, Salomon seith of Nathan the prophete þus: *Surrexit Nathan, propheta quasi adeps separatus a carne.*[3] 'Nathan' he seith, 'þe prophete, (fol. 87r) is risen as fatnes departid from þe flesch.' Be þis word 'Nathan', þou shalt undirstond an hert made fat be þe yifte of gostly wisdom. 'Nathan' is no more to sey but þe yifte of grace.

¶ Than þou shalt undirstonde it þus. ¶ An hert made fat be þe yifte of gostly love is departid fro þe flesch, þat is, from al maner fleschly and filthi carnel loves, from al maner unordinate and carnel affeccioun,[4] and so it is fully departid be þe knyf of gostly wisdom, þe wiche I calle gostly love, from al þe felaschippis, companyes, and maneris of fleschly loveris.[5]

¶ This is þat scharp knyf of charite þat Salomon spekith of þus: *Est enim dileccio Dei honorabilis sapiencia.*[6] 'The love of God' he seyth, 'is a worschipful wisdom.' And it is of so worschipful wisdom, þat it causith al þing to a clene soule for to savoure and be felt as þei ben. For þis word, *Sapiencia*, 'wisdom', is no more for to seye but a savery feling.

---

[a] Illuminated capital 'B' covering a two-line square. C leaves two-line-square space for the same. T gives two-line-square illuminated capital.

He hath a s[a]voury[a] felyng in his soule þat felith and savourith gostly   30
everyþing as it is,[7] þat is, synnes bitter, temporale goodis vile, and gostly
goodes, dere and precious.

⁋ Wherefore, Seynt Bernard seith þus: 'Thou hast founde playnly
gostly wisdom whan (fol. 87v) þou weylist and sorowist vertuously þi
synnes, and settist litelle by al wordly desires, and desirist with al þin hert   35
everlastyng blisse. Yif þou þus saverist gostly al þingis as þei ben, þou
hast founde pleynly gostly wisdom.'[8] Neverþeles, þou shalt undirstond
in þis place wisdom þat is take for þe knowleche of þe swetnes of God,
had, as it may be in þis lif, bi experience.[9] To þe wiche experientale
swetnes enduceth us þe prophete, whan he seith þus: *Gustate, et videte*   40
quoniam suavis est Dominus.[10] 'Tastith' he seyth, 'and seeth how swete
oure lord Jhesu is.' First he sayth 'tastith' and aftirward he seith 'seeth',
for þe tast of God bringeþ a soule to þe knowleche of God.

⁋ Why seyth he *gustate*, 'tastith'? Trewly, for what þat ever swetnes
þou have of God in þis lif, it is but a tastyng as fore þe swetnesse þat   45
þou shalt have in blisse. ⁋ Of þis tast had Seynt Austyn experience whan
he seyde to oure lord þus: 'Lord, oþerwhile þou ledist me into a gostly
unusid affeccioun þat never I knew afore, into a merveylous swetnes I
not what. And yif þat swetnes were complete in me, I not[b] what þing it
myght be, but yif it were heven blisse. And þan anone, within a schort   50
while, I fal doun into my ruy- (fol. 88r) nous and ponderous fleschly
body þat I bere aboute, and anone I am sopid up of myn old bodily
customes. Þan I wepe and weyle for I wold abyde[c] stil in þat swetnes
and I may not, and in my flesch I abide and I wold not. Over al I am
a wrecch; good lord, se to me.'[11]   55

Take hede, sister, to þe wordis of Seynt Austyn. He sayth þat he
was lad into a gostly unusid affeccioun, into a merveilous swetnes he
not what, and he was anone þrow doun into his corruptible body fro
þat blissid swetnes. This unusid gostly affeccioun may wel be likned to
extatik love.[12]   60

⁋ Extatik love is such a þing þat it alieneth þe soule fer fro here
mynde unto þe love of þat þing þe wich it loveth. This extatik love
oþerwhile is take for good love, as Seynt Denyse seyth, þat clepith
extatik love such love, þe wich bringeth a lover al hool into þe use and
profite of þat þing þat is lovyd. With such love oure lord loved us, yiving   65
himself al hool into oure use and profite.[13]

---

[a]   M reads 'sovoury' here erroneously.
[b]   M reads 'not ef what'.
[c]   A small hole in the vellum between these two words.

¶ Extatik love also is take in anoþer wise.[14] It is take oþerwhile for alienacioun of þe mynde be love, as ben al such fleschly loveris þat wexin mad for love, þe wiche is caused of overpassyng desire of þe hert (fol. 88v) and of afflìccioun of þoughtes set upon fleschly love. Al such love is reproveable, and it shuld be a gret confusioun to ony creature so to be aliened for such wrecchid love.

¶ Neverþeles, for to prove gostly extatik love be þe condicioun of fleschly extatik love, þou shalt undirstonde þat þer ben many toknes to know whan extatik fleschly love worchith in amourous fleschly creatures. Amonge al, seven þer ben þe wiche I shal declare to þe, þat apperin most in such amorous loveris.[15]

The first tokene is of such amorous fleschly loveris, þat þey coveyte moche and speke litel, and also spekyn here wordis unparfitly. Right so, gostly, al spiritual loveris spekyn many sentensis of love þat cannot be undirstonde unneth of ony but of such þat ben gostly loveris, as þei ben.

¶ Cristes spouse, in þe Boke of Love, rehersith many such unperfit and defectif speches. Amonge al þis is on: *Dilectus meus michi, et ego illi*.[16] That is: 'my love to me and I to him.' But þes wordis were more openly declared, it semyth right unperfit, for she tellith not what here love is to here, ne what she is to here love. But like as Aaron spake for Moyses,[17] so must gostly resoun speke for oure affeccioun, and fulfille þe (fol. 89r) unperfit wordis of a loving soule and sey þus: 'My love to me is able, and bi his mercy I am made to him able.'[18] Or þus: 'Like as my love to me is mede and reward of al my labouris, of al my sorowis, and of al my fatigaciouns, right so, I am þe reste of his laboure, sorowis, and fatigaciouns, wiche he suffred for to rawnsom me. And, þerfor, like as he suffre dissesis and tribulaciouns for to have me, so shal I gladly suffre dissesis and tribulaciouns for to have him.'[19] ¶ Or þus: 'My love to me lived and for me died, so schal I live to him and for him shal I digh.'[20]

¶ Lo, sister, þus þou mayst know how many declaraciouns a loving soule nedith for to have, in expounnyng of here defectif and unperfit wordis, and yit many mo þan here ben expounnyd. ¶ Neverþeles, it nedith never for to[a] be expounnyd to a lovyng soule, for þe schortest sentence of love is opyn inow to here.[21]

¶ The secunde tokne of an extatik lover is drinesse of al þe bodily lymes, and why þat is, I shal telle þe: because þe hert is sore applied with alle

---

[a] M reads 'never a de for to'.

þe bodily myghtes to þat þing þat it lovith. Right so to oure gostly
purpose, a lovyng soule, for þe gret passyng love þat sche hath to God,   105
is in maner dried up fro þe humorys of fleschly lust. (fol. 89v)

¶ Of þis I fynde a figure in holy writ, where I rede þus, þat oure
Lord departid þe Rede See be the blast of a gret brennyng wynde.[22]
By þis Rede See is undirstonde fleschly lust. ¶ It may wel be callid a
see, for what þat ever it pretendith of any maner fantastik swetnes, it   110
endith in bitternes. ¶ It is also callid 'rede', for it restith in þe vicious
lyvyng of þe flesch. ¶ Bi þis gret wynde and brennyng, is undirstonde a
fervent love in God þat drieth up in maner carnel affecciouns in a clene
lovyng soule. With such a gret brennyng wynde, þe holy apostelys on
Whitsonday were brennyd bi love, and dried up fro carnel affecciouns.[23]   115
¶ Bi þat wynde þou shalt undirstonde þe holy gost.

¶ Such, þat ben so dried up in maner fro fleschly lustes, ben to þe
fende right feerful.[24]

¶ The þrid token of an extatik love is holownesse of þe eyghen. Al
extatik loveris hane holow eyghen, for þe eyghen folowyn þe spirit,   120
drawyng togedres into o place where þey supposyn þat love is most
fervent.

¶ Right so, þe inward eyghen of a lovyng soule, undirstonding and
affeccioun, ben so[n]ke[a] depe into þe hert, for al þat such a soule seketh
is withinforth; al þat it lovyth is inward and not ou- (fol. 90r) teward.[25]   125
¶ Also, þe gostly eyghen of such a lovyng soule is so[n]ke in for to se
þat noþing be in þe conscience þat shuld displese[b] here lover. ¶ They ben
also so[n]k yn for to espy þe privy goyng and comyng of her lover.

¶ Oure lord comyth whan he touchith þe soule with love and
devocioun þat sche felt never afore. He goth whan he withdrawith   130
devocioun because a soule shuld know her infirmyte, þenkyng þat
such devocioun comyth only of God and not of hereself. ¶ Also, he
withdrawith such special devocioun þat, whan it comyth ayen, it myght
be kept more deyntously.[26]

¶ Many þer ben þat han such special devocioun and swetnes of love,   135
but ofte tymes þey puttyn it away from hem bi ydil occupaciouns,
ydel wordis, and oþer scurrilite, þe wich besemyth hem not, and ofte
tymes receyven outeward solaace unmoderatly. And also þey seyn her
servise of God withoute hertly attencioun,[27] and schewyn to moche

---

[a]   M erroneously reads 'souke'. 'Sonke' is supported by the Latin *De doctrina* and
by the other ME manucripts.
[b]   'l' is inserted as superscript with ^.

140   tendirnes to here carnel frendes. ¶ Al þees þinges puttyn away special
gostly swetnes.²⁸

¶ The fourth token of an extatik lover is drynes of eyghen and lakkyng
of teeris, but yif it come of somme special þought or remembraunce
of love.ᵃ In so moche þat nouþer deth (fol. 90v) of frendes ne losse of
145   temporal goodes mow in no wise make such extatik loveris for to wepe,
but it be only somme special mynde of þe love þat þei love.
¶ Right so farith a lovyng soule. Sche is not sory for no maner of
þing ne cannot wepe, but yif it be for þat þing þat sche lovith. ¶ Lo,
sister, yif þou love God tendirly, þou makist non ynly sorow for noþing,
150   but it be for þat þing þat longith to love of oure lord Jhesu, for þogh al
þing were lost fro þe, þi principale lover, Jhesu, is saf to þe.
¶ Too þinges þer ben þat maketh loveris for to wepe: on is songes of
love, anoþer is þe feere þat þei han lest þei lese here lover. ¶ As for þe
first, a lover þat is fer fro his love syngeth songes of love in mynde of his
155   lover.²⁹ ¶ So, sister, must þou do. In as moche as þi love is fer fro þe, þou
must in þis lif, synge songes of love. ¶ Songes of love I calle þe songes
of holy chirche. ¶ Such songes þou must synge devoutly in mynde of þi
lover, meltyng in swetnes of devocioun. Such a lover was Seynt Austyn,
whan he seyde þus in his confessioun: 'I wept plentevously in ympnis
160   and songes swetly sownyng in þe voice of holy chirche.'³⁰ Thus do þou,
sister, in mynde of þi lover.
¶ Somme þer ben þat syngyn in holy chirche as a belle rin- (fol. 91r)
gith in the wynde: more for praisyng of here fayre voice þan for any
special love to God. What don þei but fillyn þe eeris of þe puple wiþ
165   noyse?³¹ And wel may suche syngyng be callid noyse, for al þat sownyth
not in þe eeris of oure lord bi devocioun is but noyse. ¶ Good sister,
fille not only þe eeris of oþer, but specialy with devocioun þe eeris
of him þat biddith þe þus: *Sonet vox tua in auribus meis.*³² 'Synge so'
seith oure lord in þe Boke of Love, 'þat þi voyce may devoutly sowne
170   in myn eeris.'³³
¶ I wote wel syngyng sterith þe puple to devocioun, but yit þou
shuldist hane such devocioun in songes of holy chirch þat it sownyth
raþer in Godis eere þan in mannys eere. Therfore, whan þou shalt
synge, synge as Seynt Poule seyth: *Psallas spiritu, psallas et mente.*³⁴
175   'Synge in þi spirit and synge in þi soule.' Þou syngest wel in þi spirit,
þat is in þi gostly strengthe, whan þou syngest with devout melody of

---

ᵃ M reads 'dryness of ~~his~~ eyghen … remembraunce of ~~his~~ love.' These deletions
are done in red.

þi bodily voyce. Thou syngest wel in þi soule, whan þou syngest saverly
in gostly undirstonding of þi soule.³⁵

⁋ The secunde þing þat maketh a lover to wepe his feere þat he hath
for to lese his lover.³⁶ So wept Davith and Jonathas whan þei shuld   180
departe asondir, but (fol. 91v) yit Davith wept moche more for he lovyd
more.³⁷ ⁋ Right so, drede of separacioun þe wich is a maner of deth,
maketh a devout lover for to wepe.³⁸

⁋ The fifte token of an extatik lover is an unordinat pous. ⁋ Every
amorous lover hath ouþer to slak a pous or to swift a pous, after dyvers   185
apprehensio[n]sᵃ þat he haþe of his lover. ⁋ A slak pous he hath whan he
is in doute of here whom he lovyth. He hathe also a swift pous whan
he hopith for to have here whom he lovyth. Thus it farith in a lovyng
soule. The pous of a lovyng soule his affeccioun,³⁹ þe wiche is swift
whan a soule hoopith to have him þat sche lovith. Such apprehensioun   190
of love had Davith, whan he seyde: *Cor meum et caro mea exultaverunt
in Deum vivum.*⁴⁰ 'Myn hert' he seyde, 'and my flesch han gret joy
in God.' Bi þe hert, þou shalt undirstonde 'þought', and by þe flesch,
'affeccioun'. His þought and his affeccioun joyed so moche in God for
love, þat it skippid oute gostly from itself into God.   195

⁋ Also, þe pous of gostly affeccioun in an extatik lover goth slakly
whan a soule considerith here synnes and þe perile of gostly deth,
perceyvyng how oþer, more myghtier, more strenger in vertu, han fal in
synne. For (fol. 92r) þer sumtyme þe affeccioun of þe soule went swiftly
for love, þan it goth slakly for drede of fallyng.⁴¹   200

⁋ The sixte token of an extatik lover is whan al his þoughtes and al his
mynde is turned deply into þe hert so ferforth, þat þer may no noyse
a-dawe such a lover fro his dep þought, but only whan sche herith any
word mevid of here love.⁴² ⁋ For it is þe condicioun of an amorous
fleschly lover: speke to him of what þing þou list, but it be of his love,   205
he not what þou menist. And speke to him þe lest word þat þou canst
of his love, anone he wot what þou menyst. ⁋ Why is þis, trowist þou?
Trewly, for al his þought and entente is inwardly set upon here.
     In þe same wise, a lovyng soule þat lovith oure lord cannot undirstonde
seculer wordis, wordly tales, and wordly tithynges, for it toucheth not   210
here lover. But yif anyþing be mevid to here of Crist Jhesu, here lover,

---

ᵃ M reads 'apprehensious'. Emended reading from L. Another example of a
word where the scribe does not seem to differentiate between 'u' and 'n' (see
'sonke'/'souke' above).

or of such þing þat longith to him, sche undirstondith it quykly, for
here mynde is ful set upon him, and of him sche list to here and of no
noþer. ¶ Al þe questiouns and demawndis þat such on shal make shal
215   be of love, as Salomon seith in voyce of gostly (fol. 92v) loveris, in þe
Boke of Love, thus: *Numquid quem diligit anima mea vidistis?* [43] 'Seygh
ye not him' sche seith, 'whom my soule lovith?' It is þe maner of gostly
loveris for to heere ever and axe tithyngis of here love, Jhesu.

¶ Sory þan mow þei be þat han a dul wit to undirstonding of gostly
220   þingis, and a plyaunt wit for to undirstonde wordly þingis and wordly
tithingis. ¶ It is a verry token þat such on wantith love of God. Therfor,
sister, be not lightly wakid oute of þi lovely slep be no wordly tales, but
only whan þou herist any word or questioun of þi love, Jhesu. [44]

¶ The seventh token of an extatik lover is þat whan þe hert of such an
225   amorous fleschly lover is so tayde and festned to here þat he lovith þat,
whan þat ever he seeth anyþing þat is like to his love in here absence,
he is anone from himself in a maner of wodnes.

¶ In þe same wise, a lovyng soule, whan þat ever sche tastith, be
it never so litille, of þe excellent goodnes and swetnes of God in þis
230   lif, anone sche is from hereself, and sche begynneth to speke sche
not what. ¶ As Seynt Petir dede whan he was with oure lord in the
mownte of Thabor, and seigh him transfugured into a clernes of gret
schynyng light. [45] Anone he (fol. 93r) was from himself for joy and
seyde he nyst what, whan he seyde þus: *Domine, bonum est nos hic*
235   *esse: faciamus hic tria tabernacula, tibi unum, Moysi unum, et Helye*
unum. [46] 'Lord' he seide, 'it is best to abide here. Lete us make here
þre dwellyng places: on to þe, anoþer to Moyses, and þe þrid to
Hely.' [47] Truly, he wist not what he seyde, whan he seyde so. ¶ For,
as doctouris seyn: 'he herd how oure lord seyde afore þat he shuld
240   suffre deth in Jerusalem, and yit he seyde þat it were best to abide
þer.' [48] Be þis þou mayst undirstonde þat Petir was from himself, for
he was gostly drunke of þe swetnes of Cristes presence and þerfor, he
axid þer[a] to abide. [49] He had foryete þat tyme what Crist seyde afore,
how he shuld suffre passioun in Jerusalem.

245   ¶ Of o þing take hede. He desired no dwellyng place for himself
but for oþer, in token þat al such, þe wiche ben so gostly drunke, ben
more liberal and large to oþer in hert þan to hemself. [50] ¶ He seyde not:
'to me on' but, 'to þe on, to Moyses on, and to Hely on.' He reservid
noþing to himself, and þat was a gret charite, þe wiche sekith raþer þe

---

[a]   M reads 'þerfor'. The 'for' is deleted in red.

eese of oþer þan of itself.[51] ¶ Also, he wist not what he seyde for o þing:		250
for he[a] was so drunke in love þat he wende þe joy þe (fol. 93v) wich
he sigh, had be þe same joy þat schal be had in heven. ¶ And þat was
not so, but a liknes þerof. For þe prophete seyth: 'None eygh may se
in erth þat excellent joy in blisse, þe wiche oure lord hath ordeynid for
hem þat lovyn him.'[52] That joy þat lovyng soules shul have shal be to		255
hem an opyn clere knowyng of perfit love, and of þe goodnes of God,
and siker possessioun of everlastyng blisse.[53] To þe wiche blisse and joy
þat never shal have ende, bringe us he þat bought us on þe rode tre.[54]
AMEN.[55b]

---

[a]	A small gap follows 'for he', due to an erasure.
[b]	These capital letters are spread out to fill the remainder of the line.

Textual Commentary

Abbreviated references

The Latin *De doctrina cordis*, and Middle English *Doctrine of the Hert*

De doctrina: *De doctrina cordis*, Gerardus Leodiensis, *Speculum
                    concionatorum ad illustrandum pectora auditorum, in
                    septem libros distributum* [...] (Naples, 1607). Oxford,
                    Bodleian Library, 8° L 12 Th. BS. All references to
                    pagination and to numbers of pages are to this edition.
                    Abbreviations have been silently expanded. Spellings and
                    punctuation marks have been retained.

The Naples 1607 edition is practically identical to the first printed edition of
Paris, 1506 (Oxford, Bodleian Library, Vet. E1.f.1) which differs only in some
divisions and chapter headings from one of the earliest manuscripts of *De
doctrina*: Oxford, Bodleian Library, MS Lat. th.f.6, s. xiii (last third).

Candon, *Doctrine*: Sister M.P. Candon (ed.), '*The Doctrine of the Hert*,
                    Edited from the Manuscripts with Introduction and
                    Notes' (unpublished doctoral dissertation, Fordham
                    University, 1963).

The Bible

Douai Bible: *The Holy Bible, Douai Version Translated from the Latin
                    Vulgate (Douay, A.D. 1609; Rheims, A.D. 1582)* (London,
                    1956).

Vulgate: *Biblia sacra*, ed. by A. Colunga and L. Turrado (Madrid,
                    8th edn 1985). The numbering of the Psalms follows the
                    Vulgate numeration.

Abbreviations of the titles of biblical books follow the English abbreviations
given in *The Revised English Bible with the Apocrypha* (Oxford and Cambridge,
1989), p. x.

Principal source texts

Ancrene Wisse: _Ancrene Wisse. A Corrected Edition of the Text in Cambridge, Corpus Christi College, MS 402_, ed. by B. Millett, EETS 325 (2005).

Book for a Simple and Devout Woman: _Book for a Simple and Devout Woman_, ed. by F.N.M. Diekstra (Groningen, 1998).

The Book of Vices and Virtues: _The Book of Vices and Virtues_, ed. by W. Nelson Francis, EETS OS 217 (repr. 1998).

Desert of Religion: A. McGovern-Mouron (ed.), 'An Edition of the _Desert of Religion_ and its Theological Background' (unpublished doctoral dissertation, University of Oxford, 1996).

Hugh, _Postillae_: Ugonis de S. Charo, S. Romanae Ecclesiae tit. S. Sabinae Cardinalis primi Ordinis Praedicatorum, _Opera omnia in universum Vetus & Novum Testamentum_, 8 parts in 5 vols (Cologne, 1621).

Peraldus, _Summa de vitiis et virtutibus_: Guilielmo Peraldo, _Summae Virtutum ac Vitiorum_, 2 vols (Antwerp, 1588). Oxford, Bodleian Library, Douce P 806, 807.

Sawles Warde: _Medieval English Prose for Women: Selections from the Katherine Group and Ancrene Wisse_, ed. and tr. by B. Millett and J. Wogan-Browne (Oxford, 1990), pp. 86–109.

Speculum Vitae: William of Nassington, _Speculum vitae_, ed. by R. Hanna, 2 vols, EETS OS 331, 332 (2008).

Principal critical texts

D'Avray, _Medieval Marriage Sermons_: D.L. D'Avray, _Medieval Marriage Sermons: Mass Communication in a Culture without Print_ (Oxford, 2001).

Hendrix, _Hugo I_: Guido Hendrix, _Hugo De Sancto Caro's traktaat De doctrina Cordis. Vol. I: Handschriften, receptie, tekstgeschiedenis en authenticiteitskritiek_, Documenta Libraria 16/1 (Louvain, 1995).

Jager, *Book of the Heart*:   E. Jager, *The Book of the Heart* (Chicago, 2000).

Renevey and Whitehead (eds), *Companion*:   D. Renevey and C. Whitehead (eds), *A Companion to the Doctrine of the Hert: The Middle English Translation and its Latin and European Contexts* (Exeter, 2010).

Journals and edited series

CCCM   *Corpus christianorum, continuatio medievalis*

CCSL   *Corpus christianorum, series latina*

CSEL   *Corpus scriptorum ecclesiasticorum latinorum*

EETS   Early English Text Society; volume numbers in the Original Series are prefixed OS, those in the Extra Series are prefixed ES, those in the Supplementary Series are prefixed SS.

PL   *Patrologia latina*, ed. by J.-P. Migne 221 vols (Paris, 1842–80).

PG   *Patrologia graeca*, ed. by J.-P. Migne (Paris, 1857–76).

RTAM   *Recherches de théologie ancienne et médiévale*

SC   *Sources chrétiennes*

Additional prefatory notes

We are indebted to Guido Hendrix (Hendrix, *Hugo I*) for all references to Hugh of St Cher's *Postillae* as a potential source or analogue to passages from the *Doctrine*, and for a number of additional patristic references.

In the commentary, we have followed the policy of drawing attention to material present within the Latin *De doctrina* but omitted by the Middle English translator, when the material in question covers *one page or more* within the Latin *De doctrina*. In addition, there are a small number of occasions where, because of some point of particular interest, we have also included a comment on material present within the Latin but absent from the Middle English, where the material in question is *less* than a page.

A note is also required on our rationale for providing supplementary modern English translations of some Latin source material. We do *not* provide translations of the extracts from *De doctrina cordis* in the light of the fact that an edition of the Latin text with facing page modern English translation is planned in the future. Additionally, we do *not* provide translations of direct and indirect patristic sources owing to the fact that most such sources are readily available in modern English translation. References to these translations have been included in the bibliography. However, in order to aid ease of reading, in accordance with the policy of University of Exeter Press we have provided supplementary translations of relatively obscure Latin source texts, including Hugh of St Cher's *Postillae*, which does not exist in modern edition or translation, the *De venerabili sacramento altaris* of Pseudo-Thomas Aquinas and the Pseudo-Bernardine *Liber de modo bene vivendi ad sororem*. We give English translations of the Vulgate from the Douai Bible in those instances where the Middle English translation in the *Doctrine* is noticeably distant from the Latin Vulgate text. In addition, we have also provided supplementary translations of all the medieval French extracts for which no modern English translation exists.

All modern English translations of Latin and medieval French extracts are the work of Anne Mouron.

A note on the title

M and L give no title to the treatise. C entitles it 'Doctrina cordis'. T entitles it 'The doctrine of the harte', and refers to it again as 'the doctrine of the hert' in a closing colophon (fol. 75v).

Prologue

This English prologue to the *Doctrine* is original to the Middle English translation. It bears very little relation to the Latin prologue to the treatise, which is largely concerned with beneficial preaching and the appropriate reception of the preached word. See Mouron, '*The Doctrine of the Hert*: a Middle English Translation', in Renevey and Whitehead (eds), *Companion*, pp. 99–104. The first part of the Latin prologue as given in the Naples 1607 edition (the 'HV' prologue according to the classification proposed by Hendrix) is provided in Appendix A.

1 Ps. 93:8. 'Understand, ye senseless among the people: and, you fools, be wise at last' (*Douai Bible*).

2 Peter Lombard, *Commentaria in Psalmos*, *PL* 191, col. 868C: '[Aug. Gl. int.] Vel ita: Vos insipientes, id est nescii, intelligite, qui jam bene vivendo, estis in populo, id est in numero bonorum, et vos, stulti, id est improvidi; et si scitis, aliquando sapite.'

3 The phrase 'symple soules', which occurs repeatedly in the Middle English translator's prologue, has complex resonances. On the one hand, taking into account the aggressive opening quotation from Ps. 93:8, it can be interpreted in markedly disparaging terms: the translator minimizes the intellectual capacities of his audience in line with a consistent desire to exercise authority over his reader. The same gloss can be given to the word 'unkunnyng' which is also used a number of times in relation to the envisaged audience in the Middle English prologue. On the other hand, bearing in mind the ways in which late medieval mystical treatises such as *The Cloud of Unknowing* and Marguerite Porete's *Mirouer des simples ames* position the concepts of 'unkunnyng' and simplicity, it is possible that both adjectives may be intended to carry more positive, anti-scholastic resonances.

4 Isa. 40:2.

5 The translator indicates that he is a member of a religious order.

6 A simplified allusion to the 'four causes' that structure the scholastic Aristotelian prologue. Here, the translator appears to indicate the 'fynal cause' of his work of translation: it is 'to the worship of God principally, and to edificacioun of symple soules'. For an assessment of the four Aristotelian causes in medieval prologues, see A.J. Minnis and A.B. Scott, assist. D. Wallace, *Medieval Literary Theory and Criticism c.1100–c.1375* (Oxford, rev. edn 1991), pp. 1–11.

7 The recommendation of a 'savourly' or 'hertly redyng' is characteristic of an *affective* approach to spirituality. Very popular throughout the fifteenth century, this model, which emphasizes the use of the spiritual senses and affections in the apprehension of God, can ultimately be traced back to the writings of St Anselm and St Bernard of Clairvaux. The affective model recommended in the prologue is somewhat at odds with the more scholastic exegetical approach employed throughout the rest of the treatise.

8 1 John 2:27. Note that Vulgate reads 'unctio eius docet vos de omnibus'. The Vulgate has the 2nd person pronoun 'vos', the text has the 1st person pronoun 'nos'.

9 St Gregory the Great, *Homiliae in Evangelia*, Bk 2, Hom. 30, lines 81–2, ed. by R. Étaix, *CCSL* 141 (Turnhout, 1999), pp. 258–9: 'Per uocem ergo non instruitur, quando mens per Spiritum non ungitur.'

10 The seven gifts referred to here are the seven gifts of the Holy Spirit: wisdom, understanding, counsel, fortitude, knowledge, piety, and fear of the lord (Isa. 11:2–3). These seven gifts, intended for the sanctification of the person who receives them, are especially attributed to the Holy Ghost as a consequence of his procession from the Father and the Son through their mutual love. The last five gifts are generally associated with the active life, while the first two (understanding and wisdom), are more closely linked with contemplation.

O. Lottin writes that the seven gifts first became associated with various other listings of seven in the *De quinque septenis seu septenariis opusculum* of Hugh of St-Victor in the twelfth century, where they were harmonized with equivalent listings, such as the seven deadly sins and the seven petitions of the *Pater noster*. *Psychologie et morale aux XIIe et XIIIe siècles* (Leuven-Glembloux, 1942–60), Part III, pp. 434–56. Cited in Hendrix, *Hugo I*, pp. 338–9. In this treatise, each gift is allied systematically with a corresponding action of the heart. It should be noted that the contemporary French Dominican treatise, *La Somme le Roi* of Lorens d'Orléans, which bears some relation to *De doctrina*, contains a long central section similarly structured around the seven gifts of the Holy Spirit. For another text partly divided into an examination of the seven gifts, see William of Nassington, *Speculum vitae: A Reading Edition*, ed. by R. Hanna, 2 vols, EETS OS 331, 332 (2008). A brief account of Nassington's sources is given on pp. lxx–lxxiv. A longer account of the history of the seven gifts and other such lists is provided in an earlier edition: William of Nassington, *Speculum vitae*, ed. by J.W. Smeltz, microfilm (Ann Arbor, MI, 1977), pp. 1–18.

11 The actions of keeping the heart via the gift of piety and of opening the heart via the gift of knowledge invert the equations of the Latin treatise, in which the heart is kept or guarded through the gift of *scientiae* (knowledge), and opened through the gift of *pietatis* (piety). The Middle English text corrects itself in the repetition of the equations on p. 6, lines 32–3, but then reverts to its original inversions throughout books 2 and 3.

12 'a mynchen …'. These are the first words of the Bodleian Laud manuscript (L). It is likely that earlier folios containing the rest of the Middle English prologue were lost at some point in the manuscript's history.

Capitulum primum

1 See *The Book of Vices and Virtues*, p. 126: 'þe ȝifte of drede is þe first of alle þe ȝiftes þat casteþ out al synne of a mannes herte or a wommanes … propreliche he destroieþ þe rote of pride, and sett in his stede þe vertue of humblenesse'. *The Book of Vices and Virtues* is one of the late Middle English translations of the *Somme le Roi*. See also, *Speculum vitae*, lines 3473–510, 3600–843, respectively, pp. 118–19, 122–30.

2 1 Sam. 7:3.

3 Prov. 4:23.

4 2 Macc. 1:4. Note that Vulgate reads 'Adaperiat cor vestrum'. 'Deus' is implied. See 2 Macc. 1:2.

5 Heb. 13:9. Note that Vulgate reads 'Optimum est enim gratia stabilire cor', and that MS McClean translates 'stabilire' rather than 'stabiliri'.

6 Ecclus. 39:6. Note that Vulgate reads 'Cor suum tradet ad vigilandum

diluculo ad Dominum, qui fecit illum'. Ecclus. 39:6 omits 'justus'; 'sapiens', though, features in Ecclus. 39:1. The book of Ecclesiasticus is consistently attributed to Solomon by the Middle English translator. Its author was, in fact, Jesus, son of Sirach.

7   Lam. 3:41. Note that Vulgate reads 'Levemus corda nostra cum manibus ad Dominum'.

8   Joel 2:13.

9   Here, exceptionally, the order of 'opening' and 'keeping' is inverted. In all other lists of the actions of the heart and in the order in which they are examined in the chapters, 'keeping' the heart is placed second, 'opening' it, third.

10   Isa. 11:2–3.

11   The material from the book opening up until this point forms the last part of the prologue in *De doctrina*. The first chapter follows in *De doctrina* at this point: 'De Praeparatione cordis ad similitudinem domus praeparandae' (p. 6).

12   Isa. 28:12. Note that Vulgate reads 'Haec est requies mea. Reficite lassum'. The *Doctrine* omits the verb 'est', i.e. 'is'.

13   The image of Christ as a bloodied and exhausted fighter, seeking rest after doing battle with the devil on the cross, appears many times in medieval devotional texts. Notable examples include *Ancrene Wisse*, Part VII, *Þe Wohunge of Ure Lauerd*, and *Piers Plowman*, Passus XVIII. See R. Woolf, 'The Theme of Christ the Lover-Knight in Medieval English Literature', *Review of English Studies*, 13 (1962), 1–16; C. Innes-Parker, '*Ancrene Wisse* and *Þe Wohunge of Ure Laurerd*: The Thirteenth-Century Female Reader and the Lover-Knight', in J. Taylor and L. Smith (eds), *Women, the Book and the Godly* (London, 1995), pp. 137–47.

14   Isa. 63:1. A poetic expansion of Isaiah 63:1–7, of considerable relevance to the *Doctrine*'s extended allegory of Christ as a bloodied warrior, occurs in William Herebert's well-known lyric, 'What ys he, thys lordling, that cometh crom the vyht' (D. Gray (ed.), *A Selection of Religious Lyrics* (Oxford, 1975), no. 40). The biblical passage in question was known through its application to the post-crucifixional appearance of Christ in the liturgical readings for the Wednesday of Holy Week.

15   'O, yif angelis … werynesse?' These rhetorical and affective lines are original to the Middle English translation.

16   Matt. 25:43. Note that Vulgate reads 'Hospes eram, et non collegistis me'. The *Doctrine* uses the past tense 'fui', whereas the Vulgate has the imperfect 'eram'.

17   The trope in which the fight against sin is succeeded by domestic hospitality can be paralleled with a passage from the *Tractatus de interiori domo*, an anonymous late twelfth-century Cistercian treatise: 'Redeamus ergo

ad nos, et discutiamus conscientiam nostram. Nam sicut corpus nostrum tabernaculum dicitur, in quo militamus, sic conscientia nostra domus vocatur, in qua post militiam requiescimus.' *PL* 184, col. 507C. (Therefore let us come back to ourselves and discuss our conscience. For as our body is said to be a tent in which to serve as soldiers, thus our conscience is called a house in which we rest after military service.) See also *The Book of Vices and Virtues*, p. 126: 'Þe ȝifte of drede is þe first of alle þe ȝiftes þat casteþ out al synne of a mannes herte or a wommannes, as we han seid tofore.' A new chapter follows in *De doctrina*, p. 7: 'Primum praeparatorium domus, est Mundare'.

18 Ecclus. 1:27.

19 *De doctrina*: 'Anima enim peccata sua cognoscens, et ex cognitione eorum pertimescens inducitur ad confitendum' (p. 7). Reference untraced.

20 See Hugh, *Postillae*, II, 196va (Ps. 76:7): 'Scopabo eam in scopa terens dicit Dominus, id est prius teram et comminuam glebas per contritionem, et postea scopabo per confessionem. Notandum quod multae sunt proprietates scopae quare per scopam significatur confessio … Item loca plana purgat scopa, similiter confessio planas conscientias, non scrupulosas, in quibus semper remanent aliquae sordes.' (Rubbing away, I shall sweep it with a broom, says the Lord, that is, I shall first rub away and break up lumps of earth by contrition, and after this I shall sweep them by confession. One must note that the broom has many properties, for which reason confession is signified by the broom … Just as a broom makes a flat area clean, similarly confession cleanses smooth consciences, and not rough ones, in which some filth always remains.) For well-know vernacular analogues to this image, see *Ancrene Wisse*, Part V, lines 212–19, p. 119: 'Þe poure widewe hwen ha wule hire hus cleansin, ha gedereð al þe greaste on an heap on alre earst, ant schuueð hit ut þenne. Þrefter kimeð eft aȝein ant heapeð eft togederes þet wes ear ileauet, ant schuueð hit ut efter. Þrefter o þe smeale dust, ȝef hit dusteð swiðe, ha flaskeð weater, ant swopeð ut efter al þet oðer. Alswa schal þe schriueð him efter þe greate schuuen ut te smealre. Ȝef dust of lihte þohtes windeð to swiðe up, flaski teares on ham; ne schulen ha nawt þenne ablende þe heorte ehnen.' See also Lorens d'Orléans, *La Somme le Roi*, in which confession is figured as house sweeping: 'Tex larmes chacent le deable fors dou cuers aussi comme liaue chaude chace le chien de la cuisine. Apres la repentance doit venir la confession. Cest la bone chamberiere qui netoie lostel & giete toute lordure hors au balai de la langue si comme parole Dauid ou sautier.' London, British Library, MS Add. 28162, fol. 94ra. The psalm verse in question is Ps. 76:7, the same that the *De doctrina* author goes on to quote. See further the anonymous Middle English prose recension of Guillaume de Deguileville's *Pèlerinage de la vie humaine*, Part I. The personification of Penitence speaks: 'I am chaumberere to Grace Dieu my maistresse, I wole holde clene hire hous withoute withholdinge of any filthe. My beesme is my tunge and my palet, with which I sweepe alle filthes, and remeeve and clense: þer is nothing þerinne up ne doun, neiþer in corner ne in hole, þat al I ne wole remeeve and seeche and caste out bi hol shrifte withoute fraude and withoute outtakinge anything.' *The Pilgrimage of the Lyfe of the Manhode*, ed. by A. Henry, EETS 288 (1985), p. 30.

21 Ps. 76:7.

22 This striking image refers to the widespread medieval medical practice of bloodletting. Based upon the theories of Galen, the procedure involved removing 'excess' blood from the veins in order to balance the humours.

23 These three paragraphs abbreviate just over a page in *De doctrina*, examining the process of confession via three similitudes of cleaning and of medical expulsion.

24 Prov. 10:11.

25 L and T identify this prophet as David.

26 Ps. 50:16.

27 The gifts of nature are endowments of the body and soul; the gifts of fortune are riches and social position, and the gifts of grace are mental powers and spiritual strength. The idea of the three gifts of God is also found in Lorens d'Orléans' *La Somme le Roi*. A Middle English translation of the relevant passages can be found in *The Book of Vices and Virtues*, pp. 75–9. See also *Book for a Simple and Devout Woman*, pp. 111–12.

28 This simile for the process of confession – 'Of o þing be war: thow mayst never yif trew rekenyng in confessioun … sittyng ther in thi lordis name' – conflates two separate similes, described as the fourth and fifth similitudes for the process of confession in *De doctrina*. They are respectively: 'Item, sit praemeditata confessio tua ad similitudinem dispensatoris patris familias, qui de expensis coram domino suo comparet, suae vilicationis rationem redditurus … Item, sit et praemeditata confessio ad similitudinem Oratoris, siue Aduocati, qui antequam coram iudice compareat, rationes, et allegationes suas ordinat, et affirmat …' (pp. 9–10). For a further analogue see *The Book of Vices and Virtues*, pp. 173–4: 'Þe synful man or womman schal entre in-to here house, þat is in-to his herte … and loke all þe defautes of whiche þei schulle ȝelde acountes & answer of to God and to his bailif, þat is his schrifte-fadre, and schulle þenk also on hemself, as he þat is a-iorned to ȝelde acounte of his receiȝtes and of his dispences to-fore his lord, wher-for euery man and womman schulle biþenk hem straiteliche to-fore, and loke wel to þe stirop of his conscience þat it faile not at þe countes.'

29 The distinction here would seem to be between mortal and venial sins. In medieval and modern moral theology, mortal sins condemn a person's soul to Hell after death, unless confessed and absolved, whereas venial sins are forgivable. The distinction between types of sin originates in 1 John 5:16–17. *The*

Clensyng of Mannes Sowle explains that there are eight 'distinctiouns' of sins.
The eighth is that 'a man synneth either in venial synnes or in dedelly synnes.
Synne may be cleped venyal in thre maners. Oon is whan a man hath synned
and is sory, and in will to take and do penaunce; þerfore by þat repentaunce,
he shall have forȝevenesse þerfor, and in such maner hit is cleped venial as
thus. That synne is made venial by confessioun which was before deadly in þe
dede doing; for albeit þat suche a grete synne is nat clene purged anone wiþ
full satisfaction, ȝet be þe merci of God he þat synned is received to grace and
saved fro goostly deth as for þat trespass. And so þat synne is made venial wich
was deadly before. Anoþer maner may synne be cleped venial as when a man
hat some cause or skyl joined to him wherby he may somewhat be excusable
and have forȝevenesse, as when a man synneth be infirmite or be ignoruance.
He þat synne venially infirmite excusith in partye, but not in al, for hit excusith
not from original synne. In þe same maner ignoraunce excusith, but hit so
be þat a man is to necligent or to wilfully necligent, as if a man doth not or
will not doo his besinesse to knowe þat he is bounde to knowe. Also in þe
þride maner þat synne is cleped venial which is so litel, or so light of himself
þat hit deservith nat everlasting deth. In þese thre maners venial synne may
be understonde in general. Which be þe dedely synnes I schewed ȝow tofore
in general, as pride and lecheri and all þe oþer as thei stonden. But ȝet all
þe spices of pride, ne all the spices of þe sevene dedely synnes, ben nat alwey
dedely synnes, and to tell ȝow a special knowynge clerely of dedely synne from
venial sikerly I kan nought. Natheles, what som clerkes seyen in this mater, I
will seye ȝow. Seint Austyn seith there is no synne so venial but þat hit may
be dedely while it plesith. Also in þe contrarye wiese þer is synne so dedely but
þat hit may be venial with desplesaunce of the sinner. To þe more declaracioun
of þese words, Seint Austyn seiþ þat synne comith of unreasonable desire and
will ...' Oxford, Bodleian Library, MS Bodley 923, fols 15v–16v.

30   Again, this paragraph conflates two extended similitudes from *De doctrina*:
that of the 'ancilla negligentia', and that of the 'ancilla pigra' (pp. 11–12). *De
doctrina* also turns to natural history to elucidate the function of the heart,
quoting the 'Philosophus': 'Primum membrum, quod formatur in animali est
cor ... a quo quidam calor vitalis procedit cooperans aliorum membrorum
formationem' (p. 11).

31   This paragraph on the cleansing water of contrition is substituted for
approximately four pages in *De doctrina*, exhorting religious not to imitate the
children of Israel who preferred the flour of the Egyptians to the manna of the
Lord (Exod. 16), or to be like the captured kings with severed hands and feet
who ate the remnants beneath the table of Adoni-Bezek (Judg. 1:7). Religious
are also exhorted not to allow desire for sin to become rooted in their hearts,
and reminded of the root of juniper of Job 30:4, which tastes sweet but has

spiky fruit (pp. 12–16). With regard to the substituted paragraph on contrition, again, the similarity to *Ancrene Wisse*, Part V, lines 215–19, p. 119, is pronounced (see note 20): 'Þrefter o þe smeale dust, ȝef hit dusteð swiðe, ha flaskeð weater, ant swopeð ut efter al þet oðer. Alswa schal þe schriueð him efter þe greate schuuen ut te smealre. Ȝef dust of lihte þohtes windeð to swiðe up, flaski teares on ham; ne schulen ha nawt þenne ablende þe heorte ehnen.'

32 Ecclus. 2:20. Note that Vulgate reads 'Qui timent Dominum praeparabunt corda sua'.

33 A new chapter follows in *De doctrina* at this point: 'Secundum ad praeparationem domus requisitum, est Ornatus' (p. 16).

34 A variation on this household allegory can be found in *Le Livre de Seyntz Medicines* of Henry, duke of Lancaster (1354), similarly informed by early thirteenth-century Dominican pentitential manuals, in which the narrator readies the house of the heart for the visit of a great lord (Christ). After sweeping it thoroughly and dousing it with hot water, he hopes that the lord will send help to clear the house of the furniture of sin and make it fit for his arrival. Ruefully, the narrator relates that: 'quant le signur s'en va, les ostiementz sont remys ariere en son lieu come ils estoient et sovent de pire aray q'ils devant ne feurent, et plus encombrent l'ostiel ... Tresdouz Sires, les ostiementz sont les maveis pechés qe sont en moy.' *Le Livre de Seyntz Medicines: The Unpublished Devotional Treatise of Henry of Lancaster*, ed. by E. J. Arnould, Anglo-Norman Text Society 2 (1940), p. 101. (When the lord goes away, the furniture is put back as it was, and often in a worse order than it had been before, and it clutters the house more ... Very sweet lord, the furniture is the bad sins which are in me.) Cited in C. Batt, D. Renevey and C. Whitehead, 'Domesticity and Medieval Devotional Literature', *Leeds Studies in English*, NS 36 (2005), 195–250 (p. 217).

35 The prophet Elisha.

36 The story is told in 2 Kgs. 4:8–10.

37 For a reading of these significations as domesticizations of significations formerly applied to the sacred furnitures of the Old Testament temple and tabernacle and of the Christian church, see C. Whitehead, *Castles of the Mind: A Study of Medieval Architectural Allegory* (Cardiff, 2003), chs 1, 4 and 7. A new chapter follows in *De doctrina*: 'De utensilibus domus cordis, et primo de Lectulo' (p. 17).

38 Ps. 75:3. Note that Vulgate reads 'Et factus est in pace locus eius'. See Hugh, *Postillae*, I, 288vab (2 Kgs. 4:10): 'Et ponamus in eo lectulum]: id est quietem contemplationis.' (And in it let us place a little bed]: that is, the repose of contemplation.)

39 See twelfth-century interpretations of the bed of S. of S. 1:16: 'lectulus noster floridus' (our bed is verdant.) The *Glossa ordinaria* interprets this bed allegorically as the peace of the church which rests in Christ, while St Bernard of Clairvaux, William of Saint-Thierry and Hugh of Folieto interpret it more tropologically as the virtuous human conscience (Whitehead, *Castles of the Mind*, p. 138). A fifteenth-century Middle English allegorical treatise, *An Honest Bede*, possibly originating from Syon or Sheen, develops the idea that, after cleansing the chamber of the soul through confession, one must prepare a bed on which Christ will be pleased to rest. The text is edited by A. I. Doyle, '"Lectulus noster floridus": An Allegory of the Penitent Soul', in R. G. Newhauser and J. A. Alford (eds), *Literature and Religion in the Later Middle Ages: Philological Studies in Honor of Siegfried Wenzel*, Medieval and Renaissance Texts and Studies 118 (New York, 1995), pp. 179–90. The version of the text given in *Disce mori* is discussed in its Syon context in *The 'Exhortacion' from Disce Mori, edited from Oxford, Jesus College, MS 39*, ed. by E.A. Jones, Middle English Texts 36 (Heidelberg, 2006), pp. xxviii–xxxii.

40 *De doctrina* reads slightly differently here: '... quando ipse animus non turbatur ex memoria praeteritorum, nec inquietatur ex desiderio futurorum ...' (p. 17).

41 The youth of those concerned is only emphasized in the English translation. *De doctrina* reads: 'imo in tempore pacis magis solent torneamenta frequentari' (p. 17).

42 2 Cor. 11:23–27.

43 Again, the mentions of youth and of lawlessness are confined to the ME translation. Tournaments were denounced by Pope Innocent III in 1130. They were intermittently banned in England by Henry II, and by King John and Henry III. In France, they were banned by Louis IX in 1260; this ban was upheld by most of his successors.

44 The debate or battle between body and soul has a long history within medieval Latin and vernacular moral writing. Notable examples include the Middle English *Desputisoun bitwen þe Bodi and þe Soule* and the Old English *Soul and Body*. See further, P. Boitani and A. Torti (eds), *The Body and the Soul in Medieval Literature* (Cambridge, 1999). Such battles bear a close relation to the strife between the virtues and the vices which originates from Prudentius' *Psychomachia* and the *De spectaculis* of Tertullian. *De doctrina* continues to expand upon this theme for a further page.

45 Guido Hendrix relates this reference to 'consent' to the *consensus* theory of sin which was being formulated in the early years of the thirteenth century. He offers a series of further examples of references to consent in *De doctrina* in *Hugo I*, pp. 354–6.

46 2 Kgs. 5:2.

47 The idea of guarding the soul within the house of the body against thieving vices who attempt to force entry is also found in the twelfth-century

Pseudo-Anselmian Latin dialogue *De custodia interioris hominis* (in R.W. Southern and F.S. Schmitt (eds), *Memorials of St Anselm*, Auctores britannici medii aevi 1 (Oxford, 1969), pp. 354–60), and its free Middle English reworking, *Sawles Warde* (c.1200–20), (in *Medieval English Prose for Women: Selections from the Katherine Group and Ancrene Wisse*, ed. and tr. by B. Millett and J. Wogan-Browne (Oxford, 1990), pp. 86–109).

48 Job 19:12. Note that Vulgate reads 'Simul venerunt latrones eius, et fecerunt sibi viam per me'. 'His troops have come together, and have made themselves a way by me' (*Douai Bible*).

49 The concept of the soul as a closed garden derives ultimately from S. of S. 4:12. It often occurs in texts aimed at female religious. See *Liber de modo bene vivendi ad sororem* (*PL* 184, col. 1297C): 'Si te incluseris in claustro, amaberis a Christo. Quod bene in Canticis canticorum sponsus insinuat, cum sponsae loquitur, dicens: "Hortus conclusus, soror mea, hortus conclusus, fons signatus" (Cantic. IV, 12). Unaquaeque sancta anima, hortus conclusus esse intelligitur, quia dum virtutes nutrit, flores gignit, virtutibus se nutrit, reficit: fructus quos germinat, eosdem custodit.' (If you enclose yourself in the cloister, you will be loved by Christ. The bridegroom in the Song of Songs makes that known well, when he speaks to the bride, saying: my sister, you are an enclosed garden, an enclosed garden, a spring sealed up (Cantic. IV, 12). Each holy soul is understood to be an enclosed garden, for, when it nourishes virtues, it brings forth flowers, it nourishes and refreshes itself with virtues: the fruits which it [i.e. the holy soul] puts forth, the same it protects.)

50 The associated idea of a hedged garden is also encountered in religious texts. *The Desert of Religion*, for instance, states in its prologue: 'Righte so, þe state of religioune, / þat falls to þe lyve of perfeccioune, / suld be scharp in all thinge / thurgh scharpnes of strait living. / Þat is als a thorne garth to tell / againe þe wikked gast of Hell, / with þe whilk þe herte is closed about / to hald þaes wikkede bestes out.' *Desert of Religion*, vol. 2, p. 253, lines 29–36.

51 Ecclus. 36:27.

52 'esy and softe' is a translation of the Latin *tranquillitas*.

53 Ps. 75:3. Note that Vulgate reads 'Et factus est in pace locus eius'. 'And his place is in peace' (*Douai Bible*).

54 See Hugh, *Postillae*, II, 193 vb (Ps. 75:3): 'Et habitatio etc.] id est, in contemplationibus. Pax enim necessaria est actiuis, ne in actibus suis turbent proximos, uel seipsos, secundum quod dicit Aug. in omnibus motibus uestris nihil fiat quod cuiusquam offendat aspectum. Et si pacem habeant possunt de facili contemplari, aliter non. In aqua enim turbata non resultet imago nec turbatus oculus clara uidere potest.' (And his dwelling place etc.] that is, in contemplations. Peace is indeed necessary in active people, lest you disturb your neighbours or yourselves by your actions, according to what Augustine says, in all your movements and actions let there be nothing which may offend anyone's eyes. And if they have peace, they can contemplate easily, otherwise they cannot. For an image cannot be reflected in water which has been disturbed, neither can a troubled eye see things clearly.)

55 Isa. 66:2. The quote in question comes from an ancient version of the Vulgate. The standard version reads 'ad quem autem respiciam, nisi ad pauperculum, et contritum spiritu' (Candon, *Doctrine*, pp. 163–4). 'But to whom shall I have respect, but to him that is poor and little and of a contrite spirit' (*Douai Bible*). The Naples 1607 edition of *De doctrina* offers the standard version of the quotation (p. 21).

56 *De doctrina* continues to explore the theme of peace for just under a further page. A new chapter follows: 'Taciturnitas pacis est Custodia' (p. 22).

57 Luke 7:39. With regard to the slightly awkward translation of the sentence opening, the Vulgate reads 'Hic si esset propheta, sciret utique, quae, et qualis est mulier, quae tangit eum: quia peccatrix est'. 'This man, if he were a prophet, would know surely who and what manner of woman this is that toucheth him, that she is a sinner' (*Douai Bible*). 'This' in MS McClean appears to translate 'hic', and to be a demonstrative pronoun. It should be understood as 'this one, this man'.

58 Luke 10:38–42. The example is given in greater detail in *De doctrina*: 'Item, contra sororem conquerentem, quae satagebat circa frequens ministerium, solicita de coquina, et dicebat: Domine, non est tibi curae, quod soror mea reliquit me solam ministrare? non respondit: sed aduocatus eius defendens causam suam statim intulit: Martha, Martha, etc.' (p. 22). See Hugh, *Postillae*, VI, 196va (Luke 10:41): 'Et respondens dixit illi Dominus Martha etc.] Ecce Martha uolebat constituere Dominum iudicem, sed ipse iam fit aduocatus Mariae.' (And answering her, the Lord said about Martha etc.] See how Martha wanted to establish the Lord as a judge, but in fact he made himself Mary's advocate.) It is clear from this passage that Mary Magdalen has been conflated with Mary of Bethany, the sister of Martha and Lazarus. For an explication of the medieval confusion between Mary of Bethany and Mary Magdalen, see G. Constable, 'The Interpretation of Mary and Martha', in his *Three Studies in Medieval Religious and Social Thought* (Cambridge, 2nd edn 1998), pp. 6–8.

59 Matt. 26:8–9. The Vulgate reads for these verses 'Ut quid perditio haec? Potuit enim istud venundari multo, et dari pauperibus'. 'To what purpose is this waste? For this might have been sold for much and given to the poor' (*Douai Bible*).

60 *De doctrina* continues for an additional three pages, offering further advice on the custody of the tongue supported by quotations from the Bible, Cassiodorus, Augustine and Seneca (pp. 23–6). The Middle English translator switches the order of the next two chapters. Hence, the next chapter which is translated is 'De tertio ornatu domus, scilicet Mensa' (p. 34).

61 In *De doctrina*, the stool is discussed second and the meat table third.

62 'Cibus eius paenitentia mea, cibus eius salus mea, cibus eius ego ipse'. St Bernard of Clairvaux, *Sermones super Cantica canticorum*, Sermo 71, in *Sancti Bernardi Opera*, ed. by J. Leclercq, C.H. Talbot and H.M. Rochais, 8 vols (Rome, 1957–77), vol. 2, p. 217, line 12. The trope of preparing a feast of glad penitential action to serve the guest, Christ, evokes and inverts the eucharistic feast in which Christ offers himself as our food.

63 *De doctrina*: 'Nam … si tibi placet tua poenitentia, ei placet; si tibi displicet, nec ei placet' (p. 34). Source unidentified. There seems to be some confusion with the attribution. The French translation of *De doctrina* in Douai, Bibliothèque municipale, MS 514, also attributes the quotation to Chrysostom (fol. 18r). A second manuscript of the French translation: Troyes, Bibliothèque muncipale, MS 1384, does not quote the Latin here and attributes the saying to St Gregory (fol. 15r).

64 Ecclus. 29:33. Note that *De doctrina* and Vulgate read 'Transi, hospes, et orna mensam' (*De doctrina*, p. 35). The Vulgate omits the possessive adjective 'tuam, i.e. 'thi' and adds 'hospes', i.e. 'host'. 'Go, stranger, and furnish the table' (*Douai Bible*, Ecclus. 29:32).

65 Ecclus. 35:11. Note that Vulgate reads 'Et omni dato hilarem fac vultum tuum'.

66 A section is omitted from L from this point due to a lost folio or folios.

67 2 Sam. 9:6–7. Note that Vulgate reads 'faciam in te misericordiam propter Ionathan patrem tuum et restituam tibi omnes agros Saul patris tui, et tu comedes panem in mensa mea semper'. The *Doctrine* omits 'propter Ionathan patrem tuam', i.e. 'for Jonathan's sake, your father'. It also omits 'Saul', i.e. King Saul, Jonathan's father. Mephibosheth is in fact, the crippled son of Jonathan.

68 The etymological reading is correct. Mephibosheth means 'he who scatters shame', or 'from the mouth of shame'. W.E. Mills and R.A. Bullard, *Mercer Dictionary of the Bible* (Macon, GA, 1990), p. 568.

69 *De doctrina*: 'Paenitentia, ablata omnia restituit … Et tu comedes panem in mensa mea semper' (p. 36). Hendrix suggests that this bears similarities to St Augustine, *Epistola* 153, 20: 'Si enim res aliena, propter quam peccatum est, cum reddi possit, non redditur, non agitur poenitentia, sed fingitur: si autem veraciter agitur, non remittetur peccatum, nisi restituatur ablatum.' *PL* 33, col. 662 (Hendrix, *Hugo I*, p. 285).

70 'He' here refers to King David. The quotation is a repetition of 2 Sam. 9:7.

71 See Hugh, *Postillae*, VI, 324 rb (John 6): 'Possunt autem plures panes assignari qui proponendi sunt in mensa Domini spirituali. Primus est memoria mortis … Secundus est cognitio uel cogitatio miseriae praesentis, qua reficitur anima quando cogitat quod hoc sustinet propter peccata sua … Tertius est

recordatio uitae praeteritae cum dolore, siue recordatio peccatorum quam uilia, quam damnosa, quam grauia ... Quartus panis est poenitentia siue labor poenitentiae ... Quintus panis est recognitio ignorantiae uilitatis et fragilitatis propriae.' (However it is possible to identify several kinds of bread which are to be set forth on the spiritual table of the Lord. The first is the memory of death ... The second is the knowledge or thought of present wretchedness, by which the soul is refreshed when it considers that it endures this because of its sins ... The third is the painful recollection of past life, or the recollection of exceedingly base, ruinous, and offensive sins. The fourth bread is penance or the work of penance ... The fifth bread is the recognition of the baseness of ignorance and of one's frailty.)

72 *De doctrina* here reads slightly differently: 'Hic est enim panis claustralis, qui tibi datus fuit ab Abbate, quando claustrum intrasti' (p. 36). *De doctrina* continues for an additional page, reproving those who eat the bread of penance: 'cum lachrymis ... et cum murmure blasphemiae' (p. 36), along with those who delight in the sounds and sights of tourneys, of games and of hunts, but take no pleasure in becoming Christ-like through penance.

73 Ruth 2:14. Note that Vulgate reads 'et intinge buccellam tuam in aceto'. The *Doctrine* adds 'Filia', i.e. 'Daughter', at the beginning of the sentence.

74 *De doctrina*: 'Cogitatio praemij minuit vim flagelli' (p. 38). The Latin author attributes this quotation not to St Augustine but to St Gregory (p. 38), as do MS Douai, fol. 20r and MS Troyes, fol. 17r. The reference has not been identified. The interpretations of the two sauces may derive from the interpretations of the two fish in the gospel parable of the loaves and the fish, given that the quotation from St Gregory is used in connection with these interpretations, in Hugh's *Postillae. Postillae*, VI, 324 rb (John 6): '... Duo pisces sunt exempla sanctorum, quae proponuntur, et praemia beatorum quae promittuntur. His duobus condiuntur praedicti panes, et dulciores fiunt. Gregorius. Facta praecedentium recolamus, et grauia nobis non erunt quae sustinemus. Item. Grego. Consideratio praemii minuit uim flagelli.' (The two fish are the examples of the saints – which are set forth, and the rewards of the blessed which are promised. By these two, the various kinds of bread mentioned earlier are seasoned and made sweeter. Gregory: let us reflect upon the deeds of those who came before us and then the things which we endure will not be harsh to us. Likewise, Gregory: the consideration of the reward lessens the violence of the whip.)

75 S. of S. 5:1.

76 L resumes at this word after a missing folio or folios.

77 A new chapter follows in *De doctrina*: 'De cogitione sui ipsius' (p. 38). In fact, what follows in the Middle English *Doctrine* is a translation of the *previous* chapter: 'Secundus ornatus domus est Sella, vel sedes' (pp. 26–34).

78 Ps. 88:15.

79 Ps. 105:3.

80 In keeping with the way in which this allegory domesticates and secularizes the sacred furnitures of the Judiac temple and Christian church (see note 37), the stool of self-judgement appears to represent a domestication of the vacant seat of judgement within the Solomonic temple. See 1 Kgs. 7:7.

81 Job 34:17. Note that Vulgate reads 'Numquid qui non amat iudicium, sanari potest?' 'Can he be healed that loveth not judgement?' (*Douai Bible*).

82 *De doctrina* continues with an allegory of the chapter-house of the heart that seems primarily orientated towards female religious: 'Tene ergo Capitulum tibi ipsi, vt accusationem cognitionis tuae, et testimonio conscientiae, quae in capitulo cordis tanquam Abbatissa praesidet, anima tua tanquam monialis rea veniam petat; se ipsam humiliando disciplinam recipiat, de excessibus suis dolendo; et quasi ad terram sedeat, suae conditionis miseriam recolendo. Vae monacho, siue moniali nunquam istud Capitulum intranti' (pp. 26–7).

83 The passage refers to the conventual practice of making public confession within the chapter-house following the reading of the rule, and to the associated, more intermittent, practice of receiving correction from the convent's official visitor. The scriptural reference is to Heb. 12:5–7, as *De doctrina* makes explicit (p. 27). *De doctrina* continues to develop the idea of the interior chapter of self-correction for an additional page (pp. 27–8).

84 See *The Book of Vices and Virtues*, p. 177: 'so schrof hym Dauid, þat seiþ in þe Sauter, "I wole schryue me and telle alle my synnes aȝens myself," and not aȝens oþere, as doþ ypocrites, þat putten þe fairest outwarde & tellen of here goodnesses and helen here wikkednesses and accusen [o]þer of þe self þing þat þei ben hemself most gilty.'

85 1 Cor. 4:5. Note that Vulgate reads 'nolite ante tempus iudicare, quoadusque veniat Dominus: qui et illuminabit abscondita tenebrarum, et manifestabit consilia cordium'.

86 See Hugh, *Postillae*, VII, 82 (1 Cor. 4:5): 'Hoc ad humanam tentationem pertinet, i. quandoque iudicare de factis hominum suspitione, i. peccatum est veniale, iudicare autem diffinitione, et dicere cum certitudine q. ille peccat mortaliter cum possit non peccare, est mortale.' (This concerns human temptation, in other words, whenever a man's deeds are judged by suspicion, that is a venial sin, but judging decisively and saying with certainty that that person sins mortally, although he may not sin, is a mortal sin.)

87 Luke 6:37.

88 These two paragraphs using the examples of the bee and the spider are selected by the translator from five pages in *De doctrina* developing the subject of right judgment. Those who are dishonest cannot judge truly in the same way that those who are ill cannot be relied upon to appraise food accurately. We are liable to be deceived in our judgements in the same way that we see images reversed when we look into water. St Augustine and St John Chrysostom are cited extensively. See *De doctrina*, pp. 29–34.

89 A new chapter follows in *De doctrina*: 'De cognitione sui ipsius' (p. 38).

90 The candlestick of self-knowledge domesticates and secularizes the seven-branched candlestick in the *debîr* of the desert tabernacle. This candlestick was interpreted as a figure of divine illumination in patristic and scholastic commentaries on the Old Testament tabernacle and temple (see note 37). The link to the seven-branched candlestick of the tabernacle is made more explicit in *De doctrina*: 'Hic enumerata sunt septem, circa quae tua debet versari cognitio, ideo forte septem lucernae in candelabro luminis fuisse describuntur, Exodi 25' (Exod. 25:31–40) (p. 40).

91 Pseudo-Bernard, *Meditationes piisimae de cognitione humanae conditionis* (also known as *Tractatus de interiori homine*), ch. 1.1, *PL* 184, col. 485A: 'Multi multa sciunt, et se ipsos nesciunt.'

92 St Gregory the Great, *Homiliae in Evangelia*, Bk 2, Hom. 36, lines 106–8, p. 335: 'Graue namque curiositatis est uitium, quae dum cuiuslibet mentem ad inuestigandam uitam proximi exterius ducit, semper ei sua intima abscondit, ut aliena sciens, se nesciat.'

93 Cf. Matt. 5:14–16; Luke 8:16; Mark 4:21–22. These references are made explicit in *De doctrina* (p. 39).

94 2 Chr. 13:11. The Vulgate reads for this verse 'estque apud nos candelabrum aureum, et lucernae eius'. The Vulgate here is less precise than the Middle English 'et lucernae eius', i.e. 'and its light'.

95 S. of S. 6:12.

96 Isa. 46:8.

97 *De doctrina* continues for a further half page, listing seven verses of knowledge which it aligns to the seven lights on the temple lampstand (Exod. 25:37), and to the seven eyes upon a single stone (Zech. 3:9). (pp. 40–1).

98 A new chapter follows at this point in *De doctrina*: 'De custodia quinque sensuum' (p. 41).

99 See *Ancrene Wisse*, Part II, on the custody of the senses, where the apertures of the senses are persistently conflated with the entrances and windows of the anchorhold. Also, *Sawles Warde*, where the five senses are allegorized as household servants who assist in protecting the treasure of the soul against thieving vices. Also, *The Book of Vices and Virtues*, p. 153: 'Whan þes fyue wittes ben wel y-kepte, þan is þe castel siker and stedefast, for þes ben þe ȝates of þe soule. Þes ben þe wyndowes wher-by deþ comeþ in-to þe soule ofte-tyme, as þe prophete seiþ'; and *Piers Plowman*, Passus IX, ll. 1–59, in which the castle of the soul, Anima, is guarded by Sir 'Inwit' and his five sons signifying the right usages of the five senses: 'Se-Wel', 'Sey-Wel'.

'Here-Wel', 'Werch-Wel' and 'Go-Wel' (William Langland, *The Vision of Piers Plowman*, ed. by A.V.C. Schmidt (London, 2nd edn 1995), pp. 130–3.) The five wits, and how to keep them properly, often figure in didactic works composed after the Fourth Lateran Council (1215), along with other catechetical lists. Oxford, Bodleian Library, MS Rawlinson C 209, for instance, lists the Ten Commandments, the Seven Deadly Sins, the Seven Virtues against the Seven Deadly Sins, the Five Wits and so on. The section on the Five Wits reads: 'These bene the five bodily wittis: hiryng, seyng, smelling, tasting and towching. Nothinge makith men sonner falle fro the commaundementis of God than doth the entryng of the fende at the five windowis of the sowle. First as in hiring, a man sinneth, when he levith wilfully to hire the lawe of God and delitith him hire fablis, folie and foule wordis. The secounde, when his iye is unstable, beholding diverse thingis and lustis, wherthrogh he is tempted, both to lust and to coveytise. For who that hath a light iye and unstable shal have a derke sowle and sinful. As Saint Austine saith, an unchast iye is the knolege of an unchast mynde. The thirde, when he throgh a deligat smel aftir his power fulfillith the lust of his flesshe. The iiij.th, he synneth in tastyng, whan he throgh swete tast of mete or of drinke owtragiowsly fedith himself, wherthrogh he is the worse disposed to travaile, and to serve God. The fifte, he synnyth in towching, when he wilfully of his delite towchith the thynge that is forbodene bi Goddis lawe and resone' (fols 10r–11r).

100 Gen. 34:1–2. The reference to Dina is encountered in other texts. See, among others, St Bernard, *De gradibus humilitatis et superbiae*, in his examination of the First Step of Pride; also, the pseudo-Bernardine text *Liber de modo bene vivendi*, col. 1242C.

101 The same scriptural example is developed in slightly greater detail in the chapter on the custody of the senses in *Ancrene Wisse*, Part II, lines 87–100, p. 22, in the course of a discussion on the dangers of sight.

102 Gen. 27.

103 *De doctrina* offers approximately three pages of additional examples on the virtues of 'remaining within' at this point.

104 The example of the two soldiers bearing maces symbolizing the fear of hell and love of God bears a close relation to *Sawles Warde*, pp. 88–94, 98–104, in which the household of the Christian body is visited by two messengers: Fear (of hell), and Love of Life, the second more effective than the first. See also *Ancrene Wisse*, Part II, lines 668–71, p. 37: 'ʒe schulen bihalde sumcheare toward te pine[n] of helle, þet ow uggi wið ham ant fleo þe swiðere ham frommard. ʒe schulen gasteliche iseon þe blissen of heouene, þe ontenden ower heorte to hihin ham toward.' For a Middle English text exploring dread and love, see *Contemplations of the Dread and Love of God*, ed. by M. Connolly, EETS 303 (1994).

105 Prov. 16:6. Note that Vulgate reads 'in timore Domini declinatur a malo'. The *Doctrine* prefers the active voice, i.e. 'declinat omnis', whereas the Vulgate has the passive, i.e. 'declinatur'. In *De doctrina*, this quotation is placed *after* the reference in the succeeding paragraph to the Prodigal Son (p. 50).

106 *De doctrina* clarifies that these rhetorical questions paraphrase 1 John 2:16 (p. 48).

107 Luke 15:17. The MS has an abbreviation sign above the second 'e' of 'mercenarii' which may be mistaken since the Vulgate has only one 'n' for this word.

108 In selecting the verb 'asayst', the Middle English translator makes use of *De doctrina* author's reference to the French vernacular at this point. *De doctrina* reads 'Nota illam differentiam inter delectari in peccato, circa consensum, et ipsum consentire, quae est inter illud gustare, quod dicitur Gallice *assaier* et comedere' (p. 48).

109 Guido Hendrix relates the emphasis upon *consenting* to sin throughout this passage to the *consensus* theory of sin being formulated in the early years of the thirteenth century. *Hugo I*, pp. 354–6.

110 The allegory here carries reminders of the female porter of discernment within the household of the human mind in St Gregory the Great's *Moralia in Job*, Bk 1, chs 30, 32, 35 (ed. by M. Adriaen, *CCSL* 143 (Turnhout, 1979), pp. 47–8, 50–2), and to the porter of Prudence in the household of the human body, in *Sawles Warde*, p. 88. For an examination of the concept of 'discretio' in western monasticism, see A. Cabassut, 'Discrétion', *Dictionnaire de spiritualité*, 3 (1954), cols 1318–26.

111 2 Sam. 4. This scriptural example is also quoted in relation to the importance of vigilance, in *Ancrene Wisse*, Part IV, lines 1340–2, p. 103, together with Gregory's interpretation of the passage. Here also, the female door keeper is interpreted as Reason: 'Þe ȝeteward is wittes skile, þet ah to windwin hweate, schaden þe eilen ant te chef from þe cleane cornes (þet is, þurh bisi warschipe sundri god from uuel).'

112 St Gregory the Great: 'Ostiaria triticum purgat, cum mentis custodia discernendo virtutes a vitiis separat. Quae, si obdormierit, in mortem proprii Domini insidiatores admittit; quia cum discretionis sollicitudo cessaverit, ad interficiendum animum malignis spiritibus iter pandit.' *Moralia in Job*, Bk 1, ch. 35, pp. 50–2.

113 The distinction here is between private property and goods held in common ownership. The passage may also allude obliquely to the gospel story of Christ overturning the stalls of the moneychangers in the temple precinct. Matt. 21:12–13.

114 Ecclus. 10:10. Note that Vulgate reads 'animam suam venalem habet'. The *Doctrine* has 'facit', i.e. 'makes', whereas the Vulgate has 'habet', i.e. 'has'.

115 In *De doctrina* this chapter concludes with an additional three pages on the need to secure the gates of the senses. A new chapter entitled 'De Sacramento Altaris' begins at this point in *De doctrina* (p. 56).

116 Prov. 23:1. Note that Vulgate reads 'Quando sederis ut comedas cum principe, diligenter attende quae apposita sunt ante faciem tuam. Et statue cultrum in gutture tuo'.

117 *De doctrina* clarifies that this passage refers to John 6:51. 'Panis vitae' is translated here as 'hevenly liflode' (p. 57).

118 *De doctrina* identifies this lamb as the Passover lamb that must be accompanied by 'lactucis agrestibus' (wild lettuce) in Exod. 12:1–11 (p. 57).

119 *De doctrina* refers the reader to the discussions of the properties of manna in Wisd. 16 and Exod. 16.

120 Exod. 16:21; Wisd. 16:22 (pp. 57–8).

121 The concluding three pages of the chapter comparing the eucharistic host to grain beaten with a pestle, resin, frost and coriander seed ('Granum pilo tusum, Bdellium, Pruinam, et Coriandrum' p. 60), in *De doctrina* are omitted (pp. 59–62).

122 A new chapter in *De doctrina*: 'De gradibus Sacramenti Altaris' commences with this sentence (p. 62). Much of this chapter (pp. 62–5), in particular the enumeration of the four degrees of divine largess or generosity, shows a close identity with Pseudo-Thomas, *De venerabili sacramento altaris*, ch. 5 (St Thomas Aquinas, *De venerabili sacramento altaris* [Rome, 1931]). The relevant passages from Pseudo-Thomas read: 'Probatur autem eius liberalitas … quantum ad tria … Primo quantum ad magnificentiam doni: quia largitor omnium bonorum in hoc Sacramento dat seipsum, et hoc largissime, quia dat proprium Corpus in cibum, secundum quod dicit, "Accipite et comedite." [Matt. 26:26] Hic est summus gradus divinae largitatis quantum ad donum. Hic gradus quidam proponi possunt divinae largitatis, quibus homini largitus est omnia bona sua; et sic patebit quod hic est summus. Primus gradus est, quod largitus est homini coelum et terram, et omnes irrationabiles creaturas ad serviendum … Secundus gradus est, quod homini largitus est illas nobilissimas creaturas rationabiles et coelestes, scilicet sanctos Angelos ad ministrandum. Heb. 1: "Omnes sunt administratorii spiritus in ministerium missi propter eos qui haereditatem capiunt salutis" … Tertius gradus est, quod largitus est seipsum … Quartus gradus, quod dedit se in servum nostrae necessitatis … Matth. 20: "Filius hominis non venit ministrari sed ministrare." [Matt. 22:28] … Quintus gradus est, quod dedit se in pretium redemptionis nostrae … Sextus gradus est, et summus, quod dat homini Corpus suum in cibum … et in hoc est expressio summae largitatis, et praecipui amoris' (pp. 39–43). (But his generosity is proven … with regard to three things … First with regard to the magnificence of the gift: for, a liberal giver of all good things, in this sacrament gives himself, and this most liberally for he gives his own body as food, according to what he says: 'Take and eat.' [Matt. 26:26] This is the highest step of divine liberality with regard to the gift. Here certain steps of divine liberality can be set forth by which he bestowed all his goods upon man, and thus it will become clear which is here the highest. The first step is that he bestowed the heavens and earth upon man and [provided] all irrational creatures to serve him ... The second step is that he bestowed man with those most excellent heavenly creatures possessing reason, that is, the holy angels, to wait upon him. Heb. 1 [Heb. 1:14] 'Are they not all ministering spirits, sent to minister for them who shall receive the inheritance of salvation?' ... The third step is that he bestowed himself ... The fourth step is that he gave himself to serve our needs ... Matth. 20 'The Son of Man came not to be served but to serve.' [Matt. 22:28] ... The fifth step is that he gave himself as the price of our redemption ... The sixth and highest step is that he gives his own body as food ... and in this is an expression of the highest liberality and of an extraordinary love.)

123 Ps. 8:8. L and T specify the 'prophet' as David. *De doctrina* gives 'Psal.'.

124 Heb. 1:14. Note that Vulgate reads for this verse 'Nonne omnes sunt administratorii spiritus, in ministerium missi propter eos, qui haereditatem capient salutis'. 'Are they not all ministering spirits, sent to minister for them who shall receive the inheritance of salvation?' (*Douai Bible*). 'Angels' are mentioned in Heb. 1:13.

125 John 13:13. Note that Vulgate reads 'Vos vocatis me Magister et Domine, et bene dicitis: sum etenim'. This quotation is absent from *De doctrina*, p. 63, but it must have featured in the Latin manuscript the translator had in front of him, since it is also found in MS Douai, fol. 34v. The text of the 1607 edition suggests that something is missing since it jumps from 'secundo dedit se nobis Christus' to 'quarto se dedit in pretium' (pp. 63, 64). The 1506 edition of *De doctrina* has the correct reading: 'Secundo dedit se nobis Christus in magistrum in doctrina et predicatione. Unde et ipse dicit Jo. 13. "Vos vocatis me magister et Domine et bene dicitis" [John 13:13]. Tertio dedit se in exemplum in humili conversatione ut dicit Jo. 13. "Exemplum dedi vobis ut quemadmodum ego feci ita et vos faciat" [John 13:15]'. Note that the 1506 edition lacks pagination.

126 John 13:15. Note that Vulgate reads 'Exemplum enim dedi vobis, ut quemadmodum ego feci vobis, ita et vos faciatis'. The Vulgate adds 'enim' (i.e. 'indeed') and a second 'vobis' (i.e. 'to you') after 'feci'.

127 1 Cor. 6:20.

128 *De doctrina* makes more explicit the fact that this is the fourth and final largess ('quartus gradus'). The Middle English translator omits approximately a page of Latin immediately following, which elaborates on this fourth largess (pp. 64–5).

129 John 6:56. Note that Vulgate reads 'Caro enim mea vere est cibus: et sanguis meus, vere est potus'.

130 The Middle English text follows the Latin *De doctrina* in referencing back to the earlier biblical quote (*Doctrine*, p. 20, lines 573–5; *De doctrina*, p. 57). However the Latin scribe appears to have made a mistake. 'Scito quia talia te oportet preparare', which follows immediately after Prov. 23:1 in the Latin text, is *not* a part of the biblical quote. It should be noted that the translation that follows in the Middle English text *does* translate Prov. 23:1. This sentence translates material from the opening of a new chapter in *De doctrina*: 'De mortificatione sui ipsius' (p. 65).

131 For further discussion and analysis of the unconventional ideas developed throughout the next section – that we should prepare ourselves to be eaten by Christ in the same way that he offers himself as food for us – see D. Renevey, 'Household chores in the *Doctrine of the Hert*: Affective Spirituality and Subjectivity', in C. Beattie, A. Maslakovic and S. Rees Jones (eds), *The Medieval Household in Christian Europe c.850–c.1550* (Turnhout, 2003), pp. 167–85, and D. Renevey and C. Whitehead, 'Introduction', in Renevey and Whitehead (eds), *Companion*, pp. 6–7. Here, *De doctrina*'s fascination with food imagery is viewed with reference to the development of the liturgical feast of Corpus Christi, and its relation to the experimental female religious culture of the thirteenth-century Low Countries. See also V. Gillespie, 'Meat, Metaphor and Mysticism: Cooking the Books in *The Doctrine of the Hert*', in Renevey and Whitehead (eds), *Companion*, pp. 131–58, where the allegorical trope of meat preparation within a noble kitchen is considered in relation to its *distance* from the actual experience of the nun; the kitchen is 'a contradictory place, a place that contrasts with the everyday life of its target audience' (pp. 157–8).

132 Gen. 27:6–9. The Vulgate reads for these verses 'Audivi patrem tuum loquentem cum Esau fratre tuo, et dicentem ei: Affer mihi de venatione tua, et fac cibos ut comedam, et benedicam tibi coram Domino antequam moriar. Nunc ergo, fili mi, acquiesce consiliis meis: et pergens ad gregem, affer mihi duos haedos optimos, ut faciam ex eis escas patri tuo, quibus libenter vescitur'. 'I heard thy father talking with Esau thy brother, and saying to him: Bring me of thy hunting, and make me meats that I may eat, and bless thee in the sight of the Lord, before I die. Now, therefore, my son, follow my counsel: And go thy way to the flock, bring me two kids of the best, that I may make of them meat for thy father, such as he gladly eateth' (*Douai Bible*). This is one of the very few occasions on which the Latin scriptural quotation is omitted from the Middle English text.

133 Rebecca is similarly interpreted as 'grace' in *Ancrene Wisse*, Part III, lines

492–4, p. 60 (some of these lines originally functioned as marginal annotation): 'ant swa he imette wið þe eadi Rebecca, þet is, wið Godes grace. Rebecca enim interpretatur multum dedit, et / Quicquid habe[s] meriti, preuentrix gratia donat'.

134 A new chapter commences at this point in *De doctrina*: 'De Abdicatione suae propriae voluntatis' (p. 67). For the following six paragraphs see Hugh, *Postillae*, 9vb: 'Et nota, q. quanto pellis subtilior est, tanto difficilior est ad excoriandum, sic subtiliora peccata, scilicet spiritualia difficiliora sunt ad confitendum. Et sicut caput animalis difficilius excoriatur, quam alia membra, sic clerici, et litterati, et praelati, difficilius aliis excoriantur per confessionem. Et sicut anguilla quae habet lubricam pellem uix potest teneri ad excoriandum, sic quidam clerici, qui lubrici sunt, et mobiles uix possunt in confessione excoriari.' (And note that, the finer the skin is, the more more difficult it is to skin, thus finer sins, namely spiritual sins, are more difficult to confess. And as the head of an animal is more difficult to skin than other parts of the body, thus clerics, and *litterati*, and prelates, are more difficult to skin by confession. And as an eel which has a slippery skin can hardly be held to be skinned, thus some clerics, who are slippery and unsteady, can hardly be skinned in confession.) The author of *De doctrina* changes 'clerici' to 'claustrales', modifying the exegesis to fit the religious life (p. 68).

135 Eccles. 1:18: 'eo quod in multa sapientia multa sit indignatio.' Hugh, *Postillae*, III, 74vb (Eccles): 'Eo quod in multa sapientia multa sit indignatio] Iuxta litteram .i. inflatio elationis.' (In that in much wisdom there is much indignation] According to the letter, that is the inflation of pride.)

136 Isa. 5:21. *De doctrina* identifies the 'prophete' explicitly as Isaiah (p. 67).

137 Hab. 3:7.

138 *De doctrina* offers additional detail about religious of this type: 'Et tales sunt quasi homines *de terre de Marche* habentes habitum claustralem, animum vero secularem' (p. 68).

139 A new chapter: 'De sufferentia tribulationis' commences at this point in *De doctrina* (p. 69).

140 Despite the unconventionality of this image, a later partial analogue can be found in Mechthild of Hackeborn's *Liber Specialis Gratiae*, ed. by H. Oudin (Paris, 1877), Bk 2, ch. 23: 'De coquina domini'. In this chapter, Mechthild declares herself unworthy of entering the Lord's kitchen and of washing his platters. Christ then declares that his kitchen is his heart and that as a kitchen is the common room of a house, his heart is open to all and for the benefit of all. The cook is the Holy Ghost who provides things in abundance and constantly replenishes them. His platters are the hearts of the saints and the chosen ones which are filled from the overflow of the sweetness of his divine heart. Hendrix relates the section on the roasting of the heart to the writings of St Bernard of Clairvaux, citing J. Leclercq, 'San Bernardo "cuciniere di Dio"', in *Bernardo Cistercense. Atti del XXVI Convegno storico internazionale Todi* (Spoleto, 1990), p. 333 (*Hugo I*, p. 290).

141 *De doctrina* here reads 'Et sicut coquina non debet esse sine igne, sic claustrum Domini non est sine tribulatione' (p. 69). Gillespie ('Meat, Metaphor and Mysticism', pp. 151–2) explores the way in which 'domini' is repositioned in the translation so to create a more vivid and concrete figurative image of a manorial kitchen.

142 Ecclus. 43:3. Note that Vulgate reads 'Fornacem custodiens in operibus ardoris'.

143 See Hugh, *Postillae*, II, 156va (Ps. 62): '... Sicut adipe et pinguedine repleatur anima mea. Per adipem qui est in intestinis, significatur deuotio interior ... Per pinguedinem quae in carne est, significatur alacritas, quam etiam Domino offerri debet. Sicut .n. antiquitus adeps, et pinguedo placebant Deo, ita spiritualiter in nostris sacrificiis spiritualibus deuotio, et hilaritas placent ei. Et ideo petit iste animam suam his repleri.' (... As my soul is restored by animal fat and by fatness. By animal fat, which is in the intestines, interior devotion is signified ... By fatness, which is in the flesh, alacrity is signified, which must also be offered to the Lord. Indeed, just as, long ago, animal fat and fatness were pleasing to God, so, spiritually, devotion in our spiritual sacrifices and cheerfulness please him. And, for that reason, he asks for his soul to be restored by these.)

144 *De doctrina* offers some indications regarding the gender of its intended target audience at this point: 'Fac ergo pinguedinem *fratrum tuorum, siue sociorum* stillare in cor tuum' (p. 69, our emphasis).

145 Simon of Cyrene, the passer-by who was compelled by the Roman soldiers to carry Christ's cross on the way to the crucifixion. See Matt. 27:32, Mark 15:21, Luke 23:26.

146 Here and throughout the text, 'sovereynes' is used to refer to superiors in religion.

147 1 Cor. 13:3. Note that Vulgate reads 'si distribuero in cibos pauperum omnes facultates meas, et si tradidero corpus meum ita ut ardeam, charitatem autem non habuero, nichil mihi prodest'.

148 The Middle English translator omits three pages of Latin material at this point providing additional Old Testament examples regarding the need for charity to temper tribulation. The episode of the three young men in the fiery furnace (Dan. 3) is the most extended of these examples (*De doctrina*, pp. 70–3). A new chapter then commences in *De doctrina*: 'Quod pellis extractio, coctio, et pinguedo fuerunt in Christo passo' (p. 74).

149 The suggestion that the Jewish people collectively were responsible for the death of Christ appears from the early patristic period onwards, and is one of the cornerstones of traditional Christian antisemitism. See further J.J. Cohen, *Christ Killers: The Jews and the Passion from the Bible to the Big Screen* (Oxford, 2007).

150 The 'fyve gret holis' refers to the crucifixional wounds in Christ's hands and feet, and the great wound in his side.

151 This unconventional image bears some relation to more standard passion iconography in which Christ's blood flows directly from his wounds into the eucharistic chalice. The Middle English translator omits a short chapter ('De praemeditatione passionis Christi') which follows in *De doctrina* at this point, in which the association of Christ's blood with the fat of charity is elaborated further (pp. 75–6). The translation recommences at the opening of the *following* chapter: 'De Coctione, seu sustinentia correptionis' (p. 76).

152 Prov. 15:12.

153 Prov. 9:8. Note that the Middle English translator translates 'sapientem' as 'savery', not 'wise'. Both meanings are legitimate for the word, but the usual translation of this passage is 'wise'. For example, in the French translations of *De doctrina*, MS Douai translates the bible verse as 'castie le saige et il t'amera', fol. 43r (i.e. chastise the wise and he will love you); MS Troyes translates it as 'argue le sage et il t'en sara bon gre', fol. 37r (i.e. reason with the wise and he will be grateful to you).

154 A new chapter: 'De Abdicatione carnalis Amoris' commences in *De doctrina* at this point (p. 78).

155 St Ambrose: 'Ergo et jugis labor avertit affectum', *Hexaemeron*, Bk 5, ch. 15, *PL* 14, col. 228B. This is followed in *De doctrina* by approximately a page of additional material interpreting the Galileans, whose blood was mingled with their sacrifices by Pilate (Luke 13:1), as religious who confuse spiritual and carnal love (pp. 78–9).

156 This sentence is a free variation of a sentence that is attributed to St John Chrysostom in *De doctrina*: 'Quid enim prodest illi, quem mores sordidant, generatio clara? ... Melius est, vt in te glorientur parentes ... quam vt tu glorieris in parentibus' (p. 79). The quotation in question actually comes from Pseudo-Chrysostomus, *Opus imperfectum in Matthaeum*, Hom. 3, *PG* 56, col. 651.

157 These last two sentences are a homely summary added by the translator. A new chapter, 'De desiderio Mortis', opens in *De doctrina* following this sentence (p. 80).

158 'Seth it so is ... holynesse of hert.' These sentences are original to the Middle English translation.

159 Phil. 1:23.

160 'This world may wel be likned ... fro flessh.' This sentence is original to the Middle English translation. In both this sentence and the previous Middle

English addition (see note 158), there is a degree of variation between the different manuscript renditions. See variants section for further detail.

161 Prov. 14:32. Note that Vulgate reads 'Sperat autem iustus in morte sua'.

162 Eccles. 7:2. Note that Vulgate reads 'Melius est nomen bonum quam ungenta pretiosa, et dies mortis die nativitatis'. 'A good name is better than precious ointments: and the day of death than the day of one's birth' (*Douai Bible*). For this and the succeeding three paragraphs, see further Hugh, *Postillae*, III, 88va (Eccles. 7): 'Et dies mortis, quam natiuitatis] melior est, scilicet in eis, qui habent bonum nomen, quia preciosa est in conspectu Domini mors sanctorum eius. In talibus enim dies mortis est egressus de praesenti miseria, dies natiuitatis est ingressus in illam ... Mors enim nihil aliud est, quam exitus de carcere, finis exilii, laboris consummatio, ad portum applicatio, peregrinationis finitio, oneris grauissimi.' (And the day of death rather than the day of birth] is better, namely for those who have a good name, because 'the death of his saints is precious in the sight of the Lord'. Indeed, for such people, the day of death is a passage out of present wretchedness, the day of birth, a going into it [i.e. present wretchedness] ... Indeed, death is nothing else than an exit from prison, the end of exile, the end of toil, access to a haven, the ending of pilgrimage, [the ending] of a very heavy burden.)

163 *De doctrina* specifies the place where death is retitled as the Martyrology: 'Vnde mors Sanctorum, Natale eorum in Martyrologijs appellatur' (p. 81).

164 *De doctrina* specifies the doctors in question as Cassiodorus and St Augustine (p. 81). Cassiodorus, *Expositio psalmorum*, Ps. 68, lines 760–1, ed. by M. Adriaen, *CCSL* 97 (Turnhout, 1958), p. 623; St Augustine, *De civitate Dei*, Bk 13, ch. 4, lines 39–40, ed. by B. Dombart and A. Kalb, *CCSL* 48 (Turnhout, 1955), p. 388.

165 Rom. 7:24.

166 Ps. 141:8.

167 The two final paragraphs here severely compress approximately three and a half pages in *De doctrina* (pp. 81–4) which culminate with a reference to Plato's teachings upon death: 'Attende ergo, iuxta verbum Platonis, Mortem omnibus vere philosophantibus esse appetendam: nam (vt dicit quidam) Mors lux est, qua proximante tam densae tenebrae ignorantiarum fugantur, vt quam vilia sint, quae amamus in hoc mundo, in ipsa morte plenius innotescant' (p. 84). Plato, *Phaedo*, 64b, in *Platonis Opera*, ed. by E.A. Duke et al. (Oxford, 1995), vol. I, p. 98. A new chapter follows: 'De Matrimonio spirituali, et primo quomodo repellitur a matrimonio Christi' (p. 85).

168 This closing section of book I can be usefully viewed in relation to the thirteenth-century mendicant Parisian marriage sermons recently edited and analysed by D.L. D'Avray, in *Medieval Marriage Sermons: Mass Communication in a Culture without Print* (Oxford, 2001), and discussed further in *Medieval*

Marriage: Symbolism and Society (Oxford, 2005). These sermons, generally preached on the second Sunday after Epiphany to laymen as well as religious, and to women as well as men, use the image of marriage as a vehicle for discussing the soul's relation with Christ, and explore the parallels between the classifications and stages of a 'real' marriage and a symbolic marriage in considerable detail.

169 Rev. 19:7.

170 Lev. 21:13–14. Note that Vulgate reads 'Virginem ducet uxorem: viduam autem et repudiatam, et sordidam atque meretricem non accipiet'. 'Sacerdos', though, is implied from what precedes. See Lev. 21:10.

171 The precise categories indicated here are widows, divorced women, stained or unvirginal women, and prostitutes.

172 The Middle English translator adds this brief explanation to the reader.

173 *De doctrina*: 'Corruptae animae, virgines efficiuntur in Christi matrimonio: unde ponit differentiam inter matrimonium carnale, et spirituale. In carnali enim matrimonio virgines corrumpuntur, in spirituali vero, corruptae, virgines efficiuntur' (pp. 85–6). Source unidentified. An identical phrase is used in the marriage sermon of Pierre de Reims OP (D'Avray, *Medieval Marriage Sermons*, p. 104).

174 These four distinctions also play a part in various mendicant marriage sermons. In the marriage sermon of Hugh of St Cher OP, the soul is designated a widow through pride, a repudiated woman through avarice, and a prostitute through lust (D'Avray, *Medieval Marriage Sermons*, p. 160). In the marriage sermon of Gérard de Mailly OP, the soul is designated a widow when it is not dead to the world, but still gladly speaks and thinks about worldly and carnal things. It is designated as repudiated when, though it is not moved by temporal or carnal things, this is not because the soul has repudiated them – rather, it has been repudiated *by* them. It is designated as 'sordidam' when, although it abstains from mortal sins, yet it still engages in impure affections. Finally, it is designated 'meretricem' when it engages in mortal sins (D'Avray, *Medieval Marriage Sermons*, pp. 264–6).

175 In a short text on widowhood, Oxford, Bodleian Library, MS 938 states: 'þer ben þre kyndis of widewis: oon þat is moost parfit and ordeyned to hevenli mede, whiche bi ensaumple of Anne widewe ... Anoþer kynde of widewis is þe whiche han governaunce of sones and hous, whiche is not worþi so myche mede, neþeles not gilti of synnes. Þe þridde kynde of widewis is þat liveþ in plentyvous metis and delicis of þe fleisch, whiche is kepte to everlasting deeþ and peyne ... Þe þridde widewis þat is living in delicis is deed wherof it is to be undurstonden þat alle widues be not even, neþer þei plesen to God, whiche ben seen to be widewis oonli in body, not in werk.' fols 265v–266r. Widowhood is also commonly viewed as one of the states of chastity. *The Book of Vices and Virtues* categorizes it as the fourth state of chastity, positioned between marriage and virginity: 'Þe ferþe staate of chastite is of hem þat han ben in mariage and deþ haþ departed hem. He þat is left in þe lif schal kepe chastite as longe as þei ben in widowhode. For þat is an staate þat seynt Poule preiseþ moche' (p. 249). In this evaluation, widowhood is properly associated with a quiet life, religious devotion, and abstinence. See further, *Speculum vitae*, vol. 2, pp. 374–9, where the seven states of chastity are examined in more detail, and it is advised how widows should and should not behave.

176 *De doctrina* additionally likens such widows to the Amalekites whose memory God threatens to blot out, in Exod. 17:14 (p. 86).

177 1 Tim. 5:6. Note that Vulgate reads 'quae in deliciis est, vivens mortua est'. 'Vidua' is implied by what precedes. See 1 Tim. 5:5. The *Speculum vitae* also quotes 1 Tim. 5:6 in its examination of widowhood: 'whaso wil halde þam chast / Bihoues vse grete metes mast / And noght delicyous dayntees; / þat makes many Chastyte lees. / For Saynt Paul says and beres witnes / þat a womman þat widow es, / þat in delyces hir lyf ledes / Es dede thurgh synne þat men dredes.' *Speculum vitae*, vol. 2, p. 378, lines 11387–94.

178 *De doctrina* additionally likens such widows to the women lamenting Tammuz in the temple in Ezek. 8:14, and links this with the 'Gentile fiction' of Venus mourning Adonis: 'In huius significatione, dicitur Ezechielis 8. Quod inter quasdam abominationes vidit mulieres plangentes Adonidem, qui iuxta fabulas Gentilium dicitur fuisse amasius Veneris' (pp. 86–7). See Hugh, *Postillae*, V, 35va (Ezek. 8:14): 'Mulieres etc.] Quia enim iuxta gentilem fabulam in mense Iulio amasius Veneris et pulcherrimus iuuenis occisus est et deinde reuixisse narratur.' (Women etc.] Indeed because, according to the pagan story, Venus's lover and the most beautiful of youth, was killed in the month of July, and then it is said that he had come back to life.)

179 Num. 21:5.

180 See St Gregory the Great, *Moralia in Job*, Bk 20, ch. 15, lines 79–85, ed. by M. Adriaen, *CCSL* 143A (Turnhout, 1979), p. 1032: '... qui dum refectionem mannae desuper perciperet, ab Aegypto ollas carnium, pepones, porres, cepasque concupivit. Quid enim signatur in manna, nisi esca gratiae, suave sapiens, ad refectionem interioris vitae bene vacantibus desuper data? Et quid per ollas carnium, nisi carnalia opera, vix tribulationum laboribus quasi ignibus excoquenda?' A new chapter commences in *De doctrina* at this point: 'Quid intelligitur per Repudiatam' (p. 87).

181 This section is slightly amplified in *De doctrina* by allusions to Ecclus. 29 and Tobit 5 (pp. 87–8). A new chapter follows: 'Quid intelligitur per sordidam' (p. 88).

182 This sentence is not in *De doctrina*.

183 *De doctrina* reads: 'Praeclara est virginitas, et pudicitiae virtus, si non alijs macularum lapsibus infirmetur' (pp. 88–9). Despite the attribution to St Jerome, the quotation actually comes from Sedulius Scottus, *Collectaneum miscellaneum*, divisio 13, subdiv. 7.1: *De virginitate*, ed. by D. Simpson, *CCCM* 67 (Turnhout, 1988), p. 69: 'Preclara est apud Deum uirginitas et pudicitiae uirtus si non aliis peccatorum et malorum lapsibus infirmetur.' See Hugh, *Postillae*, I, 42rb (Gen. 30): 'Nam sicut in bysso bene candida, parua macula cito apparet, et magna uidetur, ita sancti paruum et ueniale peccatum magnum et se maculatos reputant.' (For as in a properly white cambric, a small stain is quickly visible, and seems big, thus the saints think a small and venial sin big, and think themselves stained.) *The Book of Vices and Virtues* expresses very similar sentiments: 'seynt Ierome seiþ þat wel fair and cler is virginite a-boue alle oþere vertues whan sche is wiþ-oute filþe of synne … Virginite is þe whiȝt robe, wher-ynne þat a spott is foulere and more y-seene þan any cloþ of oþer colour. Þis robe scholde be wel y-kepte from þre spottes: of filþe of erþe, of blod, and of fier' (pp. 252–3). The *Speculum vitae* also attributes the quotation to St Jerome: 'Wharefore Saynt Ierom says þus, / þat bifore alle othir vertus / Maydenhede es clere and fayre, / If na spotte of synne it appayre', vol. 2, p. 382, lines 11523–6. The *Speculum vitae* similarly compares virginity to a 'whyte robe', see vol. 2, p. 383, lines 11537–46.

184 'a mayde' considerably simplifies the more formal Latin phrase in *De doctrina*: 'virgo Christi, id est, quaelibet sancta anima' (p. 89). A new chapter commences at this point in *De doctrina*: 'Quid intelligitur per Meretricem'.

185 St Gregory the Great, *Moralia in Job*, Bk 25, ch. 9, lines 14–15, ed. by M. Adriaen, *CCSL* 143B (Turnhout, 1985), p. 1247: 'Peccatum namque quod poenitentia non diliuit ipso suo pondere mox ad aliud trahit.'

186 The designation of the fiend as a 'fals wrecchid lover' in the Middle English replaces the more technical Latin 'Vnde *exactor* [i.e. collector of taxes] dicitur Diabolus, quia semper vlterius procedit' (*De doctrina*, p. 89, our emphasis).

187 Jas. 4:7. Note that Vulgate reads 'resistite autem diabolo, et fugiet a vobis'.

188 Two further pages of Latin material, developing the character of the 'commune woman', are omitted. Jezebel's painted countenance (2 Kgs. 9:30) is mentioned in connection with certain religious who spend too much time on their appearance before meeting their relatives. St Bernard's *Epistola CXIII: Ad Sophiam uirginem*, criticizing the excessive adornments of secular matrons, is also quoted (pp. 91–3). Following this, a new chapter opens in *De doctrina*: 'De Matrimonio spirituali cum Virgine' (p. 93).

189 The trope of the mystic marriage between Christ and the chaste soul, developed in the first instance from allegorical exegesis of the Song of Songs, became popular in mystical and contemplative writing from the twelfth century onwards. Seminal texts treating the subject include St Bernard of Clairvaux's *Sermones super Cantica canticorum* (1135–53), Pseudo-Richard of St Victor's *In Cantica canticorum explicatio* and William of St Thierry's *Expositio super Canticum canticorum* (1139). Useful recent analyses of this commentary tradition can be found in D. Renevey, *Language, Self and Love: Hermeneutics in the Writings of Richard Rolle and the Commentaries on the Song of Songs* (Cardiff, 2001), A.W. Astell, *The Song of Songs in the Middle Ages* (Ithaca, NY and London, 1990), and D. Turner, *Eros and Allegory: Medieval Exegesis of the Song of Songs* (Kalamazoo, 1995).

190 'knytteth and onyth': one of several sets of language doublets particular to the Middle English translation. *De doctrina* reads at this point: 'quod facit charitas, cuius officium est vnire' (p. 93). It follows this sentence with a brief comment upon virgins who lack the oil of charity in their lamps, who are consequently excluded from the celestial marriage feast (Matt. 25:1–13) (pp. 93–4). See Hugh, *Postillae*, VI, 77vb (Matt. 25:3): 'Non sumpserunt oleum secum] … oleum significat charitatem.' (They did not take oil with them] … the oil signifies charity.) The same idea that virginity is not to be praised without charity is also expressed in the Pseudo-Bernardine *Liber de modo bene vivendi* (cols 1238D–1239A): 'nihil valet virginitas carnis, ubi non est integritas mentis. Virgines de suis meritis gloriantes, hypocritis comparantur, qui gloriam *boni operis* foris appetunt, quam intra conscientiam habere debuerunt. Hoc est enim in Evangelio virgines non habere oleum in vasis suis; id est non servare in conscientia testimonium *boni operis* … Virginitas in corpore nihil proderit, si *charitas* aut humilitas a corde discesserit' (our emphasis). (The virginity of the flesh is worth nothing where there is no purity of mind. Virgins priding themselves upon their merits may be compared to hypocrites, who crave glory for their good works externally which they ought to have within their consciences. Indeed, in the Gospel, this refers to the virgins who had no oil in their lamps; that is, they did not conserve the testimony of their good works in their consciences … Bodily virginity will be of no use, if love or humility have gone away from the heart.) The same example, also expounded with regard to charity, is used in the discussion of virginity in *The Book of Vices and Virtues*: 'virginite wiþ-oute þe loue of God is riʒt as þe laumpe wiþ-oute oile; wherfore þe fooles maidenes, for þei ne fillede not here laumpes of þat oile, weren y-schut wiþ-oute at þe feste of weddyng' (pp. 257–8).

191 These three conditions of virginity, listed in *De doctrina* as 'Verecundia in vultu, Paupertas in rebus, et Simplicitas in sermone' (p. 94), bear comparison with the four conditions of spiritual bride listed in the marriage sermon of Gérard de Mailly OP. They are 'uirginitatis integritatem, amorem siue charitatem, obedientie humilitatem, et ornatus spiritualis uarietatem'. The principal sign of the first, i.e. virginity, is designated 'uerecundia' (D'Avray, *Medieval Marriage Sermons*, pp. 262–8).

192 Ecclus. 26:19. Note that Vulgate reads 'Gratia super gratiam mulier sancta et pudorata'. The *Doctrine* has 'verecunda' (i.e. 'modest') instead of 'pudorata' (i.e. 'chaste').

193 This paragraph condenses approximately a page and a half of Latin material in *De doctrina*, linking 'shamefastness' or modesty to the virtue of prudence and mentioning the gospel parable of the prudent virgins who kept their lamps filled (Matt. 25:1–13) (pp. 93–5). A new chapter follows: 'Secundum signum virginitatis est Paupertas' (p. 95).

194 In Latin: 'vnde in vulgari dicitur in exemplum' (*De doctrina*, p. 95).

195 These comments invert the secular practice in which a bride is valued with reference to the material dowry she is able to bring to her marriage.

196 *De doctrina* continues in strong terms: 'Sicut quidam conuersi, qui velut canes nares applicantes circa simos, et stercora explorant de superlectili, et haereditate puellae, pro qua panis claustri petitur a parentibus vel amicis' (p. 96). The remarks in this paragraph need to be read in the context of twelfth- and early-thirteenth-century reform, stressing the imperative of apostolic poverty and criticizing the traditional monastic orders for abuses linked to the possession of private property and the sale of ecclesiastical office for money. However, they also need to be viewed with reference to a thirteenth-century climate of eccesiastical concern regarding the ability of convents to generate adequate financial support for themselves. Guido Hendrix discusses Hugh of St-Cher's stance on simony and quotes from his *Postillae* on Mark 11:15–17 (the overturning of the tables of the money-lenders). He further quotes from O. Langholm: 'Hugh of Saint-Cher joined this tradition [of criticism] in all his four Gospel commentaries. The tables of the money-changers were overthrown because of the avarice of the clergy. Those who sold doves in the Temple signify simoniacs who buy and sell sacraments and ecclesiastical benefices. The money-changers also signify clerics who engages in other forbidden trades', *Economics in the Medieval Schools. Wealth, Exchange, Value, Money and Usury according to the Paris Theological Tradition, 1200–1250* (Leiden and New York, 1992), p. 102 (*Hugo I*, pp. 361–3). A new chapter follows: 'Tertium signum virginitatis est simplicitas Vocis' (p. 96).

197 The theme of the type of speech required for confession is developed in *De doctrina* for a further page at this point (pp. 96–7).

198 Ecclus. 6:5.

199 *De doctrina* explains in this chapter that simplicity of speech, the third sign of virginity, manifests itself in three different areas: in plainness of confession, in the edification of one's neighbour, and in humble prayer (this third is omitted entirely in the Middle English translation). The Latin chapter also develops a contrast with the corrupt who have 'crassiores voces' (pp. 96–8). Following this, a six-page chapter ('De Nuptijs spiritualibus faciendis cum Christo') is entirely omitted from the Middle English translation. The chapter details the spiritual marriage of the soul with Christ, using analogies with earthly marriage and a citation from pseudo-Dionysius, and examines its subsequent protection through penance and mortification (pp. 98–104). A new chapter follows: 'De distinctione Matrimonij spiritualis' (p. 104).

200 The three stages of marriage – initiation, ratification and consummation, i.e. betrothal, consent in the present tense, and sexual intercourse – were a familiar schema within theology and canon law. The three stages were regularly mapped on to the spiritual marriage of Christ with the Church. See, for example, the marriage sermon of Pierre de Saint-Benoît OM, which states: 'Nuptiarum autem istarum matrimonium, scilicet Christi et ecclesie, fuit initiatum in filii dei promissione facta sanctis patribus, fuit ratificatum in incarnatione, fuit uero consummatum in passione' (D'Avray, *Medieval Marriage Sermons*, pp. 214–16). The specific equations utilized in *De doctrina* – i.e. that initiation corresponds to entry into the religious life, that ratification corresponds to profession, and that consummation corresponds to perseverance – are also voiced in the marriage sermons of Pierre de Saint-Benoît and Jean de la Rochelle OM: 'Nuptie hee initiantur in ingressione, ratificantur in professione, consummantur in perseuerantia' (D'Avray, *Medieval Marriage Sermons*, pp. 214, 186). See also Hugh, *Postillae*, VI, 290vab (John 2): 'Moraliter. Hee nuptiae initiantur in inchoatione poenitentiae, ratificantur in profectu iustitiae, consummantur in gloria, quando iam anima non potest separari a sponso.' (Morally. This marriage is initiated at the beginning of penance, it is ratified in the process of justice, it is consummated in glory when, now, the soul cannot be separated from the bridegroom.)

201 It is common practice for a nun to receive a ring, symbolizing eternal betrothal to Christ, at the time when she makes her vows of perpetual profession. See John Alcok's *An exhortacyon made to Relygyous systers in the tyme of theyr consecracyon by the Reuerende fader in god Johan Alcok bysshop of Ely*, printed by Wynkyn de Worde (1497): 'Also I haue, by the auctoryte gyuen vnto me by Cryst Jesu, to delyuer vnto you this daye a rynge in token of maryage indyssolyble to be made betwixt you and hym. For, as saynt Poule sayth, ye must herafter remember no thynge but that is godly.' From EEBO at http://wwwlib.umi.com/eebo.

202 'and hast receyvid þe ryng' and 'bi perseveraunce abidyng in the observaunce of the cloyster in maner tastyng of swetnes of joye' are original to the Middle English translation. The final sentence is especially illuminating with regard to the relation between the four Middle English manuscripts and their relation to the Latin. C follows M closely, whereas L retains the addition, but arranges the parts of the sentence very differently and less coherently. See Textual Variants.

203 Jer. 2:2. Note that Vulgate reads 'Recordatus sum tui, miserans adolescentiam tuam, et charitatem desponsationis tuae, quando secuta es me in deserto'.

204 S. of S. 1:2. Note that Vulgate reads 'Ideo adolescentulae dilexerunt te'. The Vulgate adds 'ideo' (i.e. 'therefore') and omits 'nimis' (i.e. 'very much').

205 The image of the school of love reappears in the fifth exercise of Gertrude the Great's *Exercitia spiritualia*, and in Marguerite Porete's *Mirouer des simples ames* (R.A. O'Sullivan, 'The School of Love: Marguerite Porete's *Mirror of Simple Souls*', *Journal of Medieval History*, 32.2 (2006), 143–62). It also seems to have be particularly associated with Cistercian spirituality. H. Blommestijn describes St Bernard's perception of the Cistercian monastery [as] a 'school of love' where the rule of life is consituted by the 'laws of love'. 'Self-Transcendence in Bernard of Clairvaux', in F. Imoda (ed.), *A Journey to Freedom* (Sterling, Va., 2000), pp. 230–65 (232). See also M.B. Pennington, *A School of Love: The Cistercian Way to Holiness* (Canterbury, 2000).

206 Ecclus. 38:25. Note that Vulgate reads 'Et qui minoratur actu sapientiam percipiet'. The Vulgate mentions here 'sapientiam', i.e. 'wisdom'. The *Doctrine* has instead the pronoun 'illam', which in the sentence replaces 'love'.

207 'But first, yif a novice wil for his love suffre tribulacioun … lest þe world fynde more with þe of his good þan of Godis good.' These paragraphs condense approximately three pages of Latin material in *De doctrina* in which the instruction to give oneself fully to God is elaborated with reference to Deut. 21, and the instruction to bring nothing from the world is developed with reference to Gen. 31, in which Rachel conceals certain idols from Laban (pp. 107–9).

208 Jer. 2:2. The Latin is quoted earlier on p. 31, lines 1020–1.

209 This passage refers to the three basic religious vows of Benedictine monasticism: obedience, stability of location, and 'conversion of manners' (which includes forgoing private ownership, and celibate chastity).

210 *De doctrina* explicitly alludes to Eph. 4 as the source for these Pauline words (p. 110). However, this reference is wrong. The Latin text can be found instead in Col. 3:14: 'Super omnia autem haec, charitatem habete, quod est vinculum perfectionis'.

211 The brief allegory which follows bears some similarity to the account of the great king who attempts to woo the recalcitrant soul with riches, fame and beauty in *Ancrene Wisse*, Part VII, lines 68–224, pp. 146–50.

212 Jer. 2:2. The Latin is quoted earlier on p. 31, lines 1020–1. *De doctrina* makes clear that this is the third stage of spiritual matrimony (p. 112).

213 Luke 15:4.

214 St Gregory the Great, *Homiliae in Evangelia*, Bk 2, Hom. 34, lines 46–7,

p. 301: 'Cur autem caelum desertum uocatur, nisi quod desertum dicitur derelictum?' This quotation, which is not in *De doctrina*, appears to have been added by the Middle English translator.

215 From the beginning of the Order, Carthusian houses were referred to as 'heremi' or 'deserts'. The Middle English poem *The Desert of Religion*, probably of Carthusian origin, emphasizes the link. However, this is not exclusively a Carthusian custom, for Cistercian houses were also sometimes referred to as such. See, for example, Aelred of Rievaulx, *Opera ascetica, Liber de speculo caritatis, Epistola beati Bernardi abbatis Clarevallis ad Ælredum abbatem* 1–5, ed. by A. Hoste and C.H. Talbot, *CCCM* 1 (Turnhout, 1971), pp. 3–4.

216 See the marriage sermon of Hugh of St Cher OP, in which the same stages of marriage are outlined with less specific reference to the stages of the religious life: 'Anima enim desponsatur deo per fidem in baptismo. Osee ii(20): "Sponsabo te michi in fide". Et bene dicit "Sponsabo": in presenti enim uita non sunt nisi sponsalia, sed, in futuro, que bene probate fuerint et parate introibunt cum sponso ad nuptias eternales' (D'Avray, *Medieval Marriage Sermons*, p. 156).

217 *De doctrina* clarifies that this phrase alludes to Rev. 21:4 (p. 112). Note that this is part of 'de statu professionis' in the Latin.

218 This closing section in which the translator discusses perfected matrimony ('By this word 'desert', þou shalt undirstond þe blisse of heven ... yif þou folow oure lord wel in þe cloyster') bears a very oblique relation to *De doctrina*. The parable of the lost sheep and the quotation from Gregory the Great are original to the Middle English translation. The translation then returns briefly to the Latin text – 'Thou folowist wel oure lord in desert whan þou art perseveraunte in the observaunce of þe cloyster' – before circling back to reiterate the similitude of a lady wedded to a lord in a far country, already used in the previous section. The penultimate paragraph – 'Than wil thi spouse, Jhesu, wipe away al the teeris fro þin eyghen ...' – is thus extracted from an earlier point in *De doctrina*, where it forms the last part of the discussion of profession as the second stage of matrimony (p. 112). A new chapter follows: 'De bonis spiritualis Matrimonij; et primo de fidelitate Cordis' (p. 113).

219 *De doctrina* specifies St Augustine as the doctor in question: 'Notandum quod tria esse bona matrimonii carnalis describit August. quae sunt, Fides, Proles, et Sacramentum' (p. 113). The idea of the 'three goods' of matrimony, used extensively in canon law and in sacramental theology, derives ultimately from St Augustine, *De Genesi ad litteram*, Bk 9, ch. 7, ed. by J. Zycha, *CSEL* 28.1 (Vindobonae, 1894), pp. 275–6: 'Hoc autem tripertitum est: fides, proles, sacramentum. In fide adtenditur, ne praeter uinculum coniugale cum altera uel altero concumbatur; in prole, ut amanter suscipiatur, benigne nutriatur, religiose educetur; in sacramento, ut coniugium non separetur et dimissus aut dimissa nec causa prolis alteri coniungatur.' See also St Augustine, *De nuptiis et concupiscentia*, Bk I, ch. 17, *PL* 44, col. 424, and Hugh of St Victor, *Quaestiones et decisiones in Epistolas D. Pauli.*, *PL* 175, col. 524D: 'Tria sunt bona conjugii: Fides, proles, sacramentum scilicet inseparabilitas.' See further, St Thomas Aquinas, *Liber de Veritate Catholicae Fidei contra errores Infidelium: Summa contra Gentiles*, ed. by D.P. Marc, C. Pera and D.P. Caramello, 3 vols (Rome, 1961), vol. 3, bk. 4, ch. 78, 4124: 'Sic igitur tria sunt bona matrimonii, secundum quod est Ecclesiae sacramentum: scilicet proles, ad cultum Dei suscipienda et educanda; fides, prout unus vir uni uxori obligatur; et sacramentum, secundum quod indivisibilitatem habet matrimonialis coniunctio, inquantum est coniunctionis Christi et Ecclesiae sacramentum.' The three goods of matrimony, interpreted symbolically, also form part of the structure of many thirteenth-century marriage sermons: see, for example, those of Pierre de Reims OP, Hugh of St Cher OP, and Gérard de Mailly OP. In all these instances children are interpreted as the offspring of good works, and the sacrament is taken to refer to the soul's inseparability from Christ (D'Avray, *Medieval Marriage Sermons*, pp. 110, 156, 252–9).

220 S. of S. 2:16. Note that *De doctrina* quotes a different verse from S. of S. 7:10 (pp. 114–15).

221 *De doctrina* devotes more space to discussing the symbolism of the ring of profession, including a brief reference to Gen. 38, in which Tamar is saved from burning through her presentation of Judah's ring (pp. 115–16).

222 Hugh, *Postillae*, VI, 290vb: 'In hiis nuptiis sunt tria bona matrimonii … Item proles bonorum operum. I Tim. 2.d.'. (In this marriage there are three goods of matrimony … Likewise the offsprings of good works. I Tim. 2.d.)

223 *De doctrina* elaborates these ideas for a further page. A new chapter follows in *De doctrina*: 'De Sacramento, quod est Perseuerantiae, siue inseparabilitatis' (p. 117).

224 'to' translates here as 'two'. See glossary.

225 This paragraph is largely an explanatory addition by the Middle English translator to *De doctrina*.

226 Matt. 24:13. Note that Vulgate reads 'qui autem perseveraverit usque in finem, hic salvus erit'.

227 *De doctrina* attributes this comment to St John Chrysostom (p. 117). It then continues for another four pages (pp. 117–21), quoting St Bernard of Clairvaux on the virtue of perseverance and offering a lengthy exposition of Hos. 2:19–20: 'Sponsabo te mihi in fide, sponsabo te mihi in iustitia, et iudicio, et in misericordia, et miserationibus, sponsabo te mihi in sempiternum.'

228 A new chapter follows in *De doctrina*: 'De Ornamentis animae, et primo de lotione animae per Baptismum, et Passionem' (p. 121).

229 Ezek. 16:9–13. Note that Vulgate reads 'Et lavi te aqua, et emundavi sanguinem tuum ex te, et unxi te oleo. Et vestivi te discoloribus, et calceavi te ianthino; et cinxi te bysso, et indui te subtilibus. Et ornavi te ornamento, et dedi armillas in manibus tuis, et torquem circa collum tuum. Et dedi inaurem super os tuum, et circulos auribus tuis, et coronam decoris in capite tuo. Et ornata es bysso et polymito et multicoloribus'. 'And I washed thee with water and cleansed away thy blood from thee: and I anointed thee with oil. And I clothed thee with embroidery and shod thee with violet-coloured shoes: and I girded thee about with fine linen and clothed thee with fine garments. I decked thee also with ornaments and put bracelets on thy hands and a chain about thy neck. And I put a jewel upon thy forehead and earrings in thy ears and a beautiful crown upon thy head. And thou wast adorned with gold and silver and wast clothed with fine linen and embroidered work and many colours' (*Douai Bible*).

230 The author of *De doctrina* speaks in the 1st person at this point: 'Nec mirum si mundasti me a sordibus peccatorum meorum tali aqua, quae ita bulliens et callida exiuit de profundo cordis, tanquam de fornace quadam succensa igne vehementis, et ardentis amoris ad me mundandum' (p. 122).

231 Rev. 1:5.

232 Jer. 4:14. Note that Vulgate reads 'Lava a malitia cor tuum, Jerusalem, ut salva fias; Usquequo morabuntur in te cogitationes noxiae?' The *Doctrine* omits 'Jerusalem, ut salva fias', i.e. 'Jerusalem, so that you may be saved'. The omission in the *Doctrine* makes sense, since the verse is addressed to the reader.

233 Reviewing the Middle English manuscript variants at this point, it is clear that M is closest to the Latin. The Latin phrase in question is: 'sudore, et lachrymis' (p. 124).

234 The passage as a whole bears comparison with the 'third love' in *Ancrene Wisse*, Part VII, lines 155–65, p. 149: 'Nu of þe þridde luue. Child þet hefde swuch uuel þet him bihofde beað of blod ear hit were ihealet, muchel þe moder luuede hit þe walde þis beað him makien. Þis dude ure Lauerd us þe weren se seke of sunne, ant swa isulet þer-wið, þet na þing ne mahte healen us ne cleansin us bute his blod ane, for swa he hit walde. His luue makeð us beað þrof – iblescet beo he eaure! Þreo beaðes he greiðede to his deore leofmon forte weschen hire in ham se hwit ant se feier þet ha were wurðe to his cleane cluppunges. Þe earste beað is fulluht. Þe oðer beoð teares, inre oðer uttre, efter þe forme beað ȝef ha hire suleð. Þe þridde is Iesu Cristes blod, þet halheð ba þe oþre, as Sein Iuhan seið i þe Apocalipse: "Qui dilexit nos et lauit nos in sanguine suo".'

235 Ps. 67:24.

236 *De doctrina* elaborates on the idea of being dyed in Christ's blood for an additional page (pp. 124–5).

237 See Hugh, *Postillae*, VI, 25ra (Matt. 6:17): '... Unge caput tuum oleo, id est festiuum et hilarem te exhibe.' (... Anoint your head with oil, that is, show yourself to be prompt and cheerful.) *Postillae*, III, 95va (Eccles. 9:8): 'Oleum de capite etc.] .i. hilaritas de mente.' (Oil from your head etc.] that is, cheerfulness from your mind.)

238 Ps. 44:8. Note that Vulgate reads 'unxit te Deus, Deus tuus, oleo laetitiae'.

239 Ecclus. 35:11. Note that Vulgate reads 'Et omni dato hilarem fac vultum tuum'.

240 The fasting, weeping and praying, mentioned here and above, are specific additions by the Middle English translator. *De doctrina* continues for a further half page, relating the oil of spiritual gladness to the oil with which Esther was anointed when she entered the bedchamber of King Xerxes (Esther 2) (pp. 126–7).

241 The *De doctrina* author specifies that he is following a gloss ('secundum glossam') in offering this interpretation (p. 127). Hugh, *Postillae*, V, 58rb (Ezek. 16:10): 'Vel secundum Septuaginta: [Variis,] id est uirtutum, et bonorum operum uarietate. Virtutes enim sunt indumenta interiora, opera sunt uestes exteriores.' (Or according to the Septuagint [Variis,] that is, in a variety of virtues and good works. For virtues are inner garments, works are outer clothes.)

242 The Middle English translator adds the final three virtues: 'devocioun ... clennes and chastite'. *De doctrina* merely says 'et sic de alijs'. *De doctrina* then adds some further comments about colour symbolism within church art: 'Ita enim varietas virtutum repraesentatur in imaginibus sanctorum, quae in vestibus diuersorum colorum in picturis Ecclesiarum depinguntur' (p. 127).

243 The meditation on the thirteen ornaments of the soul is rendered corporate and public by being linked to the principal liturgical feasts of the church calendar.

244 A passing reference to the monastic chapter-house. In this instance, Christ is disciplined on our behalf in the chapter-house of the cross. The phrase carries some reminders of the earlier allegorical scheme (p. 14, line 339 to p. 15, line 397) in which the nun is exhorted to receive correction from Christ within the chapter-house of her heart.

245 The Middle English translator adds this reference to the 'festis of confessoures'.

246 The Latin original of this passage is particularly closely indebted to Hugh's *Postillae*. *Postillae*, III, 69rb: 'In natiuitate Domini pro congruentia solemnitatis debemus indui veste humilitatis. Paruulus enim natus est nobis tunc, et filius datus est nobis ... In passione eiusdem debemus indui veste luctus et disciplinae, quia tunc disciplina pacis nostrae fuit super humerum eius ... In resurrectione debemus indui veste gaudii et exultationis. In ascensione veste spei et amoris, iuxta illud Ioan. 14.d. … In festo martyrum debemus indui ueste patientiae. In festo uirginum debemus indui ueste sanctimoniae.' (At the birth of our Lord we must be dressed in clothing of humility in accordance with the solemnity [of the feast]. For, at that very time, an infant was born for us, and a son was given to us … On [the day of] his passion we must be dressed in clothing of mourning and discipline, for then the discipline of our peace [with God] was laid upon his shoulder … On the [day of his] resurrection we must be dressed in clothing of joy and exultation. On Ascension [Day] we must be dressed in clothing of hope and love, according to [what is said in the Gospel of] St John 14.d. … On the feast of the martyrs, we must be dressed in clothing of patience. On the feast of the virgins, we must be dressed in clothing of sanctity.)

247 I Cor. 9:22. Note that Vulgate reads 'Omnibus omnia factus sum'. *De doctrina* (p. 129) bears a particularly close relation to Hugh's *Postillae*, VII, 96va, on I Cor. 9:22, at this point.

248 In *De doctrina* the discussion is extended slightly with a reference to Aaron's priestly garments (Exod. 28), which represent the 'universus orbis', signifying how we should conform ourselves to all around us (p. 129).

249 The subject is slightly differently defined in *De doctrina*: 'Sic huiusmodi picturas affabilitatis, et condescensionis exterius o Praedicator, o Praelate ad eosdem attrahendos ostendere te oportet' (p. 130). The Middle English translator emphasizes throughout this passage that these instructions apply specifically to 'sovereynes' of religion. See further, Hugh, *Postillae*, VII, 96va: '… Loquitur de sacerdotibus. Sancti enim uiri austeritates suas in occulto faciunt non debent infirmis ostendere. Sicut, qui uolunt aues capere habent picturam auis ne fugiat, sed expectet. Sic sancti uiri aliquam conformitatem in se debent infirmis ostendere. Exod. 34.d. Moyses operiebat faciem suam, quando loquebatur ad Iudaeos.' (… Speaking of priests. Thus holy men who practice austerities in secret must not reveal these things to the weak. Just as those who want to catch birds have with them a picture of a bird, so that the birds do not take flight, but wait. In the same way, holy men must show conformity with the weak to some extent. 'Moses covered his face when he spoke to the Jews.' [Exod. 34:35]) The example of Moses from Exod. 34 is used immediately following in the Middle English translation.

250 This list of mortifying practices is original to the Middle English translation.

251 Exod. 34:29–35.

252 See Mark 1:4–6; Matt. 3:1–4 etc.

253 See Hugh, *Postillae*, V, 58rb (Ezek. 16:10): 'Et calcaui te hiacyntho,] id est spei soliditate, uel desiderio coelestis beatitudinis.' (And I have shoed you with jacinth] that is, with the solidity of hope, or with desire for heavenly happiness.)

254 S. of S. 7:1. Note that Vulgate reads 'Quam pulchri sunt gressus tui in calceamentis, filia principis!' The *Doctrine* has 'pedes' (i.e. 'feet') instead of 'gressus' (i.e. 'steps'). For a detailed exploration of the foot as symbol of the spiritual affections, see V. Gillespie, 'Mystic's Foot: Rolle and Affectivity', in M. Glasscoe (ed.), *The Medieval Mystical Tradition in England* II (Exeter, 1982), pp. 199–230.

255 See Hugh, *Postillae*, VII, 179ra (Eph. 6:15): 'calciati pedes] Cant. 7.a. Quam pulchri gressus tui in calciamentis, filia principis. Ex his uidetur quod praedicatores Evangelii debent esse calciati.' (feet with shoes] 'How beautiful are thy steps in shoes, O prince's daughter.' [S. of S. 7:11] It seems from these that the priests of the Gospel must have shoes on their feet.)

256 See Hugh, *Postillae*, V, 58rb (Ezek. 16:10): 'Et cinxi te bysso] id est, dedi tibi continentiam, quae est quasi cingulum renum, quia per continentiam restringitur carnis concupiscentia. Luc. 12.e.'. (And I girded you with cambric] that is, I gave you continence which is like a girdle for your loins, for the concupiscence of the flesh is bound by continence. Luc. 12.e. [Luke 12:35]) Some additional sentences in *De doctrina* at this point mention the 'vnanimitas, et uniformitas, quae inter Religiosos esse debet' (p. 132). Nigel Palmer usefully draws attention to the way in which this phrase appears to evoke the distinctive Cistercian ideal of unanimity and uniformity in 'The Authorship of *De doctrina cordis*', in Renevey and Whitehead (eds), *Companion*, p. 50. Important Cistercian documents which stress this distinctive ideal include the early twelfth-century *Charter of Charity* ('Cartam vero caritatis et unanimitas inter novum monasterium et abbatias'), and the 1152 *Act of Confirmation*.

257 Luke 12:35.

258 A marginal note in *De doctrina* (p. 132) indicates that this interpretation comes from the homilies of St Gregory the Great. The reference in question is St Gregory the Great, *Homiliae in Evangelia*, Bk 1, Hom. 13, lines 9–10, p. 90: 'Lumbos enim praecingimus cum carnis luxuriam per continentiam coarctamus.'

259 The concept of the religious life as one of continual warfare goes back to the Desert Fathers. It is taken up in Prudentius's *Psychomachia* and re-occurs under various guises in later vernacular texts. It can either take the form of allegorical armament, as in *The Pilgrimage of the Lyfe of the Manhode*, or it can occur in treatises examing the religious life as an embattled experience. The *Desert of Religion* mentions 'sevene manere of batailes, / thurgh whilk a mane mai noȝt mys / of þe sevene crounes of endless blis. / Þe firste bataile, to begyne, / is þe bataile of dedely syne; / anoþere is penaunce herde; / þe third is of þe flesch frawarde ...' and so on. See *Desert of Religion*, vol. 2, p. 300, lines 704–26.

260 *De doctrina* continues the subject of the girdle of chastity for a further one and a quarter pages, referring to the 'mulier fortis' of Prov. 31:24 and to the putrefied linen belt of Jer. 13:1–11, which signifies the pride of Judah (pp. 133–4). A new chapter follows: 'De Camisia Sponsae, quae ad fidem pertinet' (p. 135).

261 The twelve articles of faith refer to the statements of belief that comprise the Apostles' Creed. These articles are expounded in detail in the fourth book of *De doctrina* (pp. 213–29).

262 *De doctrina* continues to discuss the 'fortis mulier' who 'sindonem fecit et vendidit' (Prov. 31:24), and who is interpreted in this instance as the church, for another one and half pages (pp. 135–6). *De doctrina*'s readings of 'sindonem fecit' replicate those in Hugh's *Postillae*.

263 The Middle English translator adds this cross-reference. A new chapter follows in *De doctrina*: 'De Ornamento Charitatis' (p. 137).

264 Matt. 22:12.

265 'is' is a possible spelling for the pronoun 'his'.

266 An indirect reference to Christ's undergarment which was allocated by casting lots rather than by being torn at the time of the crucifixion. John 19:23–24 (p. 138).

267 *De doctrina* here reads 'Hoc dicit contra seminatores discordiarum, suscitatores litium, quae Christum Deum diuidere dicuntur, dum Charitatem fraternam diuidunt' (p. 138). The reference to 'schism' is original to the Middle English translation, and probably refers obliquely to the Papal Schism of 1378–1417. It is also particularly apposite to the imagery of this passage. 'Schism' means 'tear' or 'rent', and the state of being 'in schism' is formally theologically opposed to charity.

268 *De doctrina* speaks simply of the 'principes' of the 'magna curia' (p. 138).

269 Prov. 31:13. A third reference to the 'mulier fortis' who works this wool and flax.

270 Prov. 10:12.

271 *De doctrina*, which continues for approximately a page, translates this coat more explicitly as the coat required to enter the bedchamber of spiritual matrimony, referring again to Esther's entry into the bedchamber of King Xerxes. It also aligns the garment with the linen and purple costumes of the 'mulier fortis' of Prov. 31:21–22, and the sweetly-smelling clothes which Jacob wore to receive Isaac's blessing in Gen. 27:27–29 (pp. 139–40). As such, there are clear cross-references with earlier parts of book 1. A new chapter follows: 'De ornamentis Spiritualium nuptiarum, videlicet, de ornamento Brachiorum' (p. 140).

272 'broches'. The Latin gives 'armilla', meaning arm-ring or bracelet.

273 Hugh, *Postillae*, IV, 12 ra: 'armillas] ornamenta brachiorum, i. bona opera'. (bracelets] ornaments for the arms, that is, good works.)

274 Ecclus. 7:35. Note that Vulgate reads 'Datum brachiorum tuorum, et sacrificum sanctificationis offeres Domino'.

275 The emended reading from C, and the clarification it provides, is justified by a glance at the passage in Latin: 'Datum brachiorum vocat omne opus laboriosum, quod brachijs exercetur' (p. 140), and in French: 'Dons de bras appelle y toute oeuvre traveillant que on fait as bras' (MS Douai, fol. 79v). A literal translation of both into English would read 'he calls the gift of arms every work of labour that is done with [one's] arms', 'every work of labour' being an apposition to the direct object, i.e. 'the gift of arms'. It should be noted that 'arms' should be understood as 'limbs of the body', not as 'weapons'.

276 The twin obligations of manual work and prayer refer to the Benedictine ideal of 'laborare et orare'. St Benedict says: 'Idleness is the enemy of the soul. The brethren, therefore, must be occupied at stated hours in manual labour, and again at other hours in sacred reading.' *The Rule of St Benedict*, tr. by J. McCann (London, 2nd edn 1976; repr. 1989), p. 53. Both activities, manual labour and prayer, are endorsed by most (if not all) monastic orders and often feature in religious texts. The *Liber de modo bene vivendi* (cols 1272D–1273A), for example, states: 'Jeremias propheta dicit: "Levemus corda nostra cum manibus ad Deum" (Thren. III, 41). Qui orat et laborat, cor levat ad Deum cum manibus. Qui vero orat, et non laborat, cor levat ad Deum, et non manus. Qui autem laborat, et non orat, manus levat ad Deum, et non cor. Igitur, soror charissima, necesse est nobis cor in oratio ad Deum levare, et manus cum operatione ad Deum extendere.' (The prophet Jeremiah says: 'Let us lift up our hearts with our hands to God.' [Lam. 3:41] He who prays and works, lifts up his heart to God with his hands. He who prays truly but does not work, lifts up his heart to God and not his hands. But he who works and does not pray lifts up his hands to God and not his heart. Therefore, dearest sister, it is necessary for us to lift up our heart to God in prayer, and to extend our hands to God with works.)

277 S. of S. 8:6. Note that Vulgate reads 'Pone me ut signaculum super cor tuum, ut signaculum super brachium tuum'. The *Doctrine* repeats 'pone me' and adds 'dexterum', i.e. 'right'.

278 *De doctrina* continues for a further page, referring to lay brothers, or 'conuersi', who wear the 'capa Benedicti' on their backs but are loathe to carry out manual labour (pp. 141–2). The references here strengthen the argument that *De doctrina* may have been originally intended for a Cistercian audience. See Palmer, 'Authorship', in Renevey and Whitehead (eds), *Companion*, p. 50. A new chapter follows: 'De Torque temperatae locutionis' (p. 142).

279 See Hugh, *Postillae*, V, 58vb (Ezek. 16:11): 'Et torquem circa collum tuum] ... per torquem circa collum significatur gratia praedicatoris.' (By the necklace around your neck] ... by the necklace around the neck the grace of the preacher is signified.) *Postillae*, III, 183ra (Ecclus. 6:25): 'Et in torques illius collum tuum] .i. tempera sermones tuos secundum regulam sapientiae.' (And your neck in his necklaces] that is, temper your talk according to the rule of wisdom.)

280 See *Ancrene Wisse*, Part II, lines 390–6, p. 30: 'Alswa as ȝe mahe seon weater, hwen me punt hit ant stoppeð hit biuore wel, þet hit ne mahe duneward, þenne is hit inedd aȝein forte climben uppart, ant ȝe al þisses weis pundeð ower wordes, forstoppið ower þohtes, as ȝe wulleð þet ha climben ant hehin toward heouene, ant nawt ne fallen duneward ant tofleoten ȝont te worlt, as deð muchel chaffle. Hwen ȝe nede moten, a lute wiht lowsið up ower muðes flod-ȝeten, as me deð ed mulne, ant leoteð adun sone.' See also *The Book of Vices and Virtues*, pp. 282–3: 'Þer ben some men þat mowe not holde hem stille ne take non hede whan þei seien, be it soþ, be it lees, þat fareþ as a mille wiþ-out scluse, þat euere goþ as þe watre renneþ, for þei haue so many wordes as þe mylle haþ watre. But þe wise putten and schutten þe scluse of discrecion for to wiþ-holde þe watre of folie wordes and outrageous, þat þei ne passe not bi þe mylle of þe tonge; and þerfore þe wise seiþ in his boke, "Ne lete not go þe watre," þat is to seie, wiþhalde þi wordes at þe sluse of discrecion. For as Salamon seiþ, "Who-so letteþ go þe watre at his wille & habundauntliche, he is ofte cause of plee and grete strif".' See also Chaucer, *The Clerk's Tale*, in *The Riverside Chaucer*, ed. by L.D. Benson (Oxford, 3rd edn 1987), *CT* IV, line 1200. See further, many instances throughout Hugh's *Postillae*, e.g. III, 43rb; III, 96vb; IV, 9va.

281 Prov. 17:14. See Hugh, *Postillae*, III, 37vb (Prov. 17:14): 'Qui dimittit aquam] Id est, non refrenat linguam. – Gregorius, *Moralia* VII, In caput VI B. Job: Unde bene per Salomonem dicitur: "Qui dimittit aquam caput est iurgiorum" (Prov. 17:14). Aquam quippe dimittere est linguam in fluxum eloquii relaxare ... Qui ergo, dimittit aquam, caput est iurgiorum, quia qui linguam non refrenat, concordiam dissipat.' (He who releases water] that is, he who does not restrain his tongue. – St Gregory, Moralia in Job VII, chapter 6. Job: Hence it is well said by Solomon: 'He who releases water is a source of strife.' In fact to release water is to unloose the tongue in a flow of eloquence ... Therefore, he who releases water is a source of strife, for he who does not restrain his tongue destroys concord.) (see St Gregory the Great, *Moralia in Job*, Bk 7, ch. 17, p. 347). *Postillae*, III, 37vb: 'Caput est iurgiorum] Id est, origo discordiae, et contentionis.' (The source of strife] that is, the origin of discord and of contention.)

282 See *Ancrene Wisse*, Part IV, p. 89. *De doctrina* precedes this with the example of Sarah who is rebuked by her serving-girl and runs in tears to her upper chamber. Tobit 3:7–15 (p. 144).

283 *De doctrina*: 'Optimus victoriae modus est in multis vinci' (p. 144). Reference unidentified.

284 A new chapter follows in *De doctrina*: 'De inaure Obedientiae, et de proprietatibus aurium Obedientiae, et Intelligentiae' (p. 145).

285 Prov. 25:12. Note that Vulgate reads 'Inauris aurea et margaritum fulgens qui arguit sapientem et aurem obedientem'. 'As an earring of gold and a bright pearl, so is he that reproveth the wise, and the obedient ear' (*Douai Bible*).

286 i.e. 'in *two* things'.

287 Heb. 13:17.

288 *De doctrina* continues the topic of hearing for an additional four pages (pp. 146–50). As Nature has given us one mouth and two ears, so we should observe the same ratio between speaking and hearing; as our ears are open in front and closed behind, so we should open our ears to edifying instruction but close them to vain speech; as our ears are not like those of dogs which hang down towards the earth, so we should not be distracted by earthly affairs; as human ears are smaller in proportion to the body than those of many animals, so our hearing ought to be restricted; as nature has made our ears rigid – so that they can only be moved when the head is moved, so our hearing needs to be accompanied by reason (Aristotle is cited to support this); as the asp blocks his ears with earth to block out enchanted words, which prevent receptiveness to preaching, so we should block out the words of the devil. For this last example, see *The Book of Vices and Virtues*, p. 285: 'Þer is an addre þat is cleped in Latyn aspis, þat is of þis kynde þat sche stoppeþ on of hire eeren wiþ erþe and þat oþer wiþ hire tayle, þat sche ne heere not þe whisteler or þe syngere. Þis addre techeþ vs a wel gret witt: þat we ne herkenen not þe whisteles ne syngeres, þat ben þes liers and flaterers þat enchaunten and begilen ofte þes riche men. But who-so wole stoppe on of his eeren wiþ erþe and þat oþer wiþ his tayle, he ne schulde not be a-ferd to be enchaunted ne begiled, noþer of þe deuel ne of þe wikked tonges.' See also *Liber de modo bene vivendi*, col. 1284A: 'Serpens enim astutum est animal, ut de aspide legitur, quae videns incantatorem venientem, affigit aurem unam terrae, et aliam cauda obturat, ne incantatoris vocem audiat.' (Indeed the serpent is a cunning animal: as it is written that the viper, seeing the charmer coming, fixes one ear to the ground and closes the other with its tail, lest it should hear the voice of the charmer.) See further, Hugh, *Postillae*, II, 146va (Ps. 57:5–6): '... Aspis enim serpens est, quae forte uim habet medicaminis, quae uidens incantatorem, ne uocem eius audiat, alteram aurem affigit terrae, alteram summitate caudae obturat. Sic Iudaei obturauerunt aures suas, ne Dominus sapienter incantans, eos incantaret. Obturauerunt inquam terra, id est terrenorum amore, quia Dominus praedicabat contemptum temporalium et ipsi amabant ea.' (... Indeed the viper is a snake which has, as it happens, its own power of remedy, which, seeing the enchanter, fastens one ear to the ground and closes the other with the end of its tail, lest it hear his voice. Thus the Jews closed their ears, lest the wise chanting of the Lord enchant them. They closed their ears with the ground I say, that is, with the love of terrestrial things, for the Lord preached contempt for temporal things, and they themselves loved them.) A new chapter follows in *De doctrina*: 'De Corona Virginitatis' (p. 151).

289 *De doctrina* additionally cites the reference to the Lord as a glorious crown in Isa. 28:5 (p. 151).

290 Exod. 25:23–25. See *Hali Meiðhad* in *Medieval English Prose for Women*, ed. and tr. Millett and Wogan-Browne, p. 20: 'Ant alle ha beoð icrunet þe blissið in heouene wið kempene crune; ah þe meidnes habbeð upo þeo þe is to alle iliche imeane a gerlondesche schininde schenre þen þe sunne, *aureola* ihaten o Latines ledene. Þe flurs þe beoð idrahe þron, ne þe ʒimmes þrin, te tellen of hare euene nis na monnes speche.' See also *The Book of Vices and Virtues*, p. 260: 'neuer þe later þe virgines han a special coroune aboue þe coroune of ioye þat is comune to alle þe halewen, for þe virgines han a special victorie of here flesche for to pursue þe lambe wher þat euer he goþ, to whom þei ben wedded', and *Speculum vitae*, vol. 2, pp. 399–400, lines 12067–74: 'Bot always has þis madens chast / A speciall coroun to prayse mast / Oboun þe comon coroune of blisse / þat Godde has graunted til alle his. / Forthy þat maydens specially / Has wonnen here þe victory / Of þair flesshe þat þam oft assaylles / Thurgh harde lifynge and gode trauaylles.'

291 A reference to the Legend of St Cecilia, one of the famous Roman martyrs of the early church. Cecilia, a noble Roman vowed to virginity, reputedly converted her husband, Valerian, to Christianity and to a similar adherence to perpetual virginity. The couple were visited by an angel bearing crowns to reward their virginity before their subsequent martyrdom beneath the Roman prefect, Almachius. The legend is recounted in the *Legenda aurea* of the Dominican Jacobus de Voragine (before 1267) and later, famously, in Chaucer's *Second Nun's Tale*.

292 This comment is attributed to St Jerome in *De doctrina* (p. 151). MS Douai, fol. 84r, also attributes the quotation to St Jerome, but does not give the Latin. MS Troyes, fol. 74r, does not mention St Jerome.

293 A new chapter follows in *De doctrina*: 'De ornamento aureo Obedientiae' (p. 152).

294 Ecclus. 29:14. Note that Vulgate reads 'Pone thesaurum tuum in praeceptis Altissimi, et proderit tibi magis quam aurum'. The *Doctrine* has 'cor tuum' (i.e. 'your heart') instead of 'thesaurum tuum' (i.e. 'your treasure') and prefers the synonym 'mandatis' to 'praeceptis' (both meaning 'commandments').

295 *De doctrina* specifies that one puts one's heart in God's precepts via the involvement of the affections (p. 153). The opposition in the Latin text is between the understanding and the emotions.

296 A new chapter follows in *De doctrina*: 'De Ornamento argenteo Diuini eloquij' (p. 153).

297 John 8:11. Note that Vulgate reads 'Nec ego te condemnabo: vade, et iam amplius noli peccare'. The *Doctrine* adds 'in pace' (i.e. 'in peace') and omits 'iam' (i.e. 'now').

298 This paragraph is original to the Middle English translation.

299 Luke 7:50. In *De doctrina* this example is placed *before* the example of the woman taken in adultery (p. 153).

300 Luke 23:43.

301 This paragraph is original to the Middle English and echoes the earlier addition. See note 298 above. Such additions make a direct appeal to the reader's emotions, where the Latin text usually prefers a more intellectual approach, as is the case here. The Biblical quotation (Luke 23:43) is followed by these words: 'Argentum ergo dulcissimum est doctrina Euangelij' (*De doctrina*, p. 153). MS Douai, fol. 85v, says: 'Et pour che la doctrine de l'ev[a]ngile est argent qui douchement sonne'. (And for this reason the doctrine of the gospel is like silver which sounds sweetly.) For a detailed examination of 'comfortable wordis' in *De doctrina* and the Middle English *Doctrine*, see A. Sutherland, '"Comfortable wordis" – the Role of the Bible in the *Doctrine of the Hert*', in Renevey and Whitehead (eds), *Companion*, pp. 109–30.

302 *De doctrina* reads at this point: 'Iste argento ornatur, qui doctrina, et praedicatione Euangelij afficitur, et vitam suam secundum eam regulat. Argentum habet, sed argento non ornatur, qui verba Dei nouit, et secundum verba Dei non viuit' (pp. 153–4). The extra detail supplied in the Middle English would seem to refer to late medieval female religious reading practices.

303 St Jerome, *Epistola CXXV: Ad Rusticum monachum*, *PL* 22, col. 1078: 'Ama Scientiam Scripturarum, et carnis vitia non amabis.' *De doctrina* continues to expound the properties of silver for approximately one page (pp. 154–5).

304 The Middle English translator expands this final book summary. *De doctrina* has only: 'Et haec dicta de ornamentis animae sufficiant' (p. 155).

Capitulum secundum

1 See *The Book of Vices and Virtues*, p. 143: 'Þe secunde [ȝifte of þe Holy Gost] makeþ þe herte swete and debonere & pitous, and þerfore it is cleped þe ȝifte of pite, þat is propreliche a dewe and a triacle aȝens al vilenyes'; p. 115: 'Whan we seyn, þan, "et ne nos inducas in temptacionem," þat is to seye, "my swete fadre, make oure hertes hardy and stedefast þat þei ne meue nouȝt for no temptacioun þat may come to hem þurgh helpe & grace of þe ȝifte of þe spirit of pitee." We biddeþ not þat we ne beþ not y-tempted … But we bidden hym þat he kepe oure hertes þat þey ne entre not into temptacioun, þat is þat þei consent not …'. In *De doctrina*, the heart is kept or guarded not by pity but by the gift of 'scientia' (ME: 'science' or 'kunnyng').

2 In Cambridge, Trinity College, MS B.14.15, the word 'mynche' here and
in the second chapter heading is replaced with 'menoresse'. The manuscript was
bequeathed to the Franciscan convent of St Botolph without Aldgate, London,
by their prioress, Christina St Nicholas, in 1455. These changes indicate that
the manuscript was specifically copied for minoresses.

3 Prov. 4:23.

4 The first section of the Latin text is absent from the Middle English. *De
doctrina* precedes the simile of the heart as a besieged castle with the simile of
the heart as a vessel containing all the treasure of heaven ('quasi vas omnium
thesaurorum caelestium' p. 155). This simile is developed for the remainder of
the chapter (p. 155–8), with reference to the broken vessel of Jer. 25:34 and to
the imperative of sanctifying and honouring the body in 1 Thess. 4:3–5. Seneca
is also cited: 'Vnde Seneca refert de quodam, qui cum capta patria, vxore,
et liberis ex incendio solus remansisset, interrogatus, si aliquid perdidisset?
respondit: Nihil perdidi. Bona enim me meum sunt' (p. 158). A new chapter
follows: 'De custodia Cordis ad similitudinem castri obsessi' (p. 158). Guido
Hendrix identifies the allegory of the besieged castle, developed over the
following pages, as the source of a later French spiritual treatise, *Le chastel
perilleux* of Robert de Saint-Martin. 'Le *De doctrina cordis*, source directe du
Chastel perilleux', *RTAM*, 50 (1983), 252–66.

5 'Were it not gret pite … we axe help devoutly of him.' These lines are
original to the Middle English translation. Candon suggests that they may
have been added to strengthen the link with the gift of pity (Candon, *Doctrine*,
p. 186).

6 1 Pet. 5:8. The Vulgate reads for this verse 'tanquam leo rugiens circuit,
quaerens quem devoret'. There is an interesting variation between the Middle
English manuscripts at this point. L defines the animal as a 'bore'; T, as a
'bere', possibly aiming for greater realism. C and M read 'lyon'.

7 For the commonplace religious trope of the body as a castle besieged
by the devil and assailed through the windows of the senses, see Whitehead,
Castles of the Mind, ch. 6; M. Hebron, *The Medieval Siege: Theme and Image in
Middle English Romance* (Oxford, 1997); R.D. Cornelius, *The Figurative Castle:
A Study of the Medieval Allegory of the Edifice* (Bryn Mawr, 1930); A. Wheatley,
The Idea of the Castle in Medieval England (York, 2004). For contemporary
examples of the trope, see *Ancrene Wisse*, Part II, lines 174–6, 179–81, p. 24: 'Ant
nis ha [to] muche chang, oðer to folhardi, þe hald hire heued [baltliche] [forð]
vt [i] þe opene carnel hwil me wið quarreus vtewið assailleð þe castel? … Þe
carneus of þe castel beoð hire hus-þurles.] [Ne tote ha nawt ut at ham, leste
ho þe deoueles quarreus habbe amid te ehe ear ho least wene.' See further the
early thirteenth-century Anglo-Norman poem *Le château d'amour*, by Robert
Grosseteste, in which the Virgin is imagined as a fortified castle, withstanding

the world, the flesh and the devil. *Le château d'amour de Robert Grosseteste*, ed. by J. Murray (Paris, 1918).

8 The emphasis upon sobriety accords with the positioning of the castle simile in *The Book of Vices and Virtues*, p. 283, where it is used to illustrate the third degree of 'sobrenesse'.

9 'wardis': the courtyard enclosures of a castle.

10 1 Sam. 4:8. Note that Vulgate reads 'Vae nobis: non enim fuit tanta exultatio heri et nudiustertius'.

11 The development of the allegory at this point bears some relation to the figure of the wilful soul, besieged inside an earthen castle, but loved, sustained and eventually succoured by a distant lord, in *Ancrene Wisse*, Part VII, pp. 177–82. For analyses of this influential parable, see Woolf, 'The Theme of Christ the Lover-Knight', 1–16; C. Innes-Parker, 'The Lady and the King: *Ancrene Wisse*'s Parable of the Royal Wooing Re-Examined', *English Studies*, 75 (1994), 509–22. The version in *De doctrina* differs in its emphasis upon the lord's companions, the heavenly saints, and in its stress upon the efficacy of their prayers in persuading the lord to succour the captive soul.

12 The king in question is Saul.

13 1 Sam. 11. Unusually, the scriptural text is paraphrased rather than being directly quoted.

14 *De doctrina* reads: 'Sancti sint impassibiles, non tamen omnino incompassibiles' (p. 162). St Bernard, *Sermones super Cantica canticorum*, Sermo. 26, in *Sancti Bernardi Opera*, ed. by J. Leclercq, C.H. Talbot and H.M. Rochais, 8 vols (Rome, 1957–77), vol. 1, p. 173, lines 16–17: 'Porro impassibilis est Deus, sed non incompassibilis, cui proprium est misereri semper et parcere.'

15 *De doctrina* reads: 'Grauissima enim tentatio est, omnino non tentari' (pp. 162–3). St Augustine, *Enarrationes in Psalmos*, ed. by D.E. Dekkers and J. Fraipont, Ps. 144:4, *CCSL* 40 (Turnhout, 1956), p. 2090: 'Nonne melius est tentari et probari, quam non tentatum reprobari?'

16 The gender distinction between reason (male) and affection (female) is used to similar effect in the early thirteenth-century anchoritic treatise *Sawles Warde*, a free reworking of the Pseudo-Anselmian Latin dialogue *De custodia interioris hominis*, in which Reason is master of the household of the soul and Will is his wife, aided and abetted by the careless and undisciplined servants of the senses: 'Ant te fulitohe wif mei beon Wil ihaten, þet ga þet hus efter hire, ha diht hit al to wundre, bute Wit ase lauerd chasti hire þe betere ant bineome hire ofte muchel of þet ha walde' (p. 86). Such readings contend with the commonplace religious trope of female virginity as a fortification.

17 *De doctrina* supports this reading with a reference to 1 Cor. 13:11: 'Cum essem paruulus, sapiebam vt paruulus: quando autem factus sum vir, euacuaui quae erant paruuli' (p. 164).

18 Prov. 4:23.

19 A new chapter follows in *De doctrina*: 'Stultitiae imprudentium in bello spirituali' (p. 165).

20 The following discussion, of the five follies of spiritual battle (*De doctrina* lists ten follies), makes more sense in the context of the original Latin structure in which the heart is kept or guarded by the gift of 'scientia', equated on pp. 164–5 with 'sapientia'. The Latin text thus creates a neat oppostion between 'sapientia' and 'stultitia'. For a brief comparison between the Ten Follies in the Latin and the Five Follies in the Middle English, see Mouron, '*Doctrine of the Hert*: a Middle English Translation', pp. 88–94. The trope of spiritual battle which underpins the following section derives ultimately from Paul's description of the 'miles Christi', in Eph. 6:10–18. Numbered lists of 'stultitiae' are common throughout Guillaume Peraldus, *Summa de vitiis et virtutibus*, which has close affinities with *De doctrina cordis*. See, for example, Bk 5, Part 2.4: 'De xii stultitiis otiosi hominis', and Part 4.3: 'De duodecim stultitiis indiscreti fervoris'. For a direct source, see further Bk 2, Part 3.3: 'De stultitijs quibus prudentes in bello spirituali succumbunt'. 'Prima est eorum qui ante pugnam se armare nolunt ... secunda est eorum qui sumunt arma nimis onerosa ... tertio est eorum qui in ipso conflictu arma sua proiiciunt ... quarta est eorum qui ex ea parte qua debiliores sunt ... quintus est eorum qui nolunt resistere hostibus in loco ubi facilius possent ...' (p. 103). See also Hugh, *Postillae*, III, 97ra (Eccles. 9:18): 'Melior est sapientia quam arma bellica] Multiplex insipientia in bello spirituali. Multi habent haec arma, qui tamen in bellis spiritualibus succumbunt propter insipientiam aliquando, quae multiplex est ... Secunda insipientia est, cum ante pugnam non se armant, sed tunc primum arma protectionis arripiunt, cum iam fuerint uulnerati, et fiunt eis arma oneri, quae prius fuissent defensioni ... Cum iam fuerint prostrati gladio detractionis, tunc primo uolunt arripere clypeum humilitatis, uel patientiae, tunc primo consilia quaerunt, quibus haec iacula repellere possent.' (Wisdom is better than military weapons. There are many kinds of folly in spiritual battle. Many have weapons who nevertheless sometimes succumb in spiritual battle because of these many kinds of folly ... The second folly is when they do not arm themselves before the fight, but then first seize weapons of protection when they have already been wounded, making their weapons, which would earlier have been a defence, into a burden ... When they have been overthrown by the sword of detraction, then they first want to seize the shield of humility or of patience, then they first look for the advice with which they may be able to repel these javelins.)

21 *De doctrina* links this exhortation to sufferance and silence to Job 40:1–5. It then continues for another half page, quoting St John Chrysostom on the inadvisability of fighting like women: 'quae fortes sunt in lingua, infirmae in manibus', and stressing Christ's sufferance and silence at the battle of the cross (pp. 165–6). A new chapter follows: 'Secunda stultitia' (p. 166).

22 This sentence in the Middle English translation is subtituted for a brief account in *De doctrina* (p. 166), of David being weighed down by Saul's armour. 1 Sam. 17:38–39. See Hugh, *Postillae*, III, 97ra (Eccles. 9:18): 'Primo est, quando arma nimis onerosa sunt, et supra uires, ita quod non sufficiunt ad portandum, ut sunt nimiae psalmodiae, nimiae uigiliae, nimiae disciplinae, nimiae abstinentiae, et huiusmodi, quae certandi strenuitatem magis impediunt. Propter quod, et Dauid recusauit arma Saulis. 1. Reg. 17.e.' (First it is when their weapons cannot be carried because they are too heavy, and outweigh their strength, such as is the case with too much psalm-singing, too many vigils, too much scourging, too much abstinence and other things of this kind, which impede the vigour of those who fight to a significant degree. Because of which, David refused Saul's weapons. 1 Reg. 17. [1 Sam. 17:39]) A new chapter follows in *De doctrina*: 'Tertia stultitia' (p. 167).

23 See Hugh, *Postillae*, III, 97rb (Eccles. 9:18): 'Quinta stultitia est, quod statim ubi congressus imminet, et iacula praesentimus, prorsus arma nostra rejicimus quibus poteramus nos tueri … Cum iaculum detractionis, aut contumeliae, aliquis in nos iaculauerit, statim patientiam et humilitatem, quae uelut clypeus opponenda fuerant, abjicimus. Unde Philosophia dixit Boetio. Talia tibi contuleramus arma, quae nisi prius reiecisses inuicta te firmitate tuerentur.' (The fifth folly is that, as soon as the fight menaces and we anticipate javelins, straight away we throw back our weapons with which we could have protected ourselves … When someone pierces us with the javelin of detraction or of insult, at once we throw away the patience and humility which had been set against them like a shield. Hence Philosophy said to Boethius: We had brought you such weapons, these invincible weapons would have protected you firmly if you had not thrown them back beforehand.) The same quotation from Boethius is used in *De doctrina* at this point, in relation to the third folly (p. 167).

24 S. of S. 4:4. Note that Vulgate reads 'Mille clypei pendent ex ea, omnis armatura fortium'. The *Doctrine* adds 'ibi' (i.e. 'in that place') at the beginning of the sentence.

25 A martyrology is an official register of Christian martyrs arranged in the calendar order of their anniversaries or feasts. 'Historical' martyrologies, such as those of Bede, Ado and Usuard, also include stories or biographical details of the martyr. One of the main institutional uses of the martyrology was in the chapter meeting, when it supplied information on the saints whose feasts were to be celebrated the following day.

26 The emphasis upon arming oneself with the examples of the saints correlates with the emphasis upon the efficacy of praying to saints for succour from allegorical ensiegement in the first similitude of the chapter.

27 A new chapter follows: 'Quarta stultitia' (p. 168). In the Middle English translation, the character of the fourth and fifth follies are reversed from the Latin. 'Quinta stultitia' follows on pp. 169–70.

28 At this point in C, the next twenty-one lines of transcription (up until '... yif þou wilt perfightly kepe þe') are crossed out and recommenced on the next folio.

29 See Hugh, *Postillae*, III, 97rab (Eccles. 9:18): 'Quarta insipientia est, quia differimus hostem percutere dum paruulus est, et infirmus, et debilis, quia tunc de facili potest occidi. Paruulus est hostis in primo motu, debilis quando adhuc est in sola cogitatione, infirmus etiam est, quando nondum exhibuimus membra nostra arma iniquitatis peccato, ut legitur Rom. 6.c. id est, quando peccatum nondum uenit ad opus.' (The fourth folly is when we refrain from striking the enemy hard when he is insignificant and weak and powerless, for then he can be killed easily. An enemy is insignificant in his first rising, powerless when he still exists only in the mind, he is also weak 'when we have not yielded our members as instruments of iniquity unto sin', as it is written in Rom. 6.c. [Rom. 6:13], that is, when the sin has not yet been enacted.) *De doctrina* continues for a further twelve lines, quoting from Ovid's *Remedia amoris*, Ps. 136 and St Jerome (p. 170).

30 The imagery of the spiritual siege which underpins the first part of the book remains in play here.

31 See *The Book of Vices and Virtues*, p. 225: 'kepe wel alle þe wittes of þe body. Þe ei3en from foliliche lokynges, þe eeren fro herkenynge of foly wordes, þe honden fro foliliche touchynges, þe naseþerles from to moche haue likynge in swote smelles, þe tonge from to moche haue delite in goode metes and goode sauours. Þes ben þe fyue 3ates of þe citee of a mannes or a wommanes herte, wher-bi þe deuel goþ ynne ofte.'

32 *De doctrina* continues to examine the necessity of being busy for three-quarters of a page. It quotes Judith and Jerome, and ends the chapter with a further reference to a castle under attack (p. 169).

33 The Middle English translator supplies this list of specific godly occupations. This list is more congenial to the female reader that the comparison in the Latin text to avoid arrows in a siege.

34 The Middle English translator omits the second five of the ten follies described in *De doctrina* (pp. 170–5). The sixth folly relates to those who fight against themselves and do not recognize their enemies. The seventh relates to those who fight at close range. This is particularly unadvisable if fornication is the enemy. The eighth relates to those who attempt to evade the enemy by fleeing. Two types of warfare are discussed; we should oppose vexations but flee allurements: 'Occurre ergo molestijs, delitias fuge' (p. 173). The ninth relates to those who use the same weapons as their adversaries, opposing hatred with hatred ('odio contra odium' p. 173). The tenth relates to those who expend excessive effort in fighting when they could succeed quietly. The section, as a whole, closes with an epilogue (pp. 174–5) in which all ten follies are reiterated briefly. For the Latin text of the last five follies and a translation into English, see Mouron, '*Doctrine of the Hert*: a Middle English Translation', pp. 88–9. A new chapter follows in *De doctrina*: 'De Custodia Linguae' (p. 175).

35 Prov. 4:23.

36 Prov. 13:3.

37 The sins of the tongue, usually included in the sin of gluttony, are often castigated in religious or devotional texts. The *Desert of Religion* has a whole section devoted to 'þat wicked tonge'. See *Desert of Religion*, vol. 1, pp. 297–8. The *Book for a Simple and Devout Woman* examines the twenty-two species of the Sins of the Tongue (pp. 247–99). *Ancrene Wisse*, Part II, also vituperates this sin.

38 See St Gregory the Great, *Moralia in Job*, Bk 1, chs 30, 32, 35, pp. 47–8, 50–2), where Job's household is interpreted as a figure for the human mind. The portress of this household is the quality of discernment, which differentiates between vice and virtue and holds the entrance against vices. See further, the porter of prudence in *Sawles Warde*, p. 88. See further, *The Book of Vices and Virtues*, p. 283: 'Whan enemys þat maken werre aȝens any castel or citee fynden þe castel ȝate vp, þei gon ynne þe liȝtloker; riȝt so þe deuel, þat werreþ þe castel of þe herte, whan he fyndeþ þe grete ȝate vp, þat is þe mouþ, he takeþ liȝtliche þe castel; and þerfore seiþ Dauid in þe Sauter, "I sett," he seiþ, "good kepyng to my mouþ aȝens myn enemy þat is aȝens me," þat is þe deuel. Þe kepyng of þe mouþ is resoune and discrecion, þat mowe examyne þe wordes er þei passen out of þe mouþ.' See further, the porter of discretion in *Doctrine of the Hert*, p. 19, lines 534–6 above, together with associated commentary notes.

39 Prov. 25:28. Note that Vulgate reads 'Sicut urbs patens et absque murorum ambitu, ita vir qui non potest in loquendo cohibere spiritum suum'. The *Doctrine* has the synonym 'homo' instead of 'vir' (both here mean 'man', in the sense of man or woman). *De doctrina* follows this quotation with a reference to the *Glossa*: 'Vbi dicit Glossa: Si murum silentij os non habet, patet inimici iaculis ciuitas mentis' (p. 176). The *Glossa* continues: '... et cum se per uerba extra semetipsam iacit, apertam se aduersario ostendit: quam tanto ille sine labore superat, quanto et ipsa quae uincitur, contra semetipsam per multiloquium pugnat' (*Biblia Latina cum Glossa Ordinaria, facs. repr. of editio princeps Adolph Rusch of Strassburg 1480/81*, intro. by K. Froehlich and M.T. Gibson [Turnhout, 1992], vol. 2, p. 684). (Where the Gloss says: If the mouth does not have a wall of silence, the city of the mind is thrown wide open to the enemy's darts ... The *Glossa* continues: when it [the mind] throws itself outside via words, it lays itself open to the enemy; the enemy overwhelms it effortlessly to the same degree that the conquered mind fights against itself by talkativeness.) See also, Hugh, *Postillae*, III, 57ra: 'Sicut urbs … spiritum suum] Ad literam, ad modestiam loquendi, et docendi inuitat hic Salomon. Sicut enim nimia perscrutatio in discendo reprobabilis est, ita immoderata locutio in docendo odibilis est. Vel contra uitium loquacitatis dicitur hoc. Silentium enim munitio ciuitatis est animae.' (Like a city … his spirit] literally, here Solomon invites moderation in speaking and in teaching. Indeed, although too much scholarly research deserves condemnation, yet uncontrolled speech in teaching is hateful. Or this is said against the vice of talkativeness. For, silence is the fortification of the city of the soul.)

40 Num. 19:15. Note that Vulgate reads 'Vas, quod non habuerit operculum, nec ligaturam desuper, immundum erit'. The *Doctrine* omits 'nec ligaturam desuper', i.e. 'neither a fastening on top'.

41 'Ther is no portour of discrecioun … as long as it usith such condiciouns.' These words replace two biblical quotations in *De doctrina*: Prov. 25:8 and Ecclus. 19:10 (p. 177).

42 Jas. 3:3–5. Note that Vulgate reads 'Si autem equis frena in ora mittimus ad consentiendum nobis, et omne corpus illorum circumferimus. Ecce et naves, cum magnae sint, et a ventis validis minentur, circumferentur a modico gubernaculo ubi impetus dirigentis voluerit. Ita et lingua modicum quidem membrum est, et magna exaltat'. The *Doctrine* omits 'ubi impetus dirigentis voluerit', 'whithersoever the force of the governor willeth' (*Douai Bible*).

43 For the image of the unbridled horse, see *The Book of Vices and Virtues*, p. 226: 'þe bodiliche wittes fareþ as þe hors þat renneþ vnder a man wiþ-oute bridele, for þei ouer-þrowen here maister'; p. 283: '"Put," [Solomon] seiþ, "þi wordes in a balauns and a good bridel in þy mouþ, and take hede þat þou falle not bi þe tonge tofore þin enemys þat aspien þe." Who-so weieþ not his wordes in þe balauns of discrecion and wiþhaldeþ not his tonge bi þe bridel of resoune, þat schulde wiþdrawe þe tonge from schrewed wordes, he falleþ liȝtliche into þee hondes of his enemys.' See also *Speculum vitae*, vol. 2, p. 323, lines 9705–10: 'þe wittes of a man þat es idell / Fares as a horse withouten brydell / þat rynnes ay on-heued fast / And castes his mayster at þe last./ Bot þe chaste hert of gode wille / Restreynes þe wittes with þe brydell of skille.'

44 Prov. 12:14.

45 In *De doctrina*, this fruit is 'gratiarum actio' (p. 178).

46 This section, 'De fructu oris', bears a close relation to the chapter 'De octo fructibus oris' in Peraldus, *Summa de vitiis et virtutibus*, Bk 5, Part 2.4. Peraldus's fruits are 'Dei laudatio', 'gratiarum actio', 'oratio', 'confessio', 'modestia', 'abstinentia', 'fraterna eruditio' and 'fidelis reclamatio'. See also Hugh, *Postillae*, III, 28ra (Prov. 12:14): 'De fructu oris sui] … Est autem multiplex fructus oris. Primus est modestia sermonis. Secundus, abstinentia

contra vitium gulae. Tertius, veritas. Quartus, confessio peccati. Quintus, confessio laudis. Sextus, oratio. Septimus, gratiarum actio. Octauus, reclamatio pro iure Christi … Nonus, soboles spiritualis, quae maxime requiritur a doctoribus et praelatis.' (Concerning the fruit of his mouth] … Now there are many fruits of the mouth. The first fruit is moderation of speech. The second, abstinence against the vice of gluttony. The third, truth. The fourth, the confession of sin. The fifth, confession of praise. The sixth, prayer. The seventh, rendering thanks [to God]. The eighth, claiming through Christ's righteousness … The ninth, spiritual off-shoots, which are particularly required from scholars and prelates.)

47 I Cor. 14:19. Note that Vulgate reads 'volo quinque verba sensu meo loqui, ut et alios instruam: quam decem millia verborum in lingua'. The *Doctrine* has 'malo' (i.e. 'prefer') instead of 'volo' (i.e. 'want'). It also omits 'ut et alios instruam' (i.e. 'so that I may teach others').

48 Luke 23:40–42. Note that Vulgate reads 'Neque tu times Deum, quod in eadem damnatione es. Et nos quidem iuste, nam digna factis recipimus: hic vero nihil mali gessit. Et dicebat ad Iesum: Domine, memento mei cum veneris in regnum tuum'. 'Neither dost thou fear God, seeing thou art under the same condemnation? And we indeed justly; for we receive the due reward of our deeds. But this man hath done no evil. And he said to Jesus: Lord, remember me when thou shalt come into thy kingdom' (*Douai Bible*).

49 The Latin is expressed far more economically: 'Horum quinque fructus collegit ille latro poenitens, qui iuxta Iesum pendens in Cruce socio ex altero latere pendenti dicebat, Lucae. 23. Neque tu times Deum: Ecce correctio. Quod in eadem damnatione es: Ecce instructio. Et nos quidem iuste, nam digna factis recipimus: Ecce sui ipsius accusatio. Hic vero nihil mali gessit: Ecce boni commendatio. Memento mei Domine cum veneris in regnum tuum: Ecce oratio' (*De doctrina*, p. 179). A new chapter follows: 'De sermone, siue locutione, et quae in illis inquirenda sunt. Quid loquendum' (p. 179).

50 Self-scrutiny of the conditions of speech is consistently recommended within post-Lateran IV pentitentials in much the same terms as recommended categorizations of the circumstances of sin. These circumstances were often listed following the mnemonic: 'quid', 'quis', 'ubi', 'cum', 'quot', 'quotiens', 'cur', 'quomodo' and 'quando'. See Hugh, *Postillae*, VI, 47va (Matt. 12:37): 'Et ex uerbis tuis] … Unde Proverb. 18.d. Mors, et vita in manibus linguae. Nota: in locutione quinque sunt inquirenda. Quid dicatur, cui dicatur, ubi quid dicatur, quando quid dicatur, et qualitas, id est, modus loquendi.' (And from your words] … Hence Proverb 18.d. 'Death and life are in the power of the tongue.' [Prov. 18:21] Note: there are five things to be examined in speech. What may be said, to whom it may be said, where something may be said, when something may be said, and the nature, that is, the *modus loquendi* or way of saying.) See also *The Book of Vices and Virtues*, p. 54: 'Who-so wole wyte and weye þe synnes of þe tonge, hym bihoueþ to conne weye and haue also a contrepeys of alle his wordes: wher-of þei wexen, what þei ben, and what yuele þei don. 3if þou wys be wil, six kep þou whilke I þe kenne: what þou seist, whom til, of whom, how, why, where, whenne.' The categorization of the circumstances of speaking and silence is also a feature of late twelfth- and early thirteenth-century rhetorical manuals such as Albertanus da Brescia, *Tractatus de arte loquendi et tacendi* (1245). Guido Hendrix offers the following outline of the next section of *De doctrina*, pp. 179–85 (from p. 54, line 298 to p. 56, line 352 in the Middle English):

1. Viso de custodia lingue, sunt autem quinque que inquirenda sunt in locutione. 1.1. ut tu attendas QUID dicas; triplex differentia uerborum malorum: 1.1.1. quid nociuum uerbum. ... 1.1.2. quid inhonestum. 1.1.3. quid inutile. 1.2. CUI dicas, id est cum quo loqui debeas: qualitas persone. 1.2.1. si pro te. 1.2.2. aut pro illo loquaris. 1.3. UBI dicas. ... 1.4. QUANDO dicas: 1.4.1. tempus loquendi. 1.4.2. tempus tacendi. 1.5. QUALITER dicas, id est modum loquendi. 1.5.1. quo gestu. 1.5.2. qua significatione. 1.5.3. quo sono. (*Hugo I*, pp. 358–9).

51 For an analysis of such commendable speech, see Sutherland, 'Comfortable Wordis', in Renevey and Whitehead (eds), *Companion*, pp. 109–30.

52 The order of the conditions of speech differs between the Latin and the Middle English translation. *De doctrina* follows the order: 'quid', 'cui', 'vbi', 'quando', 'qualiter' (respectively, pp. 179–82, 182–3, 183, 183–4, 184–5. Note that each represents a different chapter). The Middle English proceeds: what, when, where, to whom and how.

53 Eccles. 3:7. Note that Vulgate reads 'Tempus tacendi, et tempus loquendi'. See Hugh, *Postillae*, VI, 47va (Matt. 12:36): 'Quartum est, quando quid dicatur. Est enim tempus tacendi, scilicet, si alius loqui coeperit.' (The fourth is, when something may be said. For there is a time to be silent, namely, if someone else has begun to talk.)

54 See Hugh, *Postillae*, VI, 47va (Matt. 12:36): 'Tertium est ubi quid dicatur. Est enim locus ubi perpetuum seruandum est silentium, ut sanctuarium, dormitorium.' (The third is, where something may be said. For there are locations where silence must be observed unbroken, such as the sanctuary and the dormitory.) Orders following the Benedictine rule kept strict silence from the end of Compline each evening until the following morning in addition to times of lesser silence. Silence was also mapped onto the geography of the monastery. Speaking was forbidden in the central area of the cloister, in the refectory during meals, and in the calefactory or warming house. Conversely, rooms such as the auditorium and chapter-house were specifically designed for conversation and oral instruction.

55 Ecclus. 22:14. Note that the Vulgate reads: 'Cum stulto non multum loquaris, et cum insensato ne abieris'. The *Doctrine* omits the second phrase 'et cum insensato ne abieris', i.e. 'and go not with him that hath no sense' (*Douai Bible*).

56 See Hugh, *Postillae*, VI, 47va (Matt. 12:36): '... Secundum est, cui quid dicatur. Ecclus. 22.b. Cum stulto ne multum loquaris, quia qui arguit impium generat maculam sibi. Qui ergo cum alio loquitur, primo consideret si pro se, aut propter alium loquatur. Si propter suam utilitatem loquatur, uideat utrum ipse sit talis de cuius colloquio utilitas ei provenire possit.' (The second is, to whom something may be said. Ecclus. 22.b. [Ecclus. 22:14] 'Do not speak much with the foolish', for he who finds fault with the impious begets his own blemish. Therefore, he who speaks with someone else should first consider whether he is talking for his own sake, or on account of someone else. If he is talking because of the usefulness [of his words], let him consider which one of the two applies: whether he himself is such a person whose conversation may benefit another.)

57 'It is a yifte of þe holy gost for to have þe spirit of counseyle. Al sad folk hane not þat yifte. Þe holy gost yivith it where he wille.' These lines are original to the Middle English translation.

58 This sentence is original to the Middle English translation. A new chapter follows in *De doctrina*: 'Modus loquendi' (p. 184).

59 See Hugh, *Postillae*, VI, 47vb: 'Item qualitas, id est, modus loquendi in tribus consistit. Hoc est, quo gestu, quo sono, qua significatione quid dicatur. Sit ergo gestus modestus, humilis, sonus mitis, et suauis ... significatio uerax, et dulcis.' (Likewise the nature, that is, the *modus loquendi*, consists of three things. That is, by which gesture, by which sound, and with which meaning, something may be said. Therefore, may the gesture be moderate and and humble, the sound, soft and pleasant ... the meaning, truthful and delightful.)

60 A new chapter follows in *De doctrina*: 'De Fraterna Correctione' (p. 185).

61 Guido Hendrix offers this outline of the following, final section of book 2 of *De doctrina* (p. 56, line 353 to p. 58, line 440 in the Middle English):

1. Circa correptionem proximi ... duo inuestigare necessarium reputaui. 1.1. QUI tenentur ad correptionem alterius / et qui non / in quo casu sic et in quo casu non; 1.1.1. corripere fratrem preceptum est. 1.1.2. ad hoc tenentur omnes tam prelati quam subditi. 1.1.3. sed pro loco et tempore. 1.1.4. quod prelatus corripere debet tam corrigibilem quam incorrigibilem. 1.1.5. priuata autem persona tenetur corripere. 1.1.6. Excepties: .v. casus in quibus non obligatur aliquis ad corripiendum alium: non est spes correptionis; cum timet defectus probationis; quando culpa nota est prelato suo tamquam iudici uel quia factum notorium uel quia ille confessus, uel

conuictus; cum meliori operi uacas uel saltem eque bono; correptio plus nocet quam prodest ecclesie. 1.2. QUALIS debet esse correctio. Quatuor in correptione attendenda: discretio; lenitas siue mansuetudo; caritas; utilitas. Quatuor modis contingit male corripere: per indiscretionem; per nimiam asperitatem; uidetur correptio hostilis persecutio. 1.3. QUOMODO recipi debet correptio determinauimus supra in primo libro (*Hugo I*, pp. 359–60). This section bears some similarity to Peraldus, *Summa de vitiis et virtutibus*, Bk 1, Part 3, Part II: 'De disciplina'.

62 i.e. two things.

63 *De doctrina* specifies that there are five such cases: 'Verumtamen notandi sunt quinque casus, in quibus non obligatur quis ad alium corripiendum' (p. 185). It is quite in keeping with the less scholastic tone of the Middle English to omit this sentence. Nevertheless, the Middle English mentions all five cases, even if, contrary to the Latin, they are not numbered. The emphasis upon praying rather than speaking in all these cases, is distinct to the Middle English translation, as is the repeated phrase: 'as long as þou art a subjette and no sovereyne'. See Hugh, *Postillae*, VI, 63ra–b (Matt. 18:17): '... Nota autem, quod corripere fratrem homini est praeceptum, et ad hoc non tenentur omnes semper, sed pro loco et tempore, quando, scilicet, uacat, et licet, et credit, quod sua correctio sit utilis ei qui corripitur. Verumtamen nota, quod quinque sunt casus in quibus non obligatur aliquis hoc praecepto ... Primus est, cum non est spes correctionis ... Prov. 9.b. Noli arguere derisorem, ne forte te oderit ... Secundus est cum timetur defectus probationis; et criminaliter agitur, ubi, scilicet, obligatur actor ad talionem, si deficiat in probatione ... Tertius est, cum praelato tanquam Iudici notum est factum, quia notorium, uel ille conuictus est, uel confessus ... Quartus cum meliori operi, uel ad minus aeque bono uocat aliquis ... Quintus est, cum multitudo, uel potestas est in culpa, ubi correctio plus noceret, quam prodesset Ecclesiae ... Quidam tamen dicunt, quod Praelati tenentur corripere corrigibilem, et incorrigibilem, quia habent officium, priuata persona tantum illum de quo sperat correptionem. Et hoc uerum est de publica correptione, quae pertinet ad officium praelati ubi speratur aliorum correctio.' (... but note that a man is instructed to chastise his brother, and all men are not always bound to this, but according to the place and time, when, it is clear, there is opportunity, and when it is lawful, and when one believes that one's correction may prove useful to the one chastised. But yet note that there are five instances in which one is not bound by this commandment ... The first is when there is no hope of correction ... Prov. 9.b. 'Rebuke not a scorner lest he hate thee' [Prov. 9:8] ... The second is when failure of the proof is dreaded, and an action is brought in criminal matters, where namely the plaintiff is bound by the *lex talionis* if he fails in the proof ... The third is when the deed is as well known to the prelate as to the judge,

and he has either been convicted by those who know him, or he has confessed
... The fourth is when someone calls him to a better work, or at least to an
equally good one ... The fifth is when many people or powerful figures are
involved in the fault, when the correction would do more harm than benefit
to the Church ... Nevertheless, some people say that prelates are obliged to
chastise both those who can be corrected and those who cannot, for they have
a duty, to such a degree that a private person expects chastisement (for it). And
this is true of public chastisement, which pertains to the duty of a prelate,
where the correction of others is expected.)

64 Prov. 9:8. Note that Vulgate reads 'Noli arguere derisorem, ne oderit te'.
The *Doctrine* omits 'forte', i.e. 'perhaps'.

65 *De doctrina* reads: 'Manifesta peccata non sunt occulta purgatione
purganda, sed palam arguendi sunt, qui palam delinquunt, vt dum aperta
obiurgatione sanantur illi, qui eos imitando delinquunt, corrigantur' (pp. 186–
7). St Isidore, *Sententiae*, Bk 3, ch. 46.13, ed. by P. Cazier, *CCSL* III (Turnhout,
1998), p. 293: 'Palam enim sunt arguendi qui palam nocent, ut, dum aperta
obiurgatione sanantur, hii qui eos imitando deliquerant corrigantur.' A new
chapter follows in *De doctrina* at this point: 'Quae sunt attendenda in
correctione alterius' (p. 187).

66 See Hugh, *Postillae*, VI, 63ra–b (Matt. 18:17): '... Quatuor enim debent
attendi in correctione fraterna, scilicet discretio, lenitas, charitas, utilitas, unde
quatuor modis contingit male corripere ... Primo per indiscretionem, ut si
aliquis manifestat crimen alterius sine praemonitione, uel quod probare non
posset, uel quod posset in eum replicari ... Secundo peccat correptor per nimiam
asperitatem, siue per asperam obiurgationem ... Tertio peccat corripiens, si non
ex charitate et compassione corripiat, sed malitiose et derisorie ... Quarto
modo peccat corripiens si inutiliter corripiat, quod fit quando scienter corripit
incorrigibilem, uel multitudinem, uel potestatem, ubi magis nocet, quam prosit
correctio ... Salua pace dicitur, quia quandoque tolerandi sunt mali, et est
dissimulanda correptio pro pace ecclesie, ut dicit Augustinus.' (Indeed, four
things must be attended to in fraternal correction, namely, discretion, gentleness,
love, and usefulness, hence, bad chastising occurs in four ways ... First, through
indiscretion, such as when someone reveals the crime of another without notice,
or [a crime] which he could not prove, or which could be recounted of him ...
Secondly, a reprover sins by showing too much severity, or through a severe
rebuke. Thirdly, one sins in chastising if one does not chastise out of love and
compassion, but with bad faith and derisively ... Fourthly, one sins in chastising
if one corrects unprofitably, which happens when one knowingly chastises those
who cannot be corrected, or a great multitude or [those with] power, where the
correction harms more than it may do good ... With respect to this, it is said
that bad people should be endured for a time, and their correction concealed,

for the sake of the peace of the church, as St Augustine says.) In *De doctrina*, the addressee of the following section is intermittently identified as a prelate (p. 189: 'o Praelate', 'Sed sunt quidam praelati').

67 1 Tim. 5:1.

68 2 Tim. 2:24–25. Note that Vulgate reads 'Servum autem Domini non oportet litigare: sed mansuetum esse ad omnes, docibilem, patientem, cum modestia corripientem'. The *Doctrine* omits 'docibilem, patientem', i.e. 'apt to teach, patient'.

69 St Augustine, *Epistolae*, Epistola 185, ch. 6, *PL* 33, col. 802: '… sed sicut meliores sunt quos dirigit amor, ita plures sunt quos corrigit timor.'

70 *De doctrina* offers a further one and a half pages of scriptural and patristic citations on this subject before turning to the third mode of blame: the necessity of blaming with charity (pp. 188–9).

71 Rev. 3:19.

72 Isa. 11:1.

73 *De doctrina* identifies this 'annoþer' as 'fratri, vel sorori' (p. 190).

74 *De doctrina*: 'Nam (vt dicit Augustinus) Mali quandoque sunt tolerandi, et desistendum est a correctione eorum pro pace Ecclesiae' (p. 190). Reference unidentified. Again, the emphasis upon prayer as a substitute for correction is added by the Middle English translator.

75 *De doctrina* specifies further that the right reception of correction is discussed in more detail: 'in primo libro, in illo capitulo, vbi ponuntur signa, per quae Cor ostenditur esse coctum, tamquam cibus Domino praeparatus' (p. 190).

76 Prov. 4:23. The repetition of this seminal scriptural quotation is original to the Middle English translation. Note, however, that *De doctrina* begins book 3 with a reference to the keeping of the heart: 'Expedito tractatu de custodia cordis, et oris', which is omitted in the Middle English (p. 191).

Capitulum tercium

1 *De doctrina* does not reiterate the relevant gift of the Holy Spirit at this point. It should be noted that *De doctrina* links the opening of the heart to the gift of pity ('pietatis').

2 Guido Hendrix offers the following outline of book 3 of *De doctrina*:
1. Tanquam liber aperiendum est. 1.1. QUE sunt lectiones legende in libro cordis siue conscientie. 1.1.1. lamentatio doloris et penitentie … ut doleas. 1.1.2. carmen gaudii et letitie … ut dolor lamentationis temperetur. 1.1.3. ue dampnationis eterne … ut timeas ac fugias. … 1.2. QUE et QUOT sunt impedimenta apertionis cordis. … Septem impedimenta, que nos concientiam cognoscere non permittunt. 1.2.1. peccatorum defensio. 1.2.2. peccatorum excusatio. 1.2.3.

peccatorum alterius et non suorum consideratio. 1.2.4. peccatorum celatio per hypocrisim. 1.2.5. boni propositi extinctio / propositorum conceptorum suffocatio. 1.2.6. peccantium multitudo. 1.2.7. in mundanis occupatio. 2. Cor aperiendum est ad similitudinem domus ostii. 2.1. Quare et quomodo cor aperiendum est Deo. 2.2. Quare et quomodo cor aperiendum est proximo (*Hugo I*, pp. 366–7).

3 The image of the book of the conscience is central to Robert de Sorbonne's treatise *De Consciencia* (Robert de Sorbon, *De consciencia et De tribus dietis*, ed. by F. Chambon [Paris, 1902]); it also features importantly in the pseudo-Bernardine *Meditationes piisimae de cognitione humanae conditionis*, ch. 15: 'De libro conscientiae emendando'. For a definitive exploration of the book of the heart see E. Jager, *The Book of the Heart* (Chicago, 2000), pp. 44–64, and esp. the discussion of book 3 of *De doctrina*, on pp. 58–9. Jager writes that the interior codex of the heart 'was perfected by learned authors associated mainly with the schools of Paris and with newly founded monastic orders such as the Cistercians' (p. 44). He examines the way that, as a testament of the private self, the book of the heart becomes increasingly identified with the unique individual (p. 45), and cites a variety of twelfth- and thirteenth-century scholastic writers who mobilize this metaphor at length. Richard of St Victor, for example, writes: 'Unusquisque enim in corde suo quasi scriptum gerit unde sua eum conscientia accusat, vel defendit … Quid itaque sunt judicandorum conscientiae, nisi quaedam, ut sic dicam, actiones scriptae? … Judicandos itaque nihil aliud est actionum suarum libros coram judicibus aperire, quam conscientias illis non posse abscondere', *De judiciaria potestate in finali et universali judicio*, PL 196, col. 1182A–B. (Indeed everyone bears a book in his heart, as it were, from which his conscience accuses or defends him … And so, what are the consciences of those to be judged, if not those written actions, as I will thus say? … and so, to open the books of their actions before the judges means nothing else than to be unable to conceal their consciences from them.) The metaphor is developed in a closer and more practical fashion in a twelfth-century sermon from Durham Cathedral, MS B.IV.12, fols 37v–38v: 'Pergamena igitur in qua Deo scribimus pura conscientia est, ubi omnia bona opera nostra notas perennis memorie sumunt et Deo nos commendabiles faciunt. Cultellus quo raditur timor Dei est, qui omnem peccati asperitatem vitiorumque nodositatem a conscientia per penitentiam removet. Pumex quo planificatur disciplina est desiderii celestis que minimas etiam vanarum cogitationum neglegentias diminuat …' (The parchment on which we write for him is a pure conscience, where all our good works are everlastingly recorded to make us acceptable to God. The knife with which it is scraped is the fear of God, which removes from our conscience by penitence all the roughness of sin and the unevenness of vices. The pumice with which it is made smooth is the discipline of heavenly desire, which breaks down the

smallest carelessness arising from idle thoughts). M.A. Rouse and R.H. Rouse, 'From Flax to Parchment: A Monastic Sermon from Twelfth-Century Durham', in R. Beadle and A.J. Piper (eds), *New Science out of Old Books: Studies in Manuscripts and Early Printed Books in Honour of A.I. Doyle* (London, 1995), pp. 1–13 (7). Jager writes that in being urged to consider what lies within the book of the conscience, *De doctrina*'s reader is being 'asked to reflect on his own life as a moral narrative, as a kind of autobiography' (p. 58). In addition, in that the *De doctrina* author urges an affective response to what is written, he 'seems to model the inner book on a privately owned text intended for individual, silent reading' (p. 59).

4 Pseudo-Bernard, *Meditationes piisimae de cogitiones humanae conditionis*, ch. 1.1, *PL* 184, col. 485A: 'Multi multa sciunt, et se ipsos nesciunt.' This Latin quotation is not in *De doctrina*, p. 191.

5 'Certeyn, sister, it is ful necessarie … whereby þou shalt be demyd.' These lines are original to the Middle English translation.

6 Ezek. 2:9–10.

7 A new chapter follows in *De doctrina*: 'Secunda Lectio. Carmen' (p. 193).

8 A new chapter follows in *De doctrina*: 'Tertia Lectio. Vae' (p. 193).

9 'Thees lessouns must ofte be radde, for þogh þou have no moo bokes, it wil serve the al þi lyve.' This sentence is original to the Middle English translation. It offers some insight into the translator's assessment of fifteenth-century English nunnery library possessions.

10 St Isidore, *Synonyma de lamentatione animae peccatricis*, *PL* 83, col. 857: 'De malo alieno os tuum non coinquines' (no. 50). 'Vitia tua attende, non alterius' (no. 51). 'Quod ad te non pertinet noli quaerere' (no. 52). 'Quid inter se loquantur homines cognoscere nunquam desideres' (no. 52).

11 These final two sentences are original to the Middle English translator. *De doctrina* continues for just under a page with an analysis of Deut. 32:28–29, matching the three exclamations: 'vtinam spaerent', 'vtinam intelligerent' and 'vtinam nouissima prouiderent', with the three lessons of song, lamentation and woe (pp. 194–5). The three exclamations are then matched inversely to the three stages of reading comprehension: 'vbi primo scilicet videt oculus, deinde intelligit intellectus. Tertio saporat, et delectatur affectio. Primum tangitur, cum dicitur: Nouissima prouiderent. Secundum cum dicitur: Intelligerent. Tertium cum dicitur: Vtinam saperent' (p. 195). This is another example where the more exegetical Latin is replaced by a direct appeal to the sister. The translator here is advising her what to do. A new chapter follows: 'Sequitur de septem signaculis, quibus liber conscientiae firmatus est, siue de septem impedimentis, quae impediunt ne in libro conscientiae legatur' (p. 195).

12 The specific trope of seven impediments that prevent the opening of the book of conscience appears to be orginal to the author of *De doctrina*.

However, the trope bears a close relation to other, more common, lists of impediments, most notably the 'impediments to confession'. In Raymund of Pennaforte's *Summa de poenitentia* (c.1223–30), these impediments are listed as: the evil hope of a long life, evil shame, evil fear, and despair. In Robert de Sorbonne's *Sermo de condicionibus confessionis* they are: 'extinctio cognitionis peccati', 'suspicio recidivandi', 'timor penitentiae' and 'spes longe vite'. In the *Somme le Roi* they are: shame, fear of penance, love of sin, hope of long life, and despair. See *The Middle English 'Weye of Paradys' and the Middle French 'Voie de Paradis'*, ed. by F.N.M. Diekstra (Leiden, New York, Copenhagen, Cologne, 1991), p. 56.

13   Rev. 5:12, 5:2, and 5:5. Note that this is a composite rendering of these verses. The Vulgate reads 'Dignus est Agnus, qui occisus est, accipere virtutem, et divinitatem, et sapientiam, et fortitudinem, et honorem, et gloriam, et benedictionem' (Rev. 5:12); 'Quis est dignus aperire librum, et solvere signacula eius?' (Rev. 5:2); and 'ecce vicit leo de tribu Iuda, radix David, aperire librum, et solvere septem signacula eius' (Rev. 5:5). 'The Lamb that was slain is worthy to receive power and divinity and wisdom and strength and honour and glory and benediction' (Rev. 5:12); 'Who is worthy to open the book and to loose the seals thereof?' (Rev. 5:2); 'Behold the lion of the tribe of Juda, the root of David, hath prevailed to open the book and to loose the seven seals thereof' (Rev. 5:5) (*Douai Bible*).

14   2 Macc. 1:4. Note that Vulgate reads 'Adaperiat cor vestrum'. 'Deus' is implied in what precedes. See 2 Macc. 1:2.

15   'Therfor it was … seven claspis of youre conscience.' These lines are an interpolation by the Middle English translator of a quotation which is used later in the chapter in *De doctrina* (p. 203), in relation to the opening of the door of the heart. Hence, we will find the same quotation repeated in the Middle English at p. 65, lines 229–30.

16   'apoc. vi' is added in the margin of MS McClean 132, fol. 63r. It is noteworthy that this occurs specifically at the point where all biblical quotations are directly translated into English, without their Latin original.

17   Rev. 6:1–2. *De doctrina* reads 'quod cum aperuisset Agnus primum sigillum, audiuit vocem tanquam tonitui magni. Et ecce equus albus, et qui sedebat super eum, habebat arcum' (p. 196). The Vulgate reads for these verses 'Et vidi quod aperuisset Agnus unum de septem sigillis, et audivi unum de quatuor animalibus, dicens, tanquam vocem tonitrui: Veni, et vide. Et vidi et ecce equus albus, et qui sedebat super illum habebat arcum'. The *Doctrine* (Latin and Middle English) has the quotation in the 3rd person singular rather than in the 1st person, as it is in the Vulgate. This is true with all subsequent quotations from Revelation in this section. The *Doctrine* (Latin and Middle English) also omits 'et audivi unum de quatuor animalibus, dicens … Veni, et vide', i.e. 'and I heard one of the four beasts, saying ... come and see'. Note that the *Doctrine* (Middle English) has 'angel' rather than 'lamb'. It is likely that there was confusion between 'agnus' and 'angelus'.

18   The Middle English translator expands the explanation of the white horse slightly. *De doctrina* reads only: 'Per equum album, corpus castum significatur. Tales enim frequentius loquuntur amarius, qui de castitate corporis inaniter gloriantur, et solam exteriorem carnis munditiam sibi sufficere aestimant' (p. 197).

19   Rev. 6:3–4. *De doctrina* reads 'Cum aperuisset secundum sigillum, ecce equus rufus, et qui sedebat super illum, datum est ei, vt sumeret pacem de terra, et vt invicem se interficiant' (p. 197). The Vulgate reads for these verses 'Et cum aperuisset sigillum secundum, audivi secundum animal, dicens: Veni, et vide. Et exivit alius equus rufus: et qui sedebat super illum, datum est ei ut sumeret pacem de terra, et ut invicem se interficiant'. The *Doctrine* (Latin and Middle English) omits again the mention of the beast speaking. See note 17, above.

20   Ps. 140:4.

21   Rev. 6:5. *De doctrina* reads 'Et cum aperuisset tertium sigillum, ecce equus niger, et qui sedebat super eum, habebat stateram in manu sua' (p. 197). The Vulgate reads for this verse 'Et cum aperuisset sigillum tertium, audivi tertium animal, dicens: Veni, et vide. Et ecce equus niger: et qui sedebat super illum, habebat stateram in manu sua'. The *Doctrine* (Latin and Middle English) omits again the mention of the beast speaking. See note 17, above.

22   *De doctrina* reads 'Per equum nigrum, corpus peccati ... designatur' (p. 197).

23   Prov. 11:1. Note that *De doctrina* reads 'Proverb. 11:16 et 20. Statera dolosa abominatio est apud Deum' (p. 198). The Vulgate reads for this verse 'statera dolosa abominatio est apud Dominum'.

24   Here, and at line 125 in the *Doctrine*, *De doctrina* speaks specifically of 'Abbates' (pp. 198–9).

25   The words 'sistren and bretherin' are used with more wordplay in *De doctrina*: 'Vnde, licet vocent se omnes fratres, non tamen omnes scutellae sunt sorores' (p. 199).

26   *De doctrina* is more detailed and more vivid at this point: 'ad proprietarios excommunicandos, et praecepta cum austeritate, et imperio buccis rubentibus, et peccatori rubenti facienda' (p. 199).

27   'Good sister ... were suche.' These words are original to the Middle English translation.

28   Rev. 6:7–8. *De doctrina* reads 'Et cum aperuisset quartum sigillum, ecce equus pallidus, et qui sedebat super eum, nomen illi Mors, et Infernus sequebatur eum' (p. 199). The Vulgate reads for these verses 'Et cum aperuisset sigillum quartum, audivi vocem quarti animalis dicentis: Veni, et vide. Et ecce equus pallidus: et qui sedebat super eum, nomen illi Mors, et infernus sequebatur eum'. The *Doctrine* (Latin and Middle English) omits again the mention of the beast speaking. See note 17, above.

29 See Hugh, *Postillae*, VII, 386rb (Rev. 6:7–8): 'Et ecce equus pallidus] congregatio hypocritarum … qui recte per equum pallidum designantur … Et qui sedebat super eum, nomen illi mors] id est diabolus a quo mors.' (And behold a pale horse] a congregation of hypocrites … are rightly indicated by the pale horse … And the name of the one who sat on the horse was death] that is the devil from whom death [comes].)

30 Rev. 6:9–10. *De doctrina* reads '… cum aperuisset sigillum quintum. Vidi sub altare animas interfectorum, et clamabant voce magna. Vindica sanguinem nostrum Deus noster' (p. 200). The Vulgate reads for these verses 'Et cum aperuisset sigillum quintum, vidi subtus altare animas interfectorum propter verbum Dei, et propter testimonium, quod habebant, et clamabant voce magna dicentes: Usequequo Domine (sanctus, et verus), non iudicas, et non vindicas sanguinem nostrum?' 'And, when he had opened the fifth seal, I saw under the altar the souls of them that were slain for the word of God and for the testimony which they told. And they cried with a loud voice, saying: How long, O Lord (Holy and True), dost thou not judge and revenge our blood on them that dwell on the earth?' (*Douai Bible*). The *Doctrine* (Latin and Middle English) gives a shorter version of this verse.

31 The phrase 'good lyvyng' is added in the Middle English. The Latin simply says: 'Quid per altare nisi cor designatur, super quod omne sacrificium Deo offerri debet?' (p. 200). Note that 'good lyvyng' is often used in vernacular texts to refer to the monastic life. See, for example, *The Manere of Good Lyvyng*, a Middle English translation of *Liber de modo bene vivendi ad sororem*, Oxford, Bodleian Library, MS Laud Misc. 517. *The Manere of Good Lyvyng*, ed. by A. Mouron (Turnhout, forthcoming). 'Maner of good living' is also the 'tenthe frute' or tenth chapter, in the short treatise entitled *Twelue Frutes of þe Holy Gost*, which accompanies the *Doctrine* in MS McClean (fols 117v–198r), and MS Cosin (fols 92v–150v). *Deuout Treatyse*, ed. by Vaissier, pp. 124–31. Walter Hilton begins *The Scale of Perfection* thus: 'Goostli suster in Jhesu Crist, y praye thee that in the callynge whiche oure Lord hath callyd thee to His servyse, thu holde thee paied and stond stedefastli thereinne … to fullefille in sothfastnesse of gode lyvynge the staat whiche that thou hast take thee too in likenesse and in semynge.' Walter Hilton, *The Scale of Perfection*, ed. by T.H. Bestul (Kalamazoo, 2000), p. 31.

32 1 Thess. 5:19. *De doctrina* adds additional quotations from Isa. 37:3 and Matt. 24:19 (p. 201).

33 Rev. 6:12–13. *De doctrina* reads 'Cum aperuisset sigillum sextum, ecce terremotus magnus factus est, et Sol factus est niger tanquam saccus cilicinus:

et Luna tota facta est sicut sanguis: et stellae de caelo ceciderunt super terram' (p. 201). The Vulgate reads for these verses 'Et vidi cum aperuisset sigillum sextum: et ecce terraemotus magnus factus est, et sol factus est niger tanquam saccus cilicinus: et luna tota facta est sicut sanguis: et stellae de caelo ceciderunt super terram'. The *Doctrine* (Latin and Middle English) omits the introductory verb and conjunction 'et vidi', i.e. 'and I saw'.

34 'for þe nombre of synneris is gretter þan þe nombre of devout lyveris.' The Middle English translator adds these words of explanation.

35 *De doctrina* is more precise as to the identity of those criticized: 'Quid per Solem, nisi maiores praelati vt Episcopi, et Archiepiscopi designantur' (p. 201). L is the only Middle English MS to provide a full translation of this phrase.

36 Again, *De doctrina* provides more precise information: 'Per lunam autem minores praelati, vt Abbates, Archidiaconi, Decani, Presbyteri ...' (p. 201). L mentions 'lesse prelatis as abbotes, prioures, and prestes'. See Hugh, *Postillae*, VII, 387rb (Rev. 6:12): 'Allegorice ... Sol] id est praelatus ... luna] id est ecclesia sibi subiecta, quae ab illo illuminari debuit, amisso suo lumine fiat.' (Allegorically ... the sun] that is, a prelate ... the moon] that is, the church, which ought to have been illuminated by him [the prelate], becomes subject to itself, his light being lost.)

37 Rev. 8:1. *De doctrina* and Vulgate read for this verse 'Cum aperuisset sigillum septimum, factum est silentium in caelo, quasi media hora' (p. 202).

38 'þe moral undirstonding': a brief reference to the third of the four traditional reading levels of scripture: literal, allegorical, moral or tropological, and anagogical. For the classical discussion of these reading levels, see H. de Lubac, *Medieval Exegesis: the Four Senses of Scripture*, tr. by M. Sebanc (Grand Rapids, Michigan and Edinburgh, 1998). For a brief explanation see also 'The Four "Senses" of Scripture', in Turner, *Eros and Allegory*, pp. 89–92.

39 Job 34:30. Note that Vulgate reads 'Qui regnare facit hominem hypocritam propter peccata populi'.

40 'Perfor, I pray þe, whan þou redist ... to regne in mysselevyng.' This retraction of earlier criticisms, whereby the sins of the superiors are caused by the sins of the subjects, is added by the Middle English translator.

41 *De doctrina* includes two extra sentences expounding the importance of *emending* the book of the conscience before presenting it at the day of judgement: 'In mundo non occuperis, et sic in libro conscientiae tuae poteris legere, et eiusdem conscientiae tuae librum poteris emendare. Quid est, quod librum vnum materialem, vt puta Missale, vel Breuiarium, vis emendare, et librum concientiae tuae, secundum cuius scripturam (vt dictum est) iudicaberis, sic incorrectum dimittis?' (pp. 202–3). See Jager, *Book of the Heart*, p. 59 and pp. 54–5, discussing a similar idea in the anonymous Cistercian treatise *Tractatus de interiori domo*. The scribe of the book of the conscience must carefully check his text for errors against the exemplar of the book of life: 'Conferamus itaque libros nostros cum libro vitae: et si quid aliter habuerint, corrigantur, ne in illa ultima collatione, si quidpiam aliter inventi fuerint habentes, abjiciantur', Pseudo-Bernard, *Tractatus de interiori domo*, ch. 15, *PL* 184, col. 520B–C. (And so, let us consider our books in relation to the book of life, and if they differ in any way, let them be corrected, lest they are thrown away in the final collation, if they are then found to differ in some respect.) Other features of the *De interiori domo* show some similarities to the methodology and imagery of *De doctrina*. The treatise opens initially with the scriptural image of the conscience as a house with seven pillars (Prov. 9:1). It then focuses on the reformation of the heart and conscience through confession and penitence, via chapters such as ch. 12: 'De custodia et refrenatione cordis ad bonam conscientiam necessaria'; ch. 13: 'De mobilitate cordis restringenda per considerationem majestatis et potentiae divinae'; ch. 29: 'De cordis instabilitate confessio poenitentis, et responsio patris spiritualis'; ch. 30: 'Pergit poenitens aperire conscientiam et statum animae suae coram patre spirituali'. The last chapters of the treatise move beyond the penitential stage to expound divine love and contemplation.

42 'sentence diffynytif': a technical term taken from canon law. A sentence (the decision of the court upon any issue) is definitive or final when it defines the principal question in controversy. A definitive sentence may be absolutory, condemnatory or declaratory.

43 A new chapter follows in *De doctrina*: 'Quomodo Cor sic aperiendum ad modum ostij' (p. 203).

44 The imagery here links closely to the first similitude of the first chapter, where the heart is prepared as a house to receive Christ as a guest.

45 2 Macc. 1:4. Note that Vulgate reads 'Adaperiat cor vestrum in lege sua'. 'Deus' is implied in what precedes. See 1 Macc. 1:2.

46 Rev. 3:20. Note that Vulgate reads 'Ecce sto ad ostium, et pulso: siquis audierit vocem meam, et aperuerit mihi ianuam, intrabo ad illum'. *De doctrina* also makes reference to S. of S. 5:2 as one of the bases for the following discussion (p. 204). The *Doctrine* has reduced 'siquis audierit vocem meam et aperuerit mihi ianuam' (i.e. 'if someone hears my voice and opens his door to me') to 'si quis mihi apperuerit' (i.e. 'if someone opens to me').

47 See Hugh, *Postillae*, III, 129rb (S. of S. 5:2): 'Pulsantis] utraque sua manu, id est tam beneficiis quam flagellis.' (By striking] with both his hands, that is, as much by kindnesses as by scourges.)

48 These three short paragraphs severely condense two and a half pages in *De doctrina*. The difference between the actions of Christ's left and right hands is developed, based upon Prov. 3:16. The four names with which the bridegroom addresses the bride in S. of S. 5:16 ('Sororem, Amicam, Columbam, et Immaculatam' (p. 206)) are enumerated and interpreted (pp. 206–7).

49 *De doctrina* adds two additional parts of the body: 'manus ad operationem bonam, et eleemosynarum largitionem' (p. 207). The tone of the writing here, and in the two succeeding paragraphs, seems to slip towards a more affective and Bernardine spirituality. In particular, the exhortations here arguably invert the well-known Bernardine comment in the *Legenda aurea*, listing Christ's members on the cross: 'Uidelicet caput inclinatum ad osculum, brachia extensa ad amplexum, manus perforatas ad largiendum, latus apertum ad diligendum, pedum affixionem ad nobiscum commanendum, corporis extensionem ad se totum nobis impendendum.' *Jacopo da Varazze: Legenda aurea*, ed. by G.P. Maggioni (Florence, 1998), p. 346.

50 *De doctrina* continues for a further page, developing the idea of Christ, the rock, based upon Isa. 2:16 and Exod. 33:22 (pp. 207–8). A new chapter follows: 'De Apertione Cordis facienda proximo' (p. 208).

51 1 John 3:17. Note that Vulgate reads 'Qui habuerit substantiam huius mundi, et viderit fratrem suum necessitatem habere, et clauserit viscera sua ab eo: quomodo charitas Dei manet in eo?' The *Doctrine* omits 'habuerit substantiam huius mundi et', i.e. 'who has goods of this world and'.

52 Isa. 58:7. The emphasis upon 'pite', here and in the preceding sentence, makes more sense in relation to *De doctrina*, in which the heart is opened through 'pietatis'.

53 Ecclus. 11:31. The contrast between restriction and openness also relates to the dominant similitudes of book 1 (the guarding of the house of the heart) versus book 3.

54 *De doctrina* identifies St Jerome as the source of this comment: 'Soluit Hieronymus: Omnes introducendi sunt affectu charitatis: et non omnes, imo pauci, in secretum priuatae familiaritatis, et secretorum communicationem' (p. 209). Reference unidentified.

55 This paragraph is reduced from *De doctrina* which quotes Proverbs, Ecclesiasticus, Cicero and St Ambrose. See *De doctrina*, pp. 209–10.

56 *De doctrina* identifies 'Tullius, Libro de Amicitia' as the source of this comment (p. 210). The full reference is Cicero, *Laelius de Amicitia Liber*, ed. by K. Simbeck (Lipsia, 1917), 5, 18: 'Hoc primum sentio nisi in bonis amicitiam esse non posse.'

57 St Augustine, *Epistolae*, Epistola 258, par. 2, *PL* 33, col. 1072: 'nec hominem recte diligere noverit quisquis eum non diligit qui hominem fecit.'

58 Prov. 22:24.

59 Prov. 11:2. Note that Vulgate reads 'Ubi fuerit superbia, ibi erit et contumelia'.

60 Prov. 17:17. Note that Vulgate reads 'Omni tempore diligit qui amicus est'. The *Doctrine* adds 'seme', i.e. 'once'.

61 These two sentences derive from Ecclus. 6:15 (*De doctrina* wrongly cites

'Ecclesiastici 7', p. 212. Note that *De doctrina* attributes this to Ecclesiastes). The Vulgate reads 'amico fideli nulla est conparatio, et non est digna ponderatio auri et argenti contra bonitatem fidei illius'. 'Nothing can be compared to a faithful friend: and no weight of gold and silver is able to countervail the goodness of his fidelity' (*Douai Bible*).

62　See Hugh, *Postillae*, III, 182rb (Ecclus. 6:15): 'Et non est digna ponderatio auri et argenti contra bonitatem fidei illius] id est, contra fidelitatem illius: quia fidelis amicus semper iuuat etiam post mortem, quod non facit aurum et argentum. Fidelis amicus uitam conseruat, tam temporalem, quam spiritualem, quod non aurum nec argentum.' (And there is no adequate weight of gold and silver compared to the goodness of his loyalty] that is, compared to his fidelity: for a faithful friend always gives help, even after death, which neither gold nor silver do. A faithful friend preserves life, temporal just as much as spiritual, which neither gold nor silver do.)

63　Ecclus. 6:16.

64　*De doctrina* wrongly attributes this saying to Cicero, 'ait Tullius in Libro de Amicitia' (p. 212). The Middle English translator adds the reference to Solomon to clarify the scriptural origin of the quotation. Note that MS Douai, fol. 110r, correctly attributes the quotation: 'Et pour che est dit en che meismez livre' (i.e. referring to the previous quotation from Ecclus. 6:15).

65　The Middle English translator adds this final sentence.

Capitulum quartum

1　*De doctrina* does not reiterate the relevant gift of the Holy Spirit at this point.

2　Heb. 13:9. Note that Vulgate reads 'Optimum est enim gratia stabilire cor'.

3　Ecclus. 19:4. Note that Vulgate reads 'Qui credit cito levis corde est'.

4　See Hugh, *Postillae*, III, 205vb (Ecclus. 19:4): 'Qui credit cito] id est, subito sine deliberatione.' (He who believes quickly] that is, suddenly without deliberation.)

5　i.e. 'too soon'.

6　There were several versions of the Creed, often divided up into twelve or fourteen articles. See R.N. Swanson, *Religion and Devotion in Europe, c.1215– c.1515* (Cambridge, 1995), pp. 15–17; J.D. Gordon, 'The Articles of the Creed and the Apostles', *Speculum*, 40 (1965), 634–40. The most popular, that of twelve articles comprising the Apostles Creed, was so named following the legend of its joint composition by the apostles. Oxford, Bodleian Library, MS Hatton 12 clearly states: 'Þe apostlis made þe crede. Petir sayd þus: I trow in God Fader Almighty, maker of heven and erth. Andrew sayd þus þat es consayved of þe Haly Gast, borne of þe Virgin Marie ...' (fol. 211vb). Current from the eighth century, the Apostles Creed was employed within the daily offices of the church throughout the Middle Ages. Priests were enjoined to instruct their congregations in the twelve articles of faith, along with other catechetical listings, in Archbishop Peckham's Lambeth Constitutions of 1281: 'ut quilibet sacerdos plebi praesidens, quarter in anno, hoc est, semel in qualibet quarta anni, die uno solenni vel pluribus, per se vel per alium exponat populo vulgariter, absque cujuslibet subtilitatis textura fantastica, quatuordecim fidei articulos'. D. Wilkins, *Concilia Magnae Britanniae et Hiberniae* (London, 1737), vol. 2, p. 54. *The Book of Vices and Virtues* is one of many vernacular catechetical manuals which offers a short exposition of the twelve articles in its opening pages (pp. 6–9). See also Dan Michel's *Ayenbite of Inwyt*, Stephen Scrope's translation of Christine de Pizan's *Epistle of Othea*, and the *Speculum vitae*.

7 The reference here is to the New Jerusalem of Rev. 21. Rev. 21:14 reads in the Vulgate: 'et murus civitatis habens fundamenta duodecim, et in ipsis duodecim nomina duodecim apostolorum agni'. 'And the wall of the city had twelve foundations; and in them, the twelve names of the twelve apostles of the Lamb' (*Douai Bible*). The relevance of foundation stones to the theme of stabilization is clear.

8 *De doctrina* reads: 'Credere enim in Deum (vt dicit Augustinus) est credendo in eum ire, et credendo diligere' (p. 213). St Augustine, *Tractatus in Johannis evangelium*, Bk 29, ch. 6, lines 39–41, ed. by D. R. Willems, *CCSL* 36 (Turnhout, 1954), p. 287: 'Quid est ergo credere in eum? Credendo amare, credendo diligere, credendo in eum ire, et eius membris incorporari.'

9 i.e. 'two'.

10 *De doctrina* adds that this article is intended to combat the Manichaean error: 'Quae expressio facta est contra errorem Manichaeorum, qui dicunt, ista visibilia esse a principe tenebrarum, scilicet, Diabolo; inuisibilia vero a Deo' (p. 214).

11 The repeated phrase: 'I beleve with love', used in relation to each article, is original to the Middle English translation.

12 The repeated doublet 'moder and mayde' is original to the Middle English translation.

13 *De doctrina* dismisses the idea that Christ's soul was infused ('infusa') around forty days after conception: 'sicut dicitur fieri in alijs' (p. 216).

14 i.e. 'he died'.

15 Matt. 27:42. *De doctrina* reads 'Si Rex Israel est, descendat de Cruce: Lucae. 23' (p. 217). The Vulgate reads for this verse 'si rex Israel est, descendat nunc de cruce'. The *Doctrine* omits 'nunc', i.e. 'now'.

16 The cross is also given this interpretation in a monastic context in *The Manere of Good Lyvyng*. In its chapter upon faith, one reads: 'he þat takyth

the cros of penaunce upon hym muste be dedd to þe world. To bere the cros of penaunce is noþere but to mortifie hymself, and they þat doo not, be as ypocrytis.' Oxford, Bodleian Library, MS Laud Misc. 517, fol. 3r.

17 The recommendation to imitate or participate personally within the events of the creed, here and in many of the following articles, bears affinities to the new affective tradition of meditations upon the life and passion of Christ. Notable thirteenth-century examples include Edmund of Abingdon's *Speculum ecclesiae*, St Bonaventure's *Lignum vitae* and James of Milan's *Stimulus amoris*. Nicholas Love writes: 'For soþely þou shalt neuer finde, where man may so perfitely be taght, *first for to stable his herte* aȝeynus vanitees & deceyuable likynges of þe worlde, also to strength him amongis tribulacions & aduersitees, & forþermore to be kept fro vices & to getyng of vertues, as in þe blissede life of oure lorde Jesu … Wherefore þou þat coueytest to fele treuly þe fruyt of þis boke, þou most with all þi þought & alle þin entent, in þat manere make þe in þi soule present to þoo þinges þat bene here writen or seyd or done of oure lord Jesu, & þat bisily, likyngly & abydyngly, as þei þou herdest hem with þi bodily eres, or sey þaim with þin eyen don, puttyng awey for þe tyme, & leuyng alle oþer occupacions & bisynesses.' Nicholas Love, *The Mirror of the Blessed Life of Jesus Christ*, ed. by M.G. Sargent (Exeter, 2004), pp. 11–13, our emphasis.

18 *De doctrina* reads: 'Compatiuntur elementa conditori suo; refugit Sol, quia non poterat videre mortem Domini collaborans laboranti: Terra mouetur, petrae franguntur, velum templi diuiditur, sepulchra aperiuntur, solus miser homo non compatitur pro quo solo Christus patitur' (p. 217). The quotation correlates closely with Matt. 27:45, 51–52. It also bears a close relation to St Jerome, *Epistola XXIX, seu sermo de resurrectione Domini*, I, *PL* 30, col. 224C: 'Videtur mihi hic dies caeteris diebus esse lucidior: sol mundo clarior illuxisse: astra quoque et omnia elementa laetari: et quae, patiente Domino, proprium lumen retraxerant et fugerant, et noluerant Creatorem suum aspicere crucifixum …'

19 See Col. 3:3. Religious enclosure is viewed briefly as a sepulchre in *Ancrene Wisse*, Part VI, p. 172: 'hwon ȝe beoð ibunden wiðinnen uour large wowes. and he in a neruh kader, i neiled o rode. and ine stonene þruh, biclused heteueste. Marie wome & þeos þruh. weren his ancre huses.' See also *Liber de modo bene vivendi*, col. 1278B: 'Sicut sepultus in monumento cessat ab omni terreno negotio, ita homo contemplativus cessat ab omni terreno opera vel ministerio: et sicut homines ab activa vita ascendentes sepeliuntur in quiete contempla-tionis.' (Just as a man buried in a tomb ceases from all worldly business, thus a contemplative man ceases from all worldly works and employment: and as indeed men ascending from an active life are buried in the peace of contemplation.)

20 'Contemne diuitias, et eris diues, contemne gloriam, et eris gloriosus.' This sentence is attributed to St John Chrysostom in *De doctrina* (p. 218).

21 'In Sindone munda inuoluit Christum, qui eum pura mente suscipit.' This sentence is attributed to Bede in *De doctrina* (p. 218). See also Anselm of Laon, *Enarrationes in Matthaeum*, PL 162, col. 1491B: 'Mystice tamen Jesum sindone munda involvit, qui eum pura mente suscipit.'

22 'his derlinges'. The Latin reads simply: 'vt extraheret suos, qui erant in limbo' (*De doctrina*, p. 218). In Latin theology, limbo is the abode of souls excluded from the full blessedness of the beatific vision but not condemned to any other punishment. The author of *De doctrina* seems to refer here to the *limbus patrum*, in which the saints of the Old Covenant remained until Christ's coming and redemption of the world.

23 Luke 24:34.

24 *De doctrina* clarifies that this is a reference to Rev. 3:1 (p. 219).

25 The Middle English translation slightly obscures the meaning of the Latin in this instance. The Latin reads: 'Item integraliter surrexit Christus in corpore, vt tu integraliter per gratiam resurgas in anima' (*De doctrina*, p. 219).

26 Rom. 6:9.

27 'But now, peraventure, þou woldist wite … þe observaunces of religioun.' The Middle English translation expands considerably upon the Latin throughout this passage, and introduces the reference to the labours of the order. The Latin reads simply: 'Secundum quod homo est, sedet ad dexteram patris, et quiescit tanquam post laborem passionis: ita, si tu cum Christo laboraueris, et passa fueris illic tibi sessio concedetur. Noli ergo labores cordis deuitare, per quos tibi talem praeparas sessionem' (*De doctrina*, pp. 220–1).

28 *De doctrina* cites St Gregory the Great in relation to this sentence (p. 221). The source is *Homiliae in Evangelia*, Bk 2, Hom. 21, lines 52–3, 63, pp. 175–6: 'Quia uero omnipotens Deus et terribilis peccatoribus et blandus iustis … Deus et blandus iustis, et terribilis apparebit iniustis.'

29 This sentence is original to the Middle English translation.

30 *De doctrina* continues for a further three and a half pages, detailing seven ways in which the members of the body of Christ resemble the members of a physical body, supplemented by quotations from St Ambrose and St John Chrysostom. The mutually beneficial co-operation of members is related to life in the cloister (pp. 222–6).

31 'and also bi indulgences'. This phrase is added in the Middle English translation in MSS M, C and T. Indulgences are the remission by the Church of the temporal penalty due to forgiven sin, in virtue of the merits of Christ and the saints. The practice of granting indulgences became common from the twelfth century. In the later Middle Ages it gave rise to considerable abuses, most famously satirized by Chaucer's Pardoner.

32 *De doctrina* continues to elaborate upon the theme of the burdensome body for a further two and a half pages (pp. 227–9). It cites the customary of the addressee's order: 'Attende consuetudines Ordinis tui: Redduntur veteres panniculi vestiario, quando noua recipiuntur ab eo' (p. 227), and discusses those who make themselves ill through their fear of illness.

33 *De doctrina* terminates this chapter by referring once again to the twelve foundation stones of the New Jerusalem (Rev. 21:14), and to their prefiguration: the twelve stones transferred from the middle of the river Jordan (Josh. 4:1–9) (p. 229). A new chapter follows: 'Quae stabiliunt, et confirmant Cor' (p. 230).

34 Gen. 4:4. *De doctrina* (p. 230) and Vulgate read 'Respexit Dominus ad Abel, et ad munera eius'. 'The Lord had respect to Abel, and to his offerings' (*Douai Bible*). Interestingly, *De doctrina* follows this with a reference to an alternative version of the verse: 'Quomodo autem respexerit, determinat alia translatio, quae sic habet: Inflammauit Dominus super Abel, et super munera eius.' Hendrix cites Peter Comestor's *Scolastica historia*, which also refers to an alternative translation of this verse: 'Et respexit Deus ad Abel et ad munera eius … alia translatio aperit: Inflammauit Deus super Abel et super munera eius' (*Scolastica historia*, ch. 27, lines 6–10, ed. by A. Sylwan, *CCCM* 191 (Turnhout, 2005), pp. 49–50). Comestor identifies the alternative translation in question as that of Theodotion, the second-century translator of a Greek version of the Old Testament.

35 *De doctrina* only makes mention of Noah at this point (p. 230).

36 *De doctrina* continues for about thirteen lines, quoting St Bernard and St Gregory.

37 John 1:7. Note that Vulgate reads 'Hic venit in testimonium ut testimonium perhiberet de lumine'.

38 Heb. 11:39. Note that Vulgate reads 'testimonio fidei probati'. The *Doctrine* omits 'in testimonium', i.e. 'as a witness'.

39 *De doctrina* follows this with a comment on the witness of ancient philosophers: 'Quid etiam antiqui Philosophi, qui vnam causam omnium, vnam summam potentiam, sapientiam, et benignitatem disseruerunt?' (p. 231), and with further remarks on the witness provided by martyrs' deaths.

40 Acts 15:9. Note that Vulgate reads 'fide purificans corda eorum'. The *Doctrine* here uses a synonym: 'mundans' instead of 'purificans'. Both mean 'cleansing'. This quotation is not in *De doctrina*.

41 These two sentences condense approximately two pages of Latin detailing the doctrinal errors of other 'sects' (*De doctrina*, pp. 232–4). Jews and Muslims are mentioned in particular: 'Gens Iudaeorum, et gens Mahometi indigna sentiunt de Dei magnificentia, dum gens Iudaeorum sperat diuitias, et solam affluentiam bonorum temporalium a Deo: dum sibi dari expectat auream Ierusalem. Gens autem Mahometi solum deliliarum carnalium remunerationem expectat. Vtriusque spes fere brutalis est, et hominum, qui animas suas in vanum acceperunt: cum anima, quae inuisibilis est, sit solum bonis inuisibilibus remuneranda' (p. 233).

42 An additional chapter ('De stabilitate, siue de constantia Cordis') covering just over a page follows in *De doctrina* at this point (pp. 234–5). This chapter discusses constancy and its relevance to fortitude. It describes constancy as a mean between obstinacy ('pertinacia') and mutability ('mutabilitas'), a form of which, *De doctrina* sees in the 'pigro' of Prov. 13:4 (sluggard). A new chapter follows: 'Quatuor quae faciunt ad instabilitatem' (p. 235).

43 Ecclus. 27:12. Note that Vulgate reads 'stultus sicut luna mutatur'.

44 Lam. 1:8. Note that Vulgate reads 'Peccatum peccavit Jerusalem, propterea instabilis facta est'. The *Doctrine* uses the synonym 'ideo' instead of 'propterea'. Both mean 'therefore'.

45 The biblical quotation is followed in *De doctrina* by the following words: 'Est enim cor peccatoris', p. 236.

46 *De doctrina* quotes briefly from Boethius, *De consolatione philosophiae*, Bk 2, pr. 4.19, ed. by L. Bieler, *CCSL* 94 (Turnhout, 1984), p. 24, at this point: 'Quis est ille tam felix, qui cum dederit impatientiae manus, statum suum mutare non optet?' (p. 236).

47 Prov. 14:29. Note that Vulgate reads 'Qui patiens est multa gubernatur prudentia'. The *Doctrine* has 'sapiencia' (i.e. 'wisdom') where the Vulgate prefers 'prudentia' (i.e. 'circumspection, discretion').

48 *De doctrina* refers briefly to St Gregory the Great at this point (p. 237). The reference in question is *Moralia in Job*, Bk 6, ch. 37, p. 328: 'Anchora enim cordis est pondus timoris.'

49 *De doctrina* reads: 'Timorem mundanum habet amator auarus pecuniae, qui omnes fere, quos videt, timet, si videt pauperum, aestimat furem: ut dicit Augustinus, si vidit diuitem, reputat praedonem' (pp. 237–8). *De doctrina* attributes this saying to St Augustine. Reference untraced. MS Douai, fol. 120v, also attributes the quotation to St Augustine.

50 *De doctrina* continues for about four pages (pp. 238–42). These include a new chapter: 'De constantia in aduersis, contra instabilitatem', which opens with advice on how to overcome adverse fortune, using Seneca's 'libro … de remedijs fortuitorum' (p. 239). What follows in the Middle English: 'Yif þou wilt, þerfor, make þi soule stable … sovereynes for God', is partly taken from the first sentence of the Latin new chapter, beginning on p. 239, and partly devised by the translator to link the text to the quotation from St Jerome, which occurs later in the chapter in the Latin. See *De doctrina*, p. 242.

51 *De doctrina*: 'Haec enim … maxima securitas, nil timere praeter Deum' (p. 242). Possible source: Rufinus Aquileiensis?, *Commentarius in LXXV Psalmos*, Ps. 22, *PL* 21, col. 727B: 'Magna est securitas, secum habere Deum.'

52 This internal dialogue abbreviates a longer dialogue which takes place earlier in *De doctrina* (pp. 240–2), and is part of the four pages mentioned above in note 50. In *De doctrina* the dialogue is rendered in far more dramatic terms: 'Item. Morieris: Nec primus, nec vltimus, omnes antecesserunt, omnesque sequentur. Item. Peregre morieris: Ego quod debeo, soluere paratus sum, videat foenerator vbi me appellet. Item. Iuuenis morieris: Optimum est mori, dum delectat viuere' (p. 240). The majority of these questions and answers come from Seneca, *Naturalium quaestionum*, Bk 6, ch. 32, ed. by A. Gercke (Stuttgart, 1970), pp. 231–4. In addition, at one point Virgil is cited as the respondant: 'Quid aliud respondeam, nisi illud Virgilianum: Facilis iactura sepulchri', *De doctrina*, p. 240.

53 In *De doctrina* this sentence follows the quotation from St Jerome referred to above in note 50. The Middle English follows *De doctrina* again from this point. The author of *De doctrina* here alludes to the importance of stability of enclosure (i.e. staying within the monastery), one of the central tenets of the enclosed monastic life.

54 The reference is, in fact, not to St Bernard but to William of St-Thierry's *Epistola ad fratres de Monte Dei. Lettre aux frères du Mont-Dieu*, ed. and tr. by J. Déchanet, *SC* 223 (Paris, 1975), par. 95, pp. 218–20: 'Impossibile enim est hominem fideliter figere in uno animum suum, qui non primo alicui loco perserveranter affixerit corpus suum.'

55 *De doctrina* has only 'Sic multi claustrales …' (p. 242).

56 A reference to the times of daily prayer laid down in the Breviary. The seven commonly recognized Hours are Mattins and Lauds, Prime, Terce, Sext, None, Vespers, and Compline.

57 *De doctrina* continues for a further half page.

58 Heb. 13:9. Note that Vulgate reads 'Optimum est enim gratia stabilire cor'.

59 This paragraph is expanded from the Latin which ends book 4 thus: 'Optimum est ergo stabiliri cor. ad Hebr. 13. Et haec dicta de cordis stabilitate sufficiant' (*De doctrina*, p. 244). It is typical of the translator's direct appeal to his female reader.

Capitulum quintum

1 Ecclus. 39:6. Note that Vulgate reads 'Cor suum tradet ad vigilandum diluculo ad Dominum, qui fecit illum'. Ecclus. 39:6 omits 'justus' (i.e. 'the righteous man'); 'sapiens' (i.e. 'the wise man'), though, features in Ecclus. 39:1.

2 The repetition of this quotation (originally given on p. 5, lines 16–18) is original to the Middle English translation. The Latin says instead: 'Expedito tractatu de cordis stabilitate, quinto loco ad tractandum de ipsius cordis datione stylum conuertamus' (*De doctrina*, p. 244). The Middle English unsurprisingly prefers to reiterate the lesson of book 5 without alluding, as does the more intellectual Latin, to the writing of the treatise with the word 'stylus'.

3 'Wete right wel ... erre in þi yiving.' These references to the gift of counsel are original to the Middle English translation.

4 Prov. 23:26. Note that Vulgate reads 'Praebe, fili mi, cor tuum mihi'. The *Doctrine* omits 'fili mi', i.e. 'my son'. Note that the Middle English translates the omission in the feminine: 'Dowter ...'.

5 The Latin here specifies three ways of dealing with the heart: 'Si cor tuum est ad vendendum, emptorem instantissimum inuenisti: si ad auferendum violentissimum praedonem: si ad donandum, importunissimum rogatorem' (*De doctrina*, p. 244). These three ways are explored in the Latin and the Middle English in the following pages.

6 *De doctrina* expands this to also consider an expensive horse or pricey food (pp. 244–5).

7 *De doctrina* expands these ideas with the aid of scriptural quotations for a further page (pp. 245–6).

8 The reference is to the wound in Christ's side, sustained upon the cross, symbolically giving access to his heart.

9 These two paragraphs abbreviate one and a half pages of additional images relevant to the giving of the heart in *De doctrina* (pp. 247–8). A new chapter follows: 'Quomodo Cor sit dandum' (p. 248).

10 *De doctrina* specifies that this is related to the gift of counsel (p. 248).

11 The three vows of poverty, chastity and obedience are central to the traditional coenobitic life. See p. 126 note 209, above.

12 Luke 23:46. The Vulgate reads for this verse 'Pater, in manus tuas commendo spiritum meum'.

13 Isa. 58:3. The previous sentences: 'so shuldist þou do, being dede ... a cruel þef in þe sight of God' summarize about one page in the Latin text, which further explores the yielding of one's will into the hands of one's superior (*De doctrina*, pp. 249–50).

14 Isa. 58:3. Note that Vulgate reads 'Ecce in die ieiunii vestri invenitur voluntas vestra'. The *Doctrine* has 'quia' (i.e. 'for') instead of 'ecce' (i.e. 'behold').

15 1 Pet. 2:18.

16 *De doctrina* continues for an additional four pages, moving from the manner of accepting correction to a discussion of the manner in which superiors should give correction (pp. 251–4). The barber figure is developed further: superiors are urged not to be like barbers who shave without the water of gentleness ('lenitas') or who use a nicked razor representing stinging correction ('mordax, et vitiosa correctio'), p. 251. The relationship between superior and subject is also described in terms of an ass and his owner – the

creature should not be over-burdened – and in terms of driving a 'quadriga' pulled by horses. Prelates are urged not to be tyrannous. Those who scold and command unnecessarily are likened to those who repair old plates with hammers, causing one crack or hole to turn into many (p. 252). A section is devoted to the need to temper anger in the service of correction, with quotations from St Bernard and the bible. The address then reverts to the subject: 'Tu vero[,] o claustralis, o subdite, si tibi aliquid durum, vel dure a Praelato iniungitur, praecepti duritiam per mansuetudinem, et obedientiam studeas emollire, sicut docet Leo Papa dicens: Humilibus nihil est arduum, mitibus nihil est asperum; quia gratia praebet auxilium, et obedientia emollit imperium' (p. 254). Reference untraced.

17 'But now, peraventure ... þou comyst to religioun.' These lines, which seem to have an especial relevance to the novitiate, are original to the Middle English translator. Note that the first sentence of this paragraph is a simplification of the Latin (*De doctrina*, pp. 254–5).

Capitulum sextum

1 The repeated references to the gift of understanding at this point are original to the Middle English translation. The translator, however, omits to repeat the scriptural quote ('Leuemus corda nostra, cum manibus ad Dominum in coelos' Lam. 3:41) which serves as the key reference for this book, and which is given in the Latin. Again, the Latin prefers a more formal reference to the writing of the text: 'Dicto de cordis datione, ad tractandum de eiusdem eleuatione procedamus, ad quam nos inuitat Ieremias Thren. [3] dicens ...' (*De doctrina*, p. 255). A comparison of the discussion of this gift with *The Book of Vices and Virtues* is instructive: 'Þe ʒiftes and þe vertues þat we han spoken of tofore in þis boke belongen to þe first lif, þat is cleped actif. Þe tweie laste ʒiftes wher-of we wolen speke bi helpe of þe Holy Gost, þat is to seie þe ʒifte of vnderstondyng and þe ʒifte of wisdom, bilongen to þe secunde life, þat is cleped contemplatif ... Now wole we speke þan first of þe ʒifte of vnderstondyng, as þe Holy Gost wole teche vs. Þis ʒifte þat is cleped þe ʒifte of vnderstondyng nys no þing elles, as þe holy men and grete maistres seyn, but a liʒt and a clerenesse of grace þat þe Holy Gost sendeþ in-to þe herte of a man or a womman, *wher-bi here vnderstondyng ariseþ vp* to haue a riʒt knowynge of here maker and þe gostliche þinges þat ne mowe not be seie bodiliche and alle þinges þat longen to þe helþe of þe soule' (p. 221, our emphasis).

2 *De doctrina* and the Middle English translation cite four holy behaviours and states of mind that lift the heart to God. For an analogous list of things that lift the heart, see Hugh, *Postillae*, II, 55vb (Ps. 24:1): 'Ad te Domine leuaui animam meam] Leuatur anima bona leuatione multis modis. Primo

per conuersionem a luto peccati ... Secundo per contemplationem a mundo in coelo ... Item per humilitatem.' (Lord, I have lifted up my soul to you] the good soul is lifted up by being raised in many ways. First, by conversion from the mire of sin ... secondly, by turning from the world toward the heavens through contemplation ... Likewise, by humility.) Guido Hendrix offers the following outline of book 6 of *De doctrina*:

1. QUOMODO cor leuandum est. 1.1. Cor sursum leuatur cum superna meditatur = cognitatio. 1.1.1. Qui altum cor habere dicendus est. 1.1.2. Ab istis ... aufert Spiritus Seipsum. 1.1.3. Notabiliter dicit se meditandum cum corde. 1.1.3.1. meditari in corde. 1.1.3.2. meditari cum corde. 1.2. Secundum eleuatorium cordis est spes ... Cum ad superna spe et desiderio tendit et anhelat. 1.2.1. Qui sperat in Domino subleuabitur. 1.2.2. Spes in odore unguentorum celestium currit. ... 1.3. Tertium eleuatorium desiderium est. 1.3.1. Cor dicitur esurire quod desiderat. 1.3.2. Ve illis qui in inferioribus predam happant. 1.3.3. De corde predario et famelico sub similitudine aquile. ... 1.4. Quartum eleuatorium est intentio recta ... cuius est. 1.4.1. actiones ad Deum dirigere et quasi sursum trahere. 1.4.2. totam conuersationem ordinare. ...

2. QUARE cor eleuare. Ratio quadruplex. 2.1. Sursum est patria tua. 2.2. Quia ibi est thesaurus noster. 2.3. Quia Patrem habemus celestem. 2.4. Plenitudo et perfectio bonorum = duodecim fructus ligni uitae (Hendrix, *Hugo I*, pp. 413–14).

3 Wisd. 5:16. Note that Vulgate reads 'Cogitatio illorum apud Altissimum'.

4 Ecclus. 6:37. Note that Vulgate reads 'Cogitatum tuum habe in praeceptis Dei, et in mandatis illius maxime assiduus esto'. 'Let thy thoughts be upon the precepts of God, and meditate continually on his commandments' (*Douai Bible*).

5 Lam. 3:41. Note that Vulgate reads 'Levemus corda nostra cum manibus ad Dominum'.

6 'This is þat I sayde afore ... for to delite in hem.' These lines of additional explanation are original to the Middle English translation.

7 Ps. 75:11.

8 The Latin here speaks in more abstract terms of the psychological faculties: 'Hominis dicit, id est rationalis. Anima enim rationale homo appellatur. Sola enim cogitatio rationalis, id est, discreta, et honesta, etiam lingua tacente confitetur Deo, et laudat Deum' (*De doctrina*, p. 256).

9 *De doctrina* also mentions the horse and mule as two other animals 'quibus non est intellectus' (p. 257). See *The Book of Vices and Virtues*, p. 222: 'For he haþ lorne þe eien of þe herte, resoun and vnderstondyng, so þat he ne may not ne knowe his makere ne no þing þat may torne to helpe of his soule, but is riȝt as a best þat haþ noþer witt ne resoun in hym.'

10   Ps. 76:7. Note that Vulgate reads 'meditatus sum nocte cum corde meo'. The *Doctrine* omits 'nocte', 'in the night'.

11   See Hugh, *Postillae*, II, 196rb (Ps. 76:7): 'Et meditatus sum nocte cum corde meo …] Notabiliter autem dicit, non in corde, sed cum corde meo. Multi enim meditantur inania in corde suo, non tamen cum corde, quia cor non discernit nec aduertit quid cogitat.' (I meditated during the night with my heart] … But he clearly says, not in my heart but with my heart. Indeed, many people meditate upon idle things in their heart, nonetheless not with their heart, for their heart neither distinguishes nor notices what it thinks.)

12   *De doctrina* attributes this saying to St Gregory the Great (p. 258). The saying in question is from the *Regulae pastoralis*. Grégoire le Grand, *Règle Pastorale*, Bk 3, ch. 14, ed. and tr. by B. Judic, C. Morel and F. Rommel, *SC* 381–2 (Paris, 1992), vol. 2, p. 342, lines 24–6: 'Nil quippe in nobis est corde fugacius, quod a nobis totiens recedit, quotiens per prauas cogitationes defluit.' *De doctrina* continues to develop the theme of meditating *with* the heart for a further two pages (pp. 258–60).

13   Ps. 41:4.

14   i.e. 'loaves'. See glossary.

15   The figure of the table of penance is developed in greater detail in book 1. See p. 11, line 256 to p. 13, line 338.

16   A new chapter follows in *De doctrina*: 'Secundum eleuatorium cordis, quod est Spes' (p. 261). Note that hope, with faith and charity, is one of the three theological virtues described by St Paul in 1 Cor. 13:13. These three virtues 'ben þre hevenely vertues to reule þe upward', Oxford, Bodleian Library, MS Laud Misc. 23, fol. 41r. And they do so by 'ordain[ing] specialy / all þe herte to God Allmyghti', *Desert of Religion*, vol. 2, p. 276, lines 375–6.

17   Prov. 29:25.

18   Isa. 50:10. Note that Vulgate reads 'Qui ambulavit in tenebris, et non est lumen ei, speret in nomine Domini, et innitatur super Deum suum'.

19   *De doctrina* reads: 'Sed lumen consolationis, et gaudij in ipsa aduersitate spes praebet ei' (p. 262). The Middle English reference to the name of Jesus would appear to refer to the late medieval devotion to the Holy Name promoted by the Franciscans. This led eventually to the instigation of an official Feast of the Name of Jesus, observed in England on 7 August.

20   *De doctrina* continues to treat the lifting of the heart through hope for a further page and a half (pp. 262–3). St Augustine and St Bernard on the *Canticum canticorum* are cited. The chapter closes with a biblical list of sinners who hoped in Jesus and were helped against the odds as a result: 'Omnino propter mansuetudinem, quae in te praedicatur, currimus post te Domine Iesu, quod non spernas pauperem, id est, peccatorem non horreas. Non enim horruisti latronem confitentem, Lucae 24. Non lachrymantem peccatricem,

Lucae 7. Non Chananaeam supplicantem[,] Matthaei 15. Non deprehensam in adulterio, Ioan. 8. Non sedentem in telonio, Matthaei 9. Non negantem discipulum, Matthaei 26. Non Paulum persecutorem discipulorum, Actor. 9. Non ipsos crucifixores, Matthaei 27' (p. 263). A new chapter follows: 'De tertio cordis eleuatorio, quod est Desiderium' (p. 263).

21 Job 39:27–29. Note that Vulgate reads 'Numquid ad praeceptum tuum elevabitur aquila, et in arduis ponet nidum suum? In petris manet, et in praeruptis silicibus commoratur atque inaccessis rupibus. Inde contemplatur escam'. The *Doctrine* omits 'commoratur atque inacessis rupibus', i.e. 'remains and in inaccessible cliffs'.

22 *De doctrina* reads: 'quae ab amore, et conuersatione mundi separata est' (pp. 264–5).

23 See Hugh, *Postillae*, I, 454vb: 'Nunquid ad praeceptum tuum eleuabitur aquila, et in arduis ponet nidum suum?] ... Item sanctorum intelligentia per aquilam designatur, ut hic. Aquila enim ceteris auibus subtilius uidet, et altius uolat. In uisu aquilae, sanctorum intelligentia, in uolatu eorundem contemplatio figuratur.' (Will the eagle not be lifted up at your commandment, and build his nest in inaccessible places?] ... Likewise the understanding of the saints is indicated by the eagle, as here. Indeed, the eagle sees more acutely than all the other birds, and it flies higher. In the sight of the eagle, the understanding of the saints is figuratively represented, in its flight, contemplation.) See also *Ancrene Wisse*, Part III, lines 172–4, p. 52: 'Treowe ancres beoð briddes icleopede for ha leaueð þe eorðe, þet is, þe luue of alle worltliche þinges, ant þurh ӡirnunge of heorte to heouenliche þinges fleoð uppart toward heouene.'

24 'sad' translates 'stabilitate'. *De doctrina* reads: '... qui hic petrae appellantur, mentis stabilitate' (p. 265). See Hugh, *Postillae*, I, 455ra: 'Et in arduis ponet nidum suum,] id est in supernis figet mentis desiderium ... In petris manet] ... id est in exemplis, et dictis fortium patrum mentis statione collocatur.' (And he builds his nest in inaccessible places] that is, the mind's desire is fixed upon celestial things ... he abides in stones] that is, by the examples and sayings of the stout-hearted fathers, it is established in the abode of the mind.)

25 The reference to the fall of Lucifer and his angels is to the legendary War in Heaven and expulsion of Satan, the rebel angel, prior to the creation of the earth. This legend is found in Jewish, Christian and Islamic angelology and Christian art (see, in particular, 1 Enoch, 2 Enoch, Jude 6, and 2 Pet. 2:4). Some commentators have also interpreted the description of a war in heaven in Rev. 12:7–9 as a reference to this event.

26 'maite': the Latin here reads 'per qualitatem meriti' (*De doctrina*, p. 265).

27 See Hugh, *Postillae*, I, 455ra: 'Et in praeruptis, etc.] id est in contemplatione sanctorum angelorum, quorum gloriam adhuc in terra positus contemplatur, et cum suspirio prestolatur. Qui dicuntur praerupti quia pars eorum cedidit, pars remansit. Integri quidem per qualitatem meriti, sed praerupti per quantitatem numeri.' (And in broken flints, etc.] that is, in the contemplation of holy angels, whose glory is contemplated and waited for with sighing by the one who is still earthbound. They are said to be broken flints, for part of them fell and part of them remained. Certainly they are whole by the quality of their merit, but they are broken by the quantity of their number.)

28 See Hugh, _Postillae_, I, 455ra: '... id est post angelorum contemplationem ... Contemplatur escam] id est Christum, qui est cibus angelorum, et refectio animarum.' (that is, after the contemplation of the angels ... he looks at his food] that is, at Christ, who is the nourishment of angels and the refreshment of souls.) _De doctrina_ continues for another page and a half, amassing scriptural quotations that detail our hunger for heavenly food. A new chapter follows: 'De quarto eleuatorio Cordis, quod est Intentio recta' (p. 267).

29 Phil. 3:20. Note that Vulgate reads 'Nostra autem conversatio in caelis est'.

30 _De doctrina_ continues for another two and a half pages. After pondering the figurative image of the eye (the eye of faith, the eye of the heart), the Latin author turns to contrast the crucifixion of Christ upon the cross with the hanging of Judas. Nuns are exhorted to imitate not Judas but Christ, whose hands and feet were bound, signifying stability, but whose voice was free to sing and pray (pp. 267–70). A new chapter follows: 'Quare Cor eleuandum sit' (p. 270).

31 _De doctrina_ comments that these four 'lifters up' are signified by the four golden rings that lifted the ark of the covenant in Exod. 28 (it seems more likely that the correct reference is, in fact, Exod. 24:12–14).

32 _De doctrina_ and the Middle English translation cite four causes for lifting the heart (_De doctrina_, pp. 270–5). Again, an analogous list of causes can be found in Hugh, _Postillae_, II, 56ra (Ps. 24:1): '... Debet autem iustus animam leuare ad Deum propter multas causas. Primo ut uideat: magis enim uidemus ab alto ... Item secundo, ut audiat ... Item tertio, ut fortius pugnet ... Item ut euadat laqueos diaboli ... Item, ut in Deum requiescat, et refrigerium habeat ... Item ut se humiliet ... Item ut uirtutes amissas recuperet.' (But the just man must lift his soul up to God for many reasons. First, that he may see: for indeed, we see more from on high ... Likewise secondly, that he may hear ... Likewise thirdly, that he may fight more resolutely ... Likewise that he may escape the Devil's snares ... Likewise that he may rest in God and have refreshment ... Likewise that he may humble himself ... Likewise that he may recover lost virtues.)

33 This sentence is original to the Middle English translator. The language of royalty and of a heritage elsewhere shows close similarities with several passages from book 1, in particular p. 34, lines 1106–20. *De doctrina* continues for a further page with explanations drawn from Tullius (Cicero, *Tusculanarum disputationum*, Bk 2, 58) and the 'Philosophus' (Ovid, *Metamorphoses*, Bk 1, 84–6) (pp. 270–1). Hendrix notes that the same quotation from Ovid's *Metamorphoses* is also used in St Augustine, *De Trinitate*, Bk 2, 1, and Hugh of St-Victor, *De bestiis et aliis rebus*, Bk 3, 59 (*Hugo I*, p. 325).

34 Matt. 6:21. Note that Vulgate reads 'Ubi enim est thesaurus tuus, ibi est et cor tuum'. The *Doctrine* has 'erit' (i.e. 'will be') instead of 'est' (i.e. 'is').

35 *De doctrina* continues to elaborate upon the theme of heavenly treasure for a further three pages (pp. 271–4).

36 Matt. 6:9.

37 The addressee is also envisaged in unambiguously female terms in *De doctrina* at this point: 'Noli ergo (o charissima) a tali, et tanto patre esse degenerans, imo caelestem patrem habeas, caelestis esto filia' (p. 274). Note that this may not be the case for all Latin or vernacular manuscripts. In the French translations, MS Douai, fol. 137r, keeps the feminine; MS Troyes, fol. 135r, avoids the specific reference to the *Pater noster* but tells its reader: 'soie celestien' (be heavenly), i.e. choosing a masculine adjective; MS Paris, fol. 143v, has here its preferred formula 'ame devote' (devout soul), which does not refer to the gender of the reader, who could be masculine or feminine.

38 *De doctrina* identifies these twelve heavenly goods as the twelve fruits of the tree of life, described in Rev. 22:2 (p. 275). See Hugh, *Postillae*, VII, 427vb–428ra (Rev. 22:2): 'Afferens fructus duodecim] qui sunt duodecim fercula, quae ipse transiens ministrabit nobis in mensa resurrectionis aeternae in regno patris sui: Luc. 11.c. Quae sunt sanitas sine aegritudine … Plenitudo sine defectione … Refectio sine fastidio … Scientia sine ignorantia et dubitatione … Gaudium sine tristitia … Pax sine perturbatione … Securitas sine timore … Adimpletio omnium desideriorum … Gaudium de omni electorum congregatione … Gaudium de iustitia Dei … Gaudium de memoria boni … Gaudium de uisione Dei.' (Bearing twelve fruits] which are twelve dishes which, coming over, he serves to us himself on the table of the eternal resurrection in his father's kingdom: Luc. 11.c. [These dishes] are health without sickness … repletion without exhaustion … food without disgust … knowledge without ignorance and doubt … joy without sadness … peace without disturbance … safety without fear … the fulfilment of all desires … joy concerning the whole assembly of the elect … joy concerning the justice of God … joy concerning the memory of goodness … joy concerning the sight of God.) See also Peraldus, *Summa de vitiis et virtutibus*, Bk 2, Part 3.4: 'De xii fructibus ligni vite … sanitas absque infirmitate … inuentus sine senectute … satietas sine fastidio … libertas, ad quam faciunt corporis agilitas et subtilitas …'

(p. 75). These interpretations contrast with the better-known interpretation given within St Bonaventure's *Lignum vitae*, written around the same time, in which the twelve fruits are equated with events in the life of Christ.

39 St Augustine, *Confessionum Libri XIII*, Bk 12, ch. 15, 21, lines 59–62, ed. by L. Verheijen, *CCSL* 27 (Turnhout, 1981), p. 226: 'O domus luminosa et speciosa … Tibi suspirat peregrinatio mea, et dico ei qui fecit te, ut possideat et me in te, quia fecit et me.'

Capitulum septimum

1 Joel 2:13.

2 See *The Book of Vices and Virtues*, p. 273: 'Þe ȝifte of wisdom, þat þe Holi Gost leiþ in þe herte þat is parfiȝtliche clensed and purged of al filþe of synne and is lyfte vp, þe Holi Gost ȝeueþ hym þat he knytteþ hym to God bi a swete swolewyng of loue, so þat he is al on wiþ God … þer he forȝeteþ al his trauaile, alle his desires of þe flesch and of þe world, and also hymself, þat he ne beþenkeþ hym on no þing but on þat þat he loueþ, þat is God al onliche.'

3 Ecclus. 47:1–2. Note that Vulgate reads 'surrexit Nathan, propheta in diebus David. Et quasi adeps separatus a carne'. The *Doctrine* omits 'in diebus David', i.e. 'in the days of David'.

4 *De doctrina*, pp. 276–7. See Hugh, *Postillae*, III, 260va (Ecclus. 47:1–2): 'Et quasi adeps] per interiorem pinguedinem charitatis, de qua Hier. 31.c. Inebriabo animas sacerdotum pinguedine … Separatus a carne] Id est ab omni inquinamento carnis, uel ab omni illicito, uel inordinato affectu carnali, uel a consortio, et uita, et morib. carnalium.' (And like fat] by the internal fat of charity, about which Hier. 31.c. [Jer. 31:14] says: 'I will make the souls of the priests drunk with fatness' … separated from the flesh] that is, from all fleshly defilement, or from everything unlawful, or from excessive fleshly desire, or from cohabitation, and from the life and manners of worldly people.)

5 The language of dissevering fat from flesh carries strong reminders of the allegory of the cooked heart in book 1, in which the heart is basted with the fat of charity, and can be judged ready once it falls away easily from the bone of worldly thoughts and occupations. See p. 24, line 748 to p. 27, line 867.

6 Ecclus. 1:14. Note that Vulgate reads 'Dilectio Dei honorabilis sapientia'.

7 See Hugh, *Postillae*, III, 173rb (Ecclus. 1:14): 'Honorabilis sapientia] i. causa honorabilis sapientiae, qua sapiunt res prout sunt.' (Wisdom worthy to be honoured] that is the cause of wisdom worthy to be honoured, by which they have an understanding of things are they are.) *Postillae*, III, 182vb (Ecclus. 6:23): 'Secundum nomen eius] id est, secundum nomen sapientiae … qualis etiam significatur per nomen, scilicet sapida scientia, quia dicitur a sapore et

scientia.' (According to its name] that is, according to the name of wisdom ... its name also means 'tasty knowledge', for it is made up from 'taste' and from 'knowledge'.)

8 *Sancti Bernardi opera*, vol. 6, 1, *Sermones* 3, ed. by J. Leclercq and H. Rochais (Rome, 1970), p. 142, lines 14–16: 'Invenisti plane sapientiam, si prioris vitae peccata defleas, si huius saeculi desiderabilia parvipendas, si aeternam beatitudinem toto desiderio concupiscas. Invenisti sapientiam, si tibi horum singula sapiunt prout sunt.'

9 See *The Book of Vices and Virtues*, pp. 272–3: 'But þe ȝifte of wisdom is non oþer þing þan a sauerous knowynge, þat is a good sauour and a grete delite in þe herte. For oþer-wise knoweþ he þe wyn þat seeþ it in a faire pece or verre, and oþer-wise he þat tasteþ it, drynkeþ it, and sauoureþ it. Many philosophres knewen God ... bi symple lokyng of vnderstondyng and of kyndeliche skille; but þei ne feled neuere no þing bi taste of riȝt loue ne bi deuocion. Also þer be many cristene, clerkes and lewede, þat knowen hym wel bi bileue and bi þe bokes; but for þei han þe sauour mysordeyned bi synne, þei mowe no þing fele, no more þan a seke man may fynde sauour in good mete.'

10 Ps. 33:9.

11 St Augustine, *Confessionum Libri XIII*, Bk 10, ch. 40, 65, lines 21–7, p. 191: 'Et aliquando intromittis me in affectum multum inusitatum introrsus ad nescio quam dulcedinem, quae si perficiatur in me, nescio quid erit, quod uita ista non erit. Sed recido in haec aerumnosis ponderibus et resorbeor solitis et teneor et multum fleo ... Hic esse ualeo nec uolo, illic uolo nec ualeo, miser utrubique.' This is a rare example, where *De doctrina* identifies not only the author, but the exact source of this quotation: 'Augustinus in Libro Confessionum', p. 278. The same quotation from Augustine is used in the section of Peraldus's *Summa de vitiis et virtutibus* which discusses the two gifts of the Holy Spirit associated with contemplation: Bk 1, Part 4.12, p. 224.

12 Compare this paragraph and the previous with *The Book of Vices and Virtues*, p. 274: 'Wherfore þe countrepeis of þe flesche is so heuy þat he draweþ þe gost a-doun, wole he or non, and þerfore þe grete swetnesse þat þe contem-platif herte haþ and feleþ bi þe ȝifte of wisdom in þis dedli lif nys but a litle taste wher-by men han sauour and felen how God is swete and softe, as who-so tasteþ þe sauour of þe wyne er men drynken þer-of a ful drauȝht; but þei schulle see & come to þat gret tauerne where þat þe tunne is made al comune, þat is in þe lif wiþ-outen ende.'

13 *De doctrina* reads 'aliquando secundum quod de eo loquitur Dionysius, qui appellat amorem ecstaticum illum amorem, qui totaliter transfert amantem in usum, et profectum amati. Tali amore (sicut idem dicit) nos Deus dilexit, se totum in usum nostrum, et profectum totaliter transferens' (pp. 278–9).

14 *De doctrina* includes a reference to 'eros' (ἔρως) for this kind of love.

MS Douai, fol. 139r, also refers to 'eros': 'on prent aussi en autre maniere amour estatike pour amour qui hors met la pensee que ly mire appellant amour ereos.'

15 An influential account of seven tokens by which fleshly love can be distinguished from spiritual love is found in the popular *Formula novitiorum* of David of Augsburg, a handbook for novices of c.1250 (ed. by P.P. Collegii S. Bonaventurae (Quaracchi, 1899), III, pp. 34–5). Expounding these 'signa' or 'indicia amoris', David presents himself as a pious alternative to Ovid, the 'doctor artis amatoriae', and to thirteenth-century Ovidian love poetry such as *La Puissance d'amour* of Richard of Fournival, which also concludes with the 'signes d'amor'. In addition to the *Formula novitiorum*, there is also a body of thirteenth-century beguine poetry which adapts the trope of the secular signs of love for spiritual purposes. See, for example, *Le Regle des fins amans*, ed. by K. Christ, in B. Schädel and W. Mulertt (eds), *Philologische Studien: Karl Voretzsch Festschrift* (Halle, 1927), pp. 192–3. Whereas the *Formula novitiorum* is careful to oppose the signs of secular love-longing to the indicators of spiritual love, texts such as the *Regle des fins amans* and *De doctrina* essentially conflate the two, reading 'amor ecstaticus' with reference to the 'signa' listed in medical accounts of 'amor hereos': an unstable pulse, sunken eye sockets etc. Like *De doctrina*, the *Formula novitiorum* was translated into Middle English in the fifteenth century. Together with these translations, its listings of the seven tokens is also incorporated into *Disce mori* (Exhortation, ch. 17), and into *A litill Tretise ayence ffleshly affecciouns and all unprifty loues*. L.W. Patterson, 'Ambiguity and Interpretation: A Fifteenth-Century Reading of *Troilus and Criseyde*', *Speculum*, 54.2 (1979), 297–330. A new chapter follows in *De doctrina* at this point: 'Primum signum amoris ecstatici, est multa cogitare, et pauca loqui' (p. 279).

16 S. of S. 2:16. In the Middle English, this verse is already quoted in book 1, p. 35, line 1170, see p. 128 note 220 above. Song of Songs 2:16 is also quoted in the *Liber de modo bene vivendi* (col. 1221A–B), in order to emphasize the union with God: 'Dic, obsecro, honesta virgo, cum amore et dilectione de Christo: "Dilectus meus et ego illi, qui pascitur inter lilia, donec aspiret dies, et inclinentur umbrae (Cantic. II, 16, 17)." Sponsa Christi, rogo, ut apertius dicas: Dilectus meus mihi societur vinculo charitatis et amoris, et ego illi conjugar et socier vicissitudine mutuae dilectionis.' (Honourable virgin, I entreat you to say regarding Christ, with passionate longing and love: 'My beloved to me, and I to him, who feedeth among the lilies, till the day break and the shadows retire [S. of S. 2:16–17].' Spouse of Christ, I beseech you to speak more openly: My love is united to me by the bond of love and passionate longing, and I myself am joined and united to him by the exchange of passionate love.)

17 Exod. 4:14–16.

18 The more extended Latin in *De doctrina* helps to elucidate this phrase: 'Aaron ... dicat: Dilectus meus mihi, congruit; et ego congruo illi. Quasi dicat: si puritas, si speciositas, si generositas, si fidelitas attendatur, omnino congruit mihi, et ego illi. Omnia haec ipse habet per naturam, et ego dono misericordiae suae habeo per gratiam' (p. 280).

19 See Hugh, *Postillae*, III, 119rb (S. of S. 2:16): '... Uel sic, Dilectus meus mihi, est omnium laborum, dolorum, fatigationum pretium siue praemium ... Et ego illi, similiter sum omnium laborum, et dolorum, et fatigationum eius merces, et praemium. Omnia enim propter me habendam fecit, omnia sustinuit, et omnes labores suos, imo seipsum propter me habendam dedit.' (Or thus, my love is to me the price or reward of all my toils and pains and exhaustions ... And I am to him, in like manner, the wages and reward of all his toils and pains and exhaustions. Indeed, because he esteemed me he made everything, he endured everything and [experienced] all of his toils, certainly, he gave himself because he esteemed me.)

20 See Hugh, *Postillae*, III, 119rb (S. of S. 2:16): '... Uel sic, Dilectus meus mihi, totus uixit, et totus mihi mortuus est. Tota uita eius, et tota mors mihi fuit, id est propter me. Et ego illi, similiter tota uiuam, et tota moriar.' (Or thus, My love to me, entirely lived and entirely died for me. His entire life and entire death were for me, that is, because of me. And in a like manner, may I live entirely and die entirely to him.)

The Latin continues for a few lines with quotations from Romans and Proverbs (*De doctrina*, pp. 280–1).

21 This paragraph and the previous one replace the following lines in *De doctrina*: 'Attende verba istius animae amorosae, quanta indigeat suppletione, et, multo ampliori, quam tibi sit expositum. Sed apud dilectum non est necessaria ista suppletio, qui bene nouit intelligere amoris linguagium, apud quem crebro huiusmodi locutione defectiuae, et imperfectae sonant' (p. 281). A new chapter follows in *De doctrina*: 'Secundum signum amoris ecstatici, est Desiccatio membrorum' (p. 281).

22 Exod. 14:21. *De doctrina* reads: 'quod Dominus exiccauit mare rubrum flante vento vehementi, et vrente' (p. 281). The Vulgate reads: '... abstulit illud Dominus flante vento vehementi et urente tota nocte'. 'The Lord took it away by a strong and burning wind blowing all the night' (*Douai Bible*).

23 The reference is to the coming of the Holy Spirit upon the apostles at Pentecost recounted in Acts 2:1–4. The liturgical feast of Pentecost, which takes place seven weeks after Easter Sunday, is known as Whitsunday in England. The word derives from Old English 'hwîta sunnandaeg' (white Sunday), possibly referring to the white ceremonial robes worn by the newly baptized upon this day.

24 *De doctrina* offers additional biblical references related to the parting of the Red Sea for a further half page (p. 282). A new chapter follows: 'Tertium signum, concauitas oculorum' (p. 283).

25 The devotional trope of the 'oculus cordis' is explored in detail in W.F. Pollard, 'Richard Rolle and the "Eye of the Heart"', in W.F. Pollard and R. Boenig (eds), *Mysticism and Spirituality in Medieval England* (Cambridge, 1997), pp. 85–106.

26 The previous four paragraphs are selected from approximately two pages of additional explication and scriptural examples in *De doctrina* (pp. 283–5).

27 'servise of God'. The Latin refers more specifically to 'horas' (*De doctrina*, p. 285).

28 *De doctrina* continues for just under a page, warning the addressee not to lose the loving expression of her divine beloved ('bonus vultus') through the obstacle of sin, evoking the *mulier fortis* who 'considera semitas domus conscientiae tuae' (Prov. 31:27) and citing Anna, the wife of Tobit, who would not be consoled, but constantly watched the road her son had taken (Tobit 10:7) (pp. 285–6). A new chapter follows: 'Quartum signum, siccitas oculorum' (p. 286).

29 The emphasis upon song as a key expression of love-longing for the divine derives first from the new exegetical and homiletic prominence given to the Song of Songs from the twelfth century onwards, and second from the rise of the secular love-lyric. For further information on medieval responses to the Song of Songs, see p. 122 note 189 above.

30 St Augustine, *Confessionum Libri XIII*, Bk 9, ch. 6, 14, lines 23–5, p. 141: 'Quantum fleui in hymnis et canticis tuis suaue sonantis ecclesiae tuae uocibus commotus acriter!'

31 *De doctrina* inserts a brief reference to Amos 5:23 at this point (p. 288).

32 S. of S. 2:14.

33 *De doctrina* continues for a further two pages. It contrasts songs pleasing to God with echoes resounding from the high mountains ('Resonans de altissimis montibus Echo', Wisd. 17:18), and then goes on to discuss the cult of saints. It is pointless to visit shrines such as that of St James of Compostella, and to observe saints' days, without first loving sanctity; St John Chrysostom and St Jerome are quoted in support of this. Nuns are told that their singing should be 'integer', 'distinctus', 'plenus', 'attentus' and 'deuotus', by contrast to those who, like echoes, stammer and omit various syllables (pp. 288–90).

34 1 Cor. 14:15. Note that Vulgate reads 'psallam spiritu, psallam et mente'. The *Doctrine* uses here the 2nd person singular (i.e. 'psallas') where the Vulgate has the 1st person (i.e. 'psallam').

35 *De doctrina* attributes these two interpretations to the *Glossa ordinaria*: 'Spiritu, id est vocis melodia, dicit Glossa: et mente, id est, mentis intellectu' (p. 290).

36 i.e. 'is fear that he has'.

37 1 Sam. 20:41.

38 A new chapter follows in *De doctrina*: 'Quintum signum, Pulsus inordinatus' (p. 291).

39 i.e. 'is affection, which is swift'.

40 Ps. 83:3.

41 A new chapter follows in *De doctrina*: 'Sextum signum amoris ecstatici, Solicitudo profunda' (p. 292).

42 Feminine pronouns are changed to masculine pronouns at this point in L. L reads 'but only whan he hireth ony word mevyd of his love' (fol. 69r).

43 S. of S. 3:3. Note that Vulgate reads 'Num quem diligit anima mea vidistis?'.

44 A new chapter follows in *De doctrina*: 'Septimum, et vltimum amoris signum' (p. 293).

45 Gospel references to the events of the Transfiguration do not locate it specifically on Mount Thabor, a mountain five miles south-east of Nazareth standing above Lake Tiberias, however, oral traditions quickly seem to have associated the two. In the early third century AD, Origen declared Thabor to have been the mountain of Galilee on which Christ was tranfigured (*Comm. in Ps.* 88, 13), and by the fourth century it had become a site of pilgrimage for that reason.

46 Matt. 17:4. Note that Vulgate reads 'Domine, bonum est nos hic esse: si vis, faciamus hic tria tabernacula, tibi unum, Moysi unum, et Eliae unum'. The *Doctrine* omits 'si vis', i.e. 'if you wish'.

47 'Hely': i.e. the prophet Elijah.

48 These 'doctouris' are specified in *De doctrina* as St John Chrysostom. The Latin reads 'Nam, sicut dicit Chrysostomus, audierat in Ierusalem Christum moriturum esse, et tamen dicebat: Bonum est nos hic esse' (*De doctrina*, p. 294). See Hugh, *Postillae*, VI, 184va (Luke 9): 'Praeceptor, bonum est nos hic esse] Chrys. Quia audiuit eum moriturum in Hierusalem, ideo dicit: Bonum est nos hic esse.' (Teacher, it is good for us to be here] Chrys. For he heard he would die in Jerusalem, yet he says: It is good for us to be here.)

49 There are no references to Peter's spiritual inebriation in any of the gospel accounts of the Transfiguration. However, the final emphasis on inebriation accords well with the initial image of the wine-cellar in the Prologue to *De doctrina* (pp. 1–4), and with the comments upon the gift of wisdom in *The Book of Vices and Virtues*, pp. 274–5, 279: 'þe wyne of loue, of pees, and of ioie and solas schal be ȝeue so largeliche to euery wiȝt þat comeþ þider þat alle schul be fulfilled, as þe Sauter seiþ, þat al þe desire of þe herte schal be fulfilled whan God schal make aliȝht vpon his frendes a streme of pees, as þe prophete seiþ, wher-wiþ þei schulle be alle as drunken. Of þilke drunkenesse spekeþ Dauid in þe Sauter and seiþ þus of þe ioie of paradis: "Sire, þou schalt make hem drunke of þe plentee þat is in þin hous; and þou schalt make hem drynke of þis swetnesse and of þi delite" … þat witt put þe Holy Gost in-to þe herte whan he ȝeueþ þe ȝifte of wisdom, þat fedeþ þe herte of gostliche ioye and ȝeueþ hym drynke and makeþ hym dronke of an holy loue.'

50 Hugh, *Postillae*, VI, 104va (Mark 9:4): 'Et Heliae unum] Ecce largitas Petri. Unam solam guttam uini acceperat et tres tabernas uolebat facere.' (And one for Elijah] Behold Peter's liberality. He received one single drop of wine, and he wanted to make three tabernacles.)

51 *De doctrina* cites 1 Cor. 13 in connection with this self-forgetting (p. 295).

52 Isa. 64:4. The Vulgate reads for this verse 'Oculus non vidit, Deus, absque te, quae praeparasti expectantibus te'. 'The eye hath not seen, O God, besides thee, what things thou hast prepared for them that wait for thee' (*Douai Bible*). Although this is not the only such instance in this text, the direct rendition of the scriptural verse into Middle English without first providing the Latin is unusual. See Hugh, *Postillae*, VI, 179va (Luke 9): 'Nesciens quid diceret] … quasi ebrius de una gutta uini coelestis, quam biberat, uel uiderat, uolebat facere tres tabernas, in quo innuitur liberalitas, et largitas paradisi, quia Petrus non sibi, sed aliis uult aedificare 1 Cor. 13.b. Charitas non quaerit quae sua sunt. Nesciebat etiam Petrus quid diceret: quia speciem gloriae, quam uiderat, ueram gloriam aestimabat, Isa. 64.b. Oculus non uidit, etc.' (Not knowing what he said] … as if intoxicated from one drop of celestial wine, which he had drunk or had seen, he wanted to build three tabernacles, in which his generosity and the heavenly liberality are intimated, for Peter wanted to build them, not for himself, but for others 1 Cor. 13.b. 'Charity seeketh not her own' [I Cor. 13:5]. Also, Peter did not know what he said, for he reckoned that the splendour of the glory that he had seen was true glory, Isa. 64.b. 'The eye does not see', etc. [Isa. 64:4])

53 See Hugh, *Postillae*, IV, 162ra (Isa. 64:4): 'Oculus non uidit …] … Illa enim bona aeterna sunt cognitio tui apertae summae ueritatis, dilectio perfecta diuinae bonitatis, securitas aeternae possessionis, quae in te, et per te habebuntur.' (The eye did not see …] … Indeed, these eternal goods are your knowledge of the highest truth unveiled, perfect love of divine goodness, and security of eternal possession, which will be held in and by you.)

54 This closing reference to the rood tree is specific to the Middle English translation. 'Rode' or 'rood' derives from AS 'rod', meaning pole, crucifix or cross. A rood is generally a large crucifix, often flanked by the statues of Our Lady and St John, positioned over the entrance to the choir in a medieval church.

55 In L, the word 'Amen' is followed, a few lines below, by:

Syke and sorowe deeply,
Wepe and morne sadly,
Preye and þenk deuoutly,
Love and long contynuely.

This prayer is also used to conclude the Middle English versions of the *Mirouer des simples ames* of Marguerite Porete. The manuscripts of the ME *Mirouer* are all of Carthusian origin. In T, the following information follows 'Amen': 'Here endith a tretice made to religious wommen which is clepid the doctrine of the hert / Crist Jhesu his mede he hym rewarde that this tretice bigan and the ende made.'

Textual Variants

All additions, omissions, and substitutions of words and phrases are noted here, together with all changes in word order. All changes of number, tense and gender are also noted, together with deletions and additions in superscript or in the margin. Differences of spelling from one manuscript to another, and dialectal differences, are not noted.

Where a line contains more than one variant, a '•' is used between each consecutive variant to avoid confusion. A superscript number is used where the word in question appears more than once in a single line and the number indicates whether the variant applies to the first, second, third or fourth appearance of that word.

Prologue

11 in] *om.* C 15 be] be so T 29 desiryn] desiring C 31 or] & T • and] *om.* C 36 yif] *om.* T 39 theim] hem CT • vertue] vertuos T • of] *om.* T

41 mynche] nun C 42 here] hys C

43 mynche] nun C

45 and] and in C • mynche] nun C

48 strengthe] treuþe T

54 herte] hert to God L

Capitulum primum

4–5 'Make redy' he seith] He seith: make redy LT 7 *tuum*] *tuum*. He seith LT 8 he seith] *om.* LCT 9 that] þat boke T 11 he seith] *om.* C 13 *cor*] *cor.* He seith þus LT 14 with] *om.* LT 15 hertis] hertis to God LCT 17 *illum*] *illum*. He seith LT

• he seith] *om.* LT 21 *Deum*] *Deum.* He seith LT; *Dominum* C • we up] up we L; up T • he seith] *om.* LT 23 *vestra*] *vestra.* He seith LT • he seith] *om.* LT 26 and] *om.* C 27 þe] *om.* C 29 the³] *om.* C 30 strength] strength strength T 32 the¹] *om.* CT 33 yifte²] *om.* C 34 of¹] *om.* C 35 and] *om.* LT

38 as] *om.* T • for] *om.* C

40 shuld] schal LT 42 to] for LT • helth] *delet.* C • his] is T 43 axith] axith but C 44 wery] wery in T 48 þat is] *om.* L; wich is T 50 his] þis T 51 the] *om.* C 52 gladly] *om.* LT 53–54 with oure enemy and had the victorie and the maystry, comyng fro the batayle] *om.* LT 55 wery] weryid C 57 so is] is so LT 64 hym] *om.* T • O] *om.* LT 68 yif] *om.* C 69 seye] sey þus LT • me] *me.* He wille say LT 70 he wil sey] *om.* LT • wold] wylle C

71 yif] ȝif þat LT • receyve worthily] worthily receyve LT • blissed] *om.* C 74 of] of þi soule and of LT • shuld] schal LT 75 *peccatum*] *peccatum.* He seith LT 76–77 Seynt Austyn seith] *om.* C 82 it] it out T 85 it] it out LT 88 within] within hem LT 89 ought] out alle LT 91 not] not to C • be] be the C 93 *vite*] *vite est* L 94 *iusti*] *iusti.* He seith LT • a¹] the C 97 prophete] prophete David LT 98 That is] þat is to sey LT 99 God] good C • þou] *om.* LT 105 thow] þou be T 106 by] to C 107 confessioun] confession and LT 110 Thou wost wel also] Also þou wost wele LT; þou wotyst well so C 114 causes] cause LT 115 to²] *om.* LT 117 slow servauntes don] a slow servaunt doth LT 118 they¹] sche LT • they²] sche LT 121 so cast] he castiþ LT • the²] *om.* LT • not thou] þou not LT 123 not] no T 125 throw] strowe C 126 And] And also LT • wel] wele þat welle LT • water] watterede C • is] as C 128 filthes] filth LT 131 receyved] receyved with worschip LT 132 caused] clepid LT 133 *Deum*] *Domini* C 134 he seiþe] *om.* LT • hertis] hertis, he seith LT

136 Jhesu] Jhesu Crist L 137 be] *om.* LT • resceyved] receyve T 138 thin hous of thin hert shuld] schuld þin hous of þin hert LT 139 bi] by ense T 140 in] a LT 142 good] *om.* C 143 good] *om.* T • þe] þe þe T 145 this] þis gode LT 148 that] so C 150 Helyse] Helise, þat is LT 151 þe] þis T 158 *eius*] *eius.* He seith L; he seith T • he seyth] *om.* LT 161 shuld] schal L 162 for] *om.* T 163 wil] wil for C 164 no¹] ne LT • no²] þo LT • no is] ne LT 168 pees] in T 169 and kyngdome] *om.* C 173 wel] *om.* L 174 trew] *om.* T 177 suffryng] sofferyng of LT 178 lost] *om.* LT 181 rather þan] þan raþer LT 182 consciences] conscience LT 185 is] *om.* T 186 the] *om.* T • togedre] *om.* LT 188 stry[v]ing] strivyng LT 190 stryvyngis] stryvyng LT; steringys C 193 negligences] negligences and C 195 gretter] gret C 197 as a] *om.* LT 201 afore] befor LT 203–204 That is] þat is to sey LT 204 hem] *om.* LT 205 þe] *om.* C 206 brynging] bryngeth C 208 bringing] bringyth C • daliaunce] daliaunces

LT 209 þin] þe LT 210 as a close gardyn shuld be] as close gardyn schuld LT 211 *sepes*] *spes* LT 215 suche] *om.* LT 216 and] and suche LT 217 commun] *om.* LT 218 For it is more to] It is more for to LT • to²] *om.* T 221 *eius*] *eius*. He seith LT • he saith] *om.* LT 222 his] this C • is] *om.* LT 225 make] make a C 226 right] *om.* LT 226–227 thi face in a trobled water right so þou mayst not se] *om.* T 228 þerfore ordeyne] ordeyne þerfore C 228–229 in thin hert a place of rest] a place of rest in þin hert LT 232 *quietum*] *quietem*. He seith LT • he seyth] *om.* LT • of contemplacioun] *om.* C 233 in] of LT 236 not be] not T; 'not' added with caret in margin L 238 in al thing¹] *om.* T 245–246 she answerid noþing but she wept and oure lord answerid] he answerid T 247 Also] And also LT • hym] oure lord LT

264 begynne] be kynne C 266 of] in LT 267 for] for sake T • is] is þe LT 268 gladnes] godenes LT 273 gest] lord LT 274 þou must first honestly] first þou most LT 275 *tuam*] *tuam*. He seith LT • he seith] *om.* LT 278 ther] *om.* C 284 plater of] plate with T 286 of] in L, and C 287 Davith] *om.* T 297 thow] yif T 302 synne] synnes T 307 tymes] tyme C 309 hem] hym C 315 þat] *om.* T 317 as in hem is] as is in hem C 325 fynde] *om.* C • mete] *om.* C 327 owen] *om.* C • That] Þat þat T 328–329 trowist þou? Trewly, mynde of endeles reward. Of that sause] *om.* T 331 callid] clepid T • is ete] be eten T • therwith] þer wiþ it T 332 sause] *om.* T • the] *om.* C • Love] Songes T 333 *meis*] *meis* she seith T 333–334 she seith] *om.* CT 335 temptacioun] temptacions LT 336 Than] *om.* LT

342 *tue*] *tue*. He seith LT • he seith] *om.* LT 350 *tempore*] *tempore*. He seith LT 357 that] þe LT 359 afore] for T 362 er] ar LT • his] is T 363 þe²] *om.* LT 365 of mysdemyng] for demyng a mysse C 366 þe²] þe of LT • Al maner] Of alle maner of LT 367 inhibiteth] techith LT 369 *cordium*] *cordum*. He seith LT • he seith] *om.* LT 371 privee] pryve hidde LT 372 counseiles] counseil T 375 summe] *om.* LT 378 and] or L 380 diffinycioun] diffinycion whan we in dowty þingis ȝeve ful diffinycion LT 381 þe] þe þe T • be] of LT 382 *iudicabimini*] *iudicabimini*. He seith LT 383 he seith] *om.* LT • thow] þougth þough T 384 demyngis] demyng LT 385 ye] *om.* T 386 ye] *om.* T 388 þingis] þing to L; þingis to T 389 be ware] be ware þat LT 391 it²] *om.* C 394 other] oþer mennys LT

398 the²] þis T 399 Helyse] Helise þe prophete þat is LT 401 knowlech] knewleche for LT 402 as] as knewle T 405 Wheþer] Wher LT 411 as] *om.* T 415 þan] so LT • þe²] *om.* C • wiche] whiche þe whiche T • for] *om.* T 419 the] an LT 420 heith] hille LT • Jeroboam] *om.* T 422 he] *om.* LT 424 it] þis LT 425 he seith dere spouse] der spowse he seith C 428 merciable] merciably C • in] in in T 429 the] *om.* T 430 thus] þus Reddite T 431 cor] cor. He seith LT • he seith] *om.* LT • trespasoures] trespass C 433 light] *om.* T

436 shuld] schalle LT • wel] *om.* LT 441 oute] outward LT 446 lord] lordis LT
447 to heere, to] or LT • honest] *om.* C 448 ever have] have ever LT 449 the
wiche ben in] of C 450 of] of þe CT 452 a] *om.* C 453 Emor] Emor ~~curioste~~ T
456 on] an LT, of C 459 sekeris of] sekith LT 461 lust] lustis LT 463 be left] levith
LT 464 pessable] pesable ~~cloisteris~~ T • joy] joyes C 465 consciences] conscience
C 470 Overmore] Evermore LT • ever] *om.* LT 472 deth] deth bodily LT • or[1]]
om. T 473 fere] drede LT 477 for] of LCT 479 þe] *om.* C 481 noone] none L 484
seith Salomon] Salamon saith LT 489 profreþ] profrith þe L 490 þerof] þerfor LT
• the] *om.* C 493 is] is þe LT • the] *om.* LT • eyghen] eyne C 496 wiche wastyd]
whichid T 503 with] with þe C 505 in[2]] for LT 509 for[1]] *om.* C 509–510 For as
longe as mete is uneetyn, so longe it is uncorporate] *om.* LT 511 þat] *om.* C 514
no] *om.* LT • wise] wise þat C 517 to] *om.* T 518 ofte] of T • is] Following 'is', in
L, a later hand has added a caret and provided two words in the margin which
are difficult to decipher, but which may read 'even or'; is even or T 522 delite]
delite þe LT 523 propirly sle not] sle not propirly LT • þe] þi T 526 blasfemy]
blasfemyng LT 529 oute to] owt of to C; out of T 533 yates] wittis C 534 for] *om.*
T 536 þi] þe LCT 540 wynneweth] wenowith wete T 541 whan þat] whan L; *om.*
T • womman] woman which is LT • in] in þe C 542 Ysboseth] Ybosecch, þat is
LT 542–543 þe porter of þi yate, discrecioun] discrecion, þe porter of þi ȝatis LT;
þe porter of þin ȝate discrecioun to C 543 soule] soule and LT 547 and[3]] *om.* LT
549 wel may such a synful soule] may wele such a soule þat is synful LT 552 may
also be wel] may wel be C • callid] *om.* LT; callid also C 556 juelle] *om.* LT • þe[3]]
þi LT 557 *facit*] *facit.* He seith LT • a] *om.* T • he seith] *om.* LT 559 Be þerfor wel
war, sister] Þerfor, sister, be wele ware LT

571 aughter] auter he LT 573 techith] techeth þe LT 575 *preparare*] *preparare.* He
seith LT • he seith] *om.* LT 577 þe] þat LT 580 is] 'is' is added in the margin in
T, with a caret after 'it'. 583 right] *om.* LT • telle] 'tell' is added in the margin in
T, with a caret, possibly by a second hand. 587 it[1]] is T 589 an] as T 590 to] *om.*
T • þe[3]] *om.* C 593 þe[1]] *om.* C 597 Thus þan] Þan þus LT • manna] manna is
undirstond LT 598 is] ys ys C • is undirstonde] *om.* LT 602 or] oþer in LT • or
ellis] oþer ellis in LT • and[2]] and in C 606 þerof] þerfor LT 613 he] *om.* C • al
creatures] alle maner of creatures to be LT 614 as] as David LT 615 *eius*] *eius oves
et boves* LT 617 man] mankind and fede LT • oxyn] *om.* T • to] *om.* C • so of] so
is of alle LT 619 largnes] largenes is T • is] *om.* T 620 man] *om.* T 621 For al the
angelis that be in heven] *om.* LT • seiþ] seith: Alle þe aungelis þat ben in heven
LT 622 shuld] schul LT 626 of] *om.* C • Þat is[2]] First, þat he is LT 626 as[2]] *om.*
LT 632 *etenim*] *etenim.* He seith LT 632–633 mayster and lord] lord and mayster
C 633 he seith] *om.* LT 636 don] done so LT 639 *magno*] *magno.* He seith LT • he
seith] *om.* LT 641 he yaf] was ȝoven LT 642 *est[1]*] *om.* T • *potus*] *potus.* He seith
LT 643 he seith] *om.* LT • is[2]] *om.* T 645 his] ~~is~~ T

647 now þe nedeth] þu nedyth now C 649 *te oportet*] oportet *te* T 651–652 yive þou now þiself for his mete] *om.* C 652 now] *om.* T 653 þiself redy] redy þin self C 655 brother] brother and C 658 fro þennys] *om.* LT 660 wel] wele þat LT • gladly] *om.* C 661 synner] synner and LT • Bi] By þis LT 662 þe²] *om.* T 663 thei] hir child LT • here] his LT 664 mete able] able mete LT • ete and] *om.* LT • here] his LT 668 þerof] þerfor T • mete, able] able mete L • hym] *om.* LT 669 þe] it C 671 maner] maner of LT 672–673 here own willes] his owen wille LT 674 willes] wille LT 681 it is] is it T 682 for] *om.* C 684 þan] than the C 685 his] here C 688 Trewly] *om.* LT 689 þe] *om.* C • wittes and every sensible] *om.* T 691 and] *om.* LT 693 right] more LT • and] and to LT 694 is²] is oft LT 695 and] *om.* T 698 oþer] other men C 699 prophete] prophete Ysaye LT 700 *prudentes*] *prudentes.* He seith LT • he saith] *om.* LT 702 þat] *om.* LT • be] *om.* LT 703 new] now T 706 spekith and seith] seith thus LT 707 skynnes] skynne C 710 contradiccioun] contradiccounys C 713 away] way LT 722 seyth] seith þus LT 723 *ardoris*] ardoris. He seith LT • he seith] *om.* LT 724 he seith, be] is LT 726 religioun] religioun wyth C 729 rost] rost for defaut of bastyng LT 730 þat] þat þe LT 731 shuld] schul LT 733 þe¹] *om.* C • shuld] schul LT • be²] with LT 734 so] so for LT 735 suffre] suffre þe LT • lest þat] But þer be many þat be unpacient and for defaut rost noth kendeli C 736 bren] bren and LT 737 is] is þe LT 743 þeyme] hym T

750 And] And and T 752 propre] *om.* LT 757 for] *om.* C • poure] *om.* T 760 *pauperum*] *om.* T 761 *autem*] *om.* LT 762 he seith, to poure folk] to þe pore peple, he seith LT 763 þerto] þerto to T • þat it] for to LT 764 have þerto] þerto have C • no] *om.* T 765 noiþer¹] our LT 766 withoute] without þe LT 770–771 þe wiche] þat LT 772 flowid] folowid T 774 flowyng] folowyng T

785 affeccioun] affeccions LT 787 with] with Jhesu LT 791 þus] *om.* LT • grotchyng] grocchyng to LT; grutchyng of C 796 as] *om.* T 798 lovyth] loueth þat T 799 he] he he T 800 þe] þe, for LT 804 voyde²] empty LT 805 a voyde and] *om.* LT 808 rostid] *om.* CM • is²] is þis LT 810 affeccioun is] affeccions ben LT 811 wel rostyd in] dried up in þe rostyng of LT • it] þis C 813 affeccioun] affeccions LT • þat] þat þe gode man LT 814 seith] seith þus LT • Yis in] þis is C 817 or] and LT 819 Than shuldist þou] Thou schuldist LT 820 þei] *om.* C 821 þe] þi T 826 for] *om.* C • is¹] is rostid LT • rostid] *om.* CM • is²] *om.* C • yif flessh] þis ʒif in LT 827 be] *om.* T 828 oute of] fro LCT 829 oute of] fro C 830 so is] is so T 831 be verry nede] *om.* LT • always lyve] lyve alleway LT 832 in hert holily] holyly in herte C 834 þou desirest] desirest þou LT 835 *Christo*] Christo. He seith LT 836 he seith] *om.* LT 841 is] *om.* LT • departith] departyd C 842 vertu] vertues C 842–843 from alle vertu as a bon is fro flessh] as a bon is fro alle maner of vertu LT 845 in] at LT 847 *sua*] sua. He seith LT • he seith] *om.* LT 849 shuld] xuln C; schul LT • more] *om.* LT 850 and also þan] also LT; and also C • come] come þan C

852 blissid] *om.* LT 853 That is] þat is to sey LT • rather] more LT 855 here] *om.*
T 859 Thenk] Thyng C 860 þat] *om.* C 861 every] *om.* LT 864 seyde] seid þus LT
• *huius*] *huius.* He seid LT 865 he seyde] *om.* LT; he seyth C • also had] hadde
also T 866 prophete] prophete David LT • seyde] seid þus LT • *meam*] *meam.* He
seith LT 867 he seyde] *om.* LT

868 declared] declared to LT 869 etyn] eten and LT 870 for] *om.* C 873 *nupcie*]
numpcie L

881 she] he C 882 I] *om.* C 883 *et*²] *om.* C 884 That is] He seith LT 888–889 Bi
þis prest … clene soule¹] *om.* LT 889 bi] be þe C 890 þei] þe T 893 a virgine is]
is a virgine T 894 is¹] was LT 895 þan] *om.* LT • wymmen] woman LT 898 high]
om. LT 904 *est*] *est.* He seith LT 905 so] *om.* C 907 the wiche] þe which þe wyche
T 908 desired] desyred þe C • the wiche] þat LT 912 that] þat all C 913 And³]
And yet LT 918 for] *om.* LT 920 suffrid] suffre LT 926 matrimonye] matrimony
for LT 927 a] *om.* C 928 anoþer] any other LT 936–937 For right as a commune
womman] *om.* LT 937 be] be so T • synne] synne and LT 939 bi] with T 943
mochel] gret LT 949 and dishonest] *om.* LT 952 fendis] devylys T 954 þis] þis þat
LT 955 an] þat T 958 temptacioun] temptaciouns CLT 959 *vobis*] *vobis.* He seith
LT • he seith] *om.* LT • þan wil he] he wille LT

965 couple] *om.* T 966 afore] bifor LT 967 a²] a clene C 972 is²] *om.* LT • and] *om.*
LT 974 spouse¹] wife LT • his²] is T • spouse²] wif LT 977 *verecunda*] *veracunda.*
He seith LT 978 many] *om.* T • he seith] *om.* LT 982 hath] *om.* T 984 a] *om.* LT
988 smellith] is LT 991 besemeth] semeth LT 993 purely] trewly LT • doblenes
or] *om.* LT 997 *inimicos*] *inimicos.* He seith LT • he seith] and LT 998 an] *om.* C
• lessith or] *om.* LT 999 Thus] Than LT • shuldist þou] þou schuldist L

1001 mayst þou] þou maist LT • spouse] wif LT 1002 shal I] I schal LT 1004
of] *om.* C • is] ben LCT 1007 Jhesu] *om.* LT 1008 for] *om.* C 1010 is] *om.* C •
also] also is T 1011–1013 coupled unseparatly to þi spouse, Jhesu, bi perseveraunce
abidyng in the observaunce of the cloyster in maner tastyng of swetnes of joye]
couplid by parseveraunce abidyng in þe observaunce of þe cloistre in maner of
tastyng unseparatly to þi spouse Jhesu in endles joy L; couplid by parseveraunce
abydyng in þe observaunce in of þe cloister in maner of tastyng unseparatly to þi
spouse Jhesu in endles sorwe T 1016 þes] þe LT; *om.* C 1016–1017 þenke that thi
weddyng in perseveraunce of þe cloyster] in parseveraunce of þe cloistre, þenk þat
þi weddyng LT 1017 in maner is made] ys made in maner C 1019 into religion thus]
to religion LT 1021 *deserto*] *deserto.* He seith LT • he seith] *om.* LT 1023 because]
because þat LT 1025 take] take hede T 1025–1026 For þer] wher LT 1027 a] *om.*
C 1030 because] because he seyth C

1033 in] of LT 1037 *nimis*] *nimis.* He seith LT • he seith] *om.* LT 1040 is] *om.* T
1042 novelte] newhede LT • that] *om.* T 1043 not] 'not' is added in margin by
second hand in T, with caret. 1044 hert] hertys C 1045 hert] hertis C • tyme] tyme
in here youthe LT; time in here youthe M 1048 to¹] into LT • þan] *om.* T 1049
she¹] *om.* T • not] *om.* T 1054 the] *om.* C • for] *om.* T 1055 for²] for þe L 1056 for
his love, tribulacioun] tribulacion for his love LT 1061 *illam*] *illam.* He seith LT
1063 hemself] hymself C 1068 world] worldys LT 1070 world] worldis LT 1071
reportis] aportis LCT 1073–1074 more with þe] wyth the more C 1075 a] *om.* C
• so] *om.* T 1077 body] bodies LT • likne] likne alle LT 1079 is] he his T • þou]
þou wilt LT 1080 oute of] fro LT • affeccioun] affeccions LT

1084 thi] þe T 1087 such] þe same LT • þou] þat C 1088 after] after wyth C • the]
þi T 1090 sey] sey þat LT 1094 the] *om.* T • seith] seith hit L The 'hit' is roughly
struck through, possibly by accident or by a later hand. 1094–1095 perfightly for]
perfyth C 1097 be] art C 1098 he not] noth he C 1102 within] with þe in C •
of] in T 1103 he is] his T 1103–1104 for thou woldist have him to the] *om.* C; for
thow woldist have hym T 1104 and¹] and in T 1105 love²] have LT 1107 a] *om.*
LT 1108 fer] *om.* LT • oute of] fro C • owne] *om.* LT 1109 melody and mirthe]
myrthe and melody LT • but] *om.* LT 1112 þe²] *om.* C 1117 not] not ~~Quis ex vobis
homo qui~~ T 1118 temptacioun] temptacions LT 1119 al] *om.* LT

1121 that] as C 1124 That] That þis word LT • the] þis T 1125 thus] *om.* LT 1128
perierat] *perierat.* He seith LT • he seith] *om.* LT 1130 þat¹] þe to CM 1131 yif]
þough LT 1132 þat is] as LT 1134 is heven] þat heven is LT • for] *om.* LT 1139 in¹]
om. T • art] *om.* T 1140 þe] þi T • a] *om.* C 1141 in] *om.* LT • perseveraunce]
perseveraunte L 1142 is] *om.* C • wise] vyse ys C • coupled] complete LT 1144
So] So þou L • thow] *om.* C 1147 no] not LT 1149 tribulaciouns] tribulacion LT
• for] of LT 1151 gretter] gretter syster C • the there a gretter fest] þe a gretter fest
þere LT 1152 the] thyn C; þi T 1155 þan] *om.* T 1156 home] home in þe cloistre
LT 1158 in þe cloyster] *om.* LT

1159 sister] *om.* LT 1164 In] In þis LT 1165 shul] schuld LT • be trewe to] betwene T
• in²] in þi LT 1167 of spirit] in spyryth C • of³] of all C 1170 is] is to sey LT 1178
þou] *om.* LCT • weddyng] weddyng þou LCT 1179 werkis] werkis for LT; dedys
C 1185 done¹] y-done betwen two persones LT 1185–1186 betwene to persones]
om. LT 1191 is] is to sey LT 1195 and²] an C 1196 þees þre] *om.* LT 1197 children
of] *om.* LT 1198 thi²] *om.* T

1204 prophete] prophete Isaye LT • seyde] seith LT 1208 es] est C • argento]
argento. He seith LT • he seith] *om.* LT 1209 clensid] clense LT 1210 the] *om.*
C • of dyverse colouris] *om.* LT 1212 'with' added in margin via caret in T 1213

þe broches] broches to þe LT **1214** in] to L • eeris] heerys C **1215** araymentes]
ornamentis LT

1217 'with' added in the margin in T **1217–1218** with water of] water of L; *om.*
T **1226** a] a liȝt T **1227** *nostris*] *om.* T **1228** þer come no blode] *om.* T **1229** such]
suche a LT **1231** wilt] woldist LT • vessellis] vessell C **1233** vessellis] vessel LCT
1234 vesselle] vessel on erthe LT **1235** *noxie*] noxie. He seith LT **1236** he seith] *om.*
LT **1237** sewith] schewith T **1238** *in te*] *om.* T • That] Þis T **1242** þe] *om.* LT •
and] *om.* T **1243** bath] haþ T • swet and] swete LT; swete and devout C **1244–1245**
Into þis bath … medicinable] *om.* LT **1247** and] *om.* LT **1248** þe²] *om.* LT **1249**
feet] fote LT **1250** *sanguine*] sanguine. He seith LT • he seith] *om.* LT • feete] fote
LT **1252–1253** þe wich] that LT **1253** whiles it is þrede] whan it is cloth LT **1254**
whiles it is] in LT **1255** right] *om.* LT • But clothe, þe wiche is dighed whiles it is
þred] But þe cloth þat is died in cloth LT **1256** whiles þou art] in LT **1257** for¹]
om. LT **1259** yit] *om.* LT • love] love ȝit LT • for⁴] *om.* C **1260** and] *om.* LCT
1261 whan þou art þred] in cloth LT • lerne] lerne for C

1266 for] for þi LT **1267** for] for þi synnes and hast LT **1268** *Deus*] Deus Deus LT
• *leticie*] leticie. He seith LT • he seith] *om.* LT **1271** *tuum*] tuum. He seith LT **1272**
excercise] exersise schew glad chere LT **1273** shew glad chere] *om.* LT

1292 In] In þe LT **1293** in¹] in þe LT • with cloþis of sad] þou schalt ben arayed
in sadnes of LT • in²] in þe LT **1294** with cloþis of] þou schalt ben araied in LT
1296 can] *om.* C **1299** *sum*] sum. He seith LT • he seith] *om.* LT **1301** wite] *om.*
T **1305** and familiar] *om.* LT **1306** þat] þat þe LT • is] *om.* LT **1308** is in] be in
hire, and þan conforme hire LT **1311** to] *om.* T **1312** þis] *om.* LT **1314** lyghing]
lyvyng C **1315–1316** Moyses hid his face whan he spake to þe puple] whan Moyses
spak to þe peple he hidde his face and LT **1318** þat] *om.* C • synners] synneris
for LT **1323** never þe puple] þe peple never T • for to] *om.* C **1327** behave]
have T

1329 þe] *om.* LT **1336** þe] *om.* C **1337** That is] He seith LT • A! how faire, kynges
doughter] O kynges douȝtir, how faire LT **1339** right] *om.* C

1347 afore] before C **1350** to] to wher T • *precincti*] precincti. He seid LT **1351** up]
om. C • he seyde] *om.* LT **1360** moche] *om.* C • to] on T **1362** of] *om.* LT • away]
owt LT **1363** þou²] is LT **1366** Tho] Too LT; To C **1367** and] *om.* LT **1368** dwelle]
we ben LT **1372** we must also] also we most LT **1375** to] *om.* LT

1376 to] *om.* LT **1379** Crist his] Cristis T **1381** it never] never it to LT; yt never to
C • like as þe] riȝt as LT **1384** in] in in T • suwyng] sewyng þe LT

1386 hathe[1]] *om.* C 1393 astoned] astonyed he C 1394 þat] þat þou LT 1396 merveylous] wondir LT 1400 moche] moche for LT 1402 of] and C 1404 herte] *om.* LT • and] *om.* T 1405 myght] my3t þer LT 1406–1407 in al wisis] alle gate LT 1409 we kept] 3e kepe LT; we kepe C 1410 plesid him it was] plesith hym it is T 1411 his[2]] is CT 1413 we] we þan LCT • þan] *om.* LT 1414 and[1]] *om.* LT 1415 þat kote fro us] fro us þat coote C • þe[1]] þat C 1418 so is] is so LT • not] wite never LT 1419 oure] owre we schul be clepyd C • in] into C 1420 martires] martires and LT • yif] 3if þat LT 1421 shulle] schold T 1426 benefices wiche] benefyces þe wiche C; benefytys þat LT 1428 benefices wiche] benefyces þe wiche C; benefetis þat LT • godhede] manhode L 1429 benefices of his manhode and of his godhede] benefetis of his godhede and of his manhode LT 1431 to] unto C • in[3]] *om.* LT 1437 *caritas*] caritas. He seith LT • he seith] *om.* LT • coveryth and hydeth] hydeth and coveryth C 1438 it] it to C 1439 for] *om.* LT 1441 afore] before LT 1443 þis] *om.* T 1444 it] þat he LT 1445 she makeþ] þey make L; he ma þei make T 1445–1446 þat is, for to seke … alle creatures] *om.* LT

1447 he] *om.* C 1450 shuldist þou] þou schuldist LT 1451 *Domino*] Domino. He seith LT 1452 he seith] *om.* LT 1454 be the] *om.* MTL 1455 be þe] þi T 1459 for þees too] *om.* LT, however L adds 'for þes to' in a later hand, in the margin; for þees ii C 1461 *dexterum*] dexterum. He seith LT • he seith] *om.* LT 1463 a] a token or a LT 1466 a] *om.* LT

1468 he] he þat he T 1469 þis] þis this T • þe[2]] *om.* C 1471 moche] most C 1475 of[2]] *om.* C 1478 þe[1]] þe close T 1479 þorogh] out LT • Wheþer] Wher LT 1480 wene] wene. For LT 1482 ben cause ofte tymes] oft tymes ben cause LT 1483 *iurgiorum*] iurgiorum. He seith LT 1490 scaldyng] scaldyng hote T • with] þe T 1491 Therfor] Ther T 1492 þou] þou make T 1495 be] ys C 1497 wiche shuld be þi modir] *om.* LT 1498 þan] þan þat LT 1500 þe] *om.* LT 1504 to] *om.* LT

1506–1507 þe wiche ben ornamentes of þe eerys, þou shalt undirstonde] þou schalt undirstond, þe whiche ben ornamentis of þe eris LT 1508 *obedientem*] obedientem. He seith ri3t LT • geldyn] *om.* LT 1508–1509 he seith] *om.* LT 1512 or[1]] oþer LT; er C 1515 but] but þan T • good] *om.* LT 1516 lowly] lowly þe LT 1517 undirstonde] undirstond also LT 1518 shuldist] schalt LT 1519 *eis*] eis. He seith LT 1520 shuldist] schalt LT 1521 þer] þer þat LT 1522 subieccioun] subieccouns C 1523 reprovyng of] reproves in LT 1524 þe wiche] þat C • lowli] *om.* C 1526 at] to LT 1528 do ne suffre] suffre ne don C

1533 in þe blisse of heven þe wiche crowne] *om.* T 1536 þis] þe T 1541 þat] þe T 1542 wiche] þat LT 1543 crowne] corown corown C 1545 to] two golden LT 1548 and] and and C

1557 *aurum*] *aurum.* He seith LT • he seith] *om.* LT • to] in LT 1558 for] *om.* T 1560 in] to LT 1561 in¹] to LT • in²] to LT 1564 for to only] only for to LT

1567 he] our lord LT 1569–1570 among al] over alle L; on alle over T 1573 ben] ben clenner and LT • wordis] wordis þe LT 1574 was] wern C • þat] þe whiche LT 1575 *peccare*] *peccare.* He seid LT 1576 he seyde] *om.* LT; he seyth C 1578 soule] synner LT • to] unto C 1579 what] whiche LT • a] *om.* T 1581 *pace*] *pace.* He seith LT • he seith] *om.* LT • in me] *om.* LT 1583 also was] was also L; whas T 1584 of] on C 1585 *paradiso*] *paradiso.* He seid LT • he seyde] *om.* LT 1591 in¹] in þe L • or] oþer in LT 1595 with it] þerwith LT

1599 a] *om.* T 1601 *Cum gloria*] *om.* LT • Amen] *om.* LT

Capitulum secundum

title *Capitulum secundum*] *Secundum capitulum* L • mynche] menoresse T

1 mynche] menoresse T 4 *tuum*] *tuum.* He seith LT • he seith] *om.* LT

14 straunge] strong LT 17 of oure hertes] *om.* LT 18 lyon] bore L; bere T 19 devoure] devoure. Also LT 20 þis] þe LT • Be] To LT 21 þe eyghe] þin eyen LT 22 and] *om.* T 23 also us] us also LT • into] in LT 27 dedis] dredis L • myght] may C 32 slepe] slepe and LT 33 and] and with LT 34 þei²] þe T 35 serche] seige C 38 because] by cause þat LT 39 wel kepe] kepe wel LT 40 etyng] hetyng C 45 Serche] Seige C 47 to²] *om.* C 47–48 devoutly in the quere] in þe quere devoutly LT 50 *nobis*] *vobis* C 51 *tercius*] *tercius.* He seith LT • moche] mekyl C 53–54 in castellis] in a castell C 56 þe²] her LT 57 or] and LT 58 þe¹] þin C 60 þe¹] þy L; þi T 64 þus] þus þat LT 65 figure I fynde hereof] herof y fynde T • þus] þus that LT 66 cite] cite þe C • wiche] þat L 67 þe] þat C 70 him] hym and LT • seyde] seid þat LT 71 upon] on LT 72 tyme] tyme þat LT 73 so] aftirward LT 74 and¹] and to C • oþer] to þe LT 75 þe] þe lordis and þe LT • compassioun] compassion and pite LT 77 þat] þe LT • and¹] and to LT 79 alive] on lyve C 82 þe wiche is no more to mene but a serpente] þou schalt undirstond a crewel serpent LT 82–83 þou shalt undirstonde þe fende] þat is þe fende LT 83 þat] þe whiche LT 84 wiche] þat LT • impugnyng] undirmynyng LT 85 gret] *om.* LT • grevous] *om.* LT 86 aboute] in poynt LT 87 into] to T 88 wiche] þat LT 90 for to be in pees] *om.* T 92 oure¹] þe LT 93 knowleche] knowleche of God LT 95 feere] fere þus LT • Yis] *om.* LT 98 al þe love and gostly knowleche] þe knowleche and þe love LT • þing] þinges LT 100 þe³] *om.* L 101 þer] *om.* LT 102 þe²] *om.* L 106 compassible] uncompassyble C 108 how oure] oure C; our how T 111 and] but C • he] were LT 115 somme] summe summe C • suffreth] suffreth for C • abyde] abyde in þe

L • in] in þe T 116 be] be be T 118 and] and þat T 125 smale] *om.* LT 128 longe
be] be long LT 134 faynte] fayntise of LT • with] *om.* T 135 oute] *om.* T 140–141
also ben] ben also LT 142 of] a3enst LT 143 litel[1]] lyth C

150 þi] *om.* T 151 þe[2]] *om.* T 152 tyme] tyme þat LT 153–154 So don many in
religioun whan þei ben hurt and woundid] *om.* T 156 in al wise] alle gates LT 157
þi] þe LT 160 þin] þi gostly LT 161 speke] sey C 165 here] *om.* C 169 þe] þe for
C 170 such] such þat LT • to] to þe LT 171 þan] *om.* C 174 þan] *om.* T 175 and]
and in L 176 discrete] undyscrete C 179 *forcium*] *forcium.* He seith LT 179–180 he
seyth] *om.* LT 186 mekely and paciently suffre] suffre mekely and paciently LT 187
so] *om.* LC 190 be] with T 195 aftirward into] aftirward in L; after in T 197–198
shal þin enemy] þin enemy schal LT 200 hem] her enemyes LT 202 sister] *om.* C •
foly] foly systyr C 204 as] and C • begynneth to make] makyth C 205 syght] si3t
or LT • spekyng] spekyng or LT 206 and[1]] or LT 207 wise] wise to C 210 praying]
prayer LT 211 honest] *om.* C 213 yif] 3if þat LT 218 *suam*] *suam.* He seith LT

221 sad] *om.* T 223 do] *om.* T 225 þat[1]] þe LCT 227 portoure] keper LT 229
withoute[1]] wythowtyn a C • withoute[2]] wythowhtyn a C 230 styrne] roþer LT •
urbs patens] *patens urbs* T 231 *in loquendo*] *om.* LT 232 *suum*] *suum.* He seith LT •
Like] Ri3t LT • he seith] *om.* LT 237 yif] 3if þat LT 239 *erit*] *erit.* He seith LT 240
he seith] *om.* LT 242 what] *om.* C • what þat ever] whatsoever LT • nedis] nede
C • Ther is] thane ys ther C 244 so] so for LT • wiche] þat þat LT 245 Where]
Where it CM • of] *om.* T 246 such a] no L 248 þat] *om.* C 249 stirne] roþer LT
250 *enim*] *om.* LTC • *frena in ora*] *in ora frena* LT 251 *magne*] *valide* C 253 *et*[1]]
eciam LT • *modicum membrum*] *membrum modicum* C • *exaltat*] *exaltat.* He seith
LT • so is] is so LT 253–254 he seith] *om.* LT 254 hem] hem to C 255 bridelis]
brydyl C 256 as] *om.* C 256–257 oþerwhile] otherwyse C 258 styrne] roþer LT 259
þe[2]] þin LT; þe gret C • into] in LT 261 discretly þi tonge] thy tonge dyscretly C
• hors] hors þat is LT 262 styrneles] þat is roþerles LT • in] in a C • doth] doth
doth T • the wiche] þat LT; wiche C 263 tonge] tonge or hires whether it be LT
266 þus governe þe] governe þe þus LCT • religious] relygyous man or C

267 wynne gret frute, sister] sistir, wynne gret fruyt L 268 *replebitur*] *replebitur.*
He seith LT • he seith] *om.* LT 269 frutes?] frutes of þi mouth? LT 270 Certeyn,
þe frutis of the mowthe ben þees] Certayn, sistir, þes þei ben LT 271 þonkyng]
thonkynges LT 274 þat Seynt Poule spekith of] of Seynt Poule LT 275 *linguis*]
linguis. He seith LT • he seide] *om.* LT; he seyth C 278 first] fruyt LT • þes] þe C
279 felaw] felow þus LT • toþer] left C 279–280 þe toþer side þus] þat oþer side
LT 282 *tuum*] *tuum.* He seid LT • he seide] *om.* LT 283 he seyde] *om.* C 283–284
han trespace] have done and trespaced LT 287 charitably his felaw] blamed his
felow charitably LT • ferst] *om.* CM 288 seide] seide on C 291 shulde] schuld þe

L • sunner] *om.* C • þat þe tother shulde sunner know himself] *om.* T 292 seyde] seid þus LT • this] this lord C 293–294 at þe last, seyde] seid, at þe last LT

298 Neverþeles five þinges þer ben] Also þer ben fyve þinges LT 299 what] whane C • whan] what C 301 And] *om.* LT 303 of] þat is LT 305 to[1]] *om.* C • Inhonest] Dishonest LT • al] *om.* LT 306 or] oþer ellis L • profiteth] profytyth to C 308 dishonest] dishonest wordis LT 314 *taciendi*] *tacendi* LT • *et*] *om.* C 315 or] or ellis LT 316 þe] the þe C 320 wel] wele þat LT • spekyng] sylence C; spekyng as T 322 shalt speke] spekist LT 324 spekist] spekist to LT • fole] fole as Salomon seith LT • moche] *om.* LT 325 as Salomon seith] *om.* LT • commune] comune with T 326 or] or to LT • reformyd] enformed LT 328 hem[1]] hem of L; hym of T 330 wheþer] wher LT 331 profited] profyht C • wich] þat LT 333 yifte] ȝift of LT 334 gost] gost for he LT 337 whos] *om.* T 339 no wit for] nouht C 341 for] *om.* C • on] one scharply LT 342 for] for þe LT • for ensample of oþer] *om.* C 344 of] *om.* LT 347 manerly] namely C 348 signifiyng] significacion LT 350 speke] speke and LT • whan] whan and T 351 and[1]] *om.* C • doctrine] doctryne yf þou kepe thys doctryne C

353 now þat fallith] þat fallyth now C 354 þe[2]] *om.* C 357 not] nouþir LT 358 to þingis] *om.* LT 360 case] cause LT 363 more bounden] bowndyn more C 364 subiettis] subjectes. And LT 367 casis] causes LT 369 þan speke] for þan speke to LT; than speken to hem C • sovereyne] sovereyne as C 370 te] te. He seith LT 371 he seith] *om.* LT • hate] hate on C 372 blames] blamyng LT 373 praye] pray and LT • prof] profit T 374–375 but raþer for to praye. Also, þe nediþ not for to speke] *om.* LT 375 a] *om.* C 378 bisinessis] besynes LT 379 as[1]] a T 381 a[1]] *om.* LT • þat] þat is LCT 382 but] *om.* C 385 ben] but moche more C • as subiettis ben. For a prelate or a sovereyne is bounde] *om.* T 388 albeit] albeit þat LT 390 Isidere þus] an holy man Ysidere LT • seith] spekith þus T 391–392 opynly blamyd] y-blamed openly LT 397 states] state LT 399 Poule] *om.* T • *patrem*] *patrem*. He seith LT 400 he seith] *om.* LT 404 *corripientem*] *corripientem*. He seith LT • he seith] *om.* LT 405 blamyngis] blamyng LT 407–408 with rigerouste þat wil not be blamyd] *om.* T 409 sovereyne] sovereyne rigerouste þat wil not be blamyd and correctid with esynes so þat þe entent of a sovereyne T 410 trobel] trobil cruelnes LT 411 þe] *om.* C 413 also shuld] schuld also LT 415 *castigo*] *castigo*. He seith LT 418 blames] blame C • oute] *om.* LT • prophete] prophet Ysaie LT 419 *Jesse*] *Jesse*. He seith LT 420 of correccioun] *om.* LT 421 of[2]] *om.* LT 422 and] and of C 424 what þat ever] whatsoever þat LT 425 annoþer] anoþer persone LT 426 þerin] *om.* C • albeit] *om.* LT 428 a sovereyne shuld blame profittably] *om.* T 429 she] he C • here] hys C 430 sche] he LT 430–431 is uncorrigible where no profite is nouþer of here that] *om.* T 431 here] hym L • for] *om.* C 432 unprofittably] unprofitable T 433 wiche] þat LT 435 for] for þe LT 436 hede] *om.* T • yif] ȝif þat LT

Capitulum tercium

title wise] maner C

1 wises] wyse C 2 dore] dore þe LT

6 is] ys þat C 10 here¹] þat þe LT; the C • is¹] be C 11 Trewly] Treuly as Sent Bernard seith LT • hem] hem to LT 12 as Seynt Bernard seith] *om.* LT 13 sister þerfor] þerfor sistir LT 17 peyne or to endeles joye] joy oþer to endles peyn LT 18 þanne] *om.* C • shuldist] schul T 20 caused be] bycause of LT 22 and] and of LT 23 of] to LT 27 also] *om.* LT • þe²] *om.* C 28 þe] *om.* C • þis] þe C 30 it] it þat þou mow þe sonner dwelle þerin LT • þerin] þerin þe LT 33 Thees] The T 34 redyn rather oþer] rather redyn oþer mennys LT 35 negligently leven here owne hertes] leven here owne hertis neclygently C 36 þe] *om.* C 38 þat¹] þat þing LT; *om.* C 40 þis] þes LT 41 al day be schet] be schet al day LT

48 *eius*] *eius.* He seith LT 49 he seith] *om.* LT • most] more T 52 hert of] hert or of our LT 53 us] us whan he seid to our lord LT • to þe] þat LT 54 bi him] *om.* LT • seyde] seid þus LT 55 *vestrum*] *vestrum.* He seid LT • he seyde] *om.* LT 58 seven] *om.* LT • us] us for LT 59 for] *om.* LT • Tho] The LCT 60 oþer] other rather C 61 oure¹] to þin LT 63 in] about LT 65 closid] closeth LT • consciences] conscyence C 66 þe conscience] our consciences LT 68 þees] þe T 74 þat] *om.* C 80 or] or of C 81 and] or C • of¹] *om.* LT 85 þat] þat trowist þou] LT • Trewly] *om.* LT 92 for] *om.* C 95 wil hide eche] eche wille hide LT • oþer²] otherys C 96 his defautes] here defautes eche C 97 of²] of þe LT 98 of] of her LT 99 Eve²] sche C 100 for] *om.* C • to] to have LT 102 *peccatis*] *peccatis.* He seid L 103 he seide] *om.* L 104 in] of C 106 þe²] þe thrid L 111 and] and of L • Al þo þerfor] Therfor alle þo L 112–113 gyle such] gile also suche þat L 113 and lightly oþer] and weyen liȝtly þe gode dedis of anoþer, for as Salomon seith L • is] is an L 114 as Salomon seyth] *om.* L 116 ful] *om.* T • Therfor] They fare LT 117 taxe] taxe þe LC 118 pore folk] þe pore peple L 120 upon] on L 121 also likne] likne also L; also lykne alle C 122 kepe] kepe for L • of] with L • þe] here C 125 none] not C 126 of] with L • þe²] *om.* C 128 þough] ȝit L • sey] sey þat L • sistren and bretherin] bretheren and sisteren L • yit here] but ȝit our L 130 to¹] to þe C 132 do not þou] do not L; doo þou not C 133 be a sovereyne] come þerto L 135 þe²] our L 136 oure] oure owne C • of²] of þe C 137 in] yn here C • be] be þe L 142 hertes] hert L • face] hertis C 146 he] þe fende L • yit] *om.* C 147 wich] þat LC • folowith] followith þat is to sey L • sewith] followith L • Suche on I drede] Y drede þat L 148 folowith] folowith hym L • receyve him] swolow hym up L • he or she] sche or he T • amende] amende hem sone L 150 for] *om.* LC 158 of²] of þe L 159 cried] askid L 160 purposes] purpos L 161 of] to LT 162 religiously] wel T

164 extinguere] *extinguere*. He seith L • he seith] *om*. L 165 in] and C 170 I rede]
he seith T 173 and] and þe L 175 devout] þe good C 176–177 and governouris]
om. L 177 chirche] chirche as archebischoppis and bischoppis L • hete] herte T
178 passid] passid fro L 179 curatis of chirches, sovereynes of religioun] abbotes,
prioures and prestes L; sovereynes of religion and curatis of chirches T 181 al] *delet*.
L 183 hertis or consciences] conscience L; hertis or conscyence C 186 with] of C
• conscience] conscience to L 187 hath so tayde] is knyt for L 189 in] in þe L 190
þis] þe LCT 195 þat] þat *<illegible word>* C 196 unnethe] on ethe C 196–197 in
heven is silens] is silence in heven L 200 conscience] conscience Y have declared
to þe schortly L • þe³] thoo C 201 I have declarid to þe schortly] *om*. L; I have
declaryd to the schortly and C • Þerfor] Therfor, sistir L 205 with compassioun]
charitably L 205–206 þi synne and myn] her synne LT 206 here] þi LT • and of
myn] *om*. C 207 ypocritas] *ypocritas*. He seid L • þe¹] *om*. L 208 he seith] *om*. L • in
mysselevyng] uppon us L 215 wiche] þat LT 217 claspes] clospe C • rede withoute
any impediment clerly] clerly without ony impedement rede L 218 jugement] dome
C 220 of hym] added in superscript in a second hand C 221 withouten ende] added
in superscript in a second hand C • Amen] *om*. L

222 as] *om*. T 228 rede] fynde wretyn C 229 to] þat yt C 230 sua] *sua*. He seith L
• he seyth] *om*. L 231 in his lagh] *om*. C 232 creatures] creatures for L; creatur C
234 shalt] most L • for to receyve God] to God for to receyve hym L 239 þi] þe
L • stondith at þi dore] added in the margin in a second hand C 240 mihi] *om*.
C 241 shal] wyl C 247 nought] not T 249 bodily and gostly] goostly and bodyly
C 250 yif þou contynue in vertu] *om*. L 251 heven] heven, so þat þou continue
in vertu. L • þe] þi L 252 maner of] many C 253 offenses] offens LC 255 gode]
om. C 256 Jhesu] Jhesu to C 257 and þin armes þat] þat in his armes L 258 þe]
þe. Also L • cometh] cometh opyn C. In C at this point, the second, correcting
hand has added and then crossed out 'alle þi dores, lete no dore be schet aȝens
hym, he is þi good frend, opyn', plainly misled by the repetition of 'opyn' at this
point in the originating hand. • whan he cometh al þi dores] alle þi dores whan he
cometh L 263 þi] maner of L; *om*. C 264 openyd he not] C's second hand corrects
'opyn not he' to 'opened he not'. 265 is] is sufficient and L • þe¹] *om*. C 267 for]
to C 268 also] also þat L 269 þo] *om*. C 270 hert] hertis L • wiche] þat L 271
reprovith] reprevyth hem L 272 illo] *illo*. He seith L 273 sieth] seith T • he seith]
om. L • and] he T 275 is] it T 276 oure] þe C 276–277 þan þe gracious havyng
… to oure evencristen] *om*. by C's originating hand; added as superscript by C's
second, correcting hand. 278 as þe prophete seith, al maner of puple] alle maner
of peple, as the prophete Ysaie seith L • vagosque] *vagos* T 279 tuam] *tuam*. He
seith L • he seith] *om*. L • þe] þin L 281 wilt] wolde C 282 hert] hertis L • so is]
is so LT 283 tuam] *tuam*. He seith L 284 of þin hert] *om*. L 285 Ysaye] ~~Salomon~~
C • biddith] *om*. LT 289 to] *om*. T • indifferently] *om*. L

293 lyvyng] lyvyng and L 296 a foole] folys L • durith] endureth L • litel] *om.* L
298 wil] *om.* C 299 fayle of þis love] of hys love fayle C 301 unto þe] *om.* L 304
good folk] trewe folk and goode C 305 in effecte] *om.* L • as] *om.* C 308 on] *om.*
L 310 *iracundo*] *iracundo.* He seith L • he seith] *om.* L 312 such] suche one L 314
such] suche one L • evylle] evel, for it envenomyth alle þat ever delith þerwith L
316 al tyme] always L 319 a] a maystir or a L • on can no frende be] can be no
frend L 320 þe more] they C • be] be a C • with] to L 322 *et*] om. L • *contumelia*]
contumelia. He seith L • he seith] *om.* L 324 for] *om.* C 327 *est*] *est.* He seith L
• he seyth] more L 330 Trewly for] for truly C 331 be²] *om.* T 333–334 so seith
Salomon] Salomon seyth C 334 *fidelis*] *fidelis est* L • *vite*] *vite.* He seith L 334–335
he seith] *om.* L

336 and] and on C 337 evencristen] evyncrysten. Amen C

Capitulum quartum

2 *stabiliri*] *stabilire* C • *cor*] *cor.* He seith L • he seithe] *om.* L 4 because] because
þat L 7 ne be lad with every wynde of newe doctrines] *om.* L 8 alle suche þat ben
so variaunt] *om.* L 9 *corde*] *corde.* He seith L • he seith] *om.* L 10 sodeynly] and
credence L 14 in hem is] ys yn hem C 15 yif] *om.* L • shuld] schul L • it must
nedes have] we most have nedis L 16 strength] treuthe MC

17–18 in oure feyth. Because feith is nedful to þe stabelyng of oure undirstonding]
and L; added in superscript, in second, correcting hand, in C 19–20 twelve articles
of þe feyth after þe nombre of þe] *om.* T 20 twelve¹] *om.* L 21 cite þat is very]
om. L 23 þe¹] þo T • wich folowyn] þat folowith longith L • þo] þe LC 24 and¹]
and þe L

27 *terre*] *terre.* He seith L 29 þe] *om.* C 32 Many] Many þer ben þat L • few] few
þer ben þat L 35 to] *om.* L 37 like] riȝt L • þe] þe same L 39 supposyn] supposen
þat L • defayle] faile T 44 wiche] þat L

47 his] ys C 52 Jhesu Crist] he L • is þe] is þe only C; þe T • þe fadir and] þe
fadir and very C; and fadir is T 54 Ther] þat C 56 belevyd] beloved L 57 lord]
lord and most sovereyn god C • is] nys T

59 is] is þis L 60 Crist Jhesu] Jhesu Cryst C 62 mayde] maydyn clene C 63 beleve]
belyve also L • þat²] þe T 64 mayde] maydyn C • pure] pured T 69 was] was not
C • birthe] byrthe but ȝaf here a grete joye yn þat same tyme C

71 is] is to say L; *om.* T • with] in L 72 hard] *om.* T 73 ded] *om.* T 74 hede] *om.* T
75 creature] creature and fals juge C 76 continuede] contuned L • tyme] time þat
L 77 wiche] þat L 81 tyme] tyme þat L • and departe] *om.* L 83 light] siȝt L 88 He
was also] and also was C 92 in] in a LT 93 in] in a LT 95 so] *om.* LC 95–96 save
for þe] but for us he was beried L 96 þe²] us L • þi] oure L • soule] soules L

98 soule] soule and godhed C 100 ellis] ellis to sey L • were] þer L 101 A] A noþer
T 103 sought and] *om.* L

104–105 The þrid day he rose] he rose on þe thrid day L 105 wheþer] wher C 107
trewly] for soth L 110 gostly] hooly C 116 A] *om.* C 117 in²] and T 122 aryse] *om.*
C • soule] soule aryse from synne C 124 it] *om.* C • ligh stille in þe synne of]
lyhtly for to synne yn C 129 þis] þis is CM

133 bi] in LC 135 þe¹] *om.* C • þe²] *om.* C • Ther] Wher L 136 ful] *om.* L 138
faderis] fadir L 139–140 woldist wite] wilt sey L 140 þan] þan þat L • faderis] fadir
L 141 While] Alle þe while þat L 144 here] here tribulacion L • right] *om.* C 147
sessioun þere] ascencion L 149 in¹] for C • lik] lyk on C 153 alive] on lyve L 159
wheþer it] wher he L 162 consciencis] conscyence C 164 þat] þat þat C 166 payne
or to joy] joy or to payn L

168 *catholicam*] *catholicam.* He seith L 169 and] *om.* C • in²] *om.* L • with love
beleve] belyve with love L 170 he] *om.* L 172 Thre] Thre þerof L 174 *catholicam*]
catholicam, þat is L

177 is] is þis L

182 is] is þis L • *peccatorum*] *peccatorum*, þat is L 186 and also bi indulgences] *om.*
L; and also by yndulgence C 187 foryiveth] forȝevyth for C

190 is] is þis L 193 þe] thyn C 194 yif] ȝif þat L • mekly] mekely at C 195 now]
om. L • weyke] feble L

196 þis] *om.* C 197 lif everlastyng] everlastyng life L 201 þi] þe T

203 now] *om.* L 205 began] began first L 209 hem] his ȝiftes L • he²] se T 211
rightwis] riȝtful L 212 apostelis] apostelis for to L; apostelys to C 216 þe] *om.* C
218 to] *om.* L; to to C 220 *probati*] *probati inventi* LCT 224 touching] touchyng
to L • þe²] *om.* C 225 leved be] lyved in L; lyvyd by C; lyved be T 229 epistelis]
epistel L 230 clensith] clensyd C • bi] of L 230–231 secte undir] peple undir þe L
232 þe] *om.* C 235 þe¹] þe feyth of cryst and C

238 fynde] feynde T 239 *mutatur*] *mutatur.* He seith L 239–240 he seith] *om.*
L 240 is] is as L 243 as[1]] as it were L 244 play] place C 247 *ideo*] *propterea* C
• *est*] *est.* He seith L • Jerusalem] *om.* C 247–248 he seith] *om.* L 249 stabilnes]
unstabilnes L • unpacience] unpaciens for L 251 by a sterne] without a rother L 252
sapiencia] *sapiencia* he seyth C • pacient] pacient, he seith L • he seith] *om.* L 254
styrne] rother L • is wynde] cast and L; is C; his wynde T • hurte] hurt or lost L
255 unpacient] unpacient soule or L • tribulaciouns] tribulacion L 260–261 for a
schip withoute ankir is an hert withoute drede] *om.* L 261 is] is as T 262 to] many
T • an] *om.* L 264–265 This evyl drede may be callid wordly drede and mannys
drede] *om.* L 266 of[1]] of hys C • good] godis L 267 be] *om.* C 269 Al] Also C •
þe] *om.* C 270 wene] wene þat L 271 folk] folk and wele arayed L • wene] wene
þat L 274 þe] here C 278 only] þe C 279 to þe] into þin hert L • sey] sey þat L
281 þat] þat þing þat L 282 eschew] eschew for L • ne] no T 283 peraventure þou
shalt not] schalt L 287 bringe] brynge to T

288 Overmore] *om.* L • abidyng] abidyng evermore L 291 a[1]] for L • a[2]] *om.* L •
trewly] stedfastly T 294 þat] as L 296 and] *om.* LC 298 distemperaunces] distem-
peraunce L • heetes] hete L 299 now he lyth on þe to] but o while on þat one L;
now he lyhth on þat on C • now on þe tother] and anoþir while on þat oþer side
and L; now on þat othyr C 300 feet now his armes] armes and now his fete L 301
removeris and renneris] removers L • longe rest] rest long C 303 þe[2]] *om.* L 304
houres] hour C • hem] hem ferst C 305 also be liknéd] be likned also T 307 han]
hewe L • wyndow of here] dore of þe L 308 fro dore to dore] *om.* L • fro grate to
grate] fro gate to grate to grate C 309 be] *om.* T

312 *est*] *est enim* C • *stabiliri*] *stabilire* C • *cor*] *cor.* He seith L • þing] þing þat is
L; þyng is T 313 in] *om.* L • is] *om.* T 314 God graunte] graunte God C

Capitulum quintum

title and] *om.* T • in] *om.* C

1 The] Þis T • like] *om.* C 3 *illum*] *illum.* He seith L 4 he seith] *om.* L • lord] lord
þat made hym L

9–10 gracious yifte of] ȝyfte of gracyous C 10 þi] *om.* T • yiving] ȝevyng for L;
lyvyng C 13 þus] þus *ffilia* C 16 moche] a gret L • his] his hert L 17 bygh] bye þe
T 18 wel] wel and T 19 þe moche] *om.* C 23 Jhesu Crist] added in superscript in
C, by second, correcting hand. • revour] owner L 24 right preciously] preciously
and dere L 25 herte] hertis LC 27 þat] *om.* T 29 ayen] *delet.* C 31 Yif þin hert
also] Also ȝif þin hert L 33 wel] *om.* C • for[2]] *om.* CT 35 Neverþeles he suffreth]

and he sufferith neverþeles L 36 hucche] whuche T 38 love] love for L 40 not] not
for C 41 so] *om.* L

42 shal telle] schal telle þe L; telle þe T 43 it] þin hert L • bi] wyth C 46 þis] *om.*
C 48 do] *om.* C 51 Be] Be þou C 56 of²] yn C 57 aspexisti] *respexisti* L 58 *nescisti*]
nescisti. He seith L 59 to oure lord] *om.* L 60 wilt¹] woldyst C • lowyd] loued T
61 plesaunt] plesyng C 63 shal] *om.* T 64 had] *om.* L 70 on þe to] to þat one L;
on þat on C • now on þe toþer syde] and now to þat oþer side and L; now on þat
other syde C 71 lest] lest thenne C 77 lowly] lovly T 78 unobedience] dysobedyens
C 80 þe] the handis and C 81 *discolis*] *discolis*. He seith L

85 here] God L; *om.* C ('hym' added in margin) 86 lesse] lesse þat L; *om.* T • hast]
schal have C 88 wher] whan L 90 in yiving of þin hert to oure lord] *om.* C; in
ȝevyng of þin hert to God L 91–92 getyng and wynnyng] kepyng L

Capitulum sextum

1 of] of gostly LT 3 telle] *om.* T

6 *Altissimum*] *Altissimum*. He seith L 7 he seith] *om.* L 9 in anoþer place] *om.* C 10
esto] *esto*. He seith L 11 biddingis] biddyng L • because] by cause þat L • inow only]
only ynow L 12 on] yn C • it] þis L 16 *Deum*] *Deum*. He seith L • we] *om.* T 20
of þenkyng] of thenkynges L; þynggis T 21 sorow] sorow for L 22 repentaunces]
repentaunce L 26 upon] on L 29 synne] synne it L • on] *om.* T • is] hys C 31 *tibi*]
tibi. He seith L • he seith, in] in repentyng of L 32 oure lord] God L 34 þis] *om.*
T 35 on] in L 37 Neverþeles] Also L • þought] thouȝtes L 40 blasfemy] blasfemyng
L 41 lusti] *om.* L 44 it] is T • þat it falle not fro þe hert to þe flessh] þat þe holy
gost depart not fro þe hert L 45 þe¹] thyn C • hert] hert and L 46 cum] *in* T
• *meo*] *meo*, þat is L • with] with alle L 52 þought] thouȝt is L 53 repentauntly]
repentauntly þat L 53–54 remenaunt or þe relef] relef or þe remenaunt L 54 þo]
þe T 55 þo] þe L 56 blissid] *om.* C • whan] whom MC 57 *nocte*] *nocte*. He seith
L • he seith] *om.* L 59 spredist] laiyst forth L 60 ben] is L

66 *sublevabitur*] *sublevabitur*. He seith L • he seith] *om.* L 68 prophete] prophete
Ysay L 69 *suum*] *suum*. He seith L 71 þan] *om.* L 72 adversites] adversite L 76
þe] his L

77 for a clene] of a clene hert T 78 hungir] bryngger T 84 *suam*] *suam*. He seith
L • he seith to Job] *om.* L 85 biddyng] biddyngis L 86 fro] for C 87 egle] egle
þou schalt undirstond L • fleeth] flyyth C 88 þou schalt undirstonde] *om.* L; þou
schalt undyrstondyng C 90 in] by C 94 my biddyng] myne L 95 so lift] lyft so C

97 in²] *om.* L • þe²] *om.* C 100 o] a C • of] of þe L • in heven] *om.* C • down]
down owt of hevene C • brokyn] broken þe L 101 o] a C • stille] stille in heven L
102 maite] desert LT; myht C 104 here] *om.* C • mete] mere T 106 hungir] hungir
aftir L; hungyr wyth fervent love C

107 right¹] ryhtful C • right²] ryhtful C 109 est] *est.* He seith L • he seith] *om.* L
111 wyn] wynne heven LCT 113 þrid] thrid is LT • fourth] fourthe is T

116 kendly] of kynde L 118 wel] *om.* T 120 Be] and C • þou] *om.* T • a] þi L •
heritage] herytage and þou a C 124 tresorer] tresorere also L 125 hucch] whiche T
126 þi²] *om.* C • þer²] *om.* C 126–127 shuld þin hert] þin hert schuld L 127 *ibi*] *ibi
est* C • *erit*] *om.* C 128 non] now T 130 cause] cause ys C 131 hane] *om.* LT 138 þe]
þe the C • There] þus T 139 fulfilling withoute lothnes] ful love without haterede
L 140 servile subjeccioun] bondage L 140–141 undedlynes withoute passibilite]
om. L 143 joy] joye everlastyng C 145 þus] *om.* L 146 he] *om.* C • þe] þe to abyde
wyth hym C 147 Amen] Amen thus mote yt be C; *om.* T

Capitulum septimum

4 *vestra*] *vestra.* He seith L • he seith] *om.* L 6 cuttyng¹] kunnyng T 7–9 after my
first purpose, I shal declare unto þe be þe help of God. Thin hert is cut wel be
þe yifte of wisdom] *om.* L

12 not] not in L 14 þus] *om.* C 14–15 Nathan, he seith] He seith, Nathan L 15
fatnes] fatnes, þe whiche is L 19 þus] þus þat L 21 filthi] fylthy and C 22 fully]
om. L 25 of¹] and þat L • þat²] þe whiche L • of²] of seiyng L • of þus] thus of
and seyth C; of and seith T 26 *enim*] *om.* L • 'The love of God' he seyth] He
seith, 'þe love of God' L 27 of] *om.* C • And it is of so worschipful wisdom] *om.*
T 28 to savoure and be] to be sauvered and T 30 He hath a s[a]voury felyng] *om.*
L 31 vile and] foule and spiritual L 33 Wherefore] where of T 35 desires] desyre
C • with al þin hert] hertli T 36 þus saverist] saverist þus L • þingis] þing L 38
wisdom þat] þat wisdom L • þat is take] *om.* T 39 had as it may be] as yt may
be had C 40 prophete] prophete David L • whan] where T 41 'Tastith' he seyth]
He seith 'tasteth' L • and seeth] *om.* T 45 tastyng as fore] tastyng afore LT; tast
for C 46 had Seynt Austyn] Seynt Austyn had L 48 unusid] *om.* L 49 not what¹]
wot not whan C • not²] not of L 51 fal] fil T 52 sopid] sepyd C • old] held T 53
weyle] weyle ful sore C; weyled T 55 wrecch] wrech the C 56 þat] *om.* C 58 not]
ne wyste C 59 to] to an C 61 þe] a C 63 oþerwhile is] ys otherwhyle C 65 lovyd¹]
loveþ L • loved²] lovyth C 69 caused] cause T • overpassyng] ovyr meche passyng
C 76 declare] declare on C • þat] þe whiche L 77 amorous loveris] loveris and
fleschly C

80 al] as C • sentensis] sentence C • þat] and T 81 ony] hony C 85 is] is to say L
86 it] they C 87 here¹] hym C 90 and bi his mercy I am made to him able] *om.*
T • Like as] *om.* L 91 to me is] ys to me C 92 of al my] *om.* L 92–93 sorowis and
fatigaciouns] sorowys and fatigacions the L; sorow and fatigacion T 94 suffre¹]
suffred LCT 96 lived] livyth C • died] dyeth C 99–100 Neverþeles, it nedith
never for to be expounnyd] *om.* L 100 for¹] a dele T • lovyng] livynge C 101
here] hem T

105 purpose] purpose ryht so C 110 þat ever] *om.* C 113 in²] yn a C • maner] maner
alle LT 114 lovyng] *om.* L 115 fro] fro alle L • affecciouns] affeccions þus þan T
116 gost] gost. Alle L 117 in] yn a C

119 þe] *om.* L 121 o] a C 123 soule] soule þe L 123–124 undirstonding and
affeccioun] undirstondyngis and affeccions L 124 ben] by C 127 þat] þe whiche
L • lover] lorde C 128 privy goyng and comyng] comyng prively and þe goyng L
129 touchith] techith T 130 afore] afore and L 137 scurrilite] seculer desires L •
hem not] not to hem L 139 attencioun] entencion L • schewyn] schewyng L 140
þinges] *om.* C

142 of²] of his LT 144 of¹] of his LT • losse] lustis T 146 but] but yf C • þe] *om.*
C • þei] it LT 150 but] but yf C • to] to þe C 151 þing] þyngges CT 152 is] is his
L 153 þei lese] *om.* C 155 lover] love L 158 lover¹] love LT 160 þou] *om.* T 161 lover]
love L 162 syngyn] synggyng T 163 voice] voyces T 171 þe] *om.* C 174 *psallas et] et
psallas* L • *mente] mente.* He seith L 176 þi] *om.* C 180 lover] love L

185 ouþer] only C 185–187 after dyvers apprehensions þat he haþe of his lover. A
slak pous he hath whan he is in doute of here whom he lovyth. He hathe also a
swift pous] *om.* C 186 his lover] love L 188 for] *om.* C • whom] þat L 192 'Myn
hert' he seyde] He seid 'myn hert' L 194 joyed] joyeth C 195 skippid] skyppyth C
196 extatik] amerous L 198 myghtier] myht C

203 sche] he L 204 here] his L 205 but] but ʒif T 206 not] ne wot C 206–207
And speke to him … þou menyst] These words are added, via an asterisk, at the
top of the folio, in C, in the second, correcting hand. 208 entente] mynde L 210
it] it longgith not ne T • not] not to T 212 longith] longgith or touchith T 213
upon] on C 213–214 no noþer] none oþer L 215 in¹] in þe L 216 thus] *om.* L •
mea] om. C • *vidistis] vidistis.* Sche seith L 217 sche seith] *om.* L 218 ever] *om.* L
221 on] *om.* C • wantith] wantith þe LC • of God] *om.* T

224 an²] *om.* C 225 tayde] y-knyt L • þat²] þat is T 226 whan] what C • seeth]
seith T 231 in] on L 232 of²] of a C 233 Anone] *om.* C • himself] hymself anoon

C • for] for gret C 234 nyst] wist not L 237 and] *om.* C 243 þer] þere for LT •
what] þat C 246 þe wiche] þat L 248 to Moyses on] on to Moyses C 250 itself]
hymself L • not] never C • for o þing] *om.* L 251 in] in þe C • wende] hadde wend
þat C • þe wich] þat L; which T 253 For] For as L 256 of[3]] of goodnesse of C 257
To þe wiche blisse] *om.* C 258 ende] ende to þat C • þe] þat L

Index to Latin and English Scriptural Quotations

Note that the following references may refer only to part of a verse rather than the whole verse. Two identical references, therefore, may allude to two different parts of the same verse.

This index does not contain references to Biblical verses in the Textual Commentary when the verses in question are not quotes in the text. The reference numbers in brackets indicate the page number followed by the line number. References in italics are in Middle English in the manuscript.

Old Testament

Proverbs

Prov. 4:23 (5:7)
Prov. 4:23 (47:3–4)
Prov. 4:23 (51:147)
Prov. 4:23 (52:215)
Prov. 4:23 (58:441–2)
Prov. 9:8 (25:798–9)
Prov. 9:8 (56:370)
Prov. 10:11 (7:93–4)
Prov. 10:12 (42:1436–7)
Prov. 11:1 (62:113–14)
Prov. 11:2 (67:321–2)
Prov. 12:14 (54:268)
Prov. 13:3 (52:217–18)
Prov. 14:29 (75:251–2)
Prov. 14:32 (27:846–7)
Prov. 15:12 (25:794–5)
Prov. 16:6 (17:484)
Prov. 17:14 (43:1483)
Prov. 17:17 (67:326–7)
Prov. 22:24 (67:309–10)
Prov. 23:1 (20:573–5)
Prov. 23:2 (22:649–50)
Prov. 23:26 (77:13–14)
Prov. 25:12 (44:1507–8)
Prov. 25:28 (53:230–2)
Prov. 29:25 (81:66)
Prov. 31:13 (42:1422–3)

Ecclesiastes

Eccles. 3:7 (55:314)
Eccles. 7:2 (27:852–3)

Song of Songs

S. of S. 1:2 (32:1036–7)
S. of S. 2:14 (89:168)
S. of S. 2:16 (35:1170)
S. of S. 2:16 (87:84–5)
S. of S. 3:3 (91:216)
S. of S. 4:4 (51:178–9)
S. of S. 5:1 (13:333)
S. of S. 6:12 (16:424–5)
S. of S. 7:1 (40:1336–7)
S. of S. 8:6 (43:1460–1)

Wisdom

Wisd. 5:16 (80:6)

Ecclesiasticus

Ecclus. 1:14 (85:25–6)
Ecclus. 1:27 (7:75)
Ecclus. 2:20 (8:133)
Ecclus. 6:5 (31:996–7)
Ecclus. 6:16 (67:334)
Ecclus. 6:37 (80:9–10)
Ecclus. 7:35 (43:1450–1)
Ecclus. 10:10 (19:556–7)
Ecclus. 11:31 (66:283)
Ecclus. 19:4 (68:9)
Ecclus. 22:14 (55:324–5)
Ecclus. 26:19 (30:977)
Ecclus. 27:12 (74:239)
Ecclus. 29:14 (45:1556–7)
Ecclus. 29:33 (12:275)
Ecclus. 35:11 (12:280)
Ecclus. 35:11 (38:1271)
Ecclus. 36:27 (10:211)
Ecclus. 38:25 (32:1060–1)
Ecclus. 39:6 (5:16–17)
Ecclus. 39:6 (77:2–3)
Ecclus. 43:3 (24:722–3)
Ecclus. 47:1–2 (85:14)

Isaiah

Isa. 5:21 (23:699–700)
Isa. 11:1 (58:419)
Isa. 28:12 (6:46)
Isa. 40:2 (3:11–12)
Isa. 46:8 (16:430–1)
Isa. 50:10 (82:68–9)
Isa. 58:3 (78:57–8)
Isa. 58:3 (78:63–4)
Isa. 58:7 (66:278–9)
Isa. 63:1 (6:60–1)
Isa. 64:4 (92:253–5)
Isa. 66:2 (11:231–2)

New Testament

Transcription of the 'HV' Prologue from

De doctrina cordis

The first part of the Latin prologue given in the Naples 1607 edition of *De doctrina cordis*[1] (the 'HV' prologue according to the classification proposed by Hendrix) reads as follows:

Praeparate corda vestra Domino [1 Sam. 7:3]. Verba sunt Samuelis, I. Reg.7. Loquitur Dominus praedicatoribus per Isai. 40. dicens: *Loquimini ad cor Ierusalem* [Isa. 40:2]. In hoc verbo admonetur praedicator, vt verbum salutis diligenti, et familiari expositione studeat eliquare; vt sic ipsum verbum facilius vsque ad corda audientium transfundatur. Sunt enim verba Dei, quasi vuae, multa faecunditate repletae: vnde oportet vuam exprimere, quod est, verbum diligenter exponere, vt vinum spiritualis intelligentiae vsque in cellarium cordis fluat. Auris enim bona, torcular est (vt dicit Augustinus) vinaria verborum retinens, et vinum spiritualis intelligentiae vsque ad cellarium cordis transmittens. Quotiens ergo tibi praedicatur, totiens vinum spirituale ad cordis tui cellarium, ad te potandum, ad te inebriandum transmittitur. Vae ergo tibi, si cor tuum in huius vindemiae vbertate vacuum, et sitibundum remanserit; ac sis effectus de illis, de quibus dicitur Iob 40. *Qui calcatis torcularibus sitiunt* [Job 24:11]. Vae tibi, si canale, seu conductum auditus tui a cellario Regis, id est, diuina doctrina auerteris, ne liquor pretiosus influat in cor tuum; ad aquam turbidam, et immundam fabulationum saecularium eundem auditum conuertens cum illis, de quibus dicit Apostolus 2. ad Timoth. 4.: *A veritate auditum auertent, ad fabulas autem conuertentur* [2 Tim. 4:4]. *Narrauerunt mihi iniqui fabulationes*, (dicit Propheta) *sed non vt lex tua: supple, influxerunt in cor meum*. Psal. 118. [Ps. 118:85]. Caue ergo, ne aqua lutosa huiusmodi fabularum ad cor tuum per auditus tui vehiculum transfundatur; quin potius ad veritatem doctrinae caelestis auditus tui canale studeas applicare: vt cordis tui cellarium, vino laetificante cor

---

[1] *De doctrina*, pp. 1–4. Scriptural quotations are given in italics. Classical Latin spellings have usually been preferred; abbreviations are silently expanded.

hominis, impleatur. Secundo, *Loquimini: etc.* In hoc verbo admonetur praedicator, vt iuxta doctrinam Ecclesiastici 6. Verbi dulcedine amicos multiplicet, non exasperans auditores: sed instruens potius in spiritu lenitatis. Lenis enim consolator dicitur loqui ad cor; sicut dicit Ruth 2. ad Booz: *Consolatus es me, et locutus es ad cor ancillae tuae* [Ruth 2:13]. Vnde dicitur in vulgari: Iste locutus est ad cor meum. Non est ergo repellendum, sed amplectendum verbum doctrinae cordis, cum sit verbum solatij, quod saltem sufferre monet Apostolus ad Hebr. 13. dicens: *Rogo vos fratres, vt sufferatis verbum solatij* [Heb. 13:22]. Item, tertio: *Loquimini, etc.* In hoc verbo commonetur praedicator, vt iuxta doctrinam Ecclesiastici 4. Sapientiam in decore suo non abscondat: plus verborum compositioni, quam sententiae attendendo. Veritatis enim praedicatorem non decet huiusmodi verborum compositio per rhythmos consonantium. Vnde Seneca: Oratio, quae veritati dat operam, incomposita debet esse, et simplex. Et iuxta verbum Augustini: Bonorum ingeniorum insignis indoles est, in verbis verum amare verbum, non verba. Sunt enim quidam (vt dicit Gilbertus) qui in conuentu Fratrum student magis alta, quam apta proferre: erubescunt placida, et humilia, ne haec sola scire videantur: tales non loquuntur ad cor, sed ad aures tantum. Dicitur ergo: *Loquimini ad cor Ierusalem*; quasi non vt aures verborum ornatu mulceatis, sed potius aperta sententia cor pungatis. Vnde dicit Dominus Osee 2. de anima iusti: *Ducam eam in solitudinem, et loquar ad cor eius* [Hos. 2:14]. Attende quod non tenet colloquia sua cum corde tumultuoso, strepenti, et distracto varijs affectionibus. Ecclesiastici 32. *Vbi auditus non est, non effundas sermonem* [Eccles. 32:6]. Vt ergo ad cor tuum loquar, vt vino spiritualis intelligentiae ex racemis sacrorum verborum diligenti expositione expressum te potet, te inebriet; vt doctrina mea, imo potius Christi, te nutriat, et consoletur: vt non aures tantum tuas mulceat, sed potius cor tuum pungat: *audi filia, et vide, et inclina aurem tuam* [Ps. 44:11], attende doctrinam cordis tui propositam.

Table of chapter contents from the 1607 edition of

De doctrina cordis

Index eorum, quae summatim infra continentur.[1]

Liber Primus

---

[1] Classical Latin spellings have usually been preferred; abbreviations are silently expanded. Note that the section titles in the text are not always identical to the list of contents. If there is a significant difference, titles in the text are added in footnotes. Although not mentioned in the contents list the *Prologus* begins the text proper on pp. 1–4.

[2] The title on p. 7 reads: *Primum praeparatorium domus, est Mundare.*

[3] The title on p. 16 reads: *Secundum ad praeparationem domus requisitum, est Ornatus.*

[4] This section is on pp. 16–17.

[5] The title on p. 17 reads: *De vtensilibus domus cordis, et primo de Lectulo.*

[6] The title on p. 22 reads: *Taciturnitas pacis est Custodia.*

[7] The title on p. 26 reads: *Secundus ornatus domus est Sella, vel sedes.*

[8] The title on p. 34 reads: *De tertio ornatu domus, scilicet Mensa.*

[9] This is just one section.

---

[10] Actually this section is on pp. 56–62. There is an another section on pp. 62–5 not listed in the contents list: *De gradibus Sacramenti Altaris.*

[11] There is another section on pp. 74–5 not listed in the contents list: *Quod pellis extractio, coctio, et pinguedo fuerunt in Christo passo.*

[12] The title on p. 76 reads: *De Coctione, seu sustinentia correptionis.* Note that 'correctio' and 'correptio' are not the same word. The first means 'correction, improvement', the latter 'chastisement, reproof'.

[13] The title on p. 85 reads: *De Matrimonio spirituali, et primo quomodo repellitur a matrimonio Christi.*

[14] The following titles are added in the text: *Quid intelligitur per Repudiatam,* pp. 87–8; *Quid intelligitur per sordidam,* pp. 88–9; *Quid intelligitur per Meretricem,* pp. 89–93; *De Matrimonio spirituali cum Virgine,* pp. 93–5.

[15] The title on p. 95 reads: *Secundum signum virginitatis est Paupertas.*

[16] The following titles are added in the text: *Tertium signum virginitatis est simplicitas Vocis,* pp. 96–8; *De Nuptijs spiritualibus faciendis cum Christo,* pp. 98–104.

[17] The title on p. 113 reads: *De bonis spiritualis Matrimonij; et primo de fidelitate Cordis.*

[18] The title on p. 117 reads: *De Sacramento, quod est Perseuerantiae, siue inseparabilitatis.*

[19] This is just one section. On p. 121, it reads: *De Ornamentis animae, et primo de lotione animae per Baptismum, et Passionem.* The following titles are added in the text: *De Camisia Sponsae, quae ad fidem pertinet,* pp. 135–6; *De Ornamento Charitatis,* pp. 137–40.

[20] The title on p. 140 reads: *De ornamentis Spiritualium nuptiarum, videlicet, de ornamento Brachiorum.*

---

[21] The title on p. 142 reads: *De Torque temperatae locutionis.*

[22] The title on p. 145 reads: *De inaure Obedientiae, et de proprietatibus aurium Obedientiae, et Intelligentiae.*

[23] The title on p. 152 reads: *De ornamento aureo Obedientiae.*

[24] The title on p. 153 reads: *De Ornamento argenteo Diuini eloquij.*

[25] The title on p. 158 reads: *De custodia Cordis ad similitudinem castri obsessi.*

[26] The following titles are added in the text: *Secunda stultitia*, p. 166; *Tertia stultitia*, pp. 167–8; *Quarta stultitia*, pp. 168–9; *Quinta Stultitia*, pp. 169–70; *Sexta Stultitia*, pp. 170–1; *Septima Stultitia*, p. 171; *Octaua stultitia*, pp. 172–3; *Nona stultitia*, pp. 173–4; *Decima stultitia*, pp. 174–5.

[27] The title on p. 179 reads: *De sermone, siue locutione, et quae in illis inquirenda sunt. Quid loquendum.*

[28] Respectively, pp. 182–3, 183, 183–4, 184–5.

[29] The title on p. 192 reads: *Quid sit legendum in conscientia. Lectio prima. Lamentationes.*

[30] The following titles are: *Secunda Lectio. Carmen*, on p. 193; *Tertia Lectio. Vae*, on pp. 193–5.

[31] The title on p. 195 reads: *Sequitur de septem signaculis, quibus liber conscientiae firmatus est, siue de septem impedimentis, quae impediunt ne in libro conscientiae legatur.*

---

[32] The title on p. 203 reads: *Quomodo Cor sit aperiendum ad modum ostij.*

[33] The title on p. 208 reads: *De Apertione Cordis facienda proximo.*

[34] The title on p. 230 reads: *Quae stabiliunt et confirmant Cor.*

[35] The title on p. 234 reads: *De stabilitate, siue de constantia Cordis.*

[36] The title on p. 235 reads: *Quatuor quae faciunt ad instabilitatem.*

[37] The title on p. 239 reads: *De constantia in aduersis, contra instabilitatem.*

[38] The title on p. 261 reads: *Secundum eleuatorium cordis, quod est Spes.*

[39] The title on p. 263 reads: *De tertio cordis eleuatorio, quod est Desiderium.*

[40] The title on p. 267 reads: *De quarto eleuatorio Cordis, quod est Intentio recta.*

[41] The title on p. 276 reads: *Quomodo cor debet scindi.*

[42] The title on p. 279 reads: *Primum signum amoris ecstatici, est multa cogitare, et pauca loqui.* Although the contents list does not list the other sections in book 7, the text does: *Secundum signum amoris ecstatici, est Desiccatio membrorum*, pp. 281–2; *Tertium signum, concauitas oculorum*, pp. 283–6; *Quartum signum, siccitas oculorum*, pp. 286–90; *Quintum signum, Pulsus inordinatus*, p. 291; *Sextum signum amoris ecstatici, Solicitudo profunda*, pp. 292–3; *Septimum, et ultimum amoris signum*, pp. 293–4.

Glossary of Middle English Terms

This glossary has been compiled with the *Middle English Dictionary* and occasionally the *Oxford English Dictionary*. It is not a comprehensive glossary, but lists the unusual words or unfamiliar spellings. In many cases only a single occurrence of a given word is recorded below. The reference numbers in brackets indicate the page number followed by the line number.

The following abbreviations are used in the glossary:

abl.	ablative case	*n.*	noun
acc.	accusative case	*neg.*	negative
adj.	adjective	*neut.*	neuter
adv.	adverb	*nom.*	nominative case
adv. phras.	adverbial phrase	*pers.*	person
comp.	comparative	*poss. adj.*	possessive adjective
conj.	conjunction	*pl.*	plural
dat.	dative case	*p.ppl.*	past participle
def. art.	definite article	*pr.ppl.*	present participle
dem. adj.	demonstrative adjective	*prep.*	preposition
gen.	genitive case	*pres.*	present
imp.	imperative	*pron.*	pronoun
impers.	impersonal	*refl.*	reflexive
ind.	indicative	*rel. pron.*	relative pronoun
inf.	infinitive	*s.*	singular
int.	interjection	*subj.*	subjunctive
interr. adv.	interrogative adverb	*sup.*	superlative
interr. pron.	interrogative pronoun	*vb.*	verb
Lat.	Latin	*vbl. n.*	verbal noun
mod. aux.	modal auxiliary	*??*	word not found in M.E.D. or O.E.D.

213

ABITE, *n. s.*, (23:712) monastic habit, clothing, garment

ABLE, *adj.*, (87:90) worthy, excellent, gracious, seemly

ABOUGHT, *adv.*, (37:1231) so as to happen or to be

A-DAWE, *vb. inf.*, (90:203) awaken (from sleep), arouse

AFERDE, *vb. p.ppl.*, (48:38) frightened, terrified, apprehensive (about)

AGON, *vb. p.ppl.*, (48:52) ago, past

ALMEST, *adv.*, (48:59) mostly, very nearly, almost

AND, *conj.*, (80:18) if, when

ANGWISSE, *n. s.*, (24:741) anxiety, anguish, torment, suffering, agony

APAYED, *vb. p.ppl.*, (12:284) satisfied, content, pleased

APERITH, *vb. ind. pres. 3rd pers. s.*, (29:928) appears, is visible

APOCALIPS, *n. s.*, (64:201) The Apocalypse, the last book of the New Testament, Revelation

APORT, *n. s.*, (56:345) behaviour, deportment, bearing, appearance

APPORTES, *n. pl.*, (10:194) presents, gifts, behaviours, appearances

APPLIED, *vb. p.ppl.*, (87:103) devoted to, attached to, joined, submitted to, combined

APPREHENSIONS, *n. pl.*, (90:186) fears as to what may happen, dread, perceptions

ARAYMENT, *n. s.*, (27:872) preparation, action of decorating, clothing

ARAYTH, *vb. ind. pres. 3rd pers. s.*, (27:870) prepares, gets ready, dresses, adorns

AROMATIK, *n. s.*, (13:331) an aromatic substance, spices

ASAUGHT, *n. s.*, (52:203) armed attack, raid, temptation, affliction

ASAYST, *vb. ind. pres. 2nd pers. s.*, (18:512) test, try out, taste

ASONDRE, *adv.*, (70:85) into separate parts, in two, in pieces

ASTONED, *vb. p.ppl.*, (41:1393) bewildered, surprised, amazed, astonished

ATTENDAUNT, *adj.*, (35:1171) considerate, careful

AUDITOURE, *n. s.*, (8:115) an official who examines and verifies acounts, auditor, examiner

AUGHTER, AWGTER, *n. s.*, (20:571, 63:156) altar

AVAYLYN, *vb. ind. pres. 3rd pers. pl.*, (24:756) help, be profitable to, be of use

AVOKET, *n. s.*, (11:239) advocate, mediator, protector, champion

AVOUTRI, *n. s.*, (46:1574) adultery, idolatry

AXESSE, *n. s.*, (76:298) attack of fever, malady of lovers

AXING, *vb. pr.ppl.*, (6:67) requiring, asking for a favour

AXITH, *ind., pres. 3rd pers. s.*, (6:43) asks, begs, demands

AYSELLE, *n. s.*, (13:320) vinegar, bitter drink offered to Christ on the cross

BACHELERIS, *n. pl.*, (9:167) young men, squires, young knights

BALAUNCE, *n. s.*, (62:109) a set of scales

BARBOUR, *n. s.*, (79:69) barber, hairdresser

BARBOURIS, *n. gen. s.*, (79:68) of a barber, of a hairdresser

BAREYN, *adj.*, (27:842) sterile, fruitless, devoid, bare of

BEDE, *vb. p.ppl.*, (12:274) asked, invited

BELEFT, *vb. ind. past 3rd pers. s.*, (34:113) left, departed from, let remain

BELLE, *n. s.*, (89:162) bell

BENEFICES, *n. pl.*, (21:645) advantages, benefits, profits

BENIGNITE, *n. s.*, (69:51) kindness, mercy, meekness

BENYMME, *vb. inf.*, (49:92) take away, deprive, destroy, seize

BETYN, *vb. p.ppl.*, (9:175) beaten, flogged, whipped

BEWTE, *n. s.*, (8:121) beauty, goodness, courtesy

BIDDINGIS, *vbl. n. pl.*, (80:11) commandments

BIGH, BYGH, *n. s.*, (43:1469, 36:1213) torque, necklace

BIHEST, *n. s.*, (33:1086) promise, pledge

BIHING, BYHYNG, *vbl. n. s.*, (19:555, 19:547) buying, purchasing, acquiring

BILLES, *n. pl.*, (76:307) bills, beaks (of birds)

BISSE, *n. s.*, (36:1211) a precious kind of linen or cotton cloth, garment made of this fabric

BISYNESSIS, *n. pl.*, (3:26) diligence, efforts, tasks, exercises

BLEW, *adj.*, (6:55) blue, ash-coloured, livid

BLISSIDHODE, *n. s.*, (70:66) holiness, sacredness

BLOD, *n. s.* (26:809) blood

BODYN, *vb. p.ppl.*, (44:1525) bid, ordered, commanded

BOGHE, *n. s.*, (61:72) bow (as in Rev. 6:2)

BOLNESSE, *n. s.*, (29:941) courage, confidence, assurance

BON, *n. s.*, (27:841) bone

BORYN, *vb. p.ppl.*, (27:586) born

BOSOME, *n. s.*, (40:1363) lap (Latin: 'sinus', lap, hanging fold of the upper part of the toga, bosom of a garment)

    MAKE NO ~ (40:1356) translates Latin: 'sinum non facit', *De doctrina*, p. 132, i.e. make no breast pocket

BOUGH, *vb. inf.*, (74:232) bow, kneel, be obedient, submit to

    BOWITH, *ind. pres. 3rd pers. s.*, ~ AWAY FROM (17:485) gives up, ceases from (doing sth.), abandons, rejects

BOWELIS, *n. pl.*, (41:1404) entrails, womb, compassion, mercy

BOYLINGLY, *adv.*, (37:1221) boilingly

BOYSTOUS, BOUSTOUS, *adj.*, (53:257, 56:357) (of wind) powerful, fierce, turbulent; (of correction) crude, brutal, cruel; (of superiors) unmannerly, violent, strong, vicious

BOYSTOUSNES, *n. s.*, (31:996) rudeness, harshness, violence, coarseness

BRENNE, *vb. subj. pres. 3rd pers. s.*, (25:763) burn, roast, destroy with fire

    BRENNYD, *p.ppl.*, (25:771) burned, destroyed with fire

BRERIS, *n. pl.*, (10:209) brambles, briers

BRESTITH, *vb. ind. pres. 3rd pers. s.*, (44:1488) breaks, shatters

BRID, *n. s.*, (39:1304) bird, representation of a bird

BRIDELLE, BRIDEL, *n. s.*, (54:264, 54:265) bridle rein

BRIDILLES, *adj.*, (53:261) without a bridle

BRIST(E), *n. s.*, (37:1222, 40:1354) breast, heart

BROCHES, *n. pl.*, (36:1213) ornaments, pendants, bracelets, necklaces

BROME, *n. s.*, (7:74) broom

BYGH, BIGH, *n. s.*, (36:1213, 43:1469) torque, necklace

BYGH, *vb. inf.*, (77:17) buy, acquire sth. by effort, ransom, redeem

BYHYNG, BIHING, *vbl. n. s.*, (19:547, 19:555) buying, purchasing, acquiring

BYSIEN, *vb. ind. pres. 3rd pers. pl.*, (59:11) occupy, exert (oneself), be concerned with, undertake

CACCH, *vb. inf.*, (55:316) seize, take hold, entrap

CANDILLE, *n. s.*, (15:403) candle

CARNEL, *adj.*, (85:21) carnal, fleshly

CASTEL, CASTELLE, *n. s.*, (48:32, 47:17) fortified place, stronghold, refuge
  WARDIS OF ÞE ~ (48:35), guarded or secured sections of a castle

CATOUR, *n. s.*, (7:105) buyer of provisions, purveyor, caterer

CHALAUNGE, *n. s.*, (33:1069), FYNDE A ~ discover a blemish, find fault

CHAPELET, *n. s.*, (45:1536) wreath of flowers, leaves or branches to be worn on the head, garland, coronet, circlet

CHAPITRE, *n. s.*, (14:353) (Eccl.) an assembly of dignitaries of a religious order acting as an administrative or legislative body, an assembly of all members of a religious house
  ~ OF ÞE CROSSE (38:1287) column, pillar of the Cross

CHARGOUS, *adj.*, (51:167) heavy, burdensome, oppressive

CHAYER, *n. s.*, (32:1054) chair, throne, position of authority

CHERE, *vb. inf.*, (12:264) cheer up, comfort, encourage, entertain (sb.) with food and drink

CHERE, *n. s.*, (72:158) face, (facial) expression, attitude, display (of emotion), behaviour

CHYVETEYN, *n. s.*, (51:168) head of an armed force, commander in chief, leader

CLATERID, *vb. ind. past 3rd pers. pl.*, (70:85) broke or fell with a loud noise, were shattered, crashed

CLEPID, *vb. p.ppl.*, (3:20) called, summoned

CLIPPE, *vb. inf.*, (65:258) embrace, surround

CLOÞE, *n. s.*, (17:478) a (piece of) woven or felted fabric, cloth

CLOUSE, *n. s.*, (43:1478) milldam, floodgate or sluice

CLOYSTOR, *n. s.*, (17:460) cloister, monastery, convent

CLOYSTRERIS, *n. gen. s.*, (13:313) of a monk, of a friar, of a nun

CNOWLECHE, KNOWLECHE, *n. s.*, (7:78, 7:77) knowledge, understanding, intelligence

COMFORTABLE, *adj.*, (46:1586) (word) comforting, consoling

COMMUNE, *vb. inf.*, (46:1596) communicate, tell, meditate, disseminate (knowledge), discuss

    COMMUNYNG, *vbl. n. s.*, ~ OF SEYNTES (73:178), fellowship or community of all Christians

COMMUNE, *adj.* (19:560) common, public

    ~ GOODES (19:553) goods owned or used jointly, shared

    ~ WOMMAN (28:286–7) a promiscuous woman, prostitute

COMPASSIBLE, *adj.*, (49:106) ?? who suffers with, who feels with, full of compassion for

CONFORME, *vb. inf.*, (39:1296) comply with, dispose (sb.), adopt (oneself) to, consent

CONJUNCCIOUN, *n. s.*, (69:35) combining, uniting, union

CONTAGIOUS, *adj.*, (25:795) harmful, dangerous, wicked, evil

CORRUP, *vb. p.ppl.*, (71:119) corrupted, impure, contaminated

COSAINYS, *n. pl.*, (50:123) blood relations, relatives marriage, nephews/nieces, first cousins

COSTOME, *n. s.*, (8:140) customary practice, tradition, custom, habit

COTE, KOTE, *n. s.*, (41:1404, 41:1412) tunic, kind of surcoat

CRYING, *vbl. n. s.*, (56:347) shouting, crying, lamentation

CUTTE, *vb. inf.*, (4:54) cut, open

DAWNGER, *n. s.*, (10:199) power, control, danger, harm

DEDE, *vb. ind. past. 3rd pers. s.*, (6:66) did

DEFAYLE, *vb. inf.*, (69:39) grow feeble, deteriorate, die

DEFOULID, *vb. p.ppl.*, (28:886) dirty, soiled, morally polluted, defiled, having had sex outside marriage, raped

DEME, *vb. imp.*, (14:347) judge, censure, condemn

DEMYNGIS, *vbl. n. pl.*, (15:384) judgments, opinions, speculations

DENYGH(E), *vb. inf.*, (29:939) deny, refuse, renounce; *imp.*, (73:189) deny, refuse

DEPARTID, *vb. p.ppl.*, ~ WOMMAN (28:886), a divorced or separated woman

    DEPARTIT, *p.ppl.*, (26:836) removed (from), separated (from)

DEPENDAUNT, *adj.*, (43:1470) hanging down, suspended

DEPRESSID, *vb. p.ppl.*, (80:24) overcome, oppressed, dragged down

DERLINGES, *n. pl.*, (71:99) beloved of Christ, saints, devout Christians

DESESE, *n. s.*, (35:1149) tribulation, misery, misfortune, trouble, anxiety, pain, disease, illness

    DESESIS, *n. pl.*, (29:920) tribulations, miseries, injuries, anxieties, pains, sicknesses

DETHE, *n. s.*, (6:51) death

DETTOURE, *n. s.*, (77:27) one who owes money to another, debtor

DEVOUGHTLY, *adv.*, (8:131) devoutly, reverently

DEYNTOUSLY, *adv.*, (88:134) richly, sumptuously, elegantly

DIDE, *vb. ind. past 3rd pers. s.*, (70:76) died

DIEW, *adj.*, (7:82) conscientious, careful, correct, genuine

DIFFINYCIOUN, *n. s.*, (15:380) specific statement, declaration, judgment, decision

DIFFYNYTIF, *adj.*, (64:220) decisive, conclusive, final

DIGH, DYE, DYGH, *vb. inf.*, (27:858, 26:830, 69:39) die

   DIDE, DIGHED, *ind. past 3rd pers. s.*, (70:76, 64:215) died

   DYGHEN, *ind. pres. 3rd pers. pl.* (27:856), die

DISCEVERED, *vb. p.ppl.*, (85:9) separated from, free from, removed from

DISPERBLITH, *vb. ind. pres. 3rd pers. s.*, (50:110) scatters, disperses

   DISPERBLID, *vb. p.ppl.*, (48:63) scattered, dispersed

DISPITOUS, *adj.*, (50:119) cruel, ruthless, fierce, scornful

DISPROFIGHT, *vb. inf.*, (53:244) bring disadvantage to, injure, inconvenience

DISTEMPERAUNCES, *n. pl.*, (76:298) imbalances of humours, bodily disorders, ailments

DISTEMPERED, *vb. p.ppl.*, (76:293) indisposed or ill, upset, (physiol.) the proper balance of humours being upset

DOBLENES, *n. s.*, (31:993) duplicity, deceitfulness, treachery

DOME, *n. s.*, (9:154) judgement, punishment, order

DOUTER, DOWTER, *n. s.*, (83:131; 13:319) daughter

DOWTY, *adj.*, (14:377) ambiguous, enigmatic, obscure

DRAUGHT, *n. s.*, (18:519) drink of wine, quantity of liquid that one drinks at one time

DREPE, *vb. inf.*, (24:738) drip, fall in drops

DRINESSE, *n. s.*, (87:102) dryness, spiritual emptiness, dullness

DYE, DIGH, DYGH, *vb. inf.*, (26:830, 27:858, 69:39) die

   DIDE, DIGHED, *ind. past 3rd pers. s.*, (70:76, 64:215) died

   DYGHEN, *ind. pres. 3rd pers. pl.*, (27:856) die

DYGH, *vb. inf.*, (37:1248) dye, colour

DYGHENG, *vbl. n. s.*, (27:854) dying, death

EERE, *n. s.*, (44:1509) ear

   EERIS, EERYN, EERYS, ERYS, HERIS, *n. pl.*, (44:1517, 44:1513, 44:1507, 44:1506, 44:1510) ears

EETE, *vb. subj. pres. 2nd pers. s.*, (18:511) eat, swallow

EFTE-SONES, *adv.*, (9:148) again, back, later

ELACIOUN, *n. s.*, (7:86) arrogance, vainglory

ELDNES, *n. s.*, (83:139) old age, decrepitude

ENCOMBRED, *vb. p.ppl.*, (51:164) hindered, burdened, overpowered, overcome

ENCRESSE, *vb. inf.*, (20:594) augment, increase, intensify, enhance

ENDUCYN, *vb. ind. pres. 3rd pers. pl.*, (55:304) cause, lead to, prompt, persuade

ENFAMYNED, ENFAMYNID, *vb. p.ppl.*, (49:68, 48:55) deprived of food and drink, starved

ENFLAWMYTH, *vb. ind. pres. 3rd pers. s.*, (42:1433) sets on fire, kindles, incites, inspires with love or charity

ENFORME, *vb. inf.*, (3:10) educate, guide, instruct, teach

ENFORMYNG, *vbl. n. s.*, (54:272) training, instructing, guiding, teaching

ENSPIRED, *vb. ind. past 3rd pers. s.*, (70:65) breathed (life in a human body), endowed imbued, inspired (knowledge)

ENTRE, *n. s.*, (79:92) entrance, admission, beginning

EPISTOLIS, *n. pl.*, (9:174) letters, the apostolic letters in the New Testament

EQUYPOLLENT, *adj.*, (18:518) equal in power or degree, adequate, sufficient

EREYNE, *n. s.*, (15:391) spider

ERÞAN, *conj.*, (7:107) before, earlier than the time when

ERTHEQUAVE, ERTHEQWAVE, *n. s.* (63:174, 63:171), earth tremor, earthquake

ESCHEW, *vb. inf.*, (76:282) avoid, flee from, escape

ESE, *n. s.*, (16:416) physical comfort, peace of mind

ESY, *adj.*, (10:218) kind, gentle, peaceable, pleasant, suitable; (of correction) lenient, restrained

EVENHEDE, *n. s.*, (67:319) impartiality, equality of rank, unanimity, fairness, temperance

EXPERIENTALE, *adj.*, ~ SWETNES (86:39–40) ?? sweetness gained through experience (Latin: 'suavitas experienda', *De doctrina*, p. 277)

EXPOUNNYNG, *vbl. n. s.*, (87:98) interpretation, glossing, expounding

EYGH, *n. s.*, (8:143) eye

EYRE, *n. s.*, (17:460) air

EYTE, *adj.*, (42:1447) eighth

FANTASTIKLY, *adv.*, (71:114) not really, imaginedly

FARITH, *vb. ind. pres. 3rd pers. s.*, IT ~ (9:172), it goes, it happens, it turns out (in a certain way)

FARYN, *ind. pres. 3rd pers. pl.*, (62:115) treat, act toward, behave, deal with

FATIGACIOUNS, *n. pl.*, (87:92) fatigue, wearying, exertions

FAYNYNG, *vb. pr.ppl.*, (35:1168) false, deceiving, hypocritical

FEBLY, *adv.*, (4:35) ineffectively, poorly, badly

FEST, *n. s.*, (35:1149) feast, banquet, enjoyable occasion or event

FESTYNE, *vb. inf.*, (82:71) establish securely, be established, comfort (heart), set (one's heart or thoughts on sth.) (Latin: 'innitatur', *De doctrina*, p. 262)

FESTYVAL, *adj.*, HOLY ~ DAYES (38:1280–1), religious holidays

FILLE, *vb. ind. past 3rd pers. s.*, (82:100) fell

FYLLE, *ind. past 3rd pers. pl.*, (63:173) fell

FLEE, *vb. inf.*, (22:669) flay, skin, remove hide from (an animal)

FLEXE, *n. s.*, (42:1427) flax

FLEYNG, *vbl. n. s.*, (24:751) flaying

FLITTYNG, *vb. pr.ppl.*, (81:50) changeable, transitory, drifting

FLORE, *n. s.*, (8:122) floor, ground

FLYTE, *n. s.*, (33:1081) flight (i.e. fleeing); escape, flight (i.e. flying)

FOLIOUS, FOLYOS, *adj.*, (14:367, 29:939) foolish, sinful

FONDE, *vb. ind. past 3rd pers. s.*, (54:278) discovered, experienced, found out, learned

FORBROKYN, *vb. p.ppl.*, (75:256) broken in pieces, shattered, humbled, made penitent

FORSPRENCLID, *vb. p.ppl.*, ~ WITH BLOOD (6:54–5), spattered with blood

FREELTE, *n. s.*, (15:384) physical weakness, instability of mind, sinfulness

FRUGHTFUL, *adj.*, (32:1052) fruitful, beneficial, good, edifying

FULFILLING, *vbl. n. s.*, (83:139) satisfaction, satiety, repletion

FUSTIAN, *n. s.*, (40:1344) a kind of cloth (cotton, flax, wool)

FYLLE, *vb. ind. past 3rd pers. pl.*, (63:173) fell

FYNTE, *vb. ind. pres. 3rd pers. s.*, (11:238) finds, encounters, discovers

GALLE, *n. s.*, (25:797) gall, sore on the skin

GELDYN, *adj.*, (44:1508) made of gold, precious, glorious

GEST, *n. s.*, (12:273) guest

GIRDE, *vb. inf.*, (40:1356) put a belt about (sb.'s waist), cover, wrap, prepare oneself for, restrain (body from sin)

GIRDERIS, *n. pl.*, (40:1356) ?? belts, girdles

GIRDILLE, *n. s.*, (36:1211) girdle, belt

GODWARD, *adv.*, (33:1081) to God, toward God

GOOSTLY, *adj.*, (3:8) spiritual, devout, pious

GRATE, *n. s.*, (76:308) a grate of iron bars, grating (in a door or window)

GRENE, *adj.*, (8:118) green, freshly cut

GREVED, *vb. p.ppl.*, (7:101) injured, harmed

GROTCHYNG, *vb. pr.ppl.*, (25:791) grumbling against, murmuring against

  GRUCCHID, GRUTCHID, *ind. past 3rd pers. s.*, (11:249, 11:243) grumbled, murmured, disputed, disagreed, opposed

GROYNE, *vb. ind. pres. 3rd pers. pl.*, (26:807) murmur, grumble

GYLE, *n. s.*, (62:112) treachery, dishonesty

GYLTY, *adj.*, (72:163) guilty, culpable, blameworthy

ȜYVE, YIVE, *vb. inf.*, (4:49, 5:15) give

  YIF, *ind. pres. 3rd pers. pl.*, (68:13) give

  YIVYTH, *ind. pres. 3rd pers. s.*, (3:11) gives

HALOWYD, *vb. p.ppl.*, (73:176) sanctified, hallowed, consecrated (ritually)

HAMME, *vb. ind. pres. 1st pers. s.*, (39:1299) am

HANE, *vb. ind. pres. 3rd pers. pl.*, (16:444) have

HARBOURID, HERBOURID, *vb. p.ppl.*, BE ~ (16:428, 15:411), to be lodged, stay

HARNEYCE, *n. s.*, (51:163) personal fighting equipment, body armour, suit of mail

HAUKE, *n. s.*, (33:1078) hawk

HEETES, *n. pl.*, (76:298) heats, fevers

HEGGE, *n. s.*, (10:212) hedge, barricade

HEGGID, *vb. p.ppl.*, Y- ~ (10:210), fenced off, surrounded with a hedge

HEITH, *n. s.*, (16:420) uncultivated land, wasteland, heath

HENGE, HYNGE, *vb. ind. past. 3rd pers. s.*, (54:278, 54:279) hung, put to death by hanging on gallows

HENNES, *n. pl.*, (24:730) hens

HENNYS, *adv.*, (76:281) hence, from here

HERBERGOURE, *n. s.*, (16:429) officer of a nobleman who assigns lodging to guests, host

HERBOURID, HARBOURID, *vb. p.ppl.*, BE ~ (15:411, 16:428), to be lodged, stay

HERD, *vb. p.ppl.*, (3:31) heard, listened to (the reading of a book)

HERE, *adj. poss. 3rd pers. pl.*, (6:42) their

HERYS, EERIS, EERYN, EERYS, ERYS, *n. pl.*, (44:1510, 44:1517, 44:1513, 44:1507, 44:1506) ears

HERIS, *pron. 3rd pers. s. f. gen.*, (33:1067) hers

HERY, *adj.*, (63:172) covered with hair, rough

HEVISSOM, *adj.*, (17:460) burdensome, oppressive, discomforting

HEYRE, *n. s.*, (39:1325) stiff cloth made of haircloth, garment made of haircloth worn as a sign of asceticism or penance

HIS, *vb. ind. pres. 3rd pers. s.*, (90:179) is

HO, *interr. pron.*, (3:14) who?

HOLIS, *n. pl.*, (25:773) holes

HOLP, *vb. p.ppl.*, (50:124) helped, given spiritual aid, saved

HOMLY, *adj.*, (12:283) familiar, intimate, close, meek, simple, unassuming

HOOL, *adv.*, AL ~ (86:64), completely

HOOPITH, *vb. ind. pres. 3rd pers. s.*, (90:190) hopes, trusts, wishes

HOSOEVER, *pron. nom. s.*, (65:241) whoever, the one(s) who, whosoever

HOUSSOLD, *n. s.*, (21:620) members of a family collectively (including servants), retainers, court

HUCCH(E), *n. s.*, (83:125, 78:36) money chest, coffer

HUMORYS, *n. pl.*, (88:106) humours, one of the four fluids (blood, phlegm, choler, melancholy) which formed and nourish the body, liquids, bodily fluids

HYDEN, *vb. ind. pres. 3rd pers. pl.*, (7:87) hide, conceal, cover up

HYNGE, HENGE, *vb. ind. past. 3rd pers. s.*, (54:279, 54:278) hung, put to death by hanging on gallows

IMPUGNYNG, *vb. pr.ppl.*, (49:84) assailing, making war on, spiritually tempting

INHONEST, *adj.*, (55:305) disgraceful, obscene, improper, indecent, vile

INLY, *adj.*, (89:149) heartfelt, intense, strong, interior, spiritual

INOW, *adj.*, (26:808) (of cooking) done, cooked

JACINCTE, *n. s.*, (36:1211) a precious stone of blue (rarely red) colour

JESSIS, *n. pl.*, (33:1078) short straps fastened to the legs of a hawk (one for each leg) both attached to a leash; spiritual fetters or restraints

JUELLE, *n. s.*, (19:556) valuable object, treasure, jewel

JUES, JUIS, *n. pl.*, (25:770, 70:77) the Jews

JUSE, *n. s.*, (15:388) juice, nectar, sap

KAY, *n. s.*, (11:236) key

KEDES, KYDES, *n. pl.*, (22:667, 22:658) the young of a goat, kids

KENDLY, *adv.*, (83:116) naturally, properly, rightly

KEPYN, *vb. ind. pres. 3rd pers. pl.*, (37:1258) keep, retain, preserve

KNELIST, *vb. ind. pres. 2nd pers. s.*, (20:577) kneel (down)

KNOWLECHE, CNOWLECHE, *n. s.*, (7:77, 7:78) knowledge, understanding, intelligence

KNYTTES, *n. pl.*, (70:77) soldiers of biblical times, knights

KNYTTITH, *vb. ind. pres. 3rd pers. s.*, (30:969) fastens by a knot, binds, joins, unites

    KNET, KNETTE, KNYT, *p.ppl.*, (31:1011, 31:1003, 35:1175) fastened by a knot, bound, joined, united

KNYTTYNG, *vbl. n. s.*, (69:35) joining together, union, connection

KOKES, KOKIS, *n. pl.*, (25:779, 25:771) cooks

KOTE, COTE, *n. s.*, (41:1412, 41:1404) tunic, kind of surcoat

KUNNYNG, *vbl. n. s.*, (3:4) knowledge, understanding, wisdom, prudence

KYCHYN, *n. s.*, (23:720) kitchen

KYDES, KEDES, *n. pl.*, (22:658, 22:667) the young of a goat, kids

KYNDE, *n. s.*, (6:57) essence, nature, shape

LABOURE, *n. s.*, (6:44), work, toil, hardship, pain

LAD, *vb. p.ppl.*, (68:7) moved, tempted, misled, controlled

LAGH, *n. s.*, (65:231) set of rules prescribing conduct, law, faith, tenet of belief, justice

LAKKYNG, *vbl. n. s.*, (89:142) lack, absence, scarcity

LARDIR, *n. s.*, (24:728) ?? body fat next to the skin, animal fat (Latin: 'lardari', *De doctrina*, p. 69)

LARGE, *adj.*, (91:247) generous, open-handed

LARGELY, *adv.*, (62:122) fully, in great abundance, without prudence

LAUGHFULLY, *adv.*, (36:1185) lawfully

LAVENDIR, *n. s.*, (37:1242) washerwoman, washer, launderer

LAWNCETE, *n. s.*, (7:96) surgical instrument used for letting blood, lancet

LEESE, *vb. inf.*, (37:1254) lose

    LESE, *subj. pres. 3rd pers. pl.*, (89:153) lose

    LESYN, *ind. pres. 3rd pers. pl.*, (17:461) lose

LEETE, *n. s.*, BLOOD ~ (7:102–3), blood letting

LEFTE, *vb. inf.*, ~ UP (4:51) lift up, elevate, raise

LEGE, *adj.*, (48:60) (of a feudal superior) entitled to feudal allegiance and service

LENE, *adj.*, (24:728) lean, skinny, thin, emaciated

LESE, *vb. subj. pres. 3rd pers. pl.*, (89:153) lose

LESSITH, *vb. ind. pres. 3rd pers. s.*, (13:330) diminishes, reduces, weakens

> LESSYNNYD, *p.ppl.*, (48:63) reduced, diminished

LESYN, *vb. ind. pres. 3rd pers. pl.*, (17:461) lose

LETTYN, *vb. ind. 3rd pers. s.*, (63:166) hinder, impede, prevent, stop, thwart

LETTYNGIS, *vbl. n. pl.*, (60:43) impediments, obstacles, troubles

LETUSE, *n. s.*, (20:581) cultivated lettuce, a similar plant

LEVE, *vb. imp.*, (8:126) believe, trust, realize, be sure (that sth. is the case)

LEVED, *vb. ind. pres. 3rd pers. s.*, (81:60) is left over, stays, remains

LEWYD, *adj.*, (19:558) worthless, wicked, evil

LIGH, *vb. inf.*, (71:124) lie

> LIGTH, *ind. pres. 3rd pers. s.*, ~ IN (67:325), consists in (sth.), belongs to, lies in

LIGH, LYGH, *n. s.*, (37:1242, 37:1226) an alkaline solution made by leaching ashes, and used for washing; spiritual cleanser

LITELLE, *adv.*, (51:161) little, not much, seldom

LOKKID, *vb. p.ppl.*, ~ UP (11:236), locked up

LOTHNES, *n. s.*, (83:139) disgust, loathing

LOVES, *n. pl.*, (81:58) loaves, bread

LOWNES, LOWNESSE, *n. s.*, (79:65, 78:62) humility, meekness, obedience

LOWYD, *vb. p.ppl.*, (78:60) humbled, bowed down

LYGH, LIGH, *n. s.*, (37:1226, 37:1242) an alkaline solution made by leaching ashes, and used for washing; spiritual cleanser

LYGHING, *vbl. n. s.*, (39:1314) the action of kneeling, of being prostrate (in supplication or prayer)

LYMBO, LYMBUS, *n. s.*, (71:99, 71:100) limbo, i.e. that part of hell which bordered the pit of the eternally damned and which was the dwelling place of those who were delivered by Christ, the 'limbus patrum'.

LYMES, *n. pl.*, (51:159) limbs, agents of the devil, heathens, sinners

LYNDES, *n. pl.*, (40:1351) loins, seat of emotion, of love, of lust

LYVERIS, *n. pl.*, VERTUOS ~ (10:217), those who live righteously

LYVYN, *vb. ind. pres. 3rd pers. pl.*, (48:32) live

> LYVIST, *ind. pres. 2nd pers. s.*, (82:72) live, endure, live through

MACE, *n. s.*, (17:471) a ceremonial mace, rod of office

MAITE, *n. s.*, (82:102) might, power, knowledge, (spiritual) ability, authority, strength, virtue

MANERLY, *adj.*, (56:347) well-mannered, seemly, modest

MARCHAUNT, *n. s.*, (77:15) wholesale businessman

MARGERY, *n. s.*, ~ PERLIS (44:1509) pearls

MARTELOGE, *n. s.*, (51:183) register of martyred saints, a book containing a martyrology.

MAYNTENE, *vb. ind. pres. 3rd pers. pl.*, (23:709) keep, support, sustain, defend, persist in

MEDE, *n. s.*, (13:330) gift, salary, reward, profit, wealth

MEDICINABLE, *adj.*, (13:323) medicinal, healing, therapeutic, uplifting, spiritually edifying

MEENE, *n. s.*, (3:30) method, way

MELODOUSLY, *adv.*, (35:1156) melodiously

MENE, *vb. inf.*, (3:13) mean, signify

MENE, *n. s.*, BE ~ OF (82:75) by means of

MENNYS, *n. gen. pl.*, (14:365) of men

MENYNG, *vbl. n. s.*, (56:349) meaning

MENYS, *n. s.*, (29:918) threat, threatening by word, action or attitude

MERACLES, *n. pl.*, (74:204) miracles

MERCIABLY, *adv.*, (15:394) forgivingly, compassionately, kindly

MERITORIE, *adj.*, (55:311) deserving of spiritual merit or reward, beneficial, profitable, praiseworthy

MESSIS, *n. pl.*, (40:1341) masses, religious services

METE, *n. s.*, (6:38) food, nourishment, meal

METE-TABLE, *n. s.*, (8:147) dining table, sideboard

MEVID, *vb. p.ppl.*, ~ OF (90:204), talked of, spoken about, discussed

MONY, *n. s.*, (19:558) money, bribe

MOSSEL, *n. s.*, (13:319) mouthful, food, small meal

   MOSSELLIS, *pl.*, (29:918) small meals, dishes, morsels

MYDDIS, *n. s.*, IN THE ~ (10:204), in the middle of

MYLLE, *n. s.*, (43:1477) mill

MYNCHE, *n. s.*, (4:4) nun

MYNISTRACIOUN, *n. s.*, (16:447) (rendering of personal service), aid, duties, ministry

MYNUCIOUN, *n. s.*, (7:103) bloodletting

MYSCHEVOUS, *adj.*, (61:94) wretched, miserable, wicked, sinful, harmful

MYSCHIF, *n. s.*, (49:69) hardship, distress or duress of battle, neediness, hunger

MYSDEMYNG, *vbl. n. s.*, (14:365) false judgment, misconception, suspicion

NAPRY, *n. s.*, (37:1231) linen, sheet, napkins, tableclothes

NAREW, *adj.*, (52:200) narrow, small

NEDFUL, *adj.*, (26:837) unavoidable, necessary, needed

NETTE, *n. s.*, (39:1305) net, snare, trap

NORSHID, *vb. p.ppl.*, (24:722) nourished, fed

NORSHYN, *ind. pres. 3rd pers. pl.*, (24:725) nourish, support, maintain

NOT, *neg. vb. ind. pres. 1st pers. pl.*, (42:1418) do not know

NYST, *neg. ind. past 3rd pers. s.*, (91:234) did not know

WITE, *inf.*, (9:161) know, experience, learn, find out, be aware

WISTIST, *ind. past. 2nd pers. s.*, (17:487) knew

WOTE, *ind. pres. 1st pers. s.*, (22:660) know

NOVISHODE, *n. s.*, (32:1034) state or condition of being a novice

NOYGHES, NOYOUS, *adj.*, (37:1238, 55:304) harmful, wicked, dangerous, troublesome, distressing, painful

NOYOUS, *n. s.*, (55:303) unpleasant sound, quarrel, troublemaking, scandal, accusation

NYST, *neg. vb. ind. past 3rd pers. s.*, (91:234) did not know

OBEID, *vb. ind. past 3rd pers. s.* (20:589) obeyed, was obedient to

OFTE, *adj.*, (42:1432) frequent

OMELIE, *n. s.*, (4:34) homily, sermon

ON, *impers. pron.*, (16:420) one (person or thing)

ONED, ONHED, *n. s.*, (35:1167, 73:179) unity, accord, agreement

ONYS, *adv.*, (28:909) once

ONYTH, *vb. ind. pres. 3rd pers. s.*, (30:969) unites, joins, brings together

OPYN, *vb. subj. pres. 3rd pers. s.*, (65:230) open, unclose

ORDENAUNCE, *n. s.*, (14:342) authority, custom, practice, appointed place

OSTINACIE, *n. s.*, (20:610) obstinacy, hardness of heart, disobedience to authority

OUGHT OF, *prep.*, (8:128) out of, from within, from

OURE, *n. s.*, (42:1419) hour, time, fixed or appointed time

OUÞER, *conj.*, (48:63) either

OYNEMENT, *n. s.*, (11.250) ointment, cosmetic unguent, perfume

PALPABLE, *adj.*, (71:109) capable of being touched, tangible, visible

PANNE, *n. s.*, (25:775) caldron, pot, pan

PARTY, *n. s.*, FOR ÞE MORE ⁓ (37:1257–8), for the most part, mostly, in general

PASSIBILITE, *n. s.*, (83:141) capacity for suffering, possibility

PASSYN, *vb. ind. pres. 3rd pers. pl.*, ⁓ AWAY FROM (68:12) leave (a subject)

PAYINE, *n. s.*, (54:288) pain, torment

PERFIGHTLY, *adv.*, (5:28) flawlessly, exactly, fully

PERLIOUS, *adj.*, (15:408) dangerous, terrible, wicked, sinful

PERSHETH, *vb. ind. pres 3rd pers. s.*, (18:495) perishes, suffers spiritual death

PERSID, *vb. p.ppl.*, (41:1411) pierced, wounded

PE(S)SABLE, *adj.*, (9:172) peace-making, well-considered, measured

PEUPLE, PUPILLE, PUPLE, *n. s.*, (3:3, 42:1439, 39:1316) *n. s.*, men and women, everyone, people, nation, tribe

PEYNTYNG, *vbl. n. s.*, (31:993) representation in painting, feigning, deceiving, disguise, fabricating

PLATER, *n. s.*, (12:284) platter, plate, dish

PLAYNE, *vb. imp.*, (33:1090) complain, lament, bewail

  PLAYNID, *ind. past 3rd pers. s.*, (11:247) complained, lamented, bewailed

  PLEYNYTH, *ind. pres. 3rd pers. s.*, (10:202) complains, laments, bewails

PLYAUNT, *adj.*, (91:220) supple, flexible, compliant

PONDEROUS, *adj.*, (29:945) heavy, weighty; (86:51) (of body) viscous, of a putrid discharge

PORCHE, *n. s.*, (35:1145) entrance (hall), gate, porch

PORTOUR(E), *n. s.*, (52:221, 52:223) gatekeeper, doorkeeper

POTESTATE, *n. s.*, (57:381) ruler, lord, superior

POURE, *adj.*, (24:757) poor, destitute, needy, wretched

POUS, *n. s.*, (90:184) pulse

PRECIOSITE, *n. s.*, (45:1554) preciousness, value, great worth

PRESEDENTIS, *n. pl.*, (52:187) rulers, heads, persons who preside over the chapter of a religious house

PRESONE, *n. s.*, (47:16) prison, dungeon

PRESUMPTUES, PRESUMPTUOSE, *adj.*, (78:54, 78:57) arrogant, impertinent

PREVYS, *n. pl.*, (74:233) (pieces of) evidence, demonstrations of the truth of a belief, explanations

PREYSING, *vbl. n. s.* (80:29) worship, veneration, act of uttering praise to God

PROFIGHT, *n. s.*, (15:405) benefit, advantage, interest

PROFRES, *n. pl.*, (18:508) challenges, offers, gifts

PROMYTTITH, *vb. ind. pres. 3rd pers. s.*, (47:25) promises

PROPRETARIES, *n. pl.*, (22:677) religious who hold goods as private property in violation of the vow of poverty, property owners

PRYVE, *adj.*, (39:1321) secret, concealed, private

PUNCHITH, *vb. ind. pres. 3rd pers. s.*, (77:26) punishes, inflicts suffering on (sb.)

  PUNSHE, *imp.*, (14:347) punish

  PUNSHID, *p.ppl.*, (14:359) punished

  PUNSHING, *pr.ppl.*, (13:300) punishing, inflicting, suffering

PUPILLE, PEUPLE, PUPLE, *n. s.*, (42:1439, 3:3, 39:1316) men and women, everyone, people, nation, tribe

PUPLICANES, *n. pl.*, (34:1125) publicans of Christ's parable in Luke 18:10–14.

PURSUET, *n. s.*, (78:40) pursuit, persistence, attack, assault

QUENYS, *n. pl.*, (45:1549) queens

QUERE, *n. s.*, (48:48) choir, body of religious responsible for a particular religious institution, chapter

  ~ OF ANGELIS (34:1133), the angelic host

QUYK, *adj.*, (17:482) living, alive, vigorous, active

QUYTE, *adj.*, GO HEMSELF ~ (62:117), excuse themselves from paying

RAD, *vb. p.ppl.*, (3:31) read

   REDE, *inf.*, (3:26) read

RAVENOURES, *n. pl.*, (75:271) thieves, robbers, plunderers

RAVISCHED, *vb. p.ppl.*, (16:453) seized and carried off, raped

RAWGH, *adj.*, (24:726) uncooked, unripe, raw

RAWNSUM(M)YNG, *vbl. n.*, (42:1431, 19:563) (theol.) (price of) redemption

RAYNED, *vb. p.ppl.*, (54:263) controlled with a rein

REAWME, *n. s.*, (9:171) realm, kingdom

REBEWKYNG, *vb. pr.ppl.*, (61:84) reprimanding, chiding, reproaching

RECHELES, *adj.*, (3:15) negligent, indifferent, heedless

REDE, *vb. inf.*, (3:26) read

   RAD, *p.ppl.*, (3:31) read

REGNE, *vb. inf.*, (64:208) rule, govern, prevail, dwell, live, continue, persist

REHETE, *vb. ind. pres. 3rd pers. pl.*, (12:265) cheer up, entertain, provide good cheer for, nourish

REKENYNG, *vbl. n. s.*, (7:104) account

REKENYTH, *vb. ind. pres. 3rd pers. s.*, (7:106) enumerates, recounts

RELEF, *n. s.*, (81:32) what is left over, remnants

   RELEVES, *pl.*, (81:55) remnants, remains, leftovers

REMOVERIS, *n. pl.*, (76:301) those who change their place, restless or stirring people

RENNE., *vb. imp.*, (44:1496) run, go, flee, hasten, have recourse to (Jesus)

RENNERIS, *n. pl.*, ~ ABOUTE (76:301), those who move restlessly about, gadabouts

REPE, *vb. p.ppl.*, (13:333) harvested, reaped, received as a reward

   REPIST, *ind. pres. 2nd pers. s.*, (13:336) harvest, reap, receive as a reward

REPLETE, *adj.*, (7:103) filled with, imbued with

REPROVEABLE, *adj.*, (87:71) blameworthy, reprehensible, wicked, sinful

RESKEWE, *vb. inf.*, (49:77) rescue, deliver from a siege

RESKWYNG, *vbl. n. s.*, (48:56) rescue, deliverance from a siege

REVOLVYNG, *vb. pr.ppl.*, (42:1430) turning (sth.) over in one's mind, reflecting upon, considering

REVOUR, *n. s.*, (77:23) robber, plunderer

REVYTH, *vb. ind. pres. 3rd pers. s.*, (77:25) robs, despoils

REWDE, *adj.*, (79:79) uncouth, ignorant, harsh

REWLID, *vb. p.ppl.*, (48:46) governed, controlled, ruled

REWLY, *adj.*, (62:142) expressive of sorrow or suffering, doleful, piteous, wretched

REYNID, *vb. ind. past. 3rd pers. s.*, (20:584) sent down, rained

REYSID, *vb. p.ppl.*, ~ UP (9:165) lifted up, elevated

RIGEROUSTE, *n. s.*, (57:407) rigour (of the law), harshness, cruelty

RINGIS, *n. pl.*, (36:1214) earrings

RISSHES, *n. pl.*, (8:119) rushes or similar plants

ROTE, *n. s.*, (58:418) root

RUYNOUS, *adj.*, (86:51) going to ruin, in a state of decay

RYOT, *n. s.*, (29:919) debauchery, dissipation, revels, violence

SAD, *adj.*, (3:8) steadfast, faithful, serious, wise

SADLY, *adj.*, (56:347) grave, sober, serious, dignified, solemn (Latin: 'modestus', *De doctrina*, p. 184)

SADNES, *n. s.*, (16:443) steadfastness, constancy, seriousness, prudence

SAK, *n. s.*, (63:172) bag, sackcloth (frequently used as a sign of mourning or penitence)

SANDALYES, *n. pl.*, (40:1341) sandals, richly made shoes worn by popes and bishops

SAUSE, *n. s.*, (13:323) sauce, curative preparation

SAVERITH, *vb. ind. pres. 3rd pers. s.*, (85:11) delights (in God), takes spiritual pleasure (in God), enjoys

SAVERLY, SAVOURLY, *adv.*, (90:177, 3:30) with pleasure, with spiritual delight, with spiritual understanding

SAVERY, *adj.*, (25:799) spiritually acceptable, spiritually keen

SCABBID, *adj.*, (25:796) suffering from scabies or similar disease

SCARSE, *adj.*, (62:127) barely sufficient, lean, abstemious

SCHENSSHIP, *n. s.*, (42:1440) misfortune, harm, shame, disgrace, humiliation

SCHET, *vb. ind. pres. 3rd pers. pl.*, (51:155) close (door), lock, make secure

    SHETTITH, *ind. pres. 3rd pers. s.*, (62:135) closes

    SCHET, SCHITTE, *p.ppl.*, (60:41, 59:10) shut, closed, locked

SCHETITH, *vb. ind. pres. 3rd pers. s.*, (61:80) shoots

SCHORGID, *vb. p.ppl.*, (9:175) whipped, scourged, punished

SCHORGING, *vbl. n. s.*, (77:28) whipping, scourging

SCISME, *n. s.*, (42:1414) dissension within the church, civil disturbance or strife

SCLAKE, *vb. inf.*, (17:490) relieve, remedy, lessen, end

SCLILY, *adv.*, (17:488) cleverly, skillfully, cunningly, slyly

SCURRILITE, *n. s.*, (88:137) coarseness, indecency of language

SECED, *vb. p.ppl.*, (58:435) ceased, left off, stopped

SECTE, *n. s.*, (74:230) an organized system of religious belief and practice, esp. a non-Christian faith

SEE, *n. s.*, ÞE REDE ~ (88:108) the Red Sea

SEKERIS, *n. pl.*, (17:459) searchers, explorers, those who seek (sth.)

SELDE, SILD(E), *adv.*, (48:44, 62:130, 48:32) seldom, rarely, hardly

SEMLY, *adj.*, (6:64) handsome, beautiful

SENDEL(LE), *n. s.*, (70:93, 70:93) a kind of costly fabric (linen or cotton), this fabric used for winding sheets, esp. the sindon with which the body of Jesus was wrapped

SERJAUNTE, *n. s.*, (17:471) servant, an officer in a lord's retinue, an attendant

SERVILE, *adj.*, ~ DREDE (17:476), fear which a servant or slave has of his master, fear of punishment, a reverence for God of a fear of divine wrath or punishment

SESSIOUN, *n. s.*, (72:147) seat, bench, place for sitting, assembly

SETE, *n. s.*, (14:342) seat, throne, home

SETH, *conj.*, (3:10) inasmuch as, seeing that

SETTIST, *vb. ind. pres. 2nd pers. s.*, ~ LITELLE BY (86:35) care little about, regard with little esteem, value little

SEWE, *vb. subj. pres. 3rd pers. s.*, (80:12) follow, be practiced, be observed

SEWYNG, *pr.ppl.*, (46:1593) bringing about, striving to obtain

SEYGH, *vb. ind. past 2nd pers. pl.*, (91:216) saw

SEYN, *p.ppl.*, (30:975) seen

SIETH, *ind. pres. 3rd pers. s.*, (66:273) sees

SYGH, *ind. past 3rd pers. s.*, (61:71) saw

SHAMEFASTNES, *n. s.*, (30:975) modesty, bashfulness, shyness

SHARP, *adj.*, (39:1324) rough in texture

SHEDYNG, *vbl. n. s.*, (37:1247) shedding

SHETTITH, *vb. ind. pres. 3rd pers. s.*, (62:135) closes

SHRYVVYN, *vb. p.ppl.*, TO BE ~ (7:78), to be confessed

SIETH, *vb. ind. pres. 3rd pers. s.*, (66:273) sees

SIKER, *adj.*, (78:41) free from danger, safe

SILD(E), SELDE, *adv.*, (62:130, 48:32, 48:44) seldom, rarely, hardly

SISTREN, *n. pl.*, (62:128) sisters

SKYNNES, *n. pl.*, (23:707) skins, furs, hides

SKIPPIN, *vb. ind. pres. 3rd pers pl.*, (76:305) jump, skip, play, go, rush

SKIPPID, *ind. past. 3rd pers. s.*, ~ OUTE (90:195), rushed out, fled

SLAK, *adj.*, (36:1195) lazy, negligent, lukewarm, slow, inadequate

SLE, *vb. subj. pres. 3rd pers. pl.*, (18:523), kill, destroy

SLEITH, SLEYTHE, *n. s.*, (48:44, 48:33) prudence, ingenuity, cunning, craftiness, wisdom

SLEWTH, *n. s.*, (55:310) sloth, indolence, acedia

SLYPER, *adj.*, (23:702) having a slipping surface, deceitful, treacherous, vile

SMATERE, *vb. inf.*, (29:914) chatter, talk idly, speak foolishly about

SOBIRLY, *adv.*, (48:31) abstemiously, earnestly, dispassionately, patiently

SOCOURE, *n. s.*, (48:62) help, support, military assistance provided by an armed host

SOKETH, *vb. ind. pres. 3rd pers. s.*, (15:391) draws out nourishment from, feeds on

SOLEMPLY, *adv.*, (40:1341) reverently, in a dignified manner, seriously

SOMME, SUMME, *adj.*, (89:146, 22:656) some

SONE, *adv.*, (68:13) soon

SONK(E), *vb. p.ppl.*, (88:128, 88:124) sunk, lowered, entered

SOPHYMES, *n. pl.*, (56:349) subtle but fallacious arguments usually used to deceive, ambiguous sentences

SOPID, *vb. p.ppl.*, - UP (86:52), consumed, devoured

SOPOSE, *vb. ind. pres. 1st per. pl.*, (14:377) believe, think, assume, suspect

SORE, *adv.*, (26:819) severely, grievously, greatly, very much

SOTIL, SOTELLE, *adj.*, (22:681, 41:1380) (skin) thin, delicate, slender; (thread) intricately made, fine in texture

SOTILTEES, *n. pl.*, (36:1212) prudence, shrewdness, skills, keenness of wit or understanding

SOULEWARD, *adv.*, (10:188) to the soul, toward the soul

SOUPYNG, *vbl. n. s.*, (22:659) food (Latin: 'escae', *De doctrina*, p. 66)

SOVEREYNES, *n. pl.*, (24:743) masters, religious superiors

SOWN(E), *n. s.*, (26:806, 46:1569) sound, melody

SOWNNYN, *vb. ind. pres. 3rd pers. pl.*, (55:305) speak, say, proclaim, show, have to do with, mean

SOWNYNG, *vbl. n. s.*, (56:345) manner of speaking, style of speaking

SPITE, *n. s.*, (25:770) spit for roasting meat, short spear

SPOYLID, *vb. p.ppl.*, (23:693) stripped of clothing, deprived of

SPREDIST, *vb. ind. pres. 2nd pers. s.*, (81:59) spread, lay

STABELYNG, STABILYNG, *vbl. n. s.*, (68:18, 68:16) making morally steadfast, grounding (soul) morally, making firm

STABIL, *n. s.*, (51:155) stable

STABILID, *vb. p.ppl.*, (68:15) established

STABLE, *inf.*, (4:47) establish, make (soul) morally steadfast

STABILNES, *n. s.*, - IN THI RELIGIOUN (33:1086), (Eccl.) perseverance in monastic life avowed by a member of a monastic order

STAMYNE, *n. s.*, (41:1380) cloth of some kind, usually made of wool, undergarment made of this cloth

STEDE, *n. s.*, YIVEN - (29:935), surrender, submit, give in (to the devil)

STERNE, STYRNE, *n. s.*, (75:250, 53:230) stern, helm, rudder, guidance

STERRYS, *n. pl.*, (63:173) stars

STIRT, STIRTEN, *vb. ind. pres. 3rd pers. pl.*, (76:303, 76:308) jump, cavort, dart, hasten, go

STOLE, *vb. p.ppl.*, (51:156) stolen, robbed

STOLE, *n. s.*, (8:147) stool, seat, bench

STOMBLYNG, *vbl. n. s.*, (54:265) (of speaking) sinning, erring in judgment, blundering

STONT, *vb. ind. past 3rd pers. s.*, (13:326) was placed, was set

STREITELY, STREYGHTLY, *adv.*, (62:127, 33:1090) tightly, strictly, severely, stringently, frugally

STREYTER, *adj. comp.*, (62:131) tighter, stricter, more severe, more stringent

STROGLID, *vb. subj. past 3rd pers. s.*, (79:72) wrestled, argued, struggled

STRYVING, *vbl. n. s.*, (10:188) the action of engaging in a spiritual struggle, struggle between vices and virtues

STUFFID, *vb. p.ppl.*, (47:7) provided, supplied with, endowed with

STYHING, *vb. pr.ppl.*, (6:58) ascending, climbing, rising

STYRNE, STERNE, *n. s.*, (53:230, 75:250) stern, helm, rudder, guidance

STYRNELES, *adj.*, (53:262) without a helm or rudder

SUMME, SOMME, *adj.*, (22:656, 89:146) some

SUNGE, *vb. p.ppl.*, (35:1155) sung, chanted

SUNNER, *adv. comp.*, (41:1392) sooner

SUSPECIOUSLY, *adv.*, (14:365) suspectingly

SUWYNG, *vb. pr.ppl.*, (38:1282) following, coming after

SWAGITH, *vb. ind. pres. 3rd pers. s.*, (31:998) decreases, reduces, softens

SWETLY, *adv.*, (46:1589) sweetly

SWETYNG, *vbl. n. s.*, (37:1248) hard labour, great effort

SWOLWYNG, *vb. pr.ppl.*, (18:513) swallowing

SYGH, *vb. ind. past 3rd pers. s.*, (61:71) saw

   SEYGH, *ind. past 2nd pers. pl.*, (91:216) saw

   SEYN, *p.ppl.*, (30:975) seen

   SIETH, *ind. pres. 3rd pers. s.*, (66:273) sees

SYMONYE, *n. s.*, (30:989) simony, buying or selling of an ecclesiastical office, service or possession

SYTTYN, *vb. ind. pres. 3rd pers. pl.*, (61:81) sit

TACITURNITE, *n. s.*, (11:237) reservedness in speech, disposition to say little

TAYDE, *vb. p.ppl.*, (33:1078) fastened, tied up, fettered

TEMPERE, *vb. imp.*, (13:324) blend, assuage, soften, restrain

TEMPESTID, *vb. ind past 3rd pers. pl.*, (61:76) caused a disturbance, caused mental or spiritual turmoil, were troubled (with a condition or state)

TERIS, *n. pl.*, (20:601) tears

THO, TO, TOO, *adj.*, (40:1366, 17:475, 22:658) two

THRUST, *n. s.*, (9:176) thirst, (strong) desire

ÞAN, *adv.*, (66:266) then

ÞERAYENST, *adv.* (20:591), thereagainst

ÞEVES, *n. pl.*, (9:169) thieves, robbers

ÞEYME, *pers. pron. dat. pl.*, (24:743) them

ÞO, *pron. pl.*, (80:29) those

ÞONDRING, *vbl. n. s.*, (19:550) sound of thunder, thunderclap

ÞONKE, *vb. imp.*, (13:312) give thanks

ÞOU, *conj.*, AS ~ (39:1334), though, although

ÞOUTES, *n. pl.*, (50:130) thoughts, ideas

ÞRETNYNG, *vbl. n. s.*, (77:28) threatening

ÞUNDIR ÞOUNDIR, *n. s.*, (61:71, 72:156) thunder, thunderclap

ÞYNNE, *adj.*, (22:681) thin, gaunt, transparent

TITHINGIS *n. pl.*, (17:454) common talk, gossip, rumours, traveler's tales

TO, THO, TOO, *adj.*, (17:475, 40:1366, 22:658) two

TO, *adv.*, (26:816) too

TOGEDRES, *adv.*, (49:79) with each other, jointly

TOKNE, *n. s.*, (43:1465) token, symbol, proof, emblem

TONNE, *n. s.*, (26:804) large barrel, cask, tub

TOO, THO, TO, *adj.*, (22:658, 40:1366, 17:475) two

TORNEEMENTIS, *n. pl.*, (9:168) tournaments

TORNITH, *vb. ind. pres. 3rd pers. s.*, (26:814) changes

TORNID, *p.ppl.*, ~ IN (26:820) converted to, having undergone a spiritual conversion

TORNYNG, *vbl. n. s.*, (33.1087) spiritual conversion

TORRYN, *vb. p.ppl.*, (41:1411) torn

TROBEL, *n. s.*, (83:142) disorder, confusion, misfortune, trouble, harm, evil times

TROWE, *vb. ind. pres. 1st pers. s.*, (3:9) believe, think

TWAYN, *pron.*, (49:79) two people

TYGH, *vb. inf.*, (62:131) fasten, tie up

TYGHTH, *vb. p.ppl.*, (23:690) stretched out

UNAVISID, *vb. p.ppl.*, (3:4) imprudent, without sufficient knowledge

UNCOMPASSIBLE, *adj.*, (49:106) ?? not suffering with, lacking compassion (Latin: 'incompassibiles', *De doctrina*, p. 162)

UNCORPORATE, *adj.*, (18:510) not united into one body, not assimilated, not incorporated

UNDEDLYNES, *n. s.*, (83:141) immortality, eternal life

UNDESCRECIOUN, *n. s.*, (51:169) lack of discretion

UNEETYN, *adj.*, (18:510) not eaten

UNKUNNYNG, *vb. pr.ppl.*, (3:3) ignorant, uneducated

UNLEFFUL, *adj.*, (9:182) illegal, wicked

UNORDINATE, *adj.*, (85:21) not properly controlled, misguided, unsuitable

UNPASSIBLE, *adj.*, (49:106) ?? exempt from illness, death, suffering, impassive, without passions (Latin: 'impassibiles', *De doctrina*, p. 162)

UNSAVERY, *adj.*, (85:12) lacking in taste, distasteful, unpleasant

UNSEMLY, *adj.*, (40:1339) inappropriate, unbecoming, indecent

UNSTABLE, *adj.*, (3:7) unsteadfast in virtue, changing, unreliable

UNTRETTABLE, *adj.*, (58:433) intractable in behaviour, recalcitrant, implacable, relentless

UNUSID, *vb. p.ppl.*, (86:57) not used, not customary

VARIAUNT, *adj.*, (68:7) changeable, unstable, unreliable, contentious

VAYNE, VEYNE, *n. s.*, (7:94, 7:92) blood (vessel), heart, bodily passageway

VENYM, *n. s.*, (15:391) venom, poison

VERRE, *n. s.*, (44:1488) (vessel of) glass

VERTUES, VERTUOS, *adj.*, (38:1280, 10:217), morally good, righteous, virtuous, excellent, powerful

VERTUOS, *n. pl.*, (20:594) virtues, powers, skills

VESSELLE, *n. s.*, (37:1234) vessel, bowl

VESSELLIS, *pl.*, (37:1231) dishes, crockery

VEYNE, VAYNE, *n. s.*, (7:92, 7:94) blood (vessel), heart, bodily passageway

VISITOURE, *n. s.*, (14:359) (Eccl.) inspector, one charged with examining and reforming an ecclesiastical establishment

VOYDE, *adj.*, (26:804) empty, hollow, vacuous

WAGYD, *vb. ind. past 3rd pers. s.*, ~ BATAYLE (6:53) agreed to engage in combat, challenged to fight

WANTYD, *vb. ind. past 3rd. pers. s.*, (70:67) lacked, was without

WARD, *n. s.*, (78:41) shelter, protection, fortress

WARDIS, *pl.*, (48:35) guarded or secured sections of a castle, defensive walls, battlements

WARDID, *vb. p.ppl.*, (52:216) kept, guarded, watched

WARDLY, WORDLY, *adj.*, (30:983, 32:1059) worldly, material

WARDYN, *vb. ind. pres. 3rd pers. pl.*, (21:623) stand guard, protect, watch over

WARDYNG, *vbl. n. s.*, (10:212) guarding, protection

WASSE, *vb. ind. past 3rd pers. s.*, (37:1230) was

WASSH, *vb. p.ppl.*, (36:1217) washed

WAX, *vb. ind. past 3rd pers. s.*, (20:587) turned into, became

WEX, *p.ppl.*, (13:309) grown, increased in size

WEXITH, *ind. pres. 3rd pers. s.*, (20:604) becomes

WAYFARING, *vb. pr.ppl.*, (66:280) travelling or journeying by road

WEDEW(E), *n. s.*, (28:902, 28:886) widow

WENYN, *vb. ind. pres. 3rd pers. pl.*, (59:10) believe, suppose, expect, hope

WENYNG, *vb. pr.ppl.*, (17:489) believing, supposing, expecting, hoping

WEPYNG, *vbl. n. s.*, (37:1248) action of being stricken, beaten or attacked

WEPYNG, *vbl. n. s*, (39:1314) weeping, shedding tears as an act of penance, a show of devotion

WERYN, *vb. ind. pres. 3rd pers. pl.*, (23:712) wear, be clad in, make use of

WERYN, *vb. ind. past 3rd pers. pl.*, (72:154) were

WERYNG, *vbl. n. s.*, (39:1314) spiritual warfare, combat, fight

WERYNG, *vbl. n. s.*, (39:1314) wearing of a coarse garment as a spiritual exercise or an act of devotion. Both words fit the context, with the second slightly more likely.

WETE, *vb. imp.*, (13:319) steep in, soak, make wet

WEX, *vb. p.ppl.*, (13:309) grown, increased in size

   WAX, *ind. past 3rd pers. s.*, (20:587) turned into, became

   WEXITH, *ind. pres. 3rd pers. s.*, (20:604) becomes

WEYLIST, *vb. ind. 2nd pers. s.*, (86:34) wail aloud, express regret (for sins), utter cries of remorse

WHELE, *n. s.*, (76:308) some sort of revolving gate

WHETE, *n. s.*, (19:538) wheat

WHYGHT, WHIGHT *adj.*, (61:71, 61:81) white, pale

WICHE, *rel. pron.*, (15:415) which

WISIS, *n. pl.* (41:1406) manners, ways

WITE, *vb. inf.*, (9:161) know, experience, learn, find out, be aware

   NOT, *neg. ind. pres. 1st pers. pl.*, (42:1418) we do not know

   NYST, *neg. ind. past 3rd pers. s.*, (91:233) did not know

   WISTIST, *ind. past. 2nd pers. s.*, (17:487) knew

   WOTE, *ind. pres. 1st pers. s.*, (22:660) know

WITHOUGHTEN, *prep.*, (5:27) without

WOLLE, *n. s.*, (42:1424), wool

WOO, *n. s.*, (59:23) misery, distress, want, physical pain, torture, anguish, lamentation

WORDLY, WARDLY, *adj.*, (32:1059, 30:983) worldly, material

WYNCE, *vb. inf.*, (25:797) kick out, start, turn or move quickly

WYNDE, *n. s.*, ~ DRYVE (75:254) driven, carried, impelled or propelled by the wind

WYNNEWETH, *vb. ind. pres. 3rd pers. s.*, (19:540) winnows

   WYNWED, *ind. past 3rd pers. s.*, (19:538) winnowed

YATES, *n. pl.*, (7:73) gates, doorways

YDELLE, YDILLE, *adj.*, (52:212, 10:193) vain, sinful, idle

YERDE, *n. s.*, (58:420) branch, rod, instrument for inflicting punishment

YIF, *vb. ind. pres. 3rd pers. pl.* (68:13), give

   YIVE, ƷYVE, *inf.*, (5:15, 4:49) give

   YIVYTH, *ind. pres. 3rd pers. s.*, (3:11) gives

YIFTE, *n. s.*, (4:42), gift

YMPNIS, *n. pl.*, (89:159) hymns, psalms, songs of praise to God

YNLY, *adj.*, (89:149) inner, interior

YNOW, *adv.*, (12:283) enough, very much, completely

YOLD, *vb. p.ppl.*, ÞOU ART ALMEST ~ TO (48:59), you have almost surrendered to

   YOLDYN, *p.ppl.*, (78:51) surrendered, entrusted, submitted